THE GREAT
TOOL
EMPORIUM

THE GREAT TOOL EMPORIUM

by DAVID X. MANNERS

Designed by
Rod Lopez-Fabrega

POPULAR SCIENCE
E. P. DUTTON, NEW YORK

Library of Congress Catalog Card Number: 79-91225
ISBN: 0-525-93121-X

Manufactured in the United States of America

CONTENTS

PREFACE

Adam and Eve had no use for tools in the Garden of Eden. But things changed when they were driven out of that earthly Paradise.

"By the sweat of your brow shall you labor," they were told.

Ever since then, thinking men and women have been trying to avoid that labor and that sweat. There is an answer.

The answer is—tools.

This book is an elaboration of that answer. It's prime purpose is to tell you how to choose and use tools so they will bring you the greatest benefit and enjoyment. But it will also try to help you understand tools, showing you something of their near and distant past, and the hit-and-miss inventiveness that went into fashioning them as they are today.

Perhaps when you understand something of the long history of tool development, you'll visit your neighborhood hardware store with a touch of humility. Your ancestors had far fewer aids to do their work, and their ingenuity can only make you wag your head in wonder. You can be more than a little proud of them, at how much they accomplished with so little, and at the rich legacy you have inherited. With so much more to work with, how can we be anything but optimistic about our future?

WOODWORKING TOOLS

1.

HAMMERS

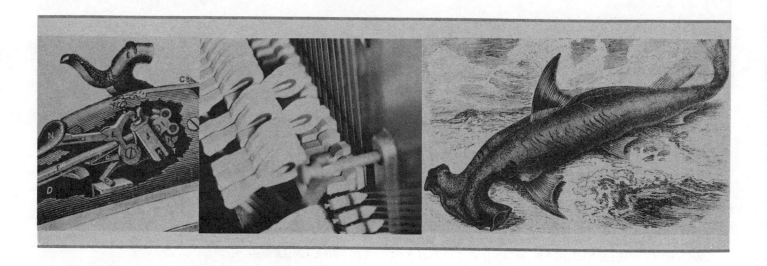

hammer/ hame(r) n [ME hamer, fr. OE hamor; akin to OHG hamar hammer, crag, Gk akmon anvil, Skt asma stone, GK akme edge—more at EDGE] la: a hand tool consisting of a solid head set crosswise on a handle and used for pounding

Guns have hammers, so do pianos, and so does the flag of one world power. It's a familiar brand of baking soda. There's even a hammer-head shark.

Hammers are so basic a tool, it isn't surprising how much the word "hammer" itself has crept into the language. To *hammer* means to shape or ornament. To *hammer* means to hit forcefully. To *hammer out* is to settle. To *hammer away* is to emphasize by repetition. To go at something *with hammer and tongs* means to attack with great noise or vigor.

TO HAMMER IS TO: assault, beat, bat, butt, bunt, blank, beetle, batter, bulldoze, blackjack, buffet, biff, bang, clip, clash, crash, cudgel, clap, cuff, club, crown, clout, clump, crack, cosh, concuss, dent, dint, dab, drive, fillip, flip, flick, flog, flail, flap, fashion, hit, impact, jolt, knock, land a blow, maul, nudge, pump, punch, pummel, pat, punt, pound, peen, plonk, plunk, ram, rap, slam, shock, smash, skelp, slock, sock, smack, slap, slug, scutch, stun, snap, stroke, stamp, swat, smite, shape, swingle, squash, tap, tamp, thwack, trounce, whop, zap.

A HAMMER IS AN ENHANCEMENT OF THE HUMAN HAND

It began as a stone held in the hand. The word "hammer" is derived from old Icelandic and Russian words meaning stone. For two million years our predecessors used stones to mash bones, crack coconuts, ward off attack, and wage aggressive battle. About a million years ago, perhaps taking their cue from the effectiveness of the ripping, slashing, tearing claws and fangs of other animals, they began to shape the stones, giving them points and sharp edges. Flint-flaking became a popular pastime.

After about a million years of this flint-flaking another idea began to sink in. About 35,000 years ago, it was found that the hands could be protected from a stone's sharp edges, and greater striking force gained, by attaching a handle. First, a stone was bound into a bent branch with thongs, later by cutting a hole so the head could be fitted to the handle.

In addition to providing protection and better control, handles also had a mechanical advantage. The added arc of their swing meant the head traveled faster, hit with more force. That's why, in hammering, you are advised to hold the handle near its end, rather than up near its head. The faster an object travels, the greater its kinetic energy—and the greater the clout on the nailhead.

After a million years of flaking flint, and perhaps somewhat more than 25,000 years after discovering the handle, our forebears discovered metal.

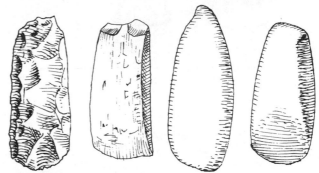

Earliest hammers were sharp-edged and pointed stones.

Stone-age hammer

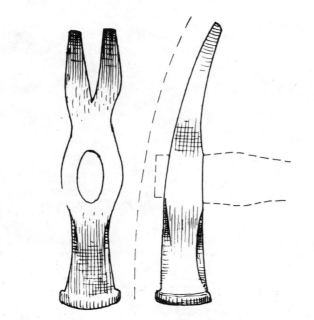

Roman hammer.

It happened not long after the last Ice Age, perhaps about 7,000 years ago. An ordinary campfire is about 1100 degrees, but when it's reduced to charcoal and there is a high wind it will get up to the 1300 to 1500 degrees needed to extract bronze. Bronze is a naturally occurring alloy that is 10 percent tin and 90 percent copper, and it's harder than either.

Soon, erstwhile stoneagers were using deer antlers as picks and pelvic bones as shovels to dig bronze ore from the ground. Later, using different ore, they began to extract iron, which was harder than copper or bronze and 500 times as plentiful. Around 1300 B.C., a messy operator spilled some molten iron in the fire and didn't bother raking out the charcoal ash. It produced the first crude steel. Soon everyone was using carbon to harden iron.

But not everyone went for the newfangled metals. A typical comment probably was: "They rust. They corrode. Give me stone."

To which the metal boosters no doubt responded: "Yeah, but there's no hand sting."

And they were right. Metal heads were three times as heavy as stone. That meant the center of gravity was nearer the head, and the center of percussion more nearly on the head—instead of in the palm of the hand!

The Romans were soon beating nails out of iron. Their square nails didn't drive easily, but actually they held better than our round ones, and they didn't split wood as readily. But, like us, Romans didn't always drive their nails straight, and bent nails were merry Jupiter to get out. Enter the claw hammer—a Roman invention. Jesus, a carpenter, probably had one in his tool box.

hammer·ma
rtillo · marte
au·malleus·
molotov·ma

A CATALOG OF OLD-TIME HAMMERS

Veneer hammer, about 1830.

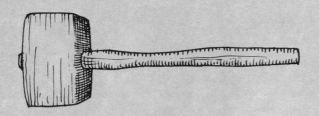

Grist-mill floodgate hammer weighed 25 pounds.

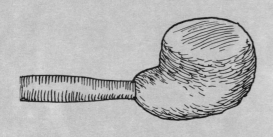

Burl hammer for wooden pegs.

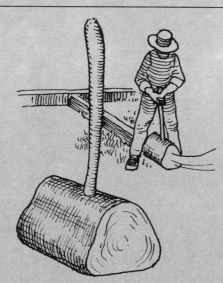

Commander hammer was for driving together the mortise-and tenon joints of beams.

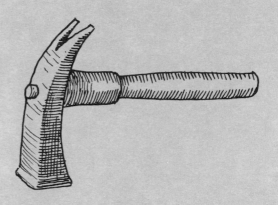

Cooper's hammer had claw for pulling wooden pegs.

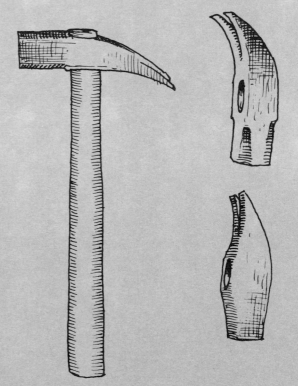

Early 18 century Pennsylvania hammers.

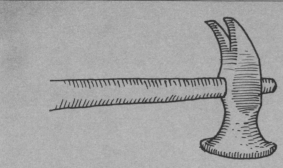

Cobbler's hammer had large face.

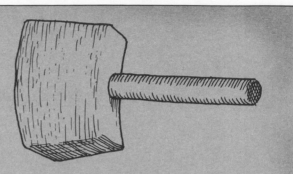

Beech burl wheelwright's mallet, 1790.

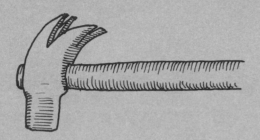

Shaker hammer had double claws for two-stage nail extraction.

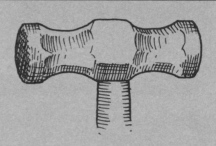

Two-faced hammer.

Shoe hammer and mold for rounding leather.

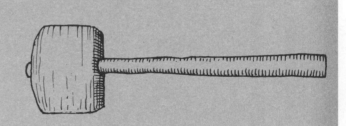

Walnut burl mallet, 1760.

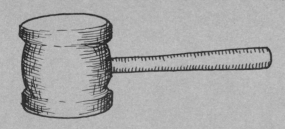

Carpenter's mallet, 1750.

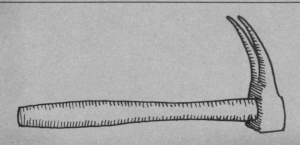

Early tack hammer.

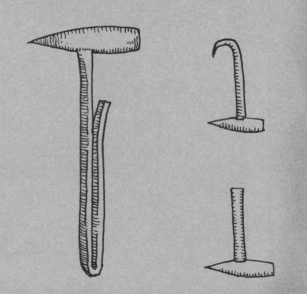

Hammers used for knocking shoes from horse's hoofs.

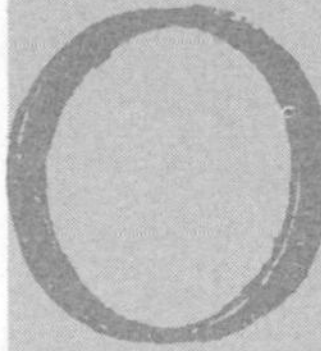

No. 35R2785 Wrought Iron Beetle Rings. Made of flat iron 1 inch wide, 5/16-inch thick.

Diameter, inches...	4½	5	6
Weight, pounds....	1¼	1½	1¾
Price, each.........	10c	12c	14c

Sears, Roebuck & Co.'s Nail Hammers.

A real good hammer gives satisfaction to the user. A poor hammer is about the meanest thing in the tool line. We sell the best hammers made and at prices that are right.

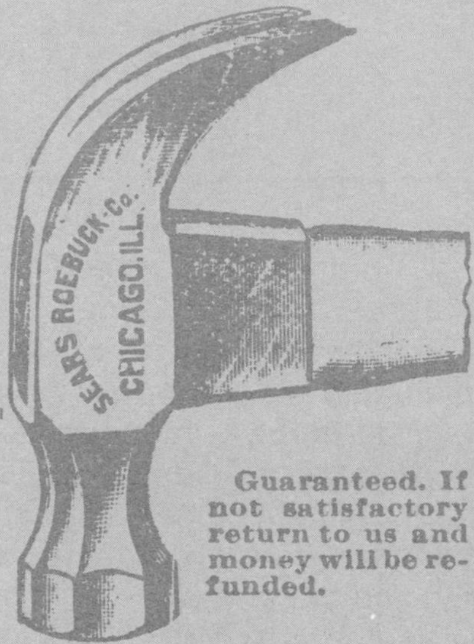

No. 35R2800 Sears, Roebuck & Co.'s Brand Nail Hammer. Octagon neck and poll. Made of the very best tool steel; finely polished and nickel plated. **OUR NAME etched on hammer. They are proportioned right; they hang right;** claws are right shape to draw a nail without breaking the claw; temper is right. Polished hickory handle. **Guaranteed. If not satisfactory return to us and money will be refunded.**

Size............................	1	1½	2
Weight, without handle.........	1¼ lb.	1 lb.	13 oz.
Price, each......................	59c	53c	50c

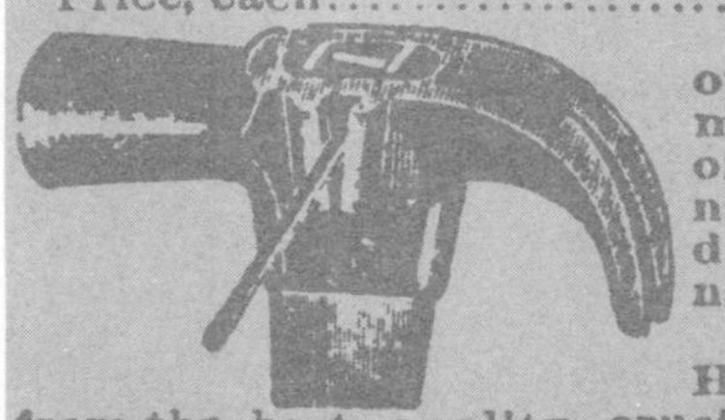

By the improved form of the groove this hammer will hold any size or shape of cut or wire nails. With it one can drive nails beyond ordinary reach.

No. 35R2803 Nail Holding Hammer, made from the best quality, crucible steel. Only one size and shape made. Weight, 1 lb. 3 oz., without handle.

Price, each, with handle................... ......73c

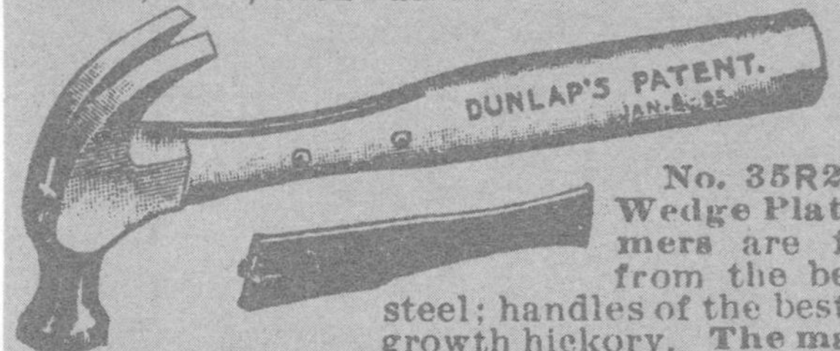

No. 35R2806 Wedge Plate Hammers are forged from the best cast steel; handles of the best second growth hickory. **The malleable wedge plate strengthens the handle and at the same time keeps the head from getting loose** or coming off. **We guarantee every hammer to be first class.** Weight of head, 1 pound; bell face. Each, **54c**

No. 35R2807 Same hammer, plain face. Each, **54c**

David Maydole's Nail Hammers.

Maydole's Hammers are made from the very best of crucible cast steel. The claws and face are not tempered the same, but each to the proper temper for the work it is required to do. The eye is left soft, so it never splits or cracks at the eye. The handles are best second growth hickory (selected stock). Every hammer is fully guaranteed.

No. 35R2810 The Genuine David Maydole's Nail Hammers.

Forged Steel Nail Hammers.

The following Hammers, No. 35R2815 and No. 35R2816, are forged from the best cast steel and are warranted against flaws and not to be soft. They are not so highly finished and polished as the higher priced goods, **but for common use they give excellent satisfaction.** Don't compare these hammers with cast iron goods like No. 35R2820. We tell you that cast iron hammers are no good and you will find them so. **We tell you that these hammers are all right and you will not be disappointed if you buy one.**

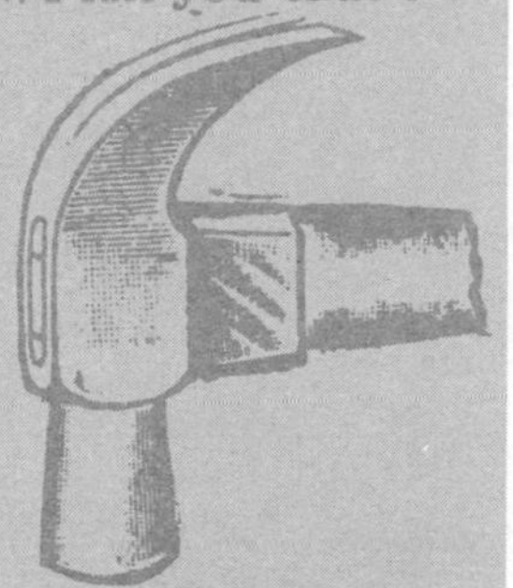

No. 35R2815 Adze Eye Plain Face Cast Steel Nail Hammer, warranted against flaws and not to be too soft.

Size	Weight	Each
1	1¼ lbs.	29c
1½	1 lb.	27c
2	13 oz.	25c

Weight of handle not included in stating weight.

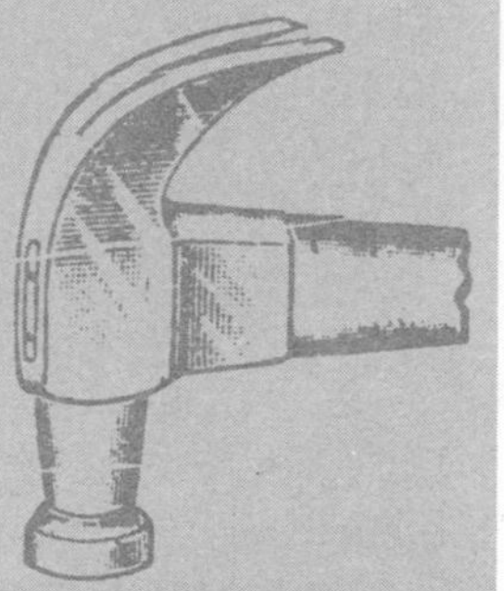

No. 35R2816 Adze Eye, Bell Face, Cast Steel Nail Hammers. Warranted against flaws and not to be too soft.

Size.......	11	11½	12
Weight...	1¼ lbs.	1 lb.	13 oz.
Price.....	29c	27c	25c

Cast Iron Nail Hammers

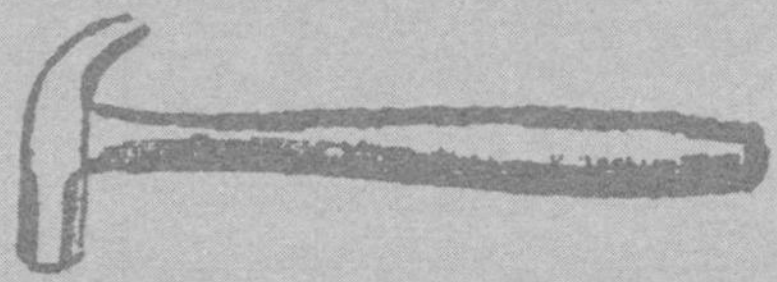

No. 35R2820 Cast Iron Hammers are positively no good. We have a few of these hammers in stock, which we would rather keep than sell to our customers. **If you must have them, we will sell you a** light one for **8 cents** or a full size for **10 cents.** You will be sorry if you buy one. **Can't you afford to buy a first class hammer at our prices for them? See how cheap they are.**

Hammer Handles.

Selected Quality Nail Hammer Handles.

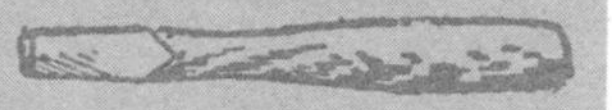

No. 35R2825 Adze Eye Nail Hammer Handles. Length, 14 inches.

Price, each..... ....4c

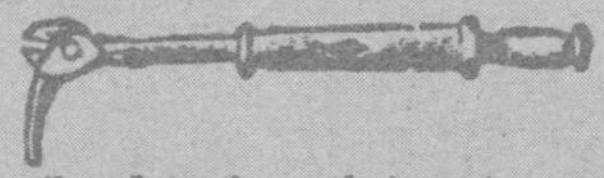

No. 35R2845 Nail Puller. Saves time, labor, cases and nails. No merchant, carpenter or plumber can afford to be without a nail puller. **It pays for itself.**

No. 1, weight 5 pounds, each...................... ..49c

Mallets.

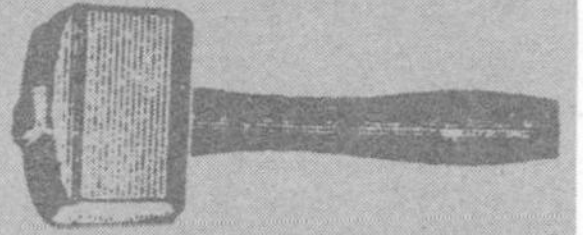

No. 35R2850 Square Hickory Mallets. Head is 6¼x2¾x3¾ inches; mortised handle. Weight, about 1¾ pounds.

Price, each.............. 11c

No. 35R2853 Square Lignum Vitæ Mallets. Head is 6½x2¾x3¾ inches. Weight, 2¼ lbs. Price, each, **22c**

Iron Bound Mallet.

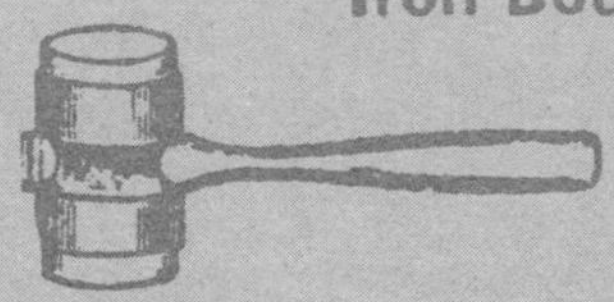

No. 35R2856 Round Malleable Iron Mallet, with inserted hickory faces. Head is 5¾x3 inches. Weight, 3½ pounds.

Price, each... ....33c

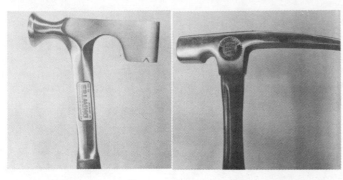

Lath Hatchet   Bricklayer's Hammer

Nail Hammer   Hand Drilling Hammer

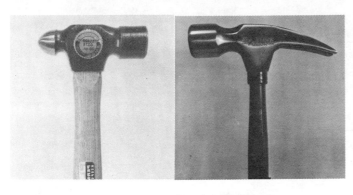

Ball Peen Hammer   Framing Hammer

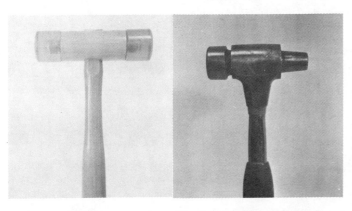

Soft Face Hammer   Shock-Absorbing Hammer

NOT ONE HAMMER BUT MANY

Our primitive ancestors used a single all-purpose tool to hammer, hack, dig, and fight. Some people still think that if you have one hammer, that's enough. Of course, you *can* use one all-purpose hammer to drive nails, take a dent out of a fender, break bricks, and flatten a rivet. But, as you can appreciate, special-purpose hammers do each of these jobs better, more easily, and more safely.

Each trade has its own special hammers. Everyone is familiar with the carpenter's hammer, the bricklayer's hammer, and the blacksmith's hammer. There are also hammers that bear the names machinist's, roofer's, tinner's, upholsterer's, bill poster's, boilermaker's, diamond cutter's, and many more, as you will find in later pages of this book.

Hammers found in a typical home workshop may include: (1) nail, (2) ball pein, (3) ripping claw, (4) hand drilling, (5) soft face, (6) blacksmith, (7) tack, (8) brick.

MANUFACTURERS

Some leading brands or manufacturers of hammers are Stanley, Plumb, Vaughan, True Temper, and Estwing. Reputable private-brand hammers, such as those of Sears, Wards, True Value, etc., are made by leading manufacturers.

THE PARTS OF A HAMMER

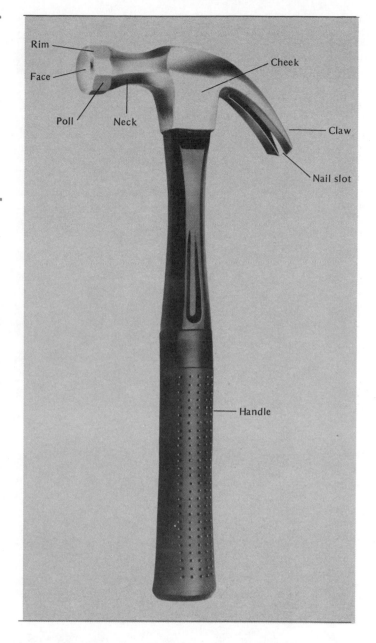

Face. May be plain, or checkered. The checkered milling is used on framing hammers, and helps prevent glancing blows and flying nails, but it leaves marks and is suitable only for rough work. A bell face (slightly convex) helps prevent marring when nails are driven flush, or even slightly below surface, and helps keep nails from flying or bending when struck at an angle.

Rim. May be tempered so it has a lower degree of hardness than rest of face. This helps prevent chipping and mushrooming. It may also be chamfered (beveled) for same reason.

Poll. This is the striking end of a hammer. It may be round or octagonal.

Neck. May be round or octagonal to match design of poll.

Wedge. Steel and/or wooden wedges may be used to expand end of handle and secure head. Many heads are bonded with epoxy resin adhesive.

Cheek. May be polished or painted. Experts usually advise against using the cheek as a striking face, but it can be used for gentle no-mar tapping.

Weight. The weight of a hammer is that of the head. This may range, typically, from 5 to 20 oz. or more. The most popular all-purpose nail hammer is 16 oz. For framing and ripping, 20 or 22 oz. is the winner. The "household" or kitchen drawer hammer is usually 7 or 12 oz.

Claw. For pulling nails. It's arched to give the required rocking motion. Straight claws fit between boards for prying.

Nail slot. Should be sharp, to take a good bite on a nail. Sears has a small secondary slot in one claw for pulling nails in tight spots.

Balance. The weight of the handle vs. the weight of the head determines point of balance on your finger. Wood balances closest to head, which is good. Fiberglass and tubular steel come next. Solid steel is farthest back.

Handle. Hickory is usually preferred for a wood handle. Tubular steel may have a hickory core to help absorb hand-stinging vibrations. Fiberglass may have hollow core for same reason. It gives better balance. Perforated grip of neoprene, nylon-vinyl, or leather also adds comfort and reduces shock hazard of metal handles.

Eye. The hole in the hammer head in which the handle fits.

THE BASICS OF HAMMER CHOICE AND USE

Get a good forged hammer with a face that has been specially heat-treated to avoid chipping and spalling. Never buy a cast hammer. You can tell it by the sand-casting marks. For the general handyman, handywoman, or apartment dweller, a 16-ounce hammer is first choice.

Should it be one with a handle of wood, fiberglass, tubular steel, or solid steel? That's largely a personal decision. Each type has its merits, as shall be explained in more detail. For all-around use, most professional carpenters prefer wood because of its greater resiliency and superior balance. But where durability is a key factor, fiberglass and tubular steel come out ahead. Solid steel is seldom selected by anyone.

For a second hammer, most people should have a ball pein. Its face is harder than that of a nail hammer and it can safely be used to strike metal, such as a chisel. If you do wrecking or rough framing, you'll need a hammer with a straight claw, 20 ounces and up. Here pro carpenters prefer fiberglass or tubular steel.

It's also a good idea to have a 7-ounce or 13-ounce nail hammer, or a 4-ounce tack hammer, to keep in the kitchen drawer.

Good, better, or best model? If by a reputable manufacturer, all can serve satisfactorily. Differences in finish, handle, and refinements account for differences in price. Now, for more details.

1. If I had a ham - mer,___
4. Well, I've got a ham - mer,___

HANDLE

If it's of wood, the preferred choice is hickory. Not all hickory is alike. It comes in four grades, which are determined by the denisty, straightness of grain, and color of the wood. Top-grade hickory tends to be white, for it is the white wood of the log that is the strongest.

Some manufacturers use ash for hammer handles. Ash is not as good as hickory. Because it is a weaker wood, it is essential that it be straight-grained. Hickory is so strong, it doesn't actually matter if it is straight-grained or not. The only thing to look for and reject is a handle that has a knot near where it joins the head. This is the weakest part of the handle and it is where the greatest stress occurs. Manufacturers generally cull out handles with knots near the head, but sometimes they slip up. A knot in the middle of the handle or in its grip section isn't of serious consequence.

All top-grade wood handles are flame hardened. It is a process of passing the handles, after they have been turned and shaped, through a gas flame. It gives the handle an attractive appearance and also removes moisture, shrinking the wood. That means the head will stay on tight no matter how much the tool dries out in the future. If the handle picks up moisture after assembly, so much the better. The head will fit even more tightly.

Handles of the best grade hammers, after flame hardening, may be cool-coated with an oil-based lacquer. Middle grade hammers may be tumble-stained to darken them and then given a clear coat of lacquer. The lowest grade usually gets an ivory-coat dip lacquer, which closes the grain of the wood and also provides a more comfortable surface for the hand.

Tubular steel and fiberglass handles are giving wood a run for the money. They cost more and are less resilient, but they are more durable. They can take abuse that would quickly wreck a wood-handled hammer. Solid steel hammers, made by Estwing and Stanley, are the most expensive hammers of all. No one can question their durability; head and handle are all one piece. But they score low on resiliency and comfort.

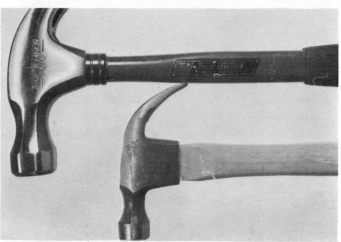

Two popular types of handles: fiberglass and wood.

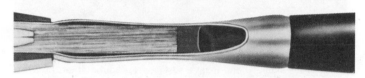

Wood plug in tubular handle of this Vaughan hammer adds strength in critical neck area, helps absorb shock and vibration.

WRONG: Gripping handle in the middle results in a short swing of meager force.

RIGHT: This grip produces a swing with a full arc and utilizes the weight of the hammer head.

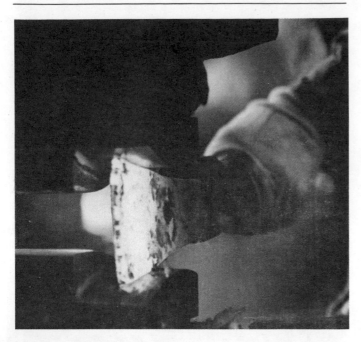

Forging a hammer head from a rod of rectangular steel. *Courtesy True Temper Corp.*

Tempering the rim of the face produces a softer surface that won't chip when it glances off a nail.

Claws are treated separately so they are harder than the eye section but softer than the face.

HEAD

Good hammer heads are forged. In forging, a heavy weight comes down on a heated rod of rectangular steel stock, mashing it between two dies which have the configuration of a hammer head. After two or three blows, the shape is roughed out. This is called drop forging, and it is an old technique. Newer is press forging, in which automated equipment is employed, but the end result is the same—stronger steel. Heads can also be made by casting—that is, pouring metal in a mold. No major manufacturer of hammer heads makes cast products. With one exception, they are found only on tools that are imported, usually from Japan or Taiwan. Such hammers are not recommended from the point of view of either safety or serviceability.

After forging, the hammer head is heat-treated to one overall hardness. The striking face, the part that hits the nail, is then dipped into a pot of molten lead to raise its hardness. The hammer's claws are treated separately to create a third degree of hardness—harder than the eye section but not as hard as the striking face. One manufacturer, Stanley, goes on to specially temper the rim or bevel around the face. Tempering gives the rim a softer surface, which helps to prevent chipping or spalling when the face glances off a nail.

Newer than lead-pot tempering is induction heat treating, or electrotempering. It is done by inserting the part of the hammer head getting the treatment into an electric coil.

Hammer heads are usually made of carbon steel. Alloy steel, a different composition, is not customarily used for nail hammers, though some manufacturers do use it for sledges. They also use it in some wrecking bars. Vanadium steel is an alloy containing vanadium, which is said to make it stronger.

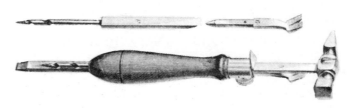

JOINING HEAD AND HANDLE

Epoxy adhesive is used in securing some handles. The advantage of epoxy is that it prevents the head from ever loosening. The particular disadvantage, with a wood handle, is that if the handle should break, you have to drill out the epoxy in order to remove the stump. It isn't easy.

The conventional method for securing wood handles is by wedging. In better hammers, one steel and two wood wedges are driven into the top face of the handle. Stanley uses an "injection molding plastic wedge" to secure some of its heads. This is a process of injecting plastic between the inside of the eye and the outside of the handle.

Typically, fiberglass handles are attached with epoxy. It almost insures the hammer head will never fly off. A flying hammer head can be deadly.

Sears, whose hammers are made by Vaughan and Bushnell, uses one head style for all its hammers. This means its fiberglass and steel handles must be the same thickness as its wood handles. To lighten the thick fiberglass, Sears gives it a hollow core, which happily also provides more flex. To keep its tubular steel handle from ringing, Sears gives it a hickory plug. Fiberglass and steel handles on True Temper and Stanley hammers are thinner and therefore lighter and more resilient.

WHY DO HANDLES BREAK?

One cause is overstrike. Instead of hitting the nail with the hammer's striking face, you hit it with the handle, usually just below the eye. As has been noted, that's the handle's weakest point. However, the major cause of breaking is pulling nails. Hammers just aren't designed for such heavy duty. If you have a lot of 16- and 20-penny nails to pull, you should use a nail puller instead of a hammer.

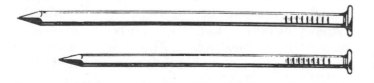

Head is attached by driving a wooden wedge into top of handle. *Courtesy True Temper Corp.*

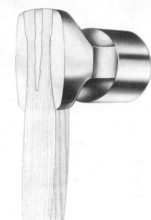

Handle of Vaughan hammer is preshrunk to fit tightly into bottom of eye, compresses into smaller center section, and then expanded at the top by a steel wedge.

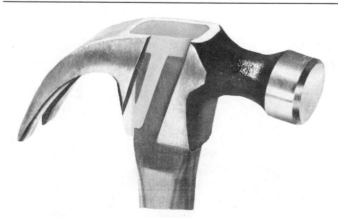

Easco's epoxy bonding is designed to assure firm, rigid attachment of handle and head. Epoxy flows into all openings to provide maximum adhesion.

The straight claw or ripping hammer is designed for taking apart forms and dismantling construction. It's sometimes called a framing hammer and can be used for that purpose. This is a 20-ounce Vaughan.

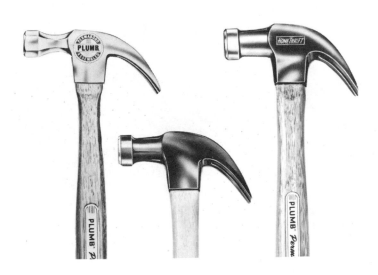

WHICH HAMMER SHALL YOU BUY?

More wood hammers are sold than any other kind. But that doesn't necessarily mean they are best for your purposes. A fiberglass or tubular steel model may be the wise choice. They offer more strength than wood, and one of middle quality need cost no more than top-quality wood.

A typical professional carpenter would probably own a 13-ounce wood hammer for cabinet work, a 16-ounce wood nail hammer for all-around use, and a 20-ounce ripping claw hammer in either fiberglass or tubular steel for rough work, such as framing, building concrete forms, etc. But there are many carpenters who choose a 16-ounce tubular steel or fiberglass nail hammer instead of a 16-ounce wood one.

The occasional do-it-yourselfer is probably best off with a 16-ounce wood hammer of medium quality. The more avid do-it-yourselfer is probably best off with a top or medium-grade hammer of tubular steel or fiberglass. He'll be using the tool strenuously, building room additions, a garage, etc. Actually, the dyed-in-the-wool do-it-yourselfer will want one of each kind. And that probably is the best way to solve the problem. It certainly is the fun way, and in working with tools that should be the aim of the game.

100 WORDS ABOUT HAMMER FINISHES

After a hammer head is forged, heat treated, and rough ground, the degree of polish and paint it gets is in keeping with its quality and price.

Typically, a lower-quality hammer will have only its striking face and chamfer polished, with the rest painted. That's the cheapest way to go. A medium-priced hammer, in addition to polished face and chamfer, will have its claws polished. If the claws are painted, some paint will come off when you pull a nail. This can be troublesome, especially on new wood. The best hammers are polished everywhere except under the claws.

ODDS AND ENDS

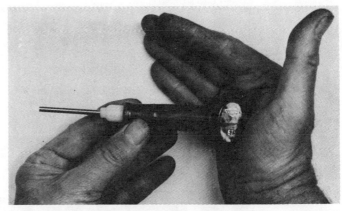

This tool, from Brookstone, drives and sets brads and finishing nails up to 1¹/₄ inches long, preventing hammer marks and mashed thumbs. Brad is held in tube by a magnet, forced into wood by pushing plastic knob.

Magnetic nail-holder permits driving nails where hammer can't reach. Stainless steel, 8 inches long. Brookstone.

Nail set drives finishing nails below the surface, ready to conceal with wood putty. Textured body gives good grip. Five sizes, from ¹/₃₂″ to ⁵/₆₄″; overall length 4″.

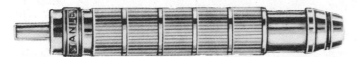

Self-centering nail set provides foolproof setting of nails and brads without marring wood surface. Comes in two sizes, one for 16, 17, 18 brads; the other for 4d and 6d finishing nails. Stanley.

The Paslode Stallion, a nailing machine, drives as many as 5,000 16d common nails an hour, weighs 11 pounds, and operates on compressed air. A quick-leading cartridge holds 120 nails.

Handyman's 14-pocket apron is made of double-stitched 10-ounce canvas, about 19¹/₂ inches long and 22 inches wide, has pockets of varied shapes and two leather hammer loops. Bolen.

Quick-draw holster holds hammer or hatchet in easy reach, allows it to swing on swivel for convenience.

Deluxe nailbag of saddle-stitched and riveted moccasin leather has three pockets, two nail-set slots and a hammer loop.

2.

AXES HATCHETS

Once, an axe was everything. It cleared the land, built the house, made the furniture, supplied the fuel, protected the family, and was used for money in trading with the Indians.

There were two kinds of axes. The woodman's axe felled the trees. It had a two-bevel "knife edge" and a long handle. The broadaxe squared the felled trees into beams and other building materials. It had a strong handle and a single-bevel "chisel edge." At the turn of the century, when sawmills were ripping out lumber of every variety, a few old-timers were still cutting and trimming logs into beams, rafters, and posts.

An eighteenth century felling axe (top) and a broadaxe.

The head of the woodsman's axe came in many patterns, and ten or more different regional styles still exist today. They reflect their origins with local blacksmiths. Two styles, Jersey and Kentucky, have "ears" extending from the eye of the axe head, where handle and head meet. They may help provide a somewhat better grip of head on handle.

Ten regional styles of axe heads that still exist today.

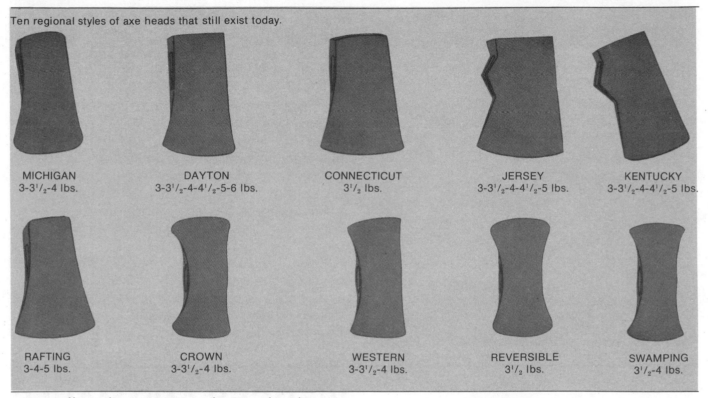

MICHIGAN	DAYTON	CONNECTICUT	JERSEY	KENTUCKY
3-3½-4 lbs.	3-3½-4-4½-5-6 lbs.	3½ lbs.	3-3½-4-4½-5 lbs.	3-3½-4-4½-5 lbs.

RAFTING	CROWN	WESTERN	REVERSIBLE	SWAMPING
3-4-5 lbs.	3-3½-4 lbs.	3-3½-4 lbs.	3½ lbs.	3½-4 lbs.

A "poll" is the extension of an axe head opposite the bit or cutting edge. It is not for striking. Its primary purpose is to provide balance and greater momentum to the swing. Early axes had no polls. They were simply a single band of iron folded over, with a narrow strip of steel inserted where the ends met to provide the cutting edge.

Instead of a poll, some of today's axes have a second cutting edge. This permits having one edge for felling and the other, sharper edge for trimming. This trimming edge should be so sharp that it would chip if used for felling. The handle on a double-bitted axe is straight, so it will work in either direction. In the South, you can also get straight handles on single-bitted axes.

Modern felling axe with poll (flat side of head) that provides balance and momentum.

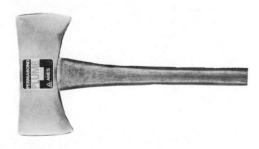

Double-bitted axe is used for felling and trimming. The trimming blade should be the sharper.

Today's standard axe comes with a head ranging in weight from 3 to 6 pounds, with a 3½-pound head the most popular. Handle length is usually 36". A lighter-weight axe, 2½ pounds, comes with a 28" handle. This is a "one-handed axe," good for clearing brush and felling small trees.

Take your pick of any of these axes at from $13 to $15 in hardware stores, or for as little as $8 in chain stores. As with most tools, the price goes up a notch or two every year. Generally, the cheapest axe is made of the same grade and hardness of steel as the most expensive. The difference is in the finish of the steel and the handle.

The big three axe manufacturers are Collins, Plumb, and True-Temper. Collins manufactures Sager and Northlund axes, and some for other manufacturers, including Stanley.

None of the axes so far described is designed for splitting logs into firewood. Nor are they made for use as a wedge, or for driving a wedge. For these purposes you need a woodchopper's maul. A maul has a narrower and heavier head than an axe, usually weighs 6 to 8 pounds, and has a straight handle. You can also use a "heavy axe" for log-splitting. Falling somewhere in between a maul and an axe, this crossbreed has a 5-pound head and a curved handle.

WEDGES AND MAULS

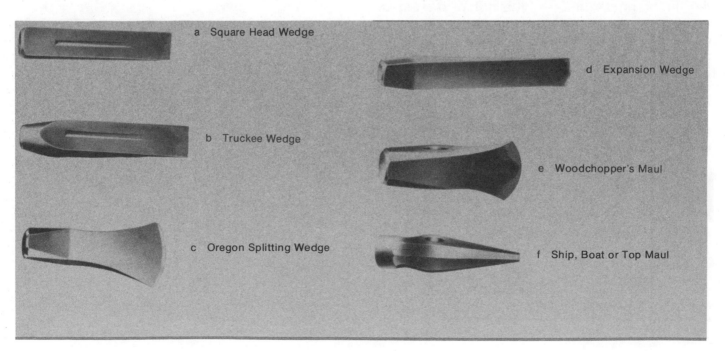

a Square Head Wedge

d Expansion Wedge

b Truckee Wedge

e Woodchopper's Maul

c Oregon Splitting Wedge

f Ship, Boat or Top Maul

HATCHETS

Hache is the French word for axe. A hatchet, literally, is a small axe. The first hatchets were used for shingling and barrel making. Earliest hatchets, factory made around 1845, had a large striking face extended to a claw for pulling nails. They were similar in design to one only recently discontinued by Plumb.

Today's carpenter uses a hatchet for rough work, like pointing a stake or taking wood off in a hurry. A hatchet is faster than a ripsaw or plane. It's good for heavy nailing, like laying sub-flooring. Eight commonly used hatchets today are the half hatchet, broad, lath, wallboard, box, rigster, car builders, and shingling hatchet.

The half hatchet is number one. It is called a "half hatchet" because its blade does not describe a full half circle, and thus appears to have been cut in half.

Hatchet blades may have a single or double bevel. Typically, their heads are forged from carbon tool steel and are heat treated. As in the case of hammers, handles may be hickory, tubular steel, solid steel, or fiberglass. Steel and fiberglass handles, and sometimes wooden ones, have a plastic, rubber, leather, or other resilient grip.

There are cheap cast hatchets and axes available. Use them only for cutting or striking wood. If you strike anything else, a nail for example, they are likely to chip and cause eye or body injury.

Modern reproductions of antiques, such as this Kent hatchet, are available for nostalgia buffs who want to recapture the frontier.

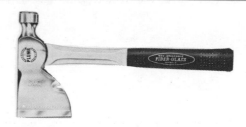

Half hatchet with polished head, red fiberglass handle and black cushion grip.

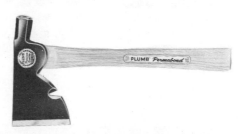

Half hatchet with black ground head, red hickory handle.

Rigster hatchet with black ground head, checkered face, red hickory handle.

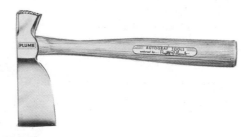

California lath hatchet, polished head with thin blade and checkered face, red hickory handle.

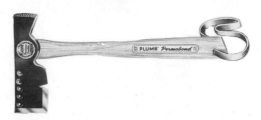

Shingling hatchet with leather wrist strap. Gauge can be adjusted every half inch to lay shingles.

3.

HANDSAWS

Ryoba Japanese saw has a crosscut edge with 9 teeth per inch and a ripsaw edge with 4½ teeth per inch. Overall length is 725mm (28½").

Steel-spined Dozuki saw is similar to our dovetail and can be used for any fine sawing. Its 210mm (8¼") cutting edge has 23 teeth per inch.

Azebiki saw can start cuts in the center of a panel and is also good for making stop cuts. One edge has 10 teeth per inch.

Saws have been in use since prehistoric times. One dating from 1450 B.C., taken from an Egyptian tomb, doesn't look too different from some saws in use today. Its principle difference is lack of "set." Set, a technique the Romans discovered, is the way the top half of teeth angle outward from the blade, to the right and left, so that the slot the saw cuts is wider than the blade. It prevents binding.

"Rake" is the angle at which the teeth incline backward or forward. If teeth have no rake, a saw cuts both on the thrust and pull strokes. Our saws rake in a direction *away* from the hand and so cut on the thrust. Teeth in some Japanese saws rake *toward* the hand and cut on the pull. Some Korean saws have teeth that rake both ways from the middle. These are two-man saws, and the arrangement means each man cuts on the pull.

During the Middle Ages, blades, being thin and flexible, were often set in the middle of a rectangular frame to keep them from buckling. These are called frame saws. Sometimes frame saws had more than one blade. They were two-man board-making instruments. In use, one man stood atop the log being cut, with a second man in a pit—hence these saws were known as "pit saws."

Saws consisting only of a blade and handle are known as "open" saws. One kind of pit saw was a single-bladed open saw with a handle at one end and a tiller at the other. Saws of this kind are still available.

Frame saws have their modern counterpart in the woodworker's bow saw. With a blade that can be turned, such a saw can cut curves. The blade may be tightened by means of a stick-tourniquet arrangement. A bow saw can do many jobs done by a power band saw.

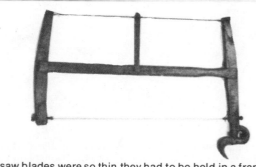

Early saw blades were so thin they had to be held in a frame to keep them from buckling.

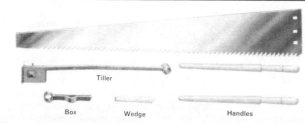

For those who want to cut their own lumber, pit saws are still available. This one has a tiller and box to accommodate handles at either end of its 7' blade.

A typical two-man pit saw used for cutting logs into planks. One man stood on the log, the other in a pit—hence the name.

Today's Saws

There are a few basic facts to know about saws. Different saws do different jobs. The two important saws in carpentry are the crosscut saw, for cutting boards across grain, and the ripsaw, for cutting with the grain. Their standard length is 26", though for drawer or toolbox, a 16" size is available.

The fewer teeth points a saw has, the rougher the cut. The number a saw has is usually stamped on the blade near the handle. Ripsaws, made for cutting with the grain, have 5½ points per inch. If you are going to buy only one saw, get a combination saw with 8 points. You can use it for ripping, as well as doing halfway decent crosscutting.

Disston professional handsaw is available as a 26" rip, with 5½ points per inch, and 16"–26" crosscut with 7 to 11 points per inch. Blade, of chrome nickel alloy steel, tapers a full four gauges from handle to tip and from tooth to back for bind-free cutting.

Stanley recommends its "Better" #1526 crosscut saw with 8 points for the do-it-yourselfer. This model, with a 26" blade, is also available (#1527) as a ripsaw with 5½ points per inch and as a finishing saw (#1528) with 11 points per inch.

All the good features of a Disston saw, plus a handle of aluminum for extra strength and a walnut grip for comfort. Note hang-up hole in toe.

Bushman Kombi includes a rule, a handle angled for marking 45° and 90° cuts, and horizontal and vertical spirit levels. Handle is plastic. Crosscut blade offered with 7, 8, or 10 points per inch. Comes in 22″, 24″ and 26″ lengths.

Disston's docking saw No. 196 is designed expressly for the roughest use. The 30″ blade has a skew back and tapers three gauges for bind-free cuts. Malleable handle is attached with stainless rivets. It has 4½ points per inch.

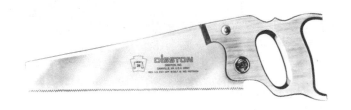

With a blade only 12″ long, this Disston saw is designed to fit right inside a toolbox. The blade has 10 points per inch and is file sharpened.

Bushman has three narrow-point lightweight handsaws. This one is coated with Teflon-S, giving good rust protection and some reduction in friction during sawing.

The best saw for crosscutting is one with 10 points, and for finishing—12 points. In the United States, crosscut saws outsell ripsaws 12 to 1.

There's a difference in the way ripsaw teeth and crosscut teeth are filed. Crosscut teeth are bevel-filed, like knives, and are designed to slice the wood's fibers. A ripsaw's teeth are cross-filed, like chisels. In effect, they chisel their way.

The method by which saw teeth are filed depends on the quality of the saw. Top of the line saws are usually "Foley-filed." The blade is set in a jig and a separate automated pass is made for each tooth. Cheaper saws are "gang-filed." A number of teeth are filed at a time. Cheapest saws are not filed at all. Teeth are merely set, and that's it.

The steel used in saw blades varies with price. To test the quality of a saw's steel, snap the toe of the blade with your thumbnail. The clearer and sharper the ring, the better. To test the blade's springiness, bend the blade and let it snap back. Some blades are Teflon-coated. The coating is intended to provide rust protection and reduce friction. The problem is that the coating wears off.

Best quality saw blades are "taper ground." That is, they taper very slightly from edge to back and from toe to handle. They cut more easily even in green or pitchy wood. The care with which a saw is set and filed is also of great importance.

Different saws fill different needs. For cutting holes, there is the compass saw, or the shorter, skinnier-blade keyhole saw. For fine cutting, there's the coping saw. For really fine finishing, there's the 13- to 15-point dovetail saw. There's also the small back or mitre saw with 13 points, or the bigger miter box saw with 11 points.

A saw of value in carpentry work, where rough cutting is desired, is the tubular steel "utility" bow saw.

The Bushman Precision combines the qualities of a backsaw, veneer saw, and a handsaw. Its small straight teeth cut both ways. The back is detachable. Its 18-inch blade has 13 points per inch.

A strong 12½-inch saw with teeth that continue around the nose and onto the back. Starts and cuts through floors and other difficult places. Frog Tool Co.

Fine teeth at the point make this Bushman Board saw easy to start. Other teeth are in groups of four and will cut both ways—thrust and pull. A fast crosscutting saw that's also adaptable to ripsawing. Blade is 24″ long.

Twin-tooth design and no set make this saw a fast and easy cutter. For logs, either green or dry, lumber, and other rough work.

This backsaw has a spine of solid brass, a blade of Sheffield steel, rolled thin to permit very fine cuts. To preserve absolute rigidity, blade is not taper-ground.

Made of European white beech, this 10″ bandsaw can cut curved patterns 5½″ deep to match the work of a heavy power bandsaw. Handles turn the blade at any angle to the frame. Replaceable blades have 14½ teeth per inch. Garrett Wade, Woodcraft.

Press the large button on the handle of this compass saw and the blade adjusts to five different positions. Allows you to get in and cut next to obstructions, ceilings, floors, etc. Has a 14″ blade, 8 points per inch.

Pad saws for awkward cuts are available with hardwood or die-cast handles that hold new or broken hacksaw blades, pieces of bandsaw, jigsaw, and other blades. Ideal for low-clearance sawing. Woodcraft.

Stanley all-purpose bow saw has tubular frame, tension clamping lever. Good for many carpentry jobs where a quick, rough saw cut is all that is needed.

For keyholes and frets, heavy 12″ blade, slim enough to cut even small holes. Has old-style lacquered wood handle. Frog Tool Co.

Stanley nest of saws answers many needs. One handle accommodates a 14″, 8-point compass blade, a 10″, 10-point finishing blade, and a 16″ blade with pruning teeth on one edge and 8-point crosscut teeth on the opposite edge. Stanley.

To make moldings fit at inside corners, you "cope the joint" with a coping saw. The saw illustrated is a Stanley, but similar ones are made by a number of manufacturers. The blade, of spring steel, can be turned to any angle.

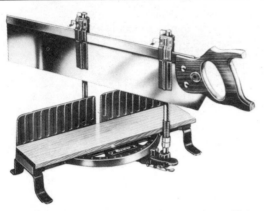

A miter box and miter saw permit cutting angles with great precision. Better boxes have greater capacity and permit cutting of more angles. Cheap boxes permit cutting only 45° and 90° angles. Best boxes will let you cut any angle from 30° to 90° with locks at ten or more most commonly used mitres.

This versatile saw cuts both wood and metal. The 16″ blade can be quickly adjusted and locked in any of nine positions, so that it is literally capable of cutting anything anywhere.

CARING FOR A SAW

Wipe a saw blade occasionally with an oily rag to help prevent rust. Once a blade rusts and becomes stained or pitted, it is almost impossible to restore. Saws are dulled by cutting painted lumber and plasterboard. Use an old saw for these materials. In sawing anything, if you come within range of a nail, stop. Switch to a saw with a metal-cutting blade. Many "nests of saws" have one.

MANUFACTURERS

Disston, Nicholson, and Stanley are the big names in U.S. saws. Stanley acquired a Pennsylvania saw company a few years ago and now makes all its own saws. You also can't overlook Sears. Their saws are made for them by Vermont-American, a Louisville company that also markets some saws on their own. Great Neck is a leading manufacturer of inexpensive saws.

European saws, despite their legend of superior steel, have never taken a big bite of the U.S. market. One reason is union carpenters tend to shun foreign tools. But they do have merit and some innovative features. Sandvik and Bushman are two top Swedish brands. Pax saws, made by a 150-year-old Sheffield firm, are a top English variety.

Most good handsaws sell for $10 to $15. If a manufacturer rates his saws as good, better, best, you'll generally do well to buy his middle grade.

WHAT THE WORDS MEAN

BACKSAW—a class of saws with a deep, thin blade stiffened by a heavy metal spine.

BOW SAW—a saw with a narrow blade which is held under tension in a bowlike frame.

COMPASS SAW—a saw, with a blade tapering from $1/8$" at the point to 2" or more at heel, for cutting curves.

COPING SAW—a small, thin-bladed frame saw for cutting sharp angles and curves.

CROSSCUT SAW—a handsaw for cutting across the grain.

DOCKING SAW—a rugged skew-back saw for rough, fast sawing.

DOVETAIL SAW—a backsaw with a thin blade.

FACE—the front or cutting edge of a tooth.

FLEAM—the side angle of a tooth.

FLOORING SAW—a saw designed for use where an occasional nail may be encountered.

GAUGE—blade thickness, usually measured as wire gauge.

GULLET—space between large saw teeth.

HEEL—end of a blade near the handle. Also called butt.

KERF—the groove cut by a saw blade.

KEYHOLE SAW—a smaller form of compass saw, for cutting curves of small radius.

MEDALLION—a large embossed screwhead on the saw handle.

MITER SAW—a backsaw especially designed for use in a miterbox.

NEST OF SAWS—a set of saws, consisting of three interchangeable blades, typically, keyhole, compass, and nail or utility blades.

PAD—a handle.

PANEL SAW—a saw 24" long or shorter.

POINTS—the number of teeth points per inch.

RAKE—the slant of a saw tooth.

RIPSAW—a saw for cutting with the grain.

SET—the amount of lateral inclination of teeth to the plane of the blade.

SKEW BACK—a curved upper edge.

SPACE—the distance between two adjoining teeth, measured from point to point.

STRAIGHT BACK—a saw with a straight upper edge.

TAPER GROUND—a blade that tapers from a thicker tooth edge to the back. Also from toe to heel. Opposite of flat ground.

4.

BIT BRACES
HAND DRILLS
PUSH DRILLS

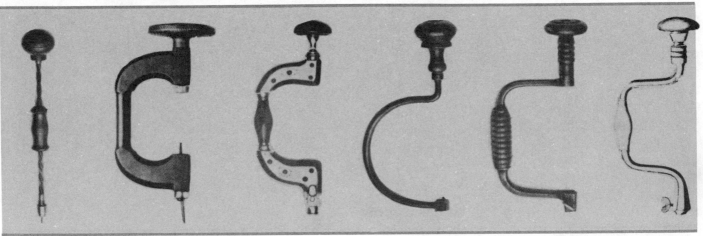

The primitive bow drill had a steel drill point at the end of its spindle. The spindle, which was held in place by hand or mouth, revolved in alternate directions as the user moved the bow back and forth.

Four thousand years after an anonymous genius invented the wheel, another anonymous genius made another great invention—the crank. It made possible the bit brace—a revolutionary tool for drilling holes.

The first drills were merely sharp objects. They were twisted back and forth to make the hole. Then, flint or bone, attached to a stick that was rotated between the palms of both hands, came into use. Later, the end of the stick opposite the drill end was held in a socket of stone, while a strap wound around the stick was pulled by a helper. Or, with the stone held in the mouth, there was not even need for a helper.

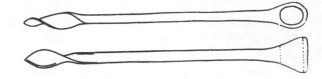

About 8000 B.C., someone got the bright idea of using a bow instead of a strap and it made continuous, uninterrupted motion possible. An early technique was to bore a small hole and then ream it larger. To bore holes the Romans used gouges and spoon bits. The spoon bit was similar to the gouge except that its bottom was spooned so it could be used to pull shavings up from the hole.

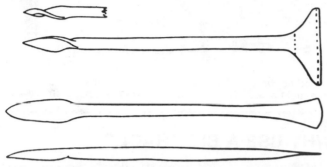

Above right: Wheelwrights of the eighteenth century used a reamer to enlarge a previously drilled hole in a wheel hub. The sharp sides of the tapered reamer do the cutting.

Above left: This anonymous fifteenth century Flemish painting of St. Joseph in his workshop is the earliest record of the bit brace. Rembrandt showed a bit brace in a 1640 painting, about a hundred years later. *Metropolitan Museum of Art, Cloisters Collection.*

Both the gouge bit and the spoon bit had tapered square tops, like the bits still used in braces today. To enlarge a hole already bored, the Romans used an auger, sharpened on one side and turned with a cross-handle. Some of these were called "pod augers" because they were shaped like a twisted seed pod. The spiral bit, ingeniously designed to discharge shavings, was not invented until 1770.

China had a bit brace in the first century, but the tool did not appear in Europe until the 15th century. In its early beginnings, a separate brace was used for each bit. No one had yet thought of the idea of interchangeable bits. A chair maker might have twenty or thirty braces, one for each size hole he wanted to drill. It took a lot of pressure to drill a hole for there was no screw to draw the bit into the wood. For extra pressure, a "brace bib" was sometimes used. Worn on the chest, it permitted body-pressure against the head of the brace.

When interchangeable bits came into use, there was a problem of holding them in place. The bit was often merely pressure-fitted into the brace, or was held there by a setscrew. Then, in 1865, a man named Milton Noble invented the chuck. It had a split sleeve, tightened by a ring, to firmly hold the bit. At the turn of the century, Barber perfected the ratchet brace, and the tool was essentially as we know it today. The ratchet, of course, makes it possible to drill in tight quarters where there is not enough space to make a complete turn of the handle.

Improved boring machine, 1883.

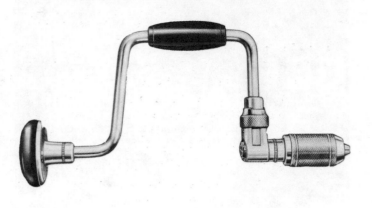

A modern bit brace.

Single-twist electrician's bit with a solid center is good for all kinds of jobs. Sizes range from ¼ to 1 inch.

Hollow-core single-twist bit is made for boring straight and true holes in heavy timbers. It comes in lengths up to 29 inches overall.

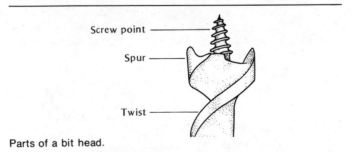

Screw point

Spur

Twist

Parts of a bit head.

The bit Russell Jennings invented has a double twist. It bores more slowly but more smoothly and accurately than single-twist bits. It's a favorite for doweled joints.

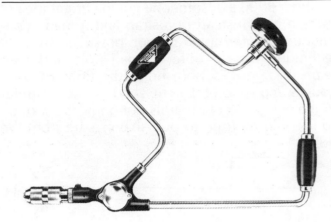

The corner brace is for drilling near beams, against walls, and in other tight places. This one, from Millers Falls, has a 10″ sweep.

WHY USE A BIT BRACE?

What can a bit brace do that a quarter-inch electric drill can't? For one thing, it has the capability of drilling large holes. It will take up to half-inch shanks. To match its capacity, you would have to have a half-inch electric drill. It also offers more control and greater accuracy. That's why it remains popular with cabinetmakers and other pros.

Requiring no electricity, the bit brace can be used where power drills are either useless (like out in the woods or up on a roof), or potentially dangerous (in wet locations). It's especially handy for drilling countersinks. It also is a powerful screwdriver. These are seven good reasons for owning a bit brace.

But for speedy drilling of small holes, a bit brace is too big and clumsy. For that there is a choice of either a hand drill or a push drill. The push drill is designed for one-hand use, and is especially good for starting screws. The hand drill, geared like an eggbeater, is a two-hand tool. It is thus more accurate than the push drill.

Hand drills are available with either one or two pinion gears. These are the small gears that engage the big gear. The two-pinion type has easier, smoother operation.

Principle manufacturers of bit braces, hand drills, and push drills are Stanley, Millers Falls, and Great Neck. Sears and Montgomery Ward braces and drills are made by Stanley, as are those of the U.S. Government.

Prices of bit braces range from about $6 to $35. Hand drills range in price from about $4 to $22, and push drills from $5 to $17.

You can buy 13 bits in graduated sizes in a protective plastic roll.

This bit is used for installing locks. Available for drilling holes 1 $^3/_4''$, 2'', and 2$^1/_8''$ in diameter. The $^5/_8''$ hex shank will also fit electric drill.

A countersink drills a tapered hole that seats the head of a flathead screw flush with the surface.

Bit extension has an overall length of 18'' and a bit capacity of 1''. Yet it is slender enough to follow a $^{11}/_{16}''$ bit through a hole.

Expansive bits solve big problems. Smaller bit will bore up to 19 standard-size holes ranging from $^5/_8$ to 1 $^3/_4''$. Larger bit bores up to 35 holes ranging from $^7/_8''$ to 3''.

Hand drill has a die-cast zinc speed gear and two steel pinions to provide smooth operation. Aluminum gear housing protects bearings, conceals gears to prevent catching clothing.

This heavy-duty hand drill has a 4'' speed gear and a $^3/_8''$ chuck. Like all good hand drills, it has two pinions, not one. Eight drill points, $^1/_{16}''$ to $^{11}/_{16}''$, are furnished in the hollow handle.

The cup on the end of this drill fits against the chest, enables you to apply your body weight while holding the lower handle.

A screwlike shaft inside this sleek chrome body converts every push into a rotary motion of the drill point. Magazine handle contains eight drill points.

Inexpensive guide keeps drills from walking or going in at an angle You can use it vertically or horizontally on any flat surface. Accommodates thirteen drill sizes up to $^1/_4''$.

5.
PLANES SPOKESHAVES DRAWKNIVES

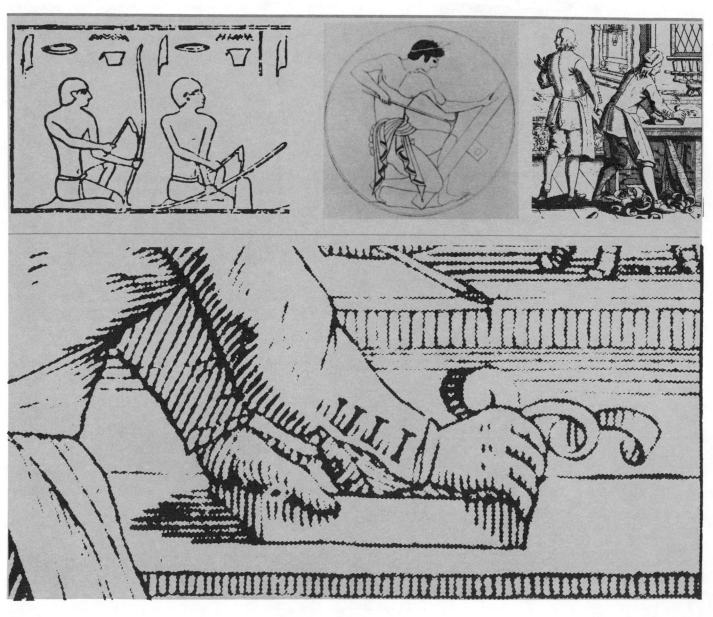

The adze, shaped like a hoe but with the cutting edge of an axe, was an ancient forerunner of the planes we know today. So was the drawknife or shave. When the blade of a shave was set in a mouth to control its depth of cut, the plane, as we most commonly think of it, was born.

Romans called the plane *runcina*. It was usually a wood block with a chisel-like blade, or iron, wedged in at an angle. They used them not just for leveling or smoothing boards, but for cutting channels, grooves, and rabbets, and for making decorative moldings.

Up until the turn of the century and beyond, the carpenter had to plane every board that came from the sawmill. He also had to make his own moldings and trim, his own doors, windows, and cabinets. He had to do fluting, beading, reeding, tongue and grooving, not to mention fillistering. Because he needed planes for so many jobs, he might have two or three dozen in his tool collection—a different one for each purpose.

Europeans lavished much love on their planes, elaborately carving and ornamenting them. Early American planes, perhaps under the influence of the Shakers, were distinguished by clean, simple designs.

Notable improvements to planes came just after the Civil War. Plane bodies were made of iron, and patented adjustments gave them new flexibility control. At the Centennial Exposition, in 1876, you could have seen planes very similar to those we have today.

The world has changed, however. The power saw and jointer-planer now do jobs that formerly would have been done by the plane. Stock millwork and trim of all kinds are available. But planes still do hold an important niche. They are still essential for fine woodworking, for custom production. They are the choice for extremely careful and accurate work, skimming off tissue-thin shavings for exact fitting, and are often faster, when power tool set-up time is considered.

Wooden planes have had a recent resurgence in popularity. The wooden body means wood-to-wood contact, and easier sliding than metal on wood. They are lighter and easier to handle than metal planes.

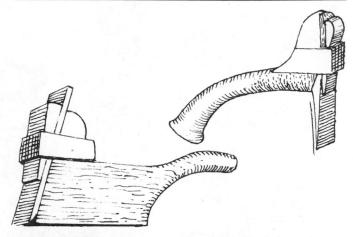

Egyptian adze of the late Ptolemaic period could be turned on its end and used as a plane.

Sometimes the board was pulled through the plane.

An early wooden plane with the date carved into the body.

A collection of modern wooden planes, from Garrett Wade.

SOME THREESOME!

Three planes are of special interest for the home workshop.

The block plane. It's a one-hand tool, typically only 7″ long. Reach for it every time you want to bevel a board, round a corner, or remove a little wood. It cuts fast.

The jack plane. Its usually 14″, with a blade 2″ wide. It's the jack of all jobs, will true boards of moderate length. The smooth plane is like the jack, but smaller and lighter, usually 8″ to 9″ with a $1^3/_4$″ blade.

The jointer plane. Its 20″ to 24″ long. Designed for truing up long boards so their edges meet almost invisibly. Good on door edges. A fore plane is like the jointer, but shorter—18″.

In addition, there are many special planes for rabbeting, routing, grooving, and molding work.

Block plane, a one-hand trimming tool, has adjustments for thickness of shaving, evenness of shaving, and for coarse or fine work. Stanley.

Wooden jack plane in traditional style is made of one solid, straight-grained piece of oiled beechwood. This 17″ plane is ideal for beginning cabinetmakers. It is $2^3/_4$″ wide and has a 2″ plane iron.

Jointer plane has long, smooth edges for making tight glue joints, perfect matching edges of long boards. Beechwood body with hornbeam sole. Length of body, about 2′. Ulmia, Denmark.

PARTS OF A PLANE

1. Handle bolt and nut.
2. Handle.
3. Lateral adjusting lever.
4. Blade.
5. Cap-iron or blade.
6. Cam lever.
7. Cap.
8. Cap-iron screw.
9. Frog.
10. Cap screw.
11. Plane bottom.
12. Knob bolt and nut.
13. Knob.
14. Face.
15. Throat.
16. Frog screw.
17. Frog clip.
18. Frog adjusting screw.
19. Frog clip screw.
20. Handle toe bolt.
21. Adjusting nut.
22. Cutter adjusting screw.
23. Y-adjustment lever.

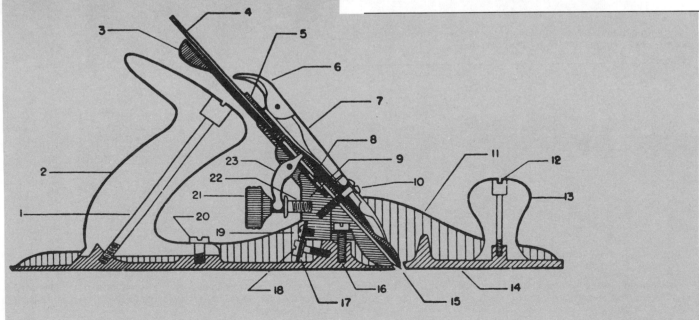

The adze is thousands of years old, and still going strong. Adze with straight edge can be used to create a hand-hewn effect on squared-up timber. Curved edge is for curved surfaces. Woodcraft.

Tonguing plane cuts a tongue which fits exactly into flat-bottomed groove cut by grooving plane. Garrett Wade.

Router plane is excellent for roughing out backgrounds on signs and for relief carving. Has a $3/16''$, $5/16''$ and $7/8''$ blade. Length of body is $9-1/2''$. Woodcraft.

Excellent reproduction of nineteenth century plough plane with adjustable fence comes with six irons. For use in ploughing grooves for tongue-and-groove panels, drawers, floorboards. Woodcraft.

A plane is used to take the rough edges off a carpenter's apprentice. The year—1681.

This plane makes moldings. A separate molding plane was used for each design shown. They are available to cut $3/8''$, $1/2''$, and $5/8''$ moldings. Woodcraft.

Smoothing plane is almost identical with one in the famed Shelburne Museum collection. It's 7¹/₂″ long, has a 2″ blade that adapts to small surfaces. Woodcraft.

Favorites since 1869, Stanley planes have a long tradition. This bench jack plane is 9¹/₄″ long, has a smooth or corrugated bottom.

When a rabbet doesn't go all the way to the end of the board, this chisel, or stop-rabbet, plane will trim and square the end. It's just over 7″, with a 1³/₈″ iron. Woodcraft.

Jack, fore, and jointer planes are 14″ to 22″ long. The biggest one costs about twice as much as the smallest one.

Japanese block plane would be called a jack plane here. It's 14¹/₄″ long and has a 2³/₈″ blade.

Rabbet plane has two blade seats. The blade in this English-made Stanley plane goes in middle seat for regular work, up front for close or bullnose jobs. Has depth gauge and adjustable fence.

This 9¹/₂″ scrub plane of oiled beechwood removes wood quickly and easily. It can be used with or across grain. Its 1¹/₄″ plane is ground convex. Woodcraft.

Bullnose plane is extremely accurate. Sides are square with the bottom, so tool can be used on all three surfaces. Take off its nose and it's a chisel plane. Beautifully made, 4″ long. Woodcraft.

Planemaster uses replaceable blades, eliminates need for sharpening. It's 10″ long, 2″ wide, comes with a fence for rabbeting. With five spare blades and rabbeting attachment. Brookstone.

Just insert a different nosepiece and this three-in-one plane shifts from regular plane to chisel plane to bullnose plane. Cutter is screw adjustable. It's 6″ long, with 1¹⁄₂″ cutter. Frog Tool Co.

They call it side rabbet plane No. 79, and it's made for trimming dados, moldings, and grooves of all kinds. Has a reversible nosepiece for working in corners. Can be used in either direction. Cutter is ¹⁄₂″ wide. Woodcraft.

Open-throat router plane comes with ¹⁄₄″ and ¹⁄₂″ square cutters and a ¹⁄₂″ V or smoothing cutter. Cutters graduated in ¹⁄₁₆ for depth adjustment. Length is 7⁵⁄₈″. Woodcraft.

This plane works on concave or convex surfaces. Its secret is a flexible steel sole that can be adjusted to a concave or convex shape. Otherwise the setting is the same as for a regular bench plane. It has a 10″ sole and a 1³⁄₄″ cutter. Woodcraft.

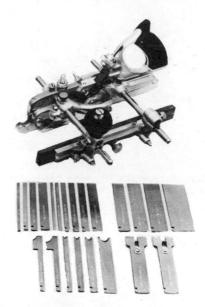

Multiplane comes with the following tungsten-steel cutting irons: 13 plough and dado, 5 beading, 1 fillister, 2 tonguing, 2 ovolo and 1 slitting—all in a wood case. Woodcraft.

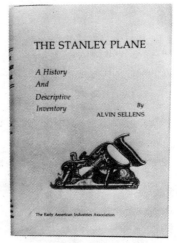

Box plane is useful in refinishing. Especially good for removing marks and defects on tabletops, floors, etc. It's 10″ long and has a 1⁷⁄₈″ cutter. Woodcraft.

Planecraft, a 255-page book, and the *Stanley Plane*, a history of all woodworking planes produced by Stanley since 1857, are available from Woodcraft.

THE ODD ONES

The spokeshave is a plane in a different kind of frame. Its handles are on the sides instead of at the ends. It derives its name from its use in smoothing wheel spokes, but it is effective on many other kinds of curved surfaces. Like most other planes, it is usually pushed.

The drawknife, or drawshave, is a simple type of plane used for making curves and cutting down edges and corners. The blade is beveled, and may be used with the bevel either up or down. The blade length is usually 8" to 10", and it may be straight or curved. Like a Chinese plane, it is designed to be pulled toward the user, not pushed. Depth of cut is regulated by tilting the blade.

TEN COMMANDMENTS FOR PLANES

1. Cut with the grain.
2. Do not use on painted or varnished wood.
3. Keep the blade razor sharp.
4. In making a rough cut, slant the plane across the board.
5. In finishing, start with pressure on the plane front, end with pressure on the rear.
6. In planing end grain, to avoid breaking corners, go from each end to the middle.
7. Store planes so they are protected from rust and damage to the cutting edge. Lay it on side when not in use.
8. Don't try to make too thick a cut.
9. Keep the blade straight for an even cut.
10. The longer the plane, the smoother the results.

MANUFACTURERS

Leading brand names of planes are Stanley, Craftsman, and Millers Falls in the United States and Record in England. Wooden planes are imported from Germany, Denmark, and Japan.

Unusual and rare planes of all kinds may be purchased from Woodcraft, Garrett Sloan, and Frog Tool Company, whose addresses are listed at the end of the book.

Another ancient tool that's still with us, and especially popular with furniture makers, is the drawknife. German styles shown here include 8", 9", and 10" sizes. Blade has a slight curve and handles are somewhat offset. Woodcraft.

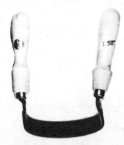

Inshave is for hollowing, scraping, and scooping out. It has a 7¾" curved cutting edge of German tool steel. Woodcraft.

It's called a scorp, and it's a roughing-out tool for concave shapes. Blade is 2¼" wide, overall length 7". Woodcraft.

This spokeshave with 10" cast-iron body and 2¹/₁₆" cutter is adjustable for very fine work. Frog Tool Co.

Japanese drawshave is different in design, but is used like a spokeshave. It has a rounded face along entire 10¼" length. Blade is 1⅝". Woodcraft.

6.

FILES/RASPS SCRAPERS

Early flint rasps from Stone Age diggings.

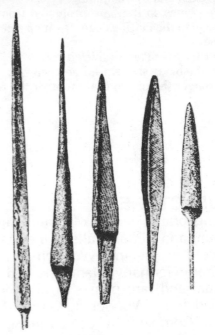

Iron files typical of the Gallo-Roman period.

In the Stone Age, our ancestors made rasps of flint. About 3,000 years ago, they began using bronze and, by hand, made the first metal files. Next, by hand, they made files of iron.

Here is how files were made by hand. A strap of metal was softened (annealed) by heating and then slow-cooled. It was next placed on a lead slab, and close, parallel grooves were chiseled on it, spaced by eye. Finally, the metal was rehardened (tempered) by heating it and thrusting it in water to cool it quickly.

The ancient Assyrians, Egyptians, Romans, Greeks, and Chinese all made files. The Roman files had a distinctive touch—a notch near the handle end. It was for twisting saw teeth and giving them "set."

Rasps differ from files in that they have teeth rather than ridges. Today, as in ancient times, they are used on wood, leather, soft metals, and horses' hoofs. In hand-making rasps, teeth are punched out with a triangular steel point.

Leonardo da Vinci, in 1490, sketched the first file-cutting machine, but file-making machinery was not introduced until the nineteenth century. Even after that, files continued to be made by hand, because handmade files were better.

Left: Handcutting of file with chisel. *Right:* File texture magnified.

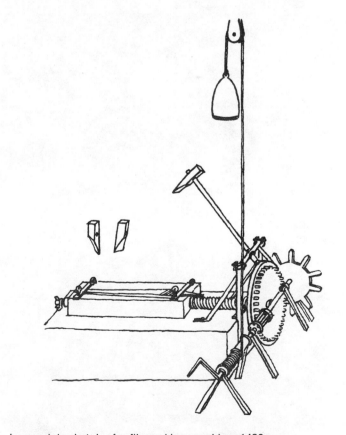

Leonardo's sketch of a file-making machine, 1490.

Today, there are over 3,000 kinds, sizes, and cuts of files. Three characteristics distinguish most of them from one another—length, shape, and cut.

The *length* of a file applies only to its cutting surface. It does not include the file's tang or handle.

The *kind* of file refers to its cross-sectional shape, which may be flat, square, round, half-round, or triangular.

The *cut* of a file refers to the kind of teeth or sharp serrations it has. A single-cut file has parallel serrations running diagonally across it. A double-cut file has a second series of serrations running at an opposite diagonal across the first. A single-cut file does smoother work and is good for sharpening knives, shears, and saws. A double-cut file is faster, but rougher. It is used for rapid removal of material.

OTHER FACTS

A file may be blunt or tapered. A tapered file is useful in enlarging openings. Because its cutting area increases from the tip, it is somewhat easier to use. A blunt shape, on the other hand, is best for inside corners.

Half-round files are good on concave surfaces, triangular files for notches, square holes and damaged threads. A single-cut triangular file is used in sharpening handsaws. Slim-tapered triangular files are good on bandsaw blades.

Files are commonly made in three different coarsenesses—smooth, second cut, and bastard. The bastard cut is fastest and roughest. As a file's length increases, its cut becomes coarser. A 4" file, for example, has many more teeth per square inch and is much smoother than a 16" file of the same type.

A curved-tooth file has teeth milled in an arc. It is used with soft metals and other materials for rapid stock removal.

A "mill" file, so-called because it was originally used in a sawmill for sharpening sawblades, typically tapers in its forward third. It may come with square or round edges or one "safe," or smooth edge. The smooth edge is so you won't rough up adjoining surfaces when you are doing close work. You can grind the teeth off an edge and make your own safe edge.

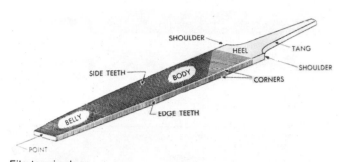

File terminology.

File length is figured from point to heel.

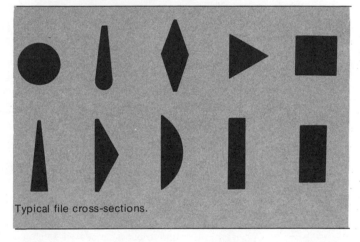

Typical file cross-sections.

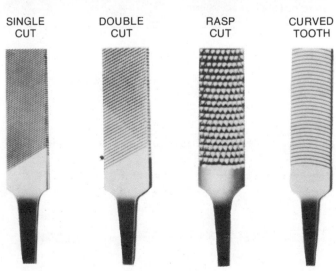

SINGLE CUT   DOUBLE CUT   RASP CUT   CURVED TOOTH

Kinds of teeth.

Top—blunt. Bottom—tapered.

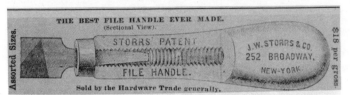

Surform tools, with hundreds of cutting teeth, work fast and do not clog. Blades are replaceable. The six varieties are shown here.

Bent riffler comes with handle, has 3¹/₂″ cut. Can be used on the most intricate work.

Checkering file is used by gunsmiths to put a checkered area on a gun to make a firm hand grip.

Knife file is generally used in slots or wedge-shaped openings. Offered with 3″, 4″, 6″ and 8″ cuts.

Wood rifflers are used by cabinetmakers.

Swiss files are similar to American files in types and shapes, but are made to more exacting tolerances and have smaller points with longer, thinner tapers. They are also made in much finer cuts. A Swiss pattern No. 00 cut is the equivalent of an American bastard, its No. 0 to a second cut, and its No. 2 to a smooth cut. From here, they go on to a No. 8, the finest.

Rifflers are small files with curved ends. One end is usually a rasp for rough cutting, the other a file for finishing. They are useful on irregular shapes, like wood carvings.

Handles. A file without a handle is more difficult to use and presents the risk of injury. Files should be equipped with a wood or metal handle. Wood handles with metal ferrules are easily force-fitted. Metal handles have a clamping device and are easier to tighten or switch from one file to another.

The Surform is a special type of file, or rasp. Distributed in this country by Stanley, it comes in a variety of styles. Its replaceable blade of Sheffield tool steel has diagonal parallel rows of razor-sharp, chisel-like individual cutting edges, each fronted by a tiny half-moon hole through which shavings pass.

It can be used on wood, aluminum, copper, plastics, tile, laminated countertops, and metals up to the hardness of mild steel.

Scrapers. Fingernails were man's first scrapers. Then came flint. The Romans made scrapers of sharp-edged squares or other pieces of steel. In pre-industrial days, carpenters, using a cold chisel, cut scrapers out of old saw blades, square-edged them on a grindstone and then sharpened them on a whetstone. They use them not only for finishing wood, but for removing paint and varnish.

Today's scrapers, closely related to drawknives and spokeshaves, come in a number of varieties. Among them are shave hooks, scraping planes, box scrapers, ship scrapers, and cabinet scrapers.

Handyman's Home File Pak, made by Nicholson, includes an 8″ mill for sharpening shears, axes and knives; a 6″ tapered triangular file to smooth angled surfaces and sharpen saw teeth; and an 8″ all-purpose 4-in-Hand that is half file, half rasp.

Typical rasp has one flat and one rounded side. Here, flat side is being used to roughen a dowel for gluing.

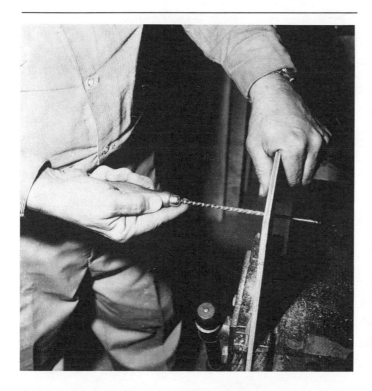

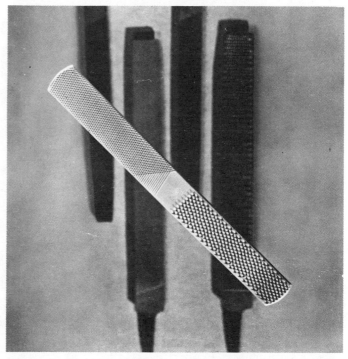

The Stickleback, made by Coastal, is a special kind of rasp with a unique kind of nonclogging teeth. For surface forming, enlarging holes, and making irregularly shaped holes in wood, hardboard, plastic. 10″ long. Available by mail order from U.S. General.

Nicholson combination tool is flat on one side, half round on other, each with a rasp and file section of different coarseness for cutting and smoothing wood, metal, or plastic. 8″ and 10″ sizes.

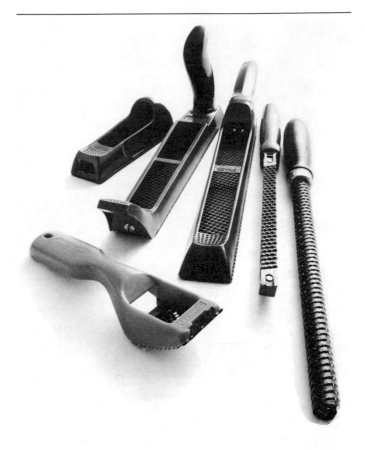

Mill file for sharpening circular saws. Comes in lengths of from 4″ to 16″.

Rotary mower file, the first file designed for sharpening rotary mower blades.

Auger bit file.

Band-saw taper file.

Chain-saw file.

Screw head file, for enlarging and cleaning out the slots in the heads of screws. 3″ long.

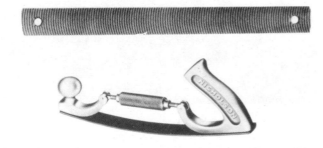

Flexible file for curved surfaces, designed for use with flexible file holder shown.

A collection of files, rasps, etc. available from Garrett Wade.

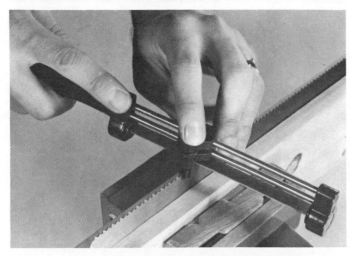

English-made Eclipse saw sharpener accurately controls pitch and angle. Can be used with almost any saw.

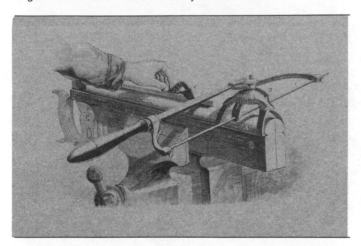

Comparative coarseness, 10″ mill files.

Channeled, serrated jaws tightly grab flat, oval, square, or round shanks. Besides files, it will hold hacksaw blades, taps, reamers, wrenches, knives. Woodcraft.

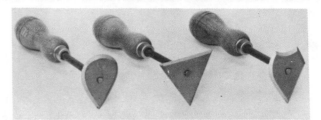

These shavehooks will handle surfaces other scrapers can't touch—convex, concave, or corners—it makes no difference. Steel shanks extend through beechwood handles. Brookstone.

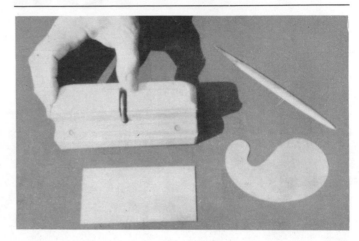

Cabinet scrapers are the tools professional cabinet and furniture makers use in getting an outstanding finish. From top left, clockwise: wheel burnisher, oval stroke burnisher, gooseneck scraper, straight scraper.

For stripping paint and for removing dried glue. Two cutting edges on replaceable blade. Handle is cast iron. Frog.

Heavy-duty scraper will tackle anything. Has tempered blade of forged steel, wooden handle. Length is 12″ overall, with a blade width of 2″. Frog.

File card keeps files free of metal chips, sawdust, and other debris, so they cut faster and better. Its semiflexible wires, set at angle, comb dirt out. U.S. General.

7.

KNIVES

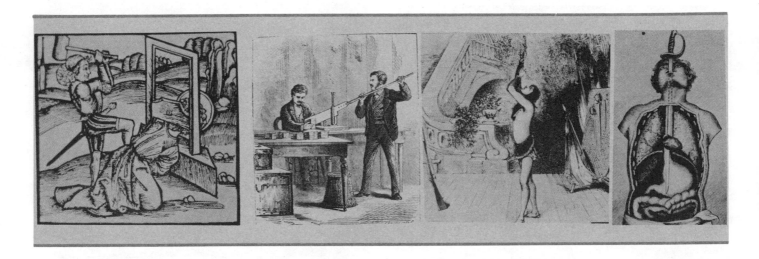

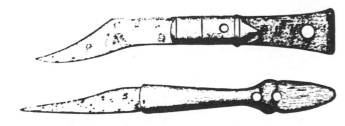

Tribal knives, Africa

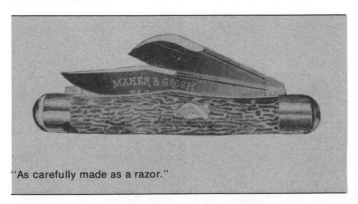

"As carefully made as a razor."

A knife was one of the first tools of the Stone Age, and it has taken many forms and been put to a wide variety of uses since then. Its role in hunting came early. So did the part it played in religious rites, notably sacrifices. It often performed a veto assignment in politics, witness Caesar's "unkindest cut of all," and the guillotine. Knife throwing and sword swallowing put it into show business.

Folding knives were known to the Romans, and it is probable that is when the love affair of the carpenter and the pocketknife began. Certainly, today, few are without one. Old-timers used a "drawing knife" to cut a groove for a saw to follow. A favorite at their bench was the "sloyd knife," used for marking wood and for small cutting jobs. Not unlike a paring knife in appearance, it is still available today.

For the handyperson, a major innovation in knife design came in 1936. In that year, the Stanley Works introduced a knife that offered razor sharpness—with high safety for the user. Its blade was only a small projecting point. Most of the blade was held in a handle of die-cast aluminum, and it was reversible, to provide a second cutting edge. When both edges became dull, the entire blade was replaceable, as in a safety razor. Replacement was easy. The two-part handle was held with a locking screw that had a "coin" slot, so it was quickly taken apart and the blade removed. Extra blades were kept in the handle.

The "Stanley knife" was a multi-purpose dream. It was used for cutting plasterboard, floor tile, carpeting, trimming wallpaper, opening cartons, cutting rope, shaving wood—everything.

In 1953, when the Stanley patent expired, everyone started making what is now called a "utility knife." All are similar in design and blades are usually interchangeable. Some blades have a single-grind edge. These are supersharp, but easier to nick. Others have a double-bevel grind that is somewhat blunter—still extremely sharp, but with greater durability. Best blades have 1.25 carbon steel. Others have .95. So they're not all alike! Special-purpose blades made to fit most utility knives include hook, linoleum, and scoring blades.

Companies offering utility knives, beside Stanley, include Allway, Cintride, Easco, General, Millers Falls, Ritco, and Red Devil. Most are in the $2.50 to $4 range.

Stanley knife, introduced in 1936, has had many imitators. Die-cast aluminum handle provides blade storage and has handy hang-hole. Comes with blade guard.

A push on projecting button adjusts blade of this Stanley knife to three positions. Aluminum handle provides blade storage.

Pocket knife with buttonhook for glove or shoe.

Left: Razor-sharp hooked ends cut to full thickness through linoleum, roofing, cartons, etc., without damage. Fits most makes.

Center: For score-cutting plastic laminates like Formica, asbestos, plastic roofing and flooring materials. Fits most makes.

Right: Linoleum blade of tempered high-carbon steel fits Stanley knives 199, 299, and 1299.

Replacement blade dispenser, designed for safety, holds 100 utility knife blades.

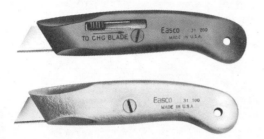

Easco offers one knife with retractable blade, one is nonadjustable. By swiveling blade, either knife can be used as a scraper. Thumb rests are a feature.

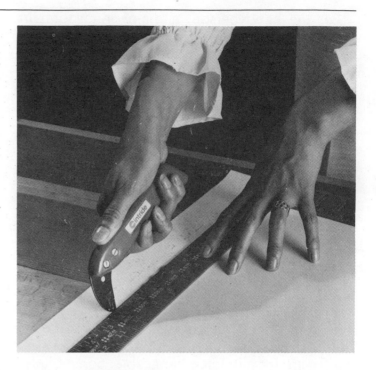

Rugged Cintride plastic-laminate knife features a double-ended tungsten-carbide-tipped cutter for plastic laminates and hard vinyl floor tiles. An English import.

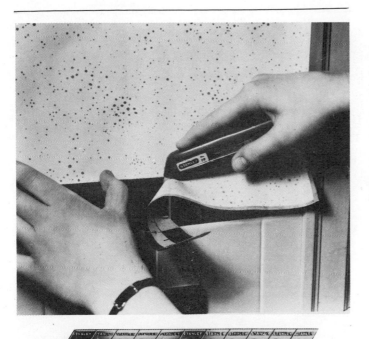

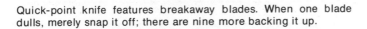

Quick-point knife features breakaway blades. When one blade dulls, merely snap it off; there are nine more backing it up.

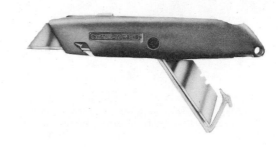

Stanley-made front-loading knife features retractable blade and automatic blade-storage magazine.

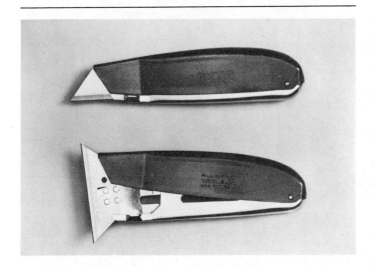

Steel body makes this knife stronger. Allway knife is so strong it can safely be hammered into Sheetrock. Unfolds for quick, screwless blade changes. Blade converts to scraper.

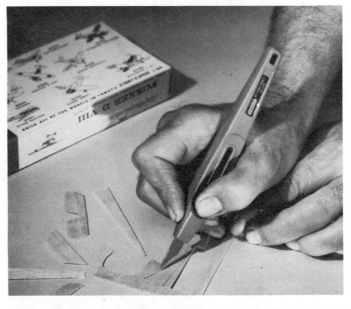

Carry this little key-chain knife in your pocket. It's only 3 ¹/₂″ long and weighs less than an ounce.

Slim Knife for fine cutting, trimming, modeling. Accommodates five different types of blades that also fit other knives of similar design.

Multi-purpose bench knife, 7″ long overall, with 1 ½″ cutting edge, hard tempered to take and hold sharpness. For fine detail work, tough cutting. Brookstone.

A line scribed with a knife is more accurate and dependable than one drawn with a pencil. This marking or striking knife has two cutting edges on one end, awl point at other. Mirror-plated stainless steel with hardwood grip. About 8″ long. Brookstone.

Forged of a single piece of tool steel 8 ½″ long, this heavy knife can safely be struck with a hammer. So tough it will even cut electrical cable. Blade is sharp on end as well as bottom edge. Brookstone.

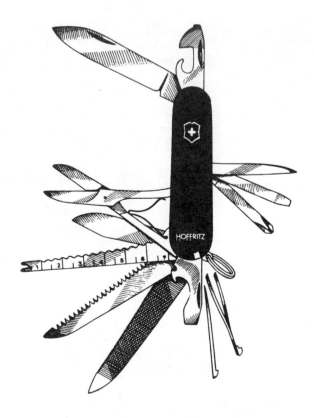

Original Swiss army knife, authorized by the government, offers thirteen tools, including wood saw, metal saw and file, regular and Phillips-head screwdrivers, shears, hole punch, tweezers, cap lifter, can opener.

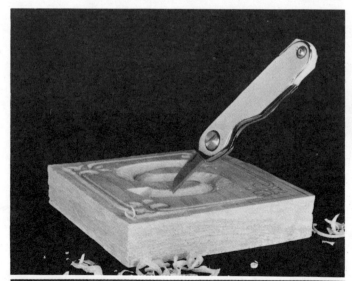

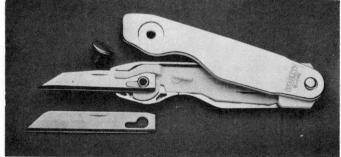

Cross between pocket and utility knife has the best elements of both. Razor-sharp fold-out stainless-steel blade (two types) is replaceable. Stanley.

What hard work 'tis crying all day, "Knives and Scissors to grind, oh!"

—George Canning (1770-1827)

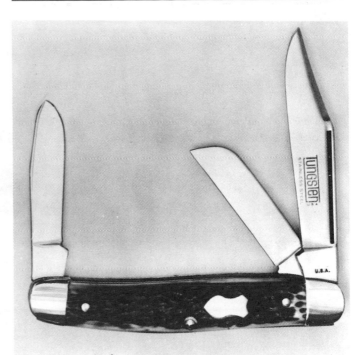

Rustproof and tough tungsten stainless-steel blades with solid nickel-silver bolsters. Solid brass linings. Virtually unbreakable handle. Medallion for initials. Brookstone.

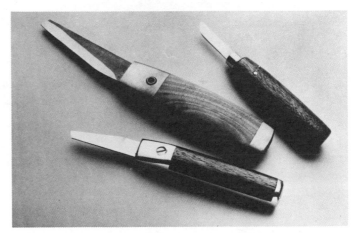

Three beautiful knives: (bottom) brass handle with rosewood grip, 6″ long, hacksaw steel blade extends through handle, (center) aluminum body with walnut grips, 6 3/4″ long; (top) whittler's knife, 5 1/2″ long. Leichtung.

Sloyd knife is old-time favorite. This design, by Dixon, has an overall length of 5 3/4″ with a 1 3/4″ blade. Dixon also makes one with an overall length of 6 5/8″ with a 2 5/8″ blade. Blades are of Swedish surgical steel.

8.

WOOD CHISELS GOUGES

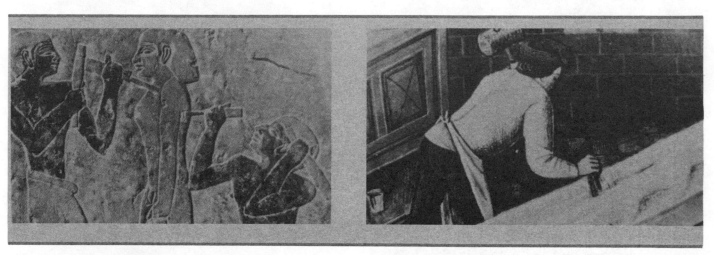

There are some things a saw, a drill, or a plane can't do. That's where the wood chisel comes in. It can remove material that can't readily be removed in any other way.

Prehistoric people on every continent used chisels made of stone. In the Bronze Age, chisels acquired wood handles. An ancient relief sculpture, dated 2540 B.C., shows two men using round wooden mallets to drive such chisels.

A century or two ago, the members of wooden structures were fitted together with mortises and tenons. This was the heyday of chisels. To make a mortise, two auger holes were drilled and then a chisel converted them into a rectangular hole. A saw could rough out a tenon, but it took a chisel to finish it off. Mortises and tenons were important not only in post-and-beam framing, but in putting together doors, windows, and shutters.

Today, chisels find most use in the installation of locks, lock strike plates, and hinges. They are used in work requiring fine craftsmanship and in wood carving and sculpture. A chisel is a free-hand tool. It may be struck with a hammer or mallet, or pushed by hand.

THE BLADE

Variations in length, width, and thickness of blades give chisels special qualities that make one chisel better than another for a particular job.

A *paring* chisel is lighter and thinner. The angle of the bevel at its cutting edge may be only 15 degrees instead of 25 degrees as in most other chisels. Because of its greater fragility, it is not for striking with a mallet. It is for light, finishing work.

A *firmer* chisel is longer and thicker than a paring chisel. It is used for both light and heavy work. A typical blade length is 4".

A *butt* chisel has the shortest blade of all chisels—usually 3". All carpenters use the butt chisel. There are few jobs it can't do. A good home shop collection would include butt chisels with blade widths of $\frac{1}{4}$", $\frac{1}{2}$", $\frac{3}{4}$", and 1".

A *mortise* chisel, as its name implies, is for cutting out mortises. This involves heavy blows by mallet or hammer and its use as a lever. Its blade is thick and strong, especially where it meets the handle. Mortise chisels most often have square rather than beveled sides, adding to their strength.

Plumbers, electricians, glaziers, lathe operators, carvers, and sculptors have their own special varieties of chisels. These are shown elsewhere in the book.

Egyptian mallet and socket chisel.

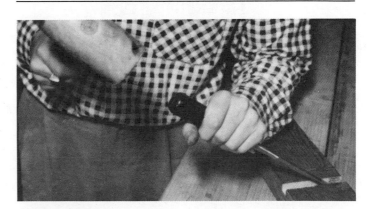

Cutting a dado.

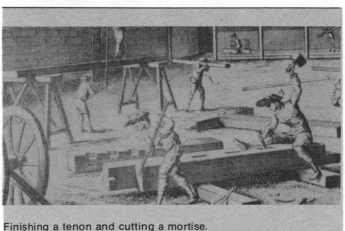

Finishing a tenon and cutting a mortise.

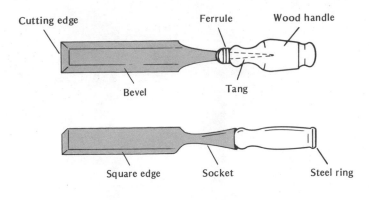

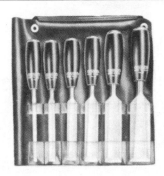

In Stanley's #40 chisels, blade and shank, forged in one piece, meet shank of steel cap.

A set of six #40 Stanley chisels come in $1/4''$, $1/2''$, $3/4''$, $1''$, $1/4''$, and $1 1/2''$.

Stanley's #60 chisels have handles of clear amber plastic. In nine widths, from $1/4''$ to $2''$.

Tang chisel with plastic handle. Butt blade, $2 1/2''$ long, forms strong conical bolster at end.

HANDLE STYLES

Wood is favored by sentiment and tradition and by those who find it has a more comfortable feel, but there is no doubt that plastic is today's material. It may be clear amber cellulose acetate, which physically is as good as you can get. Or it may be an opaque plastic, and not necessarily virgin material.

The attachment of blade to handle is important. The blade may have a tang, a tapered tail which has been driven into the wood handle or encased in a plastic one. This is a less durable arrangement than others, but it is perfectly suited to paring chisels and others not subjected to heavy pounding. Some tang chisels have an "up-set shoulder" or bolster at the blade end that takes the force of hammer blows.

For heavy duty, a continuous steel shank runs from cap to blade. Blade and shank, forged of one piece, meet the shank of the steel cap.

The technique of socketed weapons and tools was developed in the Bronze Age, and it is used effectively with one style of chisel. Socket chisels have a tapered wood or composition handle which fits into a cone-shaped socket at the blade end. The end of the handle may be fitted with a steel ring to prevent mushrooming or with a leather or metal disc. Handles are replaceable.

Bevel-edge English paring chisel, with boxwood handle, comes in six sizes, from $\frac{1}{4}$" to 1 $\frac{1}{2}$".

Mortise chisel has leather washer between bolster and ferrule that absorbs blows. Steel hoop at striking end adds durability.

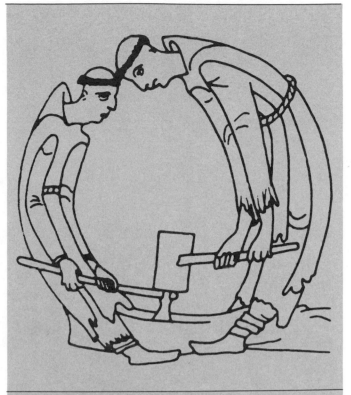

Firmer chisel with traditional machine-turned hardwood handle. Blade has square sides. Sizes in $\frac{1}{8}$"- increments to 1 $\frac{1}{2}$".

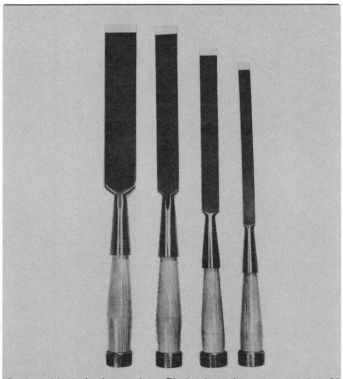

Socket chisels for heavy duty. Blades have been tempered to 62 Rockwell Hardness, insuring excellent edge-holding quality. Set of five, or sold individually. Woodcraft.

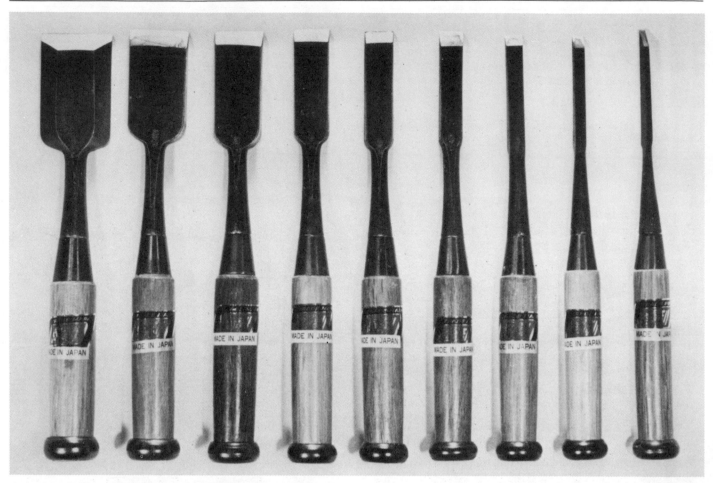

Japanese paring chisels have short butt-size blades, but are for hand use or light hammering. Set of nine in sizes from 3mm ($\frac{1}{8}$″) to 36mm (1 $\frac{1}{2}$″), or sold individually. Woodcraft.

All-steel, all-purpose Dasco chisel is recommended by manufacturer for both rough and finish work. Teardrop finger rest and smooth dome head. Sizes $\frac{1}{4}$″ to 1 $\frac{1}{4}$″.

Floor chisel for rough cutting is designed for removing tongue-and-groove flooring, but can be used for any kind of cutting or trimming. 2″, 2 $\frac{1}{2}$″, or 3″ cut. Dasco.

Kindling wood splitter.

GOUGES

Inside-ground firmer gouge. Machine-turned and polished box-wood handle is a traditional design. Available from ¹/₄″ to 1″.

Wood gouges are like chisels except that their blades are trough-shaped. They are used for cutting or smoothing grooves and other hollows.

Gouges may be firmer or paring, and are available with varying degrees of curvature or sweep.

The curved blades may be ground either on the concave side (inside-ground), or on the convex side (outside-ground). Inside-ground chisels are for paring. Outside-ground are firmer chisels and are for heavier work.

Some gouges have bent or offset shanks. This improves the handle's clearance from the work, and is especially helpful on long, shallow grooves.

Inside-ground paring gouge comes in thirteen sizes and with cutting arcs from ¹/₄″ to 1 ¹/₄″. Handle is shaped for comfortable, firm grip.

Paring gouge with offset handle. The British call an offset handle a "cranked neck" and say "in-cannel" or "out-cannel" instead of in-ground or out-ground.

Outside-ground firmer gouge. Round hardwood handle is turned in traditional style. Available in six sizes, from ¹/₄″ to 1″.

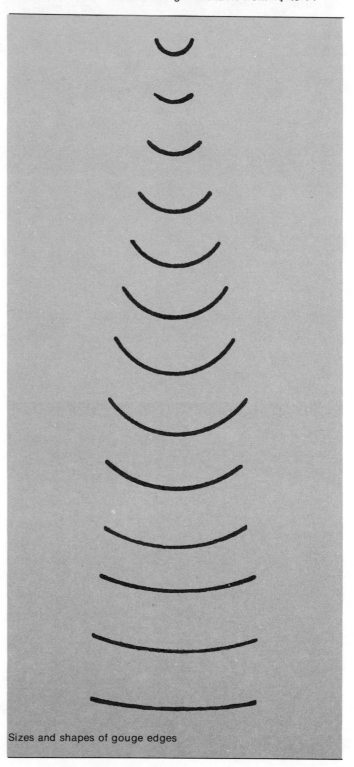

Sizes and shapes of gouge edges

ANTIQUE CHISEL TOOLS

Arnold & Walker, 112 Balham Park Raod, London SW128EA, is a gallery that sells traditional tools of carpenters and other craftsmen. Those shown here are from their Catalogue 2.

1. A paring axe, or "demi-besaigue," probably French in origin. Designed to be pushed, rather than swung. Believed used with no handle other than the iron socket itself.
2. Another paring axe, or "stossaxte," probably Swiss in origin. Functions as a chisel, and is for pushing.
3. Set of five mortise chisels.
4. French carpenter's twybil, *besaigue*, suggests a double-bitted chisel, one end for mortising, other for paring.
5. English hurdlemaker's twybil.
6. Compare this slick with the present-day replica shown among "new antique" tools.
7. A seventeenth century English socket chisel with slightly flaring blade.
8. English drawer-lock chisel.
9. Some wagon makers preferred all-metal chisels like this one.
10. Corner chisel was commonly used for squaring-up mortises.
11. Lock mortise chisel with boxwood handle.
12. "Swan neck" chisel for lock mortises. Bevel is on outside of curve. Made by William Ash in the 1830s.
13. A lock mortise chisel made by W. Staley.

OLD-TIME CHISELS

The *firmer* chisel was all-important. Its name, firmer, is a corruption of the name of an old French chisel, *fermoir,* used for cutting mortises, and that's how our forebears used the firmer chisel.

The *corner* chisel had a blade shaped like a right angle. It was used for cleaning up the corners of mortises.

The *framing* chisel was bigger than the firmer and was used for cutting tenons for the mortises.

The *clapboard* chisel was used in converting a log into wood siding.

Skew or *gooseneck* chisels were for mortising door locks.

The *slick* was a huge paring chisel, pushed by hands and shoulder. Its blade was 2" to 3" long and 2" to 4" wide. It was used like a plane for smoothing hewn beams.

The *peeling* chisel was used, along with an adze, in taking the bark off logs.

The *froe* was a chisel variation used in splitting shakes and shingles.

The *twybil* (two bill), used in the seventeenth century, was a cross between a hammer and a chisel. One end of its head was a vertical chisel edge, the other a horizontal edge. It, too, was used in cutting mortises.

THE CHISELER'S GUIDE

Used with the bevel side down, a chisel will make a rough cut. With the bevel side up, it will make a smoothing or finishing cut.

Cut with the grain. You can see its direction where it meets the edge. Cut against the grain and the wood is inclined to split.

Rock the chisel blade slightly as you cut. It's the shearing action that does the real work.

Always secure the work so it can't move.

Use a chisel smaller than the job. Don't use a 1/2" chisel to cut a 1/2" slot. It won't allow lateral movement.

Don't start cutting on your guide line. Work toward it.

Never cut toward yourself.

With a gouge, use just the tip of the cutting edge's arc, and don't try to cut a groove to its full depth in a single pass.

Always keep both hands behind the blade edge. Chisels sometimes slip unexpectedly.

MANUFACTURERS

In this country, Stanley and Buck do most of the chisel manufacturing. Millers Falls is also represented.

In England, it's Marples, and they sell all over the world. Other English chisel names are Robert Sorby and Henry Taylor.

Japanese chisels are sold in this country.

From West Germany it's Marks chisels.

NEW ANTIQUE TOOLS

Socket slick, used for paring, is held with both hands, one hand supplying the power, the other guiding the cut. Carpenters and boat builders find them useful for smoothing large areas. Maple handle is 2' long. Blade available either 3" or 3³/₄" wide. Woodcraft.

The spud has been used for nearly two centuries for taking bark off logs. It's a must for log cabin builders. Length 32". Woodcraft.

An accurate reproduction of a froe used by colonials for splitting shingles, shakes, and lumber. Long blade (15") is designed to be struck with an 18" to 24" club rather than a hammer or mallet. Hickory handle 22" long is available. Woodcraft.

Carpenter's beechwood mallet has hardwood shaft. Sizes: 4", 4¹/₂", and 5".

Lignum vitae carver's mallets should be stored in plastic bag to protect this durable wood. Four head sizes: 2¹/₂", 3", 3¹/₂", and 4". Woodcraft.

9.

RULERS MEASURING TAPES

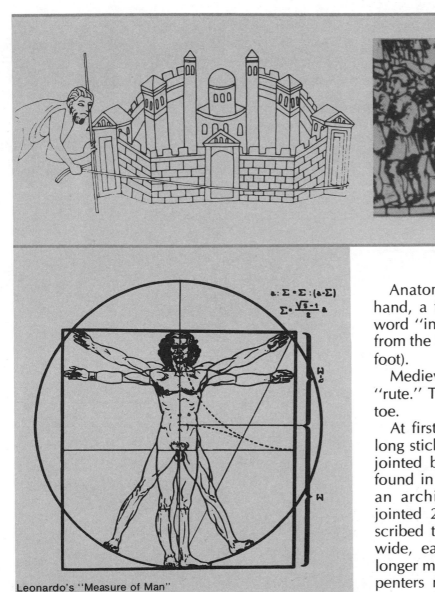

Leonardo's "Measure of Man"

Anatomical measures came first—a foot, a hand, a finger. They are still with us. Even the word "inch" has an anatomical connection. It's from the Latin *uncia,* means one-twelfth part (of a foot).

Medieval Germans had a measure called the "rute." They got it by lining up 16 men heel-to-toe.

At first, a rule was usually just a single foot-long stick. Then they began to put joints in it. A jointed bronze rule, hinged at the center, was found in a Pompeiian shop. Along about 1600, an architect, Vincenzio Scammozi, made a jointed 2' rule. In 1752, an encyclopedia described the typical ruler as 24" long and 1½" wide, each inch divided into eight parts. For longer measurements, in those days as now, carpenters made "10' rules." These were merely long sticks marked off into feet.

Brass-tipped and brass-hinged folding rulers are more than 150 years old. In their heyday, there were 1', 2', and 3' four-fold rules, some made of boxwood and brass-hinged and bound. Others were ivory and hinged and bound with German silver. The 2' size was the most popular. It was also available in 2-fold and 6-fold styles. The hinges on these rules were square, round, arch, or double arch.

Today, most folding rules come from England and the 3' (or 1-meter) four-fold boxwood rule is a standard. Traditionally, English-made rules read from left to right. American-made ones read from right to left.

Zig-zag. The zig-zag folding rule became the popular favorite after the turn of the century. Stanley introduced it in 1899 and it first appeared in their 1900 catalog. Surprisingly enough, it differed little from the ones we have today. They still aren't too popular in England, but they are popular on the Continent; a Swedish company, Mellosa Verkin, is the big name there.

Pull-push. The pull-push ruler was introduced in the 1920s by the now defunct Farrand Rule Company. It was a printed cross-curve tape that, in use, came completely out of the case. In the late 30's, it was decided to add a spring to help put the tape back.

Center pushbutton power tapes made their debut in the late 1940s. They have been largely replaced by the sliding button variety. The advantage of the sliding button is that you don't have to use it if you don't want to. For short measurements you merely hold the tape with your forefinger. A disadvantage of the pushbutton is that you have to remember to push it when you pull out the tape or you'll be pulling against the brake.

Pull-push rulers come in lengths ranging from 3' to 25', with blade widths of $1/4$" to 1". Many have thumb-locks to hold the blade extended, and springs to automatically rewind. Cases may be of metal or lightweight plastic, and may include a belt clip.

Long tapes. Commonly in 50' and 100' lengths, these tapes may be of metal or fiberglass. Some tapes are available up to 500'. In longer lengths, and in exacting work, expansion or contraction may be a significant factor, and special thermometers and scales permit correction. For accurate measurements, steel tapes must also be used under proper tension, and special tension handles can be used to counteract the effect of sag.

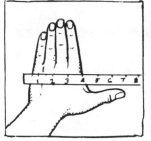

"Hand" is a linear measure equal to 4 inches. It's used especially in determining the height of a horse.

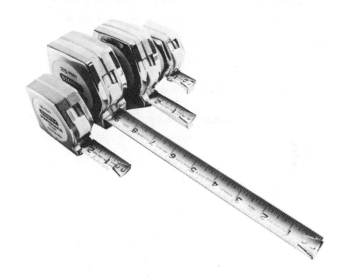

Modern tapes come in lengths to 25', and will remain rigid up to 7' for hard-to-reach measurements. They have power return and easy-to-operate thumb locks.

Folding rule is a traditional favorite. Tape rule (bottom) is quick and easy to use, has an automatic-return blade and a switch that locks the blade in any extended position. Long tape has pointed end hook and measures anything up to 50 feet.

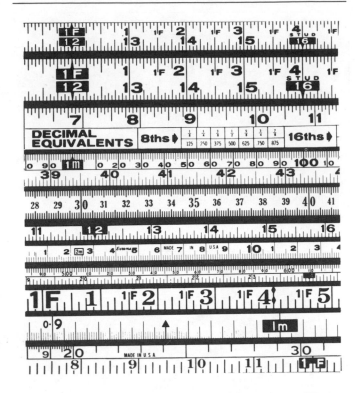

Two-section sliding rule makes it easy for one person to measure from floor to ceiling or across openings. Clamps and end-caps are brass. One variety is 5′, opening to 10′. Other is 6′, opening is 12′.

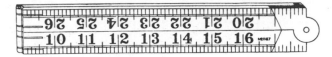

English-made folding boxwood rule, by Rabone Chesterman, is 36″ long, but folds neatly into pocket. It's marked in $1/16$″ on one side, $1/8$″ on other. Frog Tool Co.

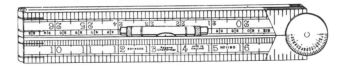

Folding boxwood rule offers two extras: a built-in spirit level and protractor. Woodcraft.

These are some of the blades available in Evans tapes. Whatever your special need you can probably find a blade to fill it.

Lufkin makes a 1-footer and a 2-footer in this brass-capped, natural-finish style. Opposite sides read from opposite ends.

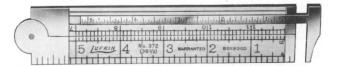

Three-foot flat wood rule is conveniently marked to read from opposite ends. It's marked on both sides, has brass end-caps to prevent wear.

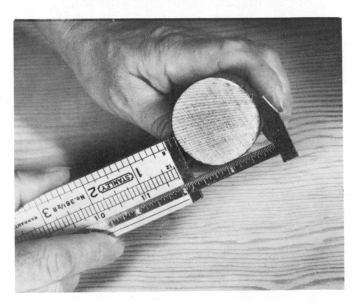

Boxwood rule is also a caliper. By extending solid-brass caliper slide, this 12′ rule provides an additional 5′ of measuring. Rule is $1^3/8$″ wide and is graduated in $1/8$″, $1/10$″, $1/12$″, and $1/16$″.

Blacksmith's measuring wheel.

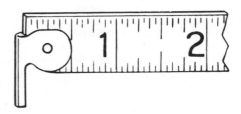

Another Lufkin "Red End" has same quality as extension rule but features a sturdy, folding brass-plated hook. Hook permits taking measurements that are beyond arm's reach.

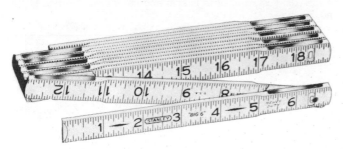

Stanley's "Big 6" is a heavy-duty classic 6' folding rule. Stud markings are located every 16".

It's a right-hand and a left-hand tape. Black graduations on a $3/4$" yellow blade. Boxed numbers indicate 16" centers. Plastic chrome case with removable belt clip. 25' length.

On this tape, exact inside measurement shows in window. Calibrated in inches and centimeters. Includes two-way bubble level, flip-out compass point for drawing circles or arcs, with hole for pencil or scriber at end of tape.

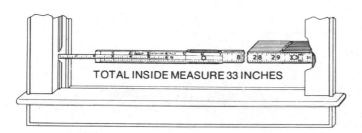

TOTAL INSIDE MEASURE 33 INCHES

Evans 6' extension rule (top) is of natural boxwood. Its brass slide extends 6", permitting inside measures.

Super-yardstick in lightweight case has a one-inch wide blade; supports itself up to 7'. Blade-holding mechanism retains blade at any length, also permits complete withdrawal from lightweight high-impact plastic case for use as an 8" yardstick. Reads from either side and also vertically in feet and inches. Metric conversion scale is on back of blade.

This tape measure is only $1/4''$ wide. Slim, compact case; comes in 6′, 8′, and 10′ sizes.

Professional steel tape, in 50′ and 100′ lengths, has white blade graduated in 8ths, with foot markings and 16″ stud markings in red. The die-cast rustproof case is slim and contour-shaped to fit the hand. Stanley.

This is one of three keychain tape rules made by Stanley. All have 3′ by $1/4''$ yellow blade. The anywhere-rule—with you when needed.

Woven fiberglass tape in 50′ or 100′ lengths. Lightweight case is of high-impact styrene. All metal parts are nickel plated.

English/metric tape is slim, trim, easy to carry and use. The $1/4''$ blade has millimeter graduations on lower edge, with inches to $1/16''$ on upper edge.

Blade has raised steel markings, is graduated in feet, $1/10''$ and $1/100''$ on one side. On the other side, diameter can be computed from circumference measurement (in inches).

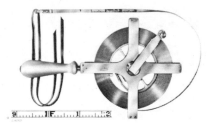

Choice of engineers and surveyors, this 100′ tape is $1/4''$ chrome-clad steel. Four-arm reel has rollers in each arm for smooth winding. Handle locks in any desired position. Thongs permit tying to stakes.

Architect's pocket tape translates scale to feet. One side has $1/4''$ scale (1 to 240). Other side has $1/8''$ scale (1 to 480).

When extreme accuracy is required—ask for Minvar, which means minimum variation. Made from a special alloy, this Lufkin tape has a coefficient of expansion $1/30$th that of high-quality steel normally used in tapes. So accurate, it is used in the space program. Comes with a "certificate of accuracy."

This wheel measures as you walk. It makes a click every 2′, sounds a bell every 100′ so you can keep a running count.

Tension handles counteract the effect of sag. Top edge shows correction required at temperatures ranging from 20° to 120°F.

Standard temperature is 68°. Provided on 100′ steel tapes on special order.

Steel tape thermometer determines accurately the temperature of the tape line itself when a measurement is taken. Thermometer bulb rests against the tape surface.

Tree tape has claw to hook into bark. One side reads left to right in $^1/_{10}$″ and $^1/_{100}$″, other right to left in $^1/_{10}$″, showing consecutive diameter inches. Tape is 20′ long.

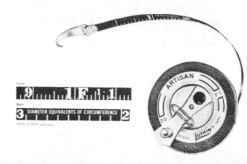

This 6″ conversion wood rule is included with all Lufkin engineer and surveyor tapes.

Rangefinder measures from 50 yards to 2 miles. Sight through eyepiece and turn dial until two images of sighted object coincide. Scale then shows you distance. Its 6 × 18 power prism binocular is detachable for birdwatching, sports, etc. Brookstone.

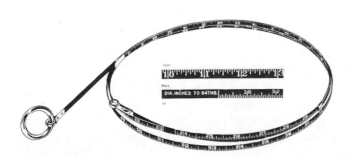

Pole tape measures both circumference and diameter. One side is marked in consecutive inches, in $^1/_{16}$″, other in diameter inches, in $^1/_{16}$″. By reading both sides of tape you get both circumference and diameter at one time. Used primarily by utilities.

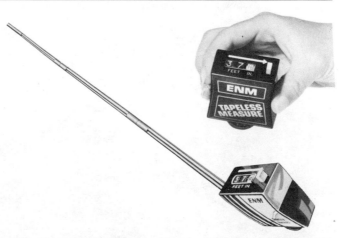

Simply roll the wheel along any surface and the measure (to 99′ 11″) shows up on magnified readout. Button snaps numbers back to zero. A 32″ extension handle optional. In English or metric.

10.

SQUARES BEVELS

Theodorus of Samos was a very successful architect. The Roman encyclopedist Pliny said he invented the square and level, but there is reason to believe he is at least partly wrong. A square appears in a picture of an Egyptian building a chair, and it is reliably dated 1490 B.C. That's at least a thousand years before Theodorus.

Squares haven't changed much through the ages. A basic square consists of two arms set at right angles to each other, and it has been used from the beginning for checking the squareness of sides, edges, or surfaces, and as a guide for drawing lines across boards for straight cuts. Squares originally were made entirely of wood, and some still are. Originally, too, they didn't have inches or other graduations marked on them. They were not a tool for measuring. You can still buy them that way.

Five kinds of squares are in common use today—steel, try, mitre, bevel, and combination.

STEEL SQUARES

These are variously referred to as carpenter's, rafter, framing, flat, mini, homeowner's, or metric squares, depending on their design features and their intended use. They are not always made of steel. Some are made of aluminum.

Typically, a steel square consists of a 24"-by-2"-body and a 1" by 1½" tongue. (If its a metric square it may have a 600 mm by 50mm body and a 400mm by 40mm tongue.) If it's a *carpenter's* square, it will be graduated in sixteenths and eighths of an inch on one side and tenths, twelfths, and sixteenths on the other. In addition it will have a brace measure, octagon scale, board measure, and a hundredths scale. If it's a *rafter* or *framing* square, it will also have rafter tables. A rafter and a framing square are the same thing. A booklet usually comes with the square that explains the carpentry tasks you can accomplish with it.

A *flat* square is a less expensive type of steel square. It is called a flat square because it is manufactured from flat stock. Better squares are not flat. They are rolled out when manufactured so that they are tapered—thicker at the point where tongue and body meet than at the ends. This makes them stronger and gives them better balance. Being heavy on the ends, they are easier and more pleasant to swing around and handle.

Squares made of aluminum are actually made of a hard aluminum alloy. They are lighter than the steel variety and don't rust. They won't take the abuse of a steel square, but if treated reasonably will hold up well.

The Stanley "Homeowners Square" is made of aluminum and has all the features a homeowner is expected to want. It has a lumber scale that gives board feet. It converts fractions to decimals, inches to meters, has a formula for squaring a foundation, 45°, 60° and 30° angle markings, volume and area formulas, a wood screw gauge table, drill sizes, nail sizes (common and finish), nail quantity per pound, and depth sizes. It is graduated in eighths on face and back.

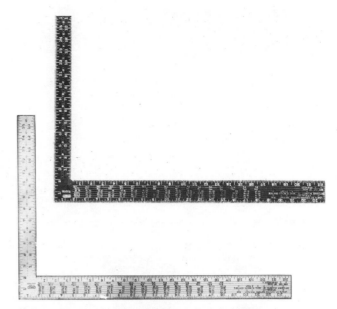

Rafter squares contain brace measure, octagon scale, rafter table, board measure, and $1/_{100}$" scale. Stanley.

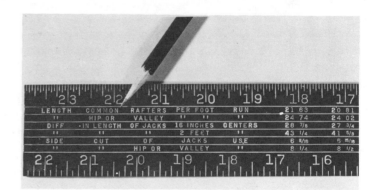

A booklet comes with most rafter squares, explaining in detail how to use rafter and framing tables.

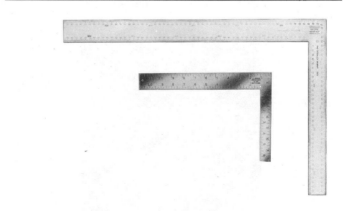

A pair of flat squares, so named because they do not taper from the center to the ends like expensive framing squares.

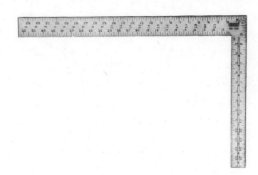

Aluminum homeowners square has valuable tables and information printed on both sides. Deep graduations assure legibility.

Minisquare has an 8″ body and a 6″ tongue, ¹/₈″ graduations on face and back. Easy to tote and use.

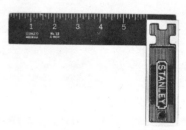

Try square speaks two languages. You can get it graduated in English, metric, or metric-English. Metric blade is 8″ long; others may be 6″, 8″, 10″, or 12″.

Here, try square is being used to align drill. Note slant-cut of handle. It enables square to make 45° as well as 90° guidelines.

Stair gauges can be attached anywhere on rafter square and act as guides for repetitive cuts on rafters, stair stringers, etc.

TRY SQUARE

It is called try because it is used to try things for squareness. It consists of a thick wood, metal, or plastic handle and a thin, metal blade 6″, 8″, 10″, or 12″ long. Once, a typical try square had an elegant rosewood handle and brass face-plates and fittings. Now these are the luxurious exceptions. They have largely given way to less expensive materials.

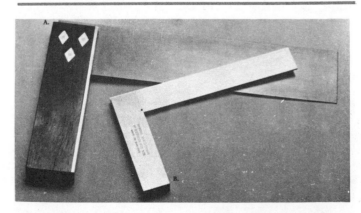

Two highly accurate squares by Rabone Chesterman in traditional style. Top square has beautifully finished wood handle faced with solid brass. In 6″, 9″, or 12″ lengths from Garrett Wade. Steel square is especially useful for setting up table saws and other power tools. In 4″, 6″, 9″, or 12″ lengths. Woodcraft.

MITER SQUARE

Actually, this is not a square at all. You can't use it to lay out a square. It is designed exclusively for laying out 45° angles (and their 135° complements).

The design on some regular try squares is such that they can be used for marking 45° as well as 90° angles.

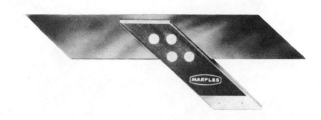

If you do a lot of mitering, this square will come in handy. Hardwood handle fastened to blued Sheffield steel blade with four steel pins and polished solid-brass inserts.

SLIDING BEVEL

This has a slotted blade which can be adjusted to any angle and locked there by means of a thumb screw or wing nut. It can be used to divide or transfer angles and check edges.

COMBINATION SQUARE

Sliding bevel adjusts to any angle. Blade may be smooth, or marked in inches. Tightened by wing nut.

As squares go, this is a relatively new development. It came in after World War II when rolled steel became commonly available. Its handle is made to slide along the blade and may be clamped in any position by means of a nut. It is not the precision tool a well-made square is, but it is more versatile.

In addition to fulfilling the functions of a try and mitre square, it can also be used as a rule, level, marking gauge, protractor, depth gauge, beam compass, and screw gauge. Its handle, or stock, may be metal or plastic. If it's metal, it may be cast iron or lighter-weight, die-cast zinc. In either case it will probably store a removeable steel scriber.

Combination square does many jobs. It can be used as a level, square, marking gauge, protractor, depth gauge, beam compass, and screw gauge. Blue-finish zinc handle. Stanley.

A centering head, a protractor head, and a square and miter head allow this tool to do everything the usual combination square does—plus a few tricks more. Woodcraft.

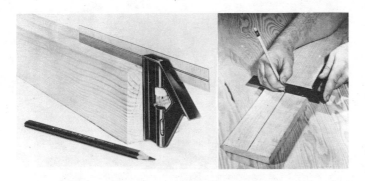

Using a square to check the trueness of a timber.

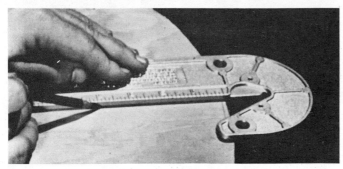

Center square is also a protractor. It will locate the center of circles, measure angles. Stanley.

Half-round stainless steel protractor for setting bevels, transferring angles, has permanently etched graduations from 0° to 180° in both directions. Knurled locking nut holds 6″ arm. General.

MARKINGS AND FINISH

These are often determining factors in establishing the quality of a square.

The markings on a square may be pressed, rolled, etched, or silk screened. Pressed or rolled markings are usually deepest and are better. They will survive rust and wear to stay legible. If a square has etched markings, be sure they are deep enough to last. Be wary of silk-screened markings. These are used on the lowest-priced squares and they may wear off sooner than you like.

Steel squares may have a black or blued finish with graduations and figures permanently impressed and filled with white enamel. Or they may be of polished steel with yellow fluorescent markings. Aluminum squares, for easy reading, may be filled with black color.

MANUFACTURERS

In the U.S. and Canada, Stanley is the big name. In addition to its own line, it makes all Sears squares. Great Neck, Sands, and Millers Falls are other names you'll encounter. Union makes a unique combination square, and General is especially noted for its aluminum alloy rafter square. Starrett and Brown and Sharpe are makers of precision squares.

Rabone Chesterman, W.H. Clay, and Marples are the tops in fine-quality English squares. All three still offer them in rosewood and brass.

Angle divider makes complicated jobs simple. Steel arms can be locked at any desired angle. Body is graduated for laying out figures with 4, 5, 6, 8, and 10-sides. It will also bisect 30°, 45°, and 60° angles. Body is 7 ³/₈″ long. Arms are 6″.

HOW TO SUCCEED IN BUSINESS

Back in 1817, a Vermont blacksmith named Silas Hawes shoed the horse of a passing peddler and received a bunch of worn saw blades in payment. It gave him an idea.

Up to that time, carpenters' squares were just two pieces of wood joined with metal, and they weren't very durable. If dropped a few times, they lost their accuracy. If dropped off a roof, they were a total loss. So Hawes welded two of the saw blades together and made an indestructible square.

But that was not all. He also added something extra. Numbers. Nobody had ever before thought of using a square for measuring, and everyone Hawes showed it to wanted one just like it. So he got a patent on it. Then he took in another blacksmith as a partner and together they began making the new squares.

Business boomed. In 1823 they left the old blacksmith shop and moved into a new stone building. It had a waterwheel that powered a triphammer, and their production took off. They kept on growing bigger and getting richer until 1834. That was the year the Hawes patent on the square expired, and everybody got in the business.

One added rafter tables to his square. Another put on board-feet measure. A third invented eccentric rolls to produce the taper on the square by machine action. But the biggest improvement was made by Norman Millington in 1854.

Up to now, all the markings on a square had to be scribed by hand. To graduate a square in eighths on just one side meant 192 cuts. To do it in eighths, tenths, twelfths, and sixteenths, plus all the other scales, tables and measures we have now, would require more than 1,900 marks. Millington made a machine to do the markings.

To make a long story short, eventually most of the competitors got together. They merged and merged again. And what came out in the end? A company which itself had its beginnings in 1842, making bolts. It absorbed them all. Its name—Stanley.

11.
LEVELS PLUMB BOBS

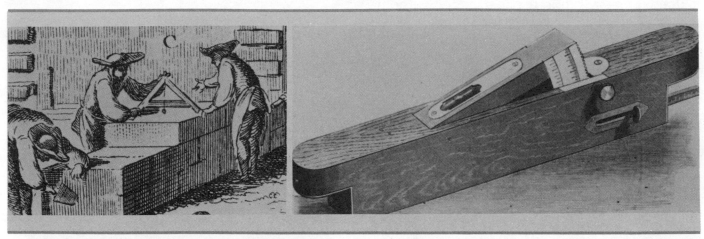

The word "level" is one with good vibes in our language. To be "level-headed" is a virtue, as is being "on the level." Then there is "finding one's own level," which gives a feeling of achievement and stability. To an airplane pilot, to "level off" means to fly parallel to the ground following ascent, and that's not all bad either.

Plumb, level, and square—that's a prescription for all good construction. The spirit level and the plumb bob play important roles in fulfilling this prescription.

LEVELS

The surface of a body of still water is nature's level. It's always a true horizontal. Aware of this principle, pioneers, building a cabin, used a glass or saucer of water to check on the level of its sill. But other ways of determining level had been developed thousands of years before.

Egyptian builders, back in 2680 B.C., suspended a lead pellet at the end of a string from a wooden triangle, a semicircle, or merely a vertical arm attached to a base. When the pellet coincided with a mark grooved on the base or a crosspiece, the work was level. Sometimes a "swinghole" was cut in the base to give the pellet clearance. Such devices were in use thoughout Roman times, the Middle Ages, and well into the last century.

The spirit level we know today was invented more than 300 years ago, but it was slow catching on. It was called a spirit level because its curved glass tube was filled with alcohol or "spirits." In the tube was a bubble. As nature has it, when the tube was level, the bubble would come to the top center of the curve.

These levels were fragile, expensive, and inaccurate, and had to be factory-made. Because most people at that time preferred to make their own tools, it was not until after the Civil War that they came into common use.

Today, most levels are made of wood, aluminum, magnesium, and plastic. Many still have the slightly curved vials filled with alcohol or ether, but more are being made in a new way. Curved vials have to be paired—one curved up, one curved down—if an accurate reading is to be taken with the level set on either edge. Now a new vial, made of plastic, has been developed with an internal bulge, so it gives an accurate reading from any position.

These new vials go under such trade names as Monovial, Du-All, 360, Versavial, and Reversovial. Typically, the vial is filled with fluorescent fluid for better visibility in poor light, and because only one vial is needed instead of two, it is about 20 percent larger.

Torpedo levels, so called for their shape, are usually 9" long and fit easily in the tool box or pocket.

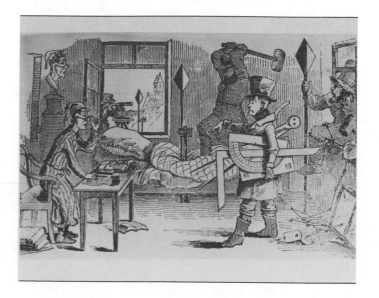

Older-style levels have two bent glass vials. Newer ones have a single plastic vial with an interior bulge and can be read correctly upside down.

This inexpensive wood level has one level and one plumb vial. End grain, especially susceptible to moisture, is sealed. Comes in 18", 24", and 28" lengths.

One-piece extruded magnesium I-beam level by Stanley has a protractor dial for determining any angle from 0° to 90°.

WHAT TO LOOK FOR

Besides the new all-direction vial, here are other special features you may want to have in your level.

Top reading. You can read this level from the top as well as from the sides, and it saves bending.

Grooved base. This is a help on tubular work, such as dowels, pipes, shafts, etc.

Magnetic. Some levels have a magnetic strip on one edge. It holds to metal surfaces, freeing hands.

Anodized finish. On aluminum, this is better than paint or enamel. The color is an integral part of the metal.

Nonconductivity. Wood and plastic levels do not conduct electricity.

Rule levels. The edge is calibrated as a ruler, so the level can be used as a straightedge and measuring tool.

Protractor. An angle-measuring tool is incorporated in some levels.

Number of vials. In addition to plumb and level vials, many designs include a 45-degree vial.

OTHER CONSIDERATIONS

Levels come in lengths ranging from a few inches to 10'. The 2' length is most popular for general carpentry and utility work.

Wood levels are a favorite of masons. Wood is not cold to the touch in winter. The best wood levels are made of mahogany or cherry, which are highly stable. Some have brass-covered ends to keep moisture from the grain.

Aluminum levels are lighter in weight than those made of wood. Magnesium ones are one-third lighter than aluminum. Less expensive aluminum levels are made of simple extruded I-beam stock. Heavier-duty levels have closed ends for added strength.

For such jobs as leveling foundation walls and laying out building sites there are levels which can be attached to lines. There are bull's-eye or target levels which give readings in all directions at once. There are two-way levels which will read in two directions at one time.

Builders use a "dumpy level." This is a surveying instrument consisting of a spirit level mounted directly under a telescope. It's used for checking level, differences in elevation, and laying out angles on an horizontal plane. Sighting is usually done on leveling rods.

In addition to doing all the preceding, a builder's transit level can also be used for plumbing, laying out, or measuring angles on a vertical plane. Dumpy levels and transit levels are almost always mounted on a tripod, which itself is equipped with a plumb bob to help in its alignment.

Starrett bench levels, of cast iron with black wrinkle finish, have that old-time look. Available in sizes from 4" to 24", they have a main vial and a double plumb vial. Bottom of the base is grooved for cylindrical work.

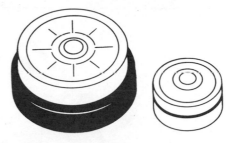

Bull's-eye, or target, levels give reading in all directions at once. Just get the bubble in the bull's-eye. Molded of clear plastic, can be permanently mounted. Empire.

Attach this three-way level and plumb to any length of board or other straightedge and you have a level of any length desired.

Aluminum line level can be slid to any desired position. Bottom is flat for surface leveling.

A level for your pocket. Made of tough plastic, this 5" Stanley level has a 360° vial, grooved base, and convenient pocket clip.

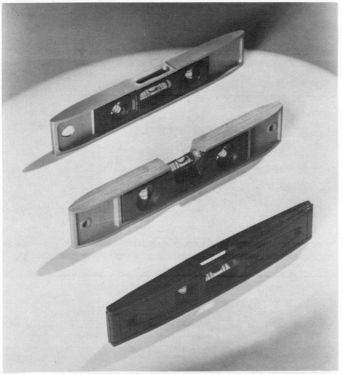

Torpedo levels, only 9" long, feature 360° vials. From top: body of die-cast aluminum, three vials, with magnetic strip in base to hold it fast to iron surfaces; plastic body, V-grooved with magnetic strip, three vials; plastic body, V-grooved, two vials. Stanley.

Cross test level and plumb, only 2″ × 3″, can be used for squaring as well as getting plumb or level. L.S. Starrett.

This cross test level permits leveling in both directions without moving the level from the work. Black wrinkle finish and nickel-plated ends. L.S. Starrett.

Hand sighting levels for outdoor work. Locke level (top) focuses on a bubble and cross hair. Good for determining grades and levels for terraces, driveways, tile lines, etc. Abney level (bottom) does all these jobs plus acts as a clinometer, accurately determining slopes and angles. Also measures height of trees, chimneys.

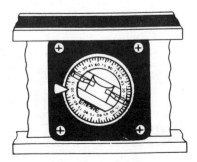

With a protractor conversion kit, many Empire mono-vial levels can be converted into accurate angle-measuring tools. Also available factory-installed on some models.

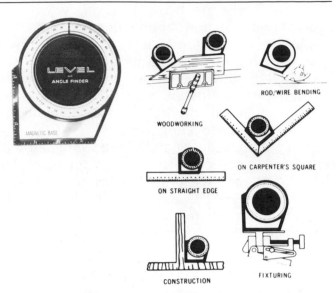

Place this inclinometer on any surface and its 4″ dial gives you an accurate reading of inclination to within $\frac{1}{2}°$.

Protractor-level attaches magnetically to any steel ruler or bar stock for greater ease and accuracy in use. Pocket-size.

Leveling rod and target is used with transits and leveling instruments. Rod is seasoned wood; target is plastic, quartered in white and bright red. Two section, 8′ extended. Starrett.

Starrett leveling instrument does everything except measure vertical angles. Fast, easy adjustments. No higher math required. Telescope is 15 power.

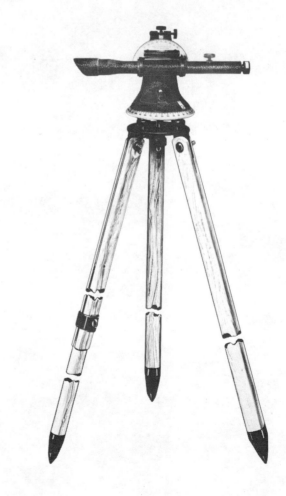

Sears' tilting transit level, for light construction work, has an 18-power telescope with lock to convert from transit to a level. Comes completely equipped with tripod and instructions.

Inexpensive, yet accurate Starrett transit No. 99, with 15-power telescope, has simple adjustments and is easy to use and read. Two spirit levels. Comes with plumb bob, tripod, carrying case.

PLUMB BOBS

The word "plumb" comes from the Latin word for lead. Attach a lead pellet to the end of a cord, and it will hang at a perfect right angle to the horizontal. If you know the true vertical, all you need is a square to get the true horizontal, and the ancients often did it that way.

Plumb bobs are seldom made of lead any more. They are usually steel, sometimes solid brass, and occasionally, for greater weight, are mercury-filled. A fairly recent development is the combination plumb bob and chalk line.

WHO MAKES THEM?

Leading manufacturers of levels and related equipment include: Berger Instruments, Empire Level Mfg. Corp., Exact Level & Tool Mfg. Co., General Hardware Mfg. Co., Goldblatt Tool Co., Johnson Products Co., Mayes Bros. Tool Mfg. Co., Millers Falls, Henry L. Hanson Co., Rabone Chesterman, Smith-Wolff Co., Stanley Tools, The L.S. Starrett Co., and The Warren Group.

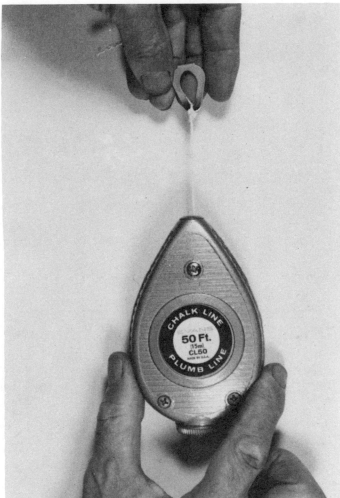

Combination chalk line and plumb bob locks at any desired length. Handle on back does rewinding. Large chalk capacity. Evans.

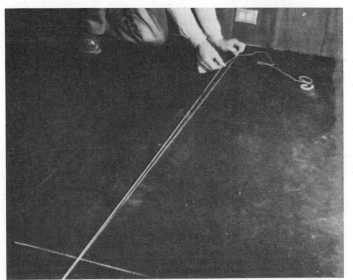

Plumb bobs are usually made of steel. Some, for greater weight, are mercury-filled.

Chalk line is stretched taut and twanged to leave mark for such jobs as laying floor tile, locating partitions, and marking courses for shingle and siding.

12. CLAMPS

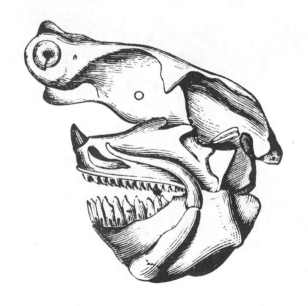

Jaws of shark are a toothed clamp.

Ancients used the screw for devising instruments of torture. Archimedes understood its power and put it to work. Today, the screw, with its strength and holding ability, is an essential feature of the clamp.

Clamps are mechanical hands. They are stronger than human hands. Their reach is bigger. They can help you in many ways.

Here are ten different kinds of clamps you should know about.

1. **Handscrews.** Made of wood, with wide, relatively soft jaws, they won't mar work, even without protective pads. Turn one of their two screws and they cock their jaws at an angle, so they're good for angular or irregular work. To open or close the jaws uniformly, hold the middle screw-handle in the left hand. Revolve the end screw clockwise to close the jaws. Revolve it counterclockwise to open them.

2. **C-clamps.** These have a C-shaped frame, so the name is appropriate. Essentially for metal work, they are also handy for wood, but put pads under their jaws to prevent marring the work. The English call them G-clamps.

C-clamps come with throat openings of $^3/_4$" to 8" (heavy duty to 12"). The depth of the throat is narrow—$1^1/_8$" to 4" is standard. But you can get deeper to 6 inches.

3. **Bar clamps.** These are indispensable in making furniture, built-ins, and in gluing work of all kinds. They have a moveable jaw at one end of their bar and a crank that turns the screw at the other. Originally, bars were made of wood, but now they are usually made of steel. This may be flat bar stock, I-shaped stock, or notched spring steel.

Pipe clamps are like bar clamps except they employ a $^1/_2$" or $^3/_4$" black iron pipe instead of a bar. You supply the pipe. The span of these clamps is limited only by the pipe length.

Double-pipe clamps are mounted on a pair of ½-inch black pipes. The distance between the individual clamps is typically about $3^1/_4$", so they spread the pressure over a wider area.

4. **Spring clamps.** These are like king-size clothespins. Though they don't have the strength of most other clamps, they are quick, easy, and handy for all kinds of holding jobs up to 4". Some have plastic-covered tips and handles.

5. **Corner/miter clamps.** Designed for holding corners of picture frames, windows, furniture, etc., especially while gluing, nailing, or screwing. It's possible to nail or screw work while the clamps are in place.

6. **Band clamps.** When work is large, irregular, or round, and you can't get in with ordinary clamps, these are the answer. Typically, a band clamp might be used to hold the four legs of a chair. A standard band is of canvas, 20' long and 2" wide. A smaller style is of nylon, 15' long and 1" wide. Self-locking cams hold the bands securely.

7. **Hold-down clamps.** These can go anywhere on a workbench or other work surface. One can be mounted on a drill press, sawhorse, side of bench, etc. Just bore a countersunk hole. Into it goes the bolt that engages the clamp frame. The clamp turns to any angle, is quickly removeable.

8. **Hinge clamps.** These have a hinged foot and are moveable sideways to any position along the length of a track, or they can be given a stationary

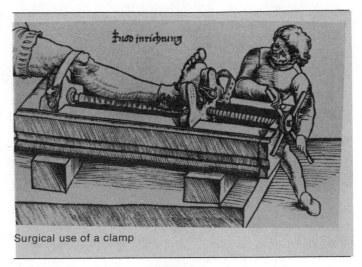
Surgical use of a clamp

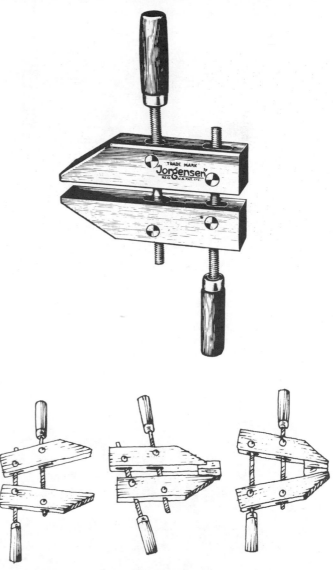
The handscrew adjusts to fit angular work; its maple jaws take a non-slip, no-mar grip on oddly shaped pieces. Used for assembling and gluing furniture, cabinet work, musical instruments, boats, etc. Available with jaws 4" to 24" long, which open 2" to 17".

Cam clamp has cork faces...

and two special attachments. Shown here are the edge-clamping attachment and extension pad which enlarges clamping surface area. Beechwood clamps are widely used by furniture and cabinet makers. They produce 330 pounds of pressure when fully cocked, and the cork faces avoid pressure marks.

Corsets and collars are clamping devices.

mount. A good spot for one is under the front edge of a workbench, where it can be swung down out of the way when not in use. They can also be used unmounted as regular bar clamps.

9. **Three-way edging clamps.** The three-screw design permits clamping countertop edges and other difficult jobs.

10. **Edge-clamp fixtures.** These are for use with bar clamps and permit pressure to be applied at right angles to the axis of the clamp bar. They come in a single and double spindle design. The double spindle straddles the clamp bar so equal pressure is applied on both sides of it.

MANUFACTURERS

Leading manufacturers are Adjustable Clamp Company, Brink and Cotton, and the Hartford Clamp Company. Jorgensen and Pony clamps are made by Adjustable. Record Ridgeway is the big English manufacturer.

Carriage clamps are probably the most widely used C-clamps. V-notch in foot of frame holds rounded sections. They come with maximum openings from 2¼" to 12". Specially treated for strength.

The best place to store clamps is where they are most often used. These C-clamps are stored on table-saw base.

Lever eliminates a lot of turning. Just press the levers and push the screw into position. Malleable iron frame with black baked-enamel finish. Openings 2½" to 8".

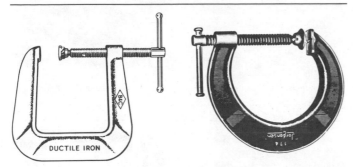

Deep-throated clamps have extra "reach." Left, Brink and Cotton design offers 3"–5" depth. Right, clamp made by Adjustable offers 4"-6" depth.

Holding edges is the specialty of a three-screw clamp. Use it to apply right-angle pressure to the edge or side of work. It has an opening capacity of 2½" and a throat depth of 2½". Adjustable.

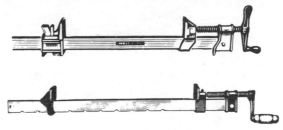

Bar clamps are used for big jobs. Openings run up to 8'! Model at top has a disc clutch that grips at any point. In the other design, foot stops at notches.

Lighter in weight and stronger than most C-clamps, the Clampco "Kant-Twist" has cantilever action that provides a 4:1 clamping ratio. Clamp Mfg. Co.

Make your own clamp with heads that fit on a 1" wooden bar. Make bar any length you like. Clamp heads are of cast-iron construction, with square-thread screws.

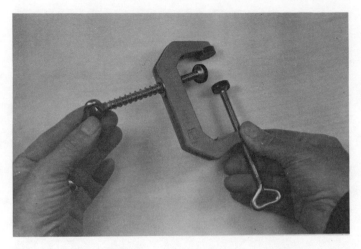
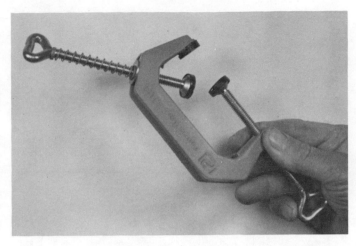

The frame of this carriage clamp is slotted so that its spring-loaded screw can be moved to hold work at almost any angle. Clamping faces have no-mar plastic pads.

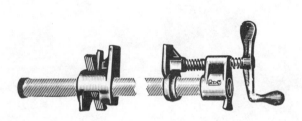

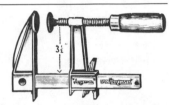

Disc-clutch clamp can instantly adjust to exact opening, so the screw is needed only to apply or release pressure. Jorgensen models available with maximum opening from 6″ to 30″. Stanley model opens to 6″.

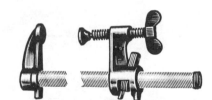

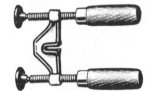

There are fixtures to convert bar clamps to edge clamps. They apply pressure at right angles to axis of clamp bar. Single spindle or double spindle styles. Adjustable.

Three styles of clamps that fit on pipes. Styles shown at top and center fit on ³/₄″ pipe. Third style (bottom) uses ¹/₂″ pipe. Adjustable.

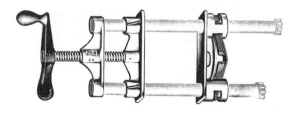

Double bar clamps distribute pressure. Mounted on ¹/₂″ pipe, these fixtures help to keep thin stock from buckling. On thick stock, they can exert greater pressure than the single-pipe variety.

Left: A hold-down clamp can be mounted anywhere: on workbench, sawhorse, machine table, etc. It's quickly removable, leaving surface free of obstruction. Adjustable.
Right: This "Kant-Twist" hold-down is designed for permanent mounting. Another model offers T-slot mounting. Maximum openings of 1″ to 6³/₈″ available. Clamp Mfg. Co.

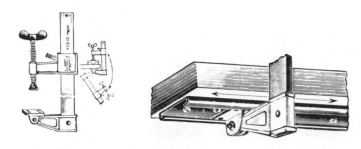

Hinged clamp can be permanently mounted, or used in track. It swings out of the way below deck when not in use. Openings 8″ to 30″. Jorgensen.

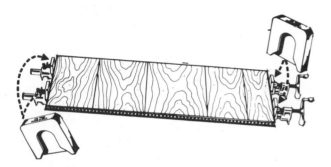

Protective pads for clamp faces slip easily on or off. Designed for Jorgensen and Pony clamps, they also fit some other clamps.

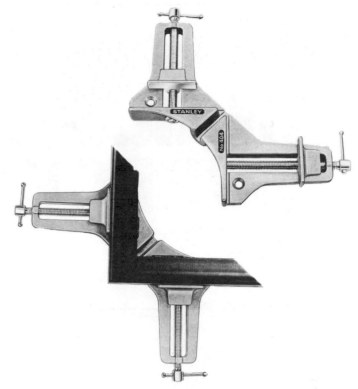

A corner clamp is indispensable for making picture frames, nailing and gluing of corner pieces. Cast of aluminum alloy. Features 3″ jaw opening and saw slot; can be mounted to workbench. Stanley.

Band clamps are used for large, irregular and round shapes. At left, 2″ by 20′ canvas band. At right, 11½′ nylon band comes with four nylon corner protectors for frames. Brookstone.

These clamp pads are magnetic! They're much easier to use than wood scraps because they adhere to the clamp. Made of hardwood with magnetic backing. Clampads.

13.
NAIL PULLERS
WRECKING BARS

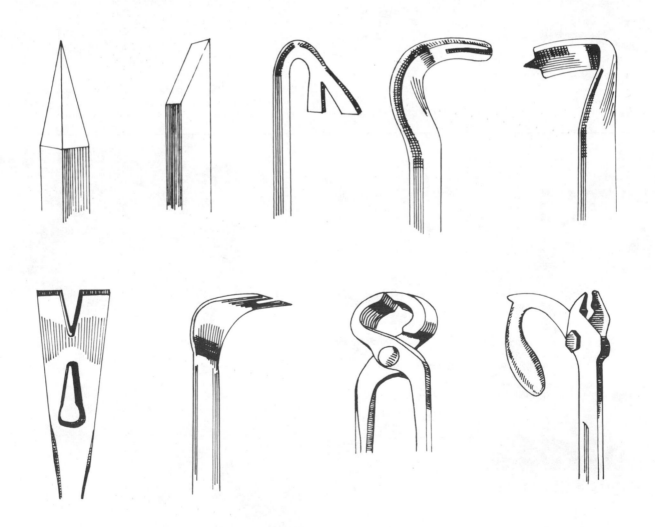

The human arm is ingeniously contrived, but its strength is extremely limited. However, team it up with a lever, and it's a different story. Long before Archimedes said he could move the world if you gave him a lever that was long enough, people were aware of the added strength a lever could give.

With a bar supported on a fulcrum, there is almost no limit to what pure muscle power can move. Put a claw on the end of the bar and it can extract nails that fingers alone could never grasp. Put a wedge on the end of the bar and almost anything can be pried apart. Give it a diamond point and it's unexcelled for breaking up concrete and masonry. For grabbing and pulling, a hook end is useful.

Not infrequently, especially during medieval times, such tools became instruments of torture.

The Romans used nails, and so also contrived nail pullers. They made some with curved ends, to provide an integral fulcrum. These rocker-heads gave maximum leverage because the support point was so close to the end of the bar.

Those clever Romans also combined two rocker head bars and made pincers, excellent for pulling, especially when a nail has lost its head. Pincers became a favorite of blacksmiths for pulling hoof nails when reshoeing horses and oxen. They also became a favorite torture tool.

Nails have been used since Roman times.

PEGS, YES. NAILS, NO.

As long as mortise-and-tenon construction was the rule, there was little need for nails. What few nails were used could be pulled with a claw hammer. But when balloon construction of houses took over, in about 1840, nails became the thing, and so did tools for pulling them. Hammers just can't take the stress of heavy-duty nail-pulling, and there are many nails they can't extract.

Nail pullers and wrecking bars make it easy.

WHO MAKES THEM?

The big eight are: Stanley, Easco, Drew, Millers Falls, Columbia, Estwing, Woodings-Verona, and Buck.

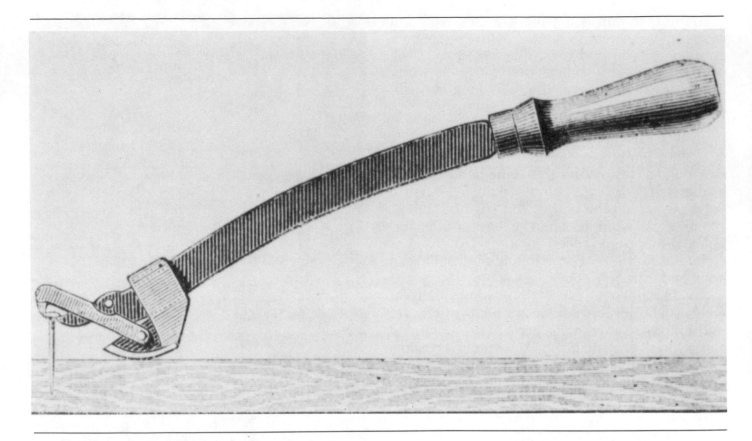

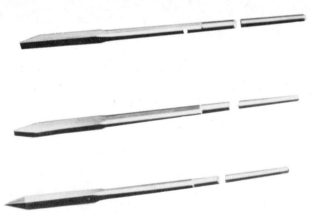

Pinchpoint, wedge, and diamond-point crowbars range from 36″ to 66″ in length, and from 6 to 26 lbs. in weight. Stock size is $^7/_8$″ to $1^1/_2$″. Woodings-Verona.

Nail pulling was an important function of this old "universal tool."

Before sunken nail heads can be pulled, they must be started. The nail claw or cat's paw, driven by a hammer, will dig under the heads of driven nails and pry them out.

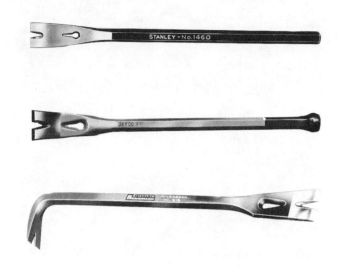

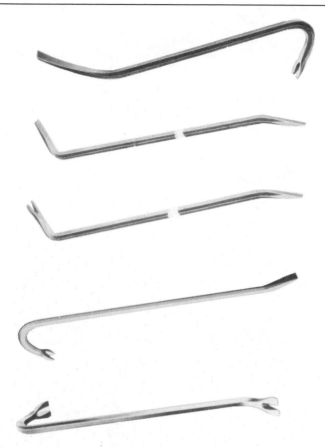

Straight (Stanley), target-head (Dasco), and offset (Stanley) ripping bars are all designed for use with a hammer. Each is 18″ long and has a beveled nail slot.

Goosenecked wrecking bars are used to wedge between boards and to pull nails. Style at top is 12″ to 48″ long; double-claw styles range from 18″ to 36″.

Ingenious old-time nail-pulling hatchet

The smooth, curved blade of a molding tool removes trim, molding, and quarter-round pieces without breaking. It can pry against finished walls without marring them. Dasco.

Nineteenth-century barrel-opener hatchet

"Wonder Bars" are made of flat stock and they're lightweight champs at lifting, prying, pulling, and scraping. The 7" Wonder Bar II (top) has a 7/8" blade width and is nickel plated. The 13³/₄" Wonder Bar (bottom) has a 1³/₄" blade. Stanley.

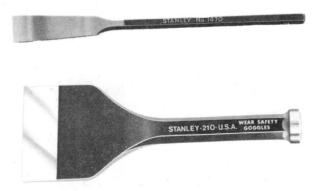

Ripping chisels for cutting-remodeling. Wide-blade style (bottom), often called a floor chisel, can be used to cut and lift tongues from floor boards without marring the surface. The thin-blade style is good for all kinds of rough cutting jobs, has excellent leverage.

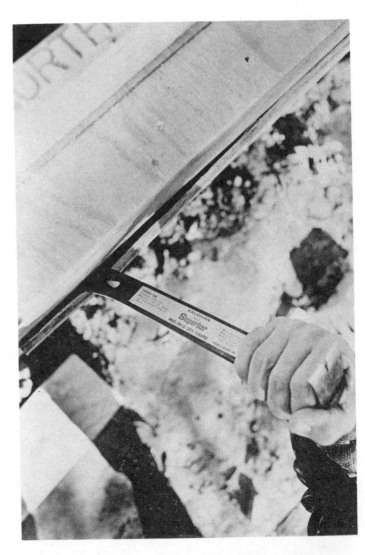

Two types of prybars used for dismantling of flooring, siding, sheeting. "Sav-in' Bar" by Dasco (top) comes in 24", 30" and 36" reverse style. Dismantles without damage to joists or studs. "Superbar," by Vaughan, is here used to remove plywood sheeting from forms. It also pulls nails, scrapes paint, lifts doors into position for attachment to frame.

Tack claw is about 7″ long, comes with easy-on-the-palm rounded wood handle. Easco.

This crate opener is drop-forged from a solid bar of tool steel. Comes in 8″ and 9¼″ sizes, weighing 10 oz. and 15 oz. respectively. Handy for all kinds of wrecking and dismantling operations. Diamond Tool and Horseshoe.

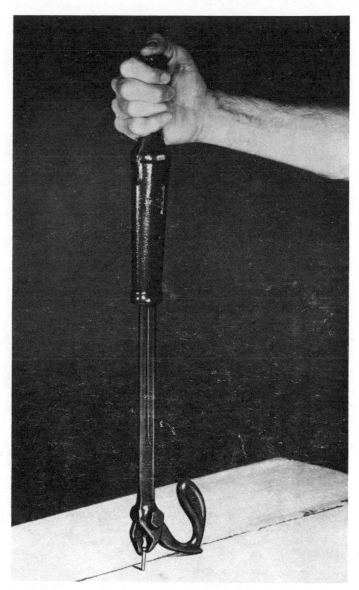

A nail puller with a powerful bite. The handle is pulled back, then rammed down to make jaws dig in around nail head. Next, levering action helps the hinged jaw to dig in under the head and pry nail out. Brookstone.

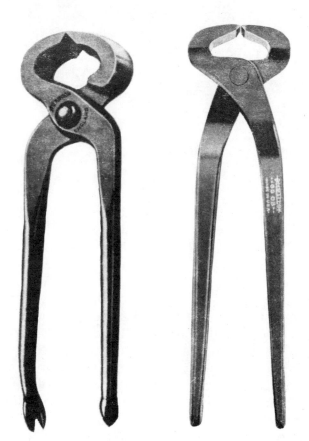

Jaws tell the story of a pincer's strength. The shorter the distance from bite to hinge, the greater the pressure you can exert. Tool with curved jaws (left) is designed primarily for pulling nails. Tool with harder bite (right) is for cutting nails, wire, etc.

This is a fence tool, used to cut wire and pull staples. Wire cutter on each side will cut double-stranded barbed wire. Puller is on one side of head, hammer face on the other. Its gripping jaws are in front. Diamond.

14.

DRILLS AND ACCESSORIES

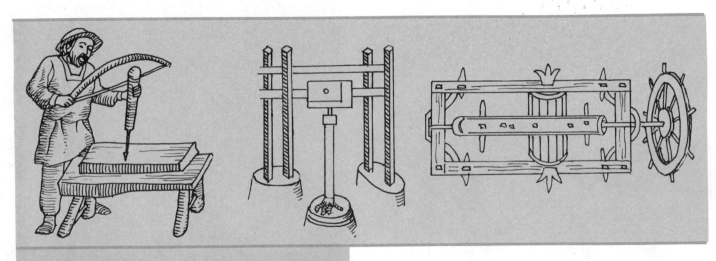

S. Duncan Black and Alonzo G. Decker talking things over in 1910.

The year was 1914, and the electric motor was still a newfangled thing. Along came two bright young fellows, S. Duncan Black and Alonzo G. Decker, who saw its possibilities. They hooked one of the new motors to a bit and the world's first electric drill was born. It had a pistol grip and a trigger switch, and it made boring holes a snap; but it didn't really catch on until more than thirty years later when, in 1946, Messers Black and Decker designed a model for consumers, and the tool took off.

Don't be fooled by its name. The drill is a do-everything tool. It is also a sander, screwdriver, wrench, hammer, chisel, scraper, gouge, paint-mixer, polisher, saw, grinder, and rust remover, and it may even supply the power for pumping water or cleaning out a clogged drain.

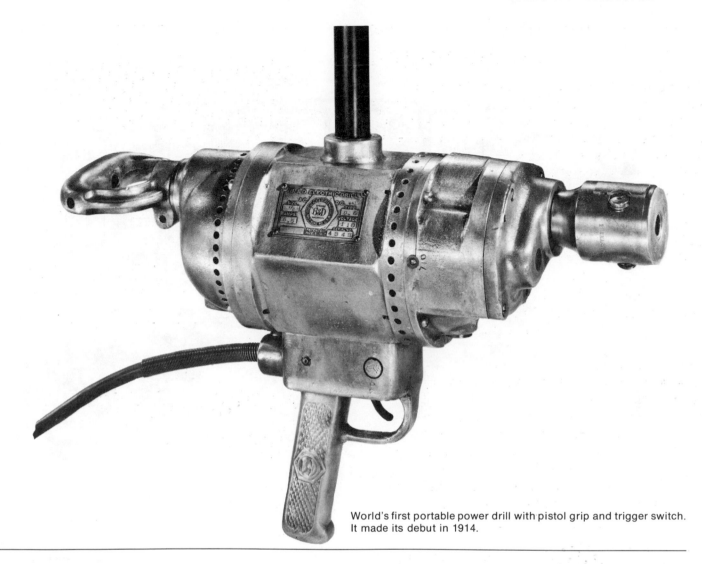

World's first portable power drill with pistol grip and trigger switch. It made its debut in 1914.

Primarily, though, a drill is a drill, and, after sawing, drilling holes is probably the most common workshop activity. That's undoubtedly why this relatively inexpensive and versatile tool is usually the first power equipment acquired by the handyman.

Drills come in a wide variety of kinds, qualities, and prices. The most common sizes are $1/4''$, $3/8''$, and $1/2''$, but you can also get $3/4''$. This inch size does not refer to the size hole the drill can make, but to the size shank that will fit in its chuck, the jawed grabber at its business end. Push it, and even a $1/4''$ drill can produce a $1 1/2''$ hole.

You can't be sure of the capacity of a tool by labels like "industrial," "commercial," or "professional." These words are sometimes used loosely. Horsepower and ampere ratings can also be deceptive. Some manufacturers offer a choice of "good," "better," and "best" drills, and this is often as good a guide as any to power and quality.

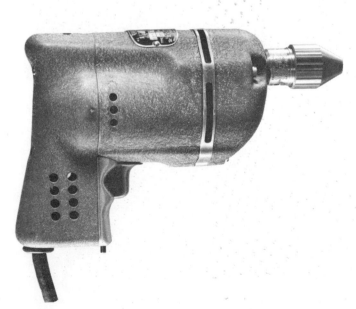

World's first portable electric drill designed for home use was introduced in 1946.

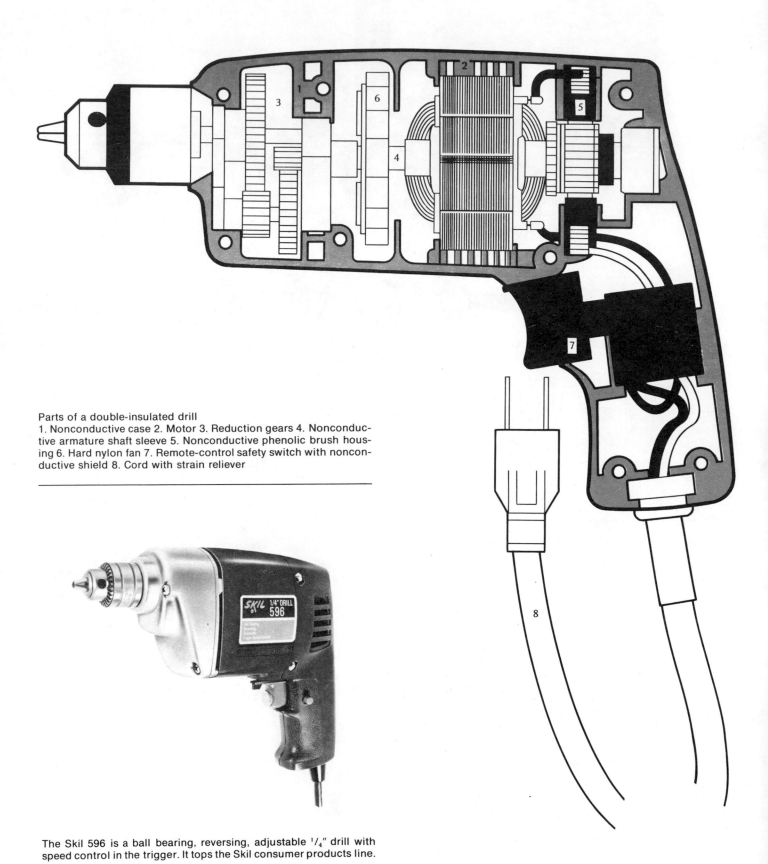

Parts of a double-insulated drill
1. Nonconductive case 2. Motor 3. Reduction gears 4. Nonconductive armature shaft sleeve 5. Nonconductive phenolic brush housing 6. Hard nylon fan 7. Remote-control safety switch with nonconductive shield 8. Cord with strain reliever

The Skil 596 is a ball bearing, reversing, adjustable ¼″ drill with speed control in the trigger. It tops the Skil consumer products line.

Training of a small power source made the electric drill possible.

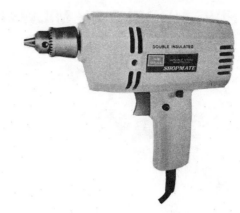

The Shopmate 2151 variable-speed, reversible ³/₈″ drill is double-insulated. Its speed adjustment dial can be set from 0-1000 rpm, and its handle is centered for better balance.

If you slave-drive your drill, get the "best," if it's within your means. If you will use the drill only occasionally and for light duty, the "good" may be good enough. But expect it to get hot and stall if you overwork it.

In comparing drills of competing manufacturers, heft them and get their feel. Drills vary in size, weight, and balance. Observe obvious signs of good finish and care in manufacture. Compare construction features. Good ventilation, easily accessible brushes, and quality and number of bearings help make one drill better than another.

Look at the information given on each tool's plate. How many amps does it pull? Greater amperage often means greater capacity. What is its guarantee—ninety days or one year? Sometimes a ³/₈″ drill may have the same motor as the ¹/₄″ drill of the same manufacturer. It's geared down for less speed and more power.

The case may be plastic, metal, or a combination of both. Because of the advantages of plastic, metal is being phased out. Plastic is tougher. It is more colorful and attractive. It is more comfortable to the touch in both hot weather and cold. And it is safer.

Plastic drills are usually "double insulated" and "shock proof." If their primary insulation barrier fails, there is still a second barrier of protective insulation between you and the electrical circuit. Shockproof tools usually have only a two-prong plug, thus making them easier to use where sockets will accept only two prongs. You don't need a grounding adapter, but some double-insulated tools may be equipped with three-prong plugs to meet safety codes that require grounding.

Stanley 91061 ¹/₄″ drill, the Super Switch, features dial speed control, a finger-tip reversing lever, and a non-slip grained handle. It has three ball bearings—and power!

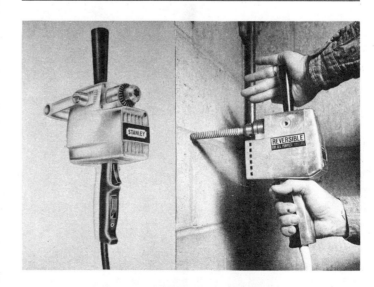

The Stanley 91722 is the perfect drill for tight places. It is a heavy-duty ¹/₂″ drill with the compactness of a ¹/₄″ drill. It will fit between studs or joists. The multi-position handle is removable. Model 91721 is reversible.

FIVE MODELS BY MILWAUKEE ILLUSTRATE DESIGN VARIETY

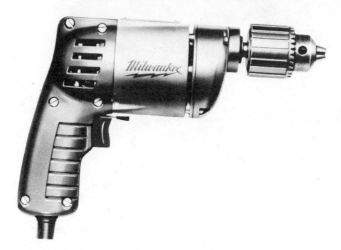

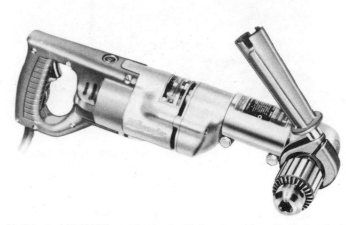

0122 ¹/₄" "Hole-Shooter" has trigger speed control and reversing switch. Handle is glass-reinforced nylon.

Half-inch drill (1101) can be had with head and handle that swivel 360° and can be locked tight in any position.

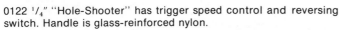

Model 1101 has a 33° angle drive. It reaches up to 30 inches.

This largest and most powerful Milwaukee model (2400) can handle 1¹/₄" in steel. Extra long handles provide maximum leverage for drilling large holes.

"Hole Hawg" 1670 (or 1675) features compact design, just the thing for drilling between studs and joists.

The speed at which a drill runs depends on its size. Typically, a $\frac{1}{4}$" drill will run at 2250 rpm, a $\frac{3}{8}$" drill at 1000 to 1250 rpm, and a $\frac{1}{2}$" drill at 700 rpm. Generally, the lower the speed the greater the power. High speed is good for small holes and soft wood. Lower speed is better for big holes and for drilling in metal, tile, and other tough or brittle materials.

Drills may have a single speed or variable speed. With variable speed you can use lower speeds for bigger bits, start holes without walking, and drive or remove screws. There is variable speed and *adjustable* variable speed. In the adjustable, you can preset and lock the speed anywhere from zero on up. This gives better control for it insures that whatever speed you select will be constant.

Some drills have a reverse feature. This is good for removing a jammed drill bit or removing screws. Reversing is usually done by means of a reversing switch.

Some drills have an auxilliary handle. This makes it easier to apply extra muscle in drilling and affords a steadier grip. The torque or twisting power, especially of larger drills, can sometimes be difficult to control.

Cords vary in color and length. High visibility colors can help prevent tripping over cords. Length of cord may vary from 6 to 10 feet. Black & Decker makes a drill with a detachable cord. You can use the cord for other things.

The Millers Falls model 8802 is 10$\frac{5}{16}$" long and weighs just 5$\frac{1}{2}$ pounds. It comes in a kit consisting of a $\frac{3}{8}$" drill, a 6" rubber backing pad and 6" wool bonnet, and 3 abrasive discs.

Two double-insulated $\frac{1}{2}$" Rockwell drills. Model 4274 (left) is reversible and has a D-handle. Model 4275 has a spade handle.

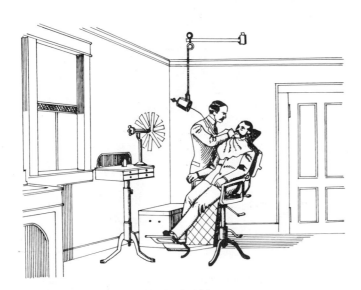

The miracle of the small motor

Piston $\frac{1}{2}$" drill is powered by a compact, lightweight gasoline engine located in its handle. You don't have to worry about finding an outlet.

Black & Decker 9001 MOD4 ¹/₄" cordless drill has a chuck speed of 750 rpm. It comes with an interchangeable energy pack and a recharger.

Black & Decker 9031 ¹/₄" cordless does 1500 rpm and is rated as "commercial duty." Battery pack is not removable. It comes with a recharger.

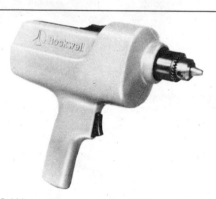

Rockwell 4008 ¹/₄" cordless develops 1300 rpm. It has a built-in recharger unit. Comes with a 13-piece twist drill set.

Skill 2006 ³/₈" cordless will drive screws without predrilling, reverses to remove them. Comes with recharger.

CORDLESS DRILLS

These never need a cord because they operate on a battery. This usually makes these drills bigger, heavier, and a little clumsier to handle, but they afford the great convenience of always being ready for immediate use without the need for an outlet. On the roof, in the woods, aboard a boat—they can't be beat, and they are totally free of shock hazard.

The nickel-cadmium batteries in a cordless drill can be recharged almost indefinitely. Some have a recharger built into the unit. Others have interchangeable power packs, so that when one runs down you can slip a fully charged one in to replace it without losing any time.

Another type of cordless drill is one that is powered by a lightweight, compact, two-cycle gasoline engine. A variable speed piston drill is no heavier or larger than the biggest ¹/₂" electric drills, but it can do the same job on its own power. It holds just 7 ounces of gas.

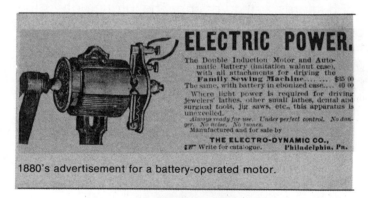

1880's advertisement for a battery-operated motor.

Low-cost Sears ¹/₄" reversible drill will drill up to 100 ¹/₄" holes through a pine 2×4 on one charge. When fully charged it has a no-load speed of 300 rpm. Comes with recharger.

THE BATTERY STORY

The nickel-cadmium batteries that power today's cordless tools have a history dating back to the 1700s. It all started with Luigi Galvani. He was an Italian physiologist who tickled a frog's leg with a metal probe and pointed the way to the discovery that electricity may result from chemical action.

His countryman, Alessandro Volta, was quick to follow up on it and make the first battery, so called because it was a battery of cells. It evolved through the lead-acid battery and the Edison alkali battery to today's nickel-cadmium power source.

Nickel-cadmium batteries, typically, can be charged in 16 hours. On a single charge they can be expected to drill about 25 $3/4$" holes in $3/4$" plywood, or 75 $3/8$" holes in a fir 2 x 4. With some tools, you can double your drilling time with an extra battery pack. A battery can be recharged at least 500 times, and is usually guaranteed for a year.

The first cordless electric drill, powered by self-contained nickel-cadmium cells, was introduced by Black & Decker in 1961.

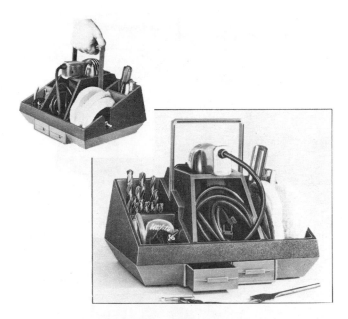

Akro-Mils Drill Mate is a portable organizer for $1/4$" and $3/8$" drills and accessories. Keeps everything in order and ready to use. Made of charcoal-gray and blue polystyrene.

No one has yet succeeded in developing a self-sufficient or "cordless" system for drilling wells.

Black & Decker 7929 Hammer Gun is a lightweight combination hammer and drill. It has a $^3/_8$" capacity chuck, and will drill $^9/_{16}$" holes in masonry, $^3/_8$" in hard brick or tile, and $^1/_4$" in steel. Weighs $4^3/_8$ lbs.

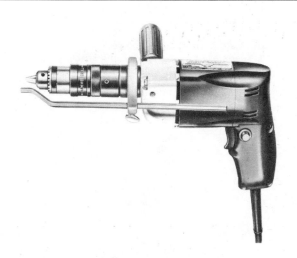

Millers Falls $^3/_8$" SP259 hammer drill has a built-in shock absorber. It will drill $^1/_2$" in steel. Double insulated. Weight is $5^3/_4$ lbs.

Milwaukee 5390 is a $^3/_8$" tool for fast percussion drilling in concrete or masonry. Light pressure against work engages the hammer mechanism. It can also drill without hammering in wood or metal. Rubber shield protects it from abrasive dust.

HAMMER DRILLS

These combine regular rotary drilling in wood, plastic, or metal with percussion drilling in concrete, brick, or tile. Typically, the shift is made by turning a locking collar located just behind the drill's chuck. Some drills convert by mere exertion of pressure against the work. The hammer action stops when not under load.

An adjustable depth gauge on the side of a hammer drill permits drilling to the exact depth desired. As a drill, it may have a trigger adjustable speed of 0–1200 rpm, or 0–800 rpm, depending on whether it is a $^3/_8$" or $^1/_2$" tool. As a hammer, it may deliver 36,000 or 24,000 blows per minute, again depending on tool size and construction.

Special hammer-drill bits are required. They are specially designed to take the impact involved. You can also get special chisels to use with some drills. Some chisels are for wood and composition materials. You can use them for mortising, grooving, dadoing, rabbeting, gouging, or sculpting. A mortar grout chisel is specially made for removal of mortar between bricks, tile grout, etc. There is also a scraper blade available. Some hammer drills are double insulated and reverse at the flick of a switch.

Black & Decker double-insulated hammer drill has two speeds— high speed for drilling small holes in wood, metal, masonry, and for using abrasive and polishing accessories; low speed for drilling larger holes.

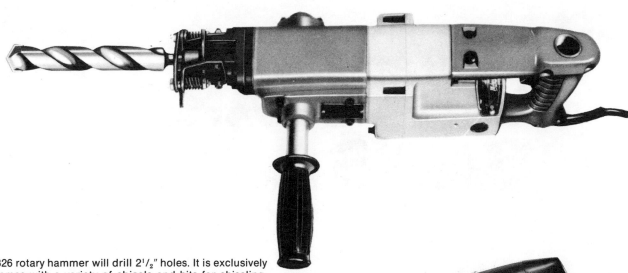

Milwaukee 5326 rotary hammer will drill 2¹/₂″ holes. It is exclusively a hammer. Comes with a variety of chisels and bits for chiseling, channeling, chipping, scaling, slotting, and tuck pointing.

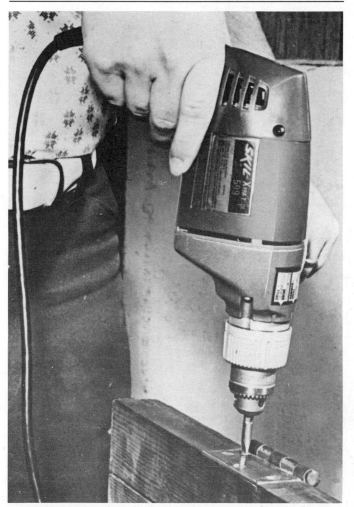

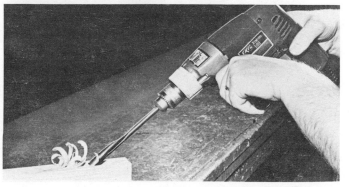

It's a screwdriver, a hammer drill, a chisel. Skil's 599 "Xtra-tool" is a hammer-drill designed especially for home use. Its accessories include wood chisels, mortar grout chisels, and scrapers. 0-800 rpm, 36,000 blows per minute.

15.

CIRCULAR SAWS

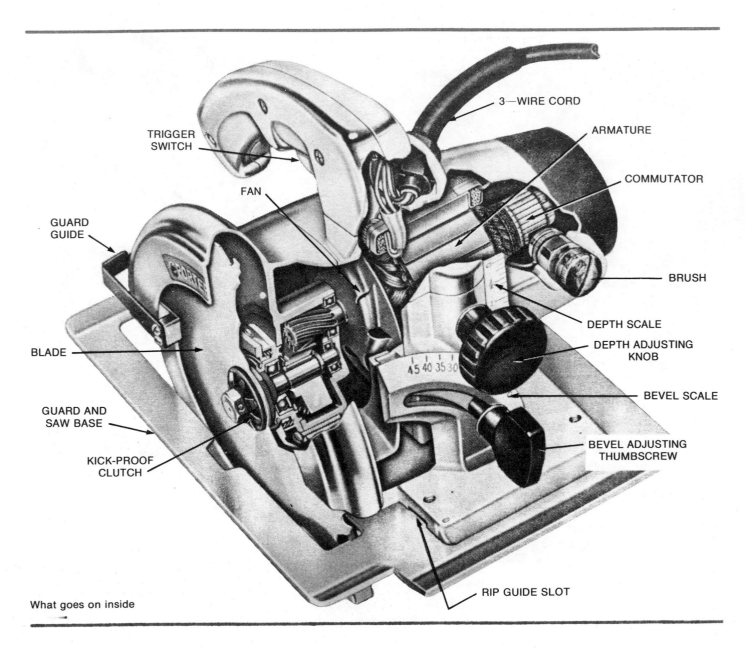

3—WIRE CORD

TRIGGER SWITCH

ARMATURE

COMMUTATOR

FAN

GUARD GUIDE

BRUSH

DEPTH SCALE

BLADE

DEPTH ADJUSTING KNOB

45 40 35 30

BEVEL SCALE

GUARD AND SAW BASE

BEVEL ADJUSTING THUMBSCREW

KICK-PROOF CLUTCH

RIP GUIDE SLOT

What goes on inside

In 1923, a New Orleans inventor named Edmond Mitchel tried to make an automated machete to cut sugar cane. He ended up by making a small, round saw blade which he hooked to a motor salvaged from a malted milk mixer. It was the first electric handsaw. Mitchel called it a "Skilsaw."

Because it was the first, many people still call all portable electric saws "Skilsaws." More, however, use the term "builder's saw," a tribute to its rough, tough cutting of 2" construction lumber.

Not as accurate as a table saw, or as easy to handle as a jig or saber saw, it has, nevertheless, certain advantages: portability, bull-strength, and speed. When you can't take work to the table saw, this is your tool. Use it to cut through walls, floors, ceiling, or roof, or make short shrift of big panels that are too cumbersome for a table saw. Its blade turns at 5000 revolutions per minute. Multiply 24 teeth by 5000 and you get 120,000 sawtooth bites per minute, which is why it's just about the world's greatest sawdust maker.

The diameter of the blade determines the saw's size. Sizes range from 4" to $8\frac{1}{4}$" and more, but the 7" and $7\frac{1}{4}$" saws are the most popular. A $6\frac{1}{2}$" saw will cut through a 2 x 4 at a 45° angle, but it means cutting practically up to the saw's arbor. A 7" or $7\frac{1}{4}$" saw breezes through with ease.

Saws are lighter in weight than they used to be, and pound-for-pound pack more punch. A good $7\frac{1}{4}$" saw may weigh only 8 pounds. The lighter weight is a special advantage in doing overhead work or working on a ladder. Heavier weight gives a saw more stability and makes it track better, but it can really be a drag when you use a saw hour after hour.

The more power a saw has, the smoother and faster it runs. You can buy $7\frac{1}{4}$" saws with $1\frac{1}{4}$, 2, and $2\frac{1}{2}$ horsepower motors. The higher the horsepower, the more drive and the less chance of stalling. Any good saw may turn at 5500 rpm, but how fast it turns under load is more important, and this is largely determined by its horsepower.

Portable saws are also safer than they used to be. Most saws today are equipped with a clutch. It's usually a spring washer under the blade. If the blade hits a knot, or is pinched, the clutch will slip, allowing the blade to stop while the arbor keeps turning. The saw won't kick back forcibly and dangerously.

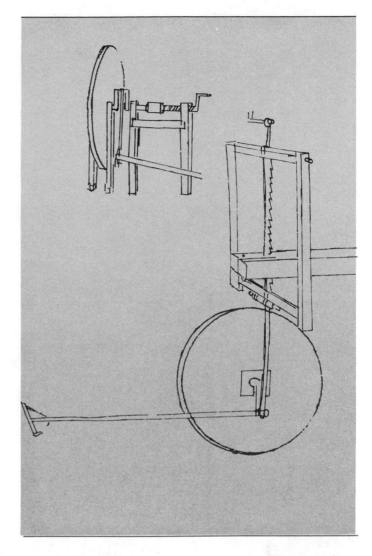

The first circular handsaw, 1923

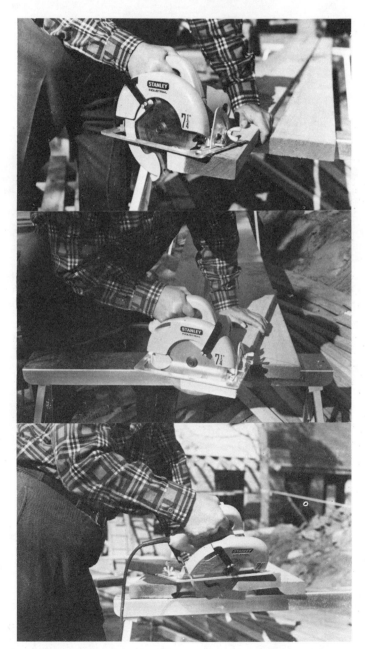

Sears best saw has a "riving knife" that trails behind the blade to prevent binding, another cause of stalling or kicking back. You'll also find saws equipped with an electronic brake that stops the blade almost the instant you take your finger off the trigger. Black & Decker introduced this feature in 1965. Most saws today also have safety switches that help prevent accidental starts.

A Skilsaw for every need

Model 574 standard duty 7¹/₄ incher is the best seller in the Skilsaw line. Die-cast aluminum housing, 10 amp, 1³/₄ hp burn-out-protected motor.

Lightweight model 534, a 6¹/₂" saw, is ideal for most home-use projects. It will cut a 2×4 at 45°

Double-insulated model 537 is a 7¹/₄" saw with a safety-guard lift that lets you raise the guard with the hand on the side away from the blade.

With a 2³/₄ hp motor and 3-ball-and-1-needle bearing, this Stanley 90714 is both beautiful and brawny. Nothing could be tougher than its plastic body or have a better feel and balance while cutting. It weighs just 12 pounds.

Heavy duty 554 is an 8¹/₄" professional saw with a 2¹/₂ hp motor. It's double insulated.

CHECKPOINTS

When doing comparative shopping for a saw, look first at obvious signs of good or poor workmanship. Is the saw crudely made or nicely finished? Are scales clearly stamped or fuzzy? Does it appear rugged or flimsy?

How about the blade guard? Is it beveled so that it won't hang up at any angle? How long and convenient is the extension lever on the guard? This is important when you pull the guard back for "plunge cuts."

Heft the saw to get a feel for its balance. Does it have an extra grab knob? This is important in making overhead cuts and provides better control on difficult cuts. How about the visibility of the blade at the cutting point? You have to be able to keep your eye on this when following a line.

A base plate that has a wraparound style gives more support for the saw when cutting, but it also gives you less clearance when making close cuts. Is it sturdy enough so that it won't bend out of alignment?

Saws may come with 6-, 8-, or 10-foot cords. If it is a shockproof or double-insulated saw it will have a cord with the extra convenience of a two-prong plug. Some cords are high-visibility yellow or orange. This is a help in preventing accidental cutting through of the cord.

The shockproof feature is characteristic of saws with plastic housing. The plastic is nonconductive. Plastic also has a thermal advantage. It feels more comfortable to the touch in broiling sun or frigid cold. Even metal saws have plastic handles because of their nonconductive quality.

Plastic has four other advantages. It is noncorrosive. It helps keep body weight down. It offers the visual appeal of color. And it also usually means more saw for the money.

Saws vary in number and size of bearings, and these are important to good operation. Note that there is a difference between "equipped with ball bearings," and "100% ball bearings."

If a saw is marked as complying with OSHA (Occupational Safety and Health Act), you know the saw is made for commercial duty. But unless you are a frequent user, you may not require the extra ruggedness and power.

Finally, in sizing up a saw, read the warranty and see what it offers. It gives you an idea what the manufacturer thinks of his own product.

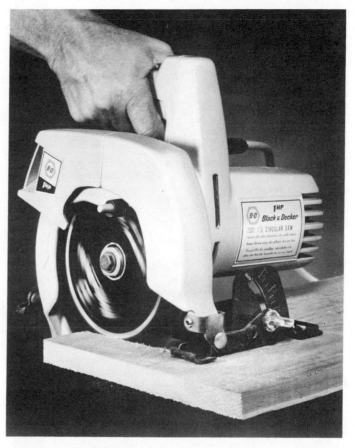

Half shoe of low-cost Black & Decker model 7399 permits cutting close to obstructions.

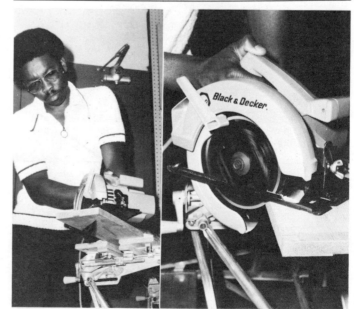

Higher-priced Black & Decker saws have a wrap-around full shoe for added support.

This 7¼" model also offers double insulation and a power-lock "off" button to guard against accidental starts. It weighs just 10 lbs., and its 1⅓ hp motor drives the blade at 5300 rpm.

Millers Falls double-insulated saw is available in 6¹/₂″, 7¹/₄″, and 8¹/₄″ sizes—all complying with OSHA (Occupational Safety and Health Act) requirements.

Lowest-cost 7¹/₄″ Rockwell model, the 4500, has a yellow plastic housing. It is double insulated and rated at 1 hp.

The best Rockwell 7¹/₄″ home-use model, the 4521, features a 9¹/₂ amp, 1¹/₂ hp motor that turns at 5800 rpm. Its housing is black and green double-insulated plastic.

Rockwell makes commercial-duty saws in all the usual sizes. This is model 4586, the 6¹/₂″ size. 100% ball bearing construction. Safety lock switch prevents accidental starting.

Two views of Milwaukee's 7¹/₄″ model 6365, the "Contractor's Saw." Handle and housing are of nonconductive glass-filled nylon. One knob adjusts for height, the other for angle.

The 7¹/₂″ Milwaukee 6370 weighs 15³/₄ lbs. Its weight gives it good tracking ability, and its worm drive makes it run smoothly. Its 2.20 hp motor is built to last forever.

Sears lightweight saw is designed especially for cutting plywood. It comes with a 4″ blade that cuts up to ⁷/₈″ at 90°, so it's suitable only for paneling, plywood and trim. It is double-insulated, with plastic motor housing.

The 7¹/₄″ cordless "Super Saw" by Piston Powered Products is gasoline powered.

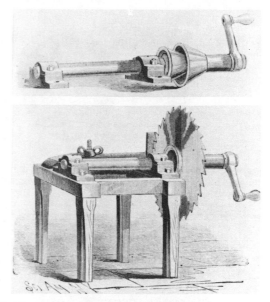

Hacket's improved saw arbor

BLADES

A new saw usually comes equipped with a chisel-tooth combination blade. This will do either crosscutting or ripping in acceptable style. But there are specialized crosscutting and ripping blades that do a somewhat better job on these operations.

As shown in the accompanying guide, there are also miter/planer blades for absolutely smooth cuts, flooring blades that will shrug off a nail or two, plywood blades, and blades for cutting nonferrous metals.

Your portable saw can cut brick, stone, metals, and hard plastics with a special cutoff wheel. It actually is a thin, plastic-reinforced grinding wheel. When using it, it is important to wear a face mask and safety glasses. Brick and ceramics can be cut more quickly, and the blade will last longer, if they are soaked for about fifteen minutes before cutting.

Many blade varieties are available with a Teflon finish. This tough plastic coating helps protect blades against rust and helps prevent blade drag.

Carbide-tip blades are recommended for cutting painted or dirty lumber. Ordinary blades lose their edge quickly on encountering grit. A carbide-tip blade won't, but it can't take nails.

A. Rip

B. Combination

C. Cutoff (crosscut)

The three most commonly used sawblades

These popular crosscut and combination blades are made of famous Sheffield steel. They come in 5″, 6″ and 7¼″ sizes, made of nickel alloy or with a Teflon-type coating.

An alternate tooth configuration for a combination blade is illustrated here.

Carbide tipped blades maintain their edge in all abrasive materials. They greatly outlast regular blades—some people claim by 50 times, others by only 12 times, and a few settle for 6 to 10 times.

The tungsten carbide tips on these blades are second only to diamonds in hardness. Left, 24-tooth general-purpose blade. Right, the 12-tooth "Nailcutter," ideal for salvaged lumber. Brookstone.

The Skil rip fence comes in sizes and styles for all saws. It attaches to the saw foot and is quickly adjustable. Eliminates the need for repeated measuring.

"Panel Crafter" saw guide attaches to either circular or table saws. It makes straight cuts to the center of a 48″ panel an easy, one-person operation. Weighs 8 lbs. Minnesota Versatil Inc.

"Trik-Trak" imparts greater accuracy and safety to portable saws. It can also be used with jigsaws and electric routers. Weighs less than 8 lbs.; can be hung on wall when not in use. Brett-Hauer Co.

BLADE SELECTION CHART

Plywood cutting

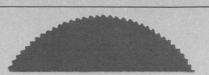

Sizing hardwood flooring

Cutting light gauge metals; Transite and Fiberglas

Thin rim blade; plywood cutting

General ripping and cross cutting

All-purpose for difficult sawing jobs

MANUFACTURERS

Skil, Black & Decker, Rockwell, McGraw-Edison (Shopmate), Wen, Electro, and Millers Falls are the names you are likely to encounter. Stanley and Milwaukee make industrial saws.

In addition to the saw companies, these are blade makers: Century, Columbia, Disston, Great Neck, Nicholson, Oldham, Remington, Simmonds, Skokie, and Vermont American.

16.

PORTABLE JIGSAWS

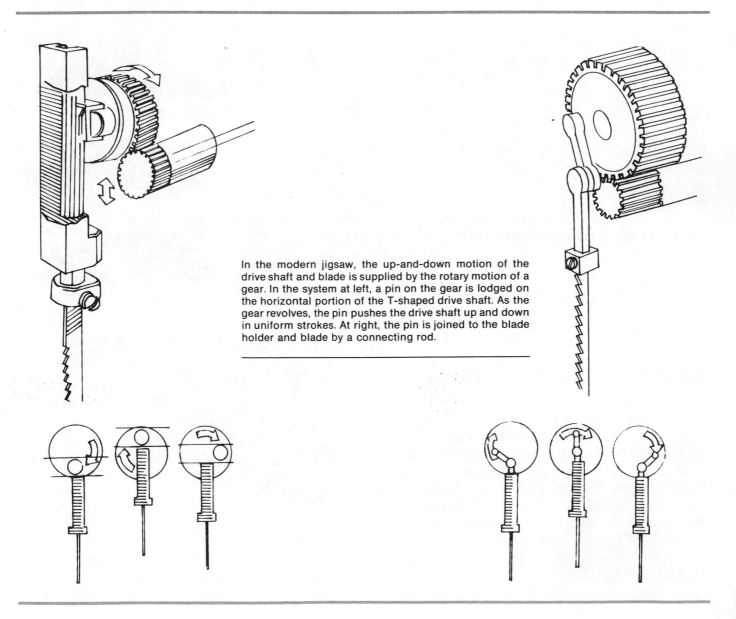

In the modern jigsaw, the up-and-down motion of the drive shaft and blade is supplied by the rotary motion of a gear. In the system at left, a pin on the gear is lodged on the horizontal portion of the T-shaped drive shaft. As the gear revolves, the pin pushes the drive shaft up and down in uniform strokes. At right, the pin is joined to the blade holder and blade by a connecting rod.

The development of small motors during World War II made the jigsaw possible. The first ones were made in Switzerland and were expensive. Now it is a mass-produced item, and its price is down. And it's no longer a novelty but an essential tool in any well-equipped shop.

The dictionary describes a jig as "a rapid, lively, springy, irregular dance for one or more persons, usually in triple meter." That definition fits this tool, which converts rotary motion to an up-and-down sawing motion. It means the jig is ready for all kinds of wood, metal, plastics, leather, and just about any other material you want to cut. It performs the operation, as the English might say, without any jiggery-pokery.

Not as fast or powerful as a circular saw, but lighter in weight and more maneuverable, the jigsaw is the answer to many jobs you can't do, or can't do as well or easily, with any other kind of saw.

It's a schizoid tool, because for everyone who calls it a jigsaw, there's another who calls it a saber saw. A saber, according to the dictionary, is a heavy, one-edge sword, usually slightly curved, used especially by cavalry. It also calls to mind the saber-toothed tiger. On the other hand, as a jigsaw, this tool has lent its name to that diverting pastime—the jigsaw puzzle.

Skil, Rockwell, Black & Decker, and Wen call their tool a jigsaw. Stanley, Millers Falls, Shopmate, and Sears call theirs a saber saw. Hoping this highly safe tool won't draw any of yours, we've opted for the fun name rather than the blood-letting one.

Really, its name is *convenience*. Weighing in at about 3 pounds, it's so light you can use it overhead, on a ladder, or in tight places, without

FOOT POWER JIG SAW.

The invention of gear systems that translate rotary motion into up-and-down motion was important to the development of the jigsaw.

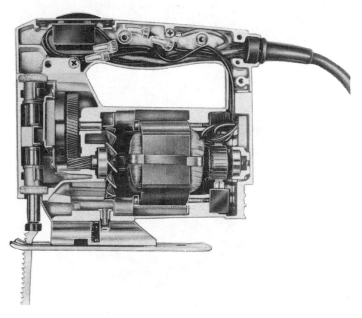

An inside view

the hazard a heavier tool might invoke. It can cut flush to obstructions and walls. It will make cutouts in countertops for sink basins, in floors for registers, and in walls for electrical outlets, without drilling. Merely tilt the tool up on its front edge and slowly lower its blade down onto the surface to be cut. Even the smallest will crosscut a 2 x 4.

Attach a jigsaw to a specially designed table, and you have a stationary tool that frees both your hands to guide material through in very intricate cuts. There is a locking button so you don't have to hold the trigger to keep it running.

For flush cutting, there is a special projecting blade. Stanley makes a model that has a push-back base for those occasions when you want to flush-cut. It will cut right up to a wall.

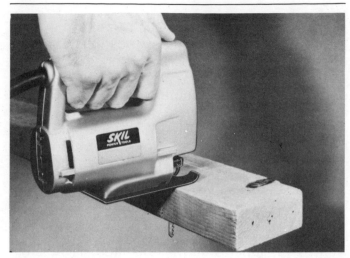

Crosscutting on wood

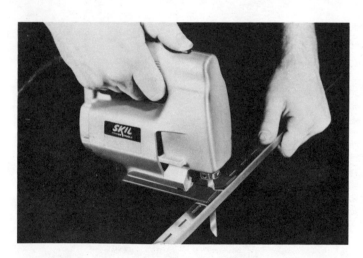

Cutting metal

Ripping

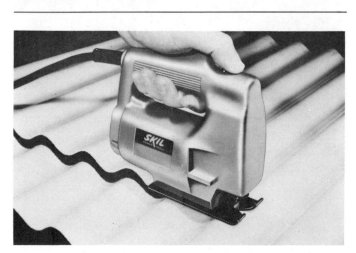

Cutting plastic

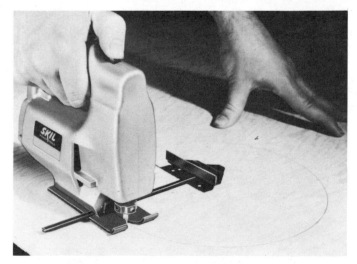

Circle cutting

SPEED AND STROKE

You can get one-speed, two-speed, multiple-speed, or completely variable speed. Typically, top speed is around 3000 strokes per minute (spm). Speed is important in effective operation. The harder the material, the slower you want to run the saw. Use high speed on a hard material and the blade will heat up and break. High speed, however, is effective for wood, plastic, and fiberboard. Medium speed is best for brass, aluminum, and copper. Low speed is best for steel, or in starting cuts.

Speed, as well as power, may be controlled by a slide switch or a trigger. With variable speed, you can slow down at the corners or speed up on the straightaway. On some saws, feedback circuitry helps keep the blade speed constant. Rockwell plays up its square drive shaft which it says eliminates blade flexing in sharp corner cuts.

In a two-speed model, you may have 2500 spm for low, and 3200 spm for high. Stanley makes a model with 7 speeds; Sears offers one with 12 speeds. These are preset by a rear-mounted control dial.

Length of blade stroke is important. It may be $\frac{1}{2}''$, $\frac{5}{8}''$, $\frac{3}{4}''$, or $1''$. Usually, the longer the stroke the greater the speed and the capacity in cutting.

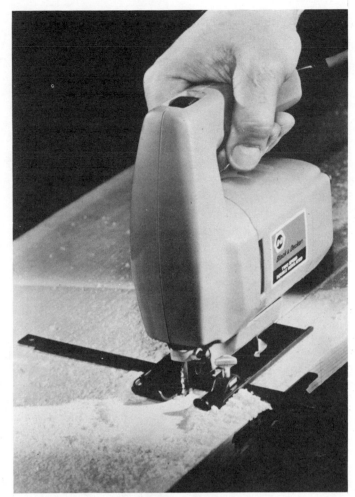

Black & Decker two-speed model is double-insulated. Shoe tilts up to 45° for bevel and compound miter cuts. Shown here with an optional accessory, a combination rip fence and circle guide.

Single speed Millers Falls SP6060 cuts at 3000 spm. It is double-insulated, 7" long overall, and weighs $3\frac{3}{4}$ lbs. Also available in a two-speed model, the SP6262.

Rockwell two-speed model 4318 comes as a set in a break-resistant carrying case that provides everything needed for all jigsaw operations. The square drive shaft eliminates blade flexing in sharp corner cuts. Double insulated.

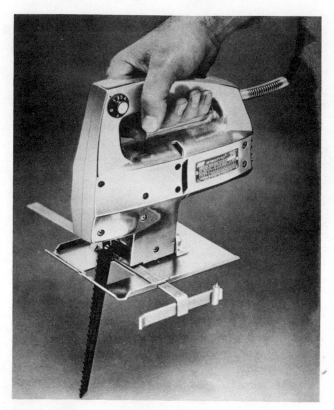

This hefty variable speed Electro saw can cut 6" logs. It comes with a combination rip-circle cut guide and an assortment of 5 blades. 0-5200 spm. 3-conductor cord.

BLADES

A blade is the key to the job the saw will do. Many saws come with only a wood-cutting blade, or one wood and one metal blade. Wen provides seven blades and there are at least two-dozen varieties of blades for specific uses, as shown in the accompanying selection guide. If your saw has a 1" or longer stroke, there is one blade that is 6" long that will cut wood up to 5" thick. It can save laborious hand sawing.

For ripping soft wood, a blade with six to seven teeth per inch is desirable. One with ten to the inch is better for crosscutting hard wood. Among metal-cutting blades, one with fourteen teeth per inch is preferred for thicker, softer metals. It is also good for wood when there is danger of running into nails.

A blade with twenty-four teeth per inch is best for hard metals and thin stock. In cutting thin stock, at least two teeth should be in contact with material or it will straddle the work and catch. To avoid this, you can sandwich thin metals between sheets of $1/4$" plywood held with clamps.

DESIGN FEATURES

In the recent past, some of the best jigsaws were of cast aluminum, but plastic tools have largely replaced them. Plastic has proved itself better. Plastic doesn't corrode. It has a better feel and better thermal qualities. It is colorful and attractive. It provides shock-safety. It is lighter in weight and less likely to break when dropped or struck. And it costs less!

But there is plastic and there is plastic. As you go up the price ladder, you'll find the plastics used are more durable. As you pay more, you'll also find an increase in tool power. At the bottom end, the motor may rate $1/6$ hp. For every added few dollars, it goes to $1/5$, $1/4$, $1/3$, and $1/2$ hp. Naturally, with more power the saw cuts quicker, easier, and smoother.

If a saw is labeled as meeting OSHA standards (Occupational Safety and Health Act), you know it is commercial duty. But if you use the saw only occasionally, and then for short periods, you may not need a tool this good—though they are nice to have if your pocketbook will allow it.

Some saws come with a combination rip fence and circle guide, but you can frequently buy one as an accessory. The rip fence permits you to make rip cuts without drawing a line. The circle guide makes it easy to cut circles up to 12" diameter. All except the lowest priced saws have tilting shoes which are calibrated up to 45° for making bevel and compound cuts.

Wen has a saw with a steering wheel knob so that you can turn the blade as you cut. That means easier maneuverability. Sears has a saw with "automatic scrolling." As you slide the saw to the right or left to follow a line, the blade pivots. Pull back and the blade pivots to the rear. Of course, if you go straight ahead, so does the blade.

The better the saw, the more bearings it has and the better they are. Sleeve bearings are the least expensive. In better saws you begin to find ball and needle bearing construction.

Millers Falls 3000 spm, single-speed 561 has a blade that can be rotated 90° in either direction for parallel cuts. Reversing shoe permits cuts within $3/4$" of a wall. Its barrel-grip design gives good control. 3-conductor cord.

A GIANT JIGSAW

Nearly 400 years ago, in the German city of Danzig, there was a giant jigsaw. A visiting Englishman in 1593 described it thus: "Without any help of hand it saweth boards, having an iron wheele which doth not only drive the saw, but hooketh in, and turneth the boards to the saw."

Here is how it worked: The workman pulled up an anchor-shaped counterweight. As the weight rose and fell, its threaded axle caused a scissorlike device to open and close, making its twin-bladed saw go up and down. Simultaneously, the workman kicked a capstan to propel the squared log past the blades, which cut the squared-off log into boards.

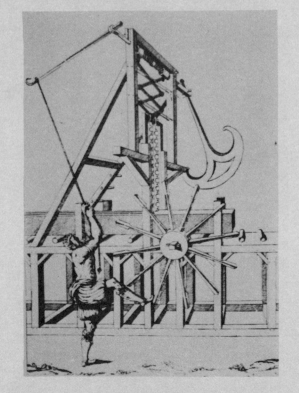

Sears "Best" cuts with a 1" stroke. It has trigger-controlled variable speed plus 12 pre-set speeds. Auto-scrolling mechanism permits accuracy in intricate cuts.

Designed for use in building and service trades, Stanley 90456 cuts with a ⁵/₈" stroke at two speeds—2400 and 3000 spm. It has a patented anti-vibration system for smooth cutting. Weighs 5 lbs.

The heads of these Milwaukee models pivot up to 45° for angle cuts. They have a ³/₄" blade stroke and all ball-and-roller bearings. Model 6272 (top) is single-speed (3900 spm), but model 6287 has trigger-control variable speed of 0-3900. They come with 10 blades, combination circle-and-rip guide, and steel carrying case.

TEN KINDS OF BLADES
AND WHAT THEY'RE GOOD FOR

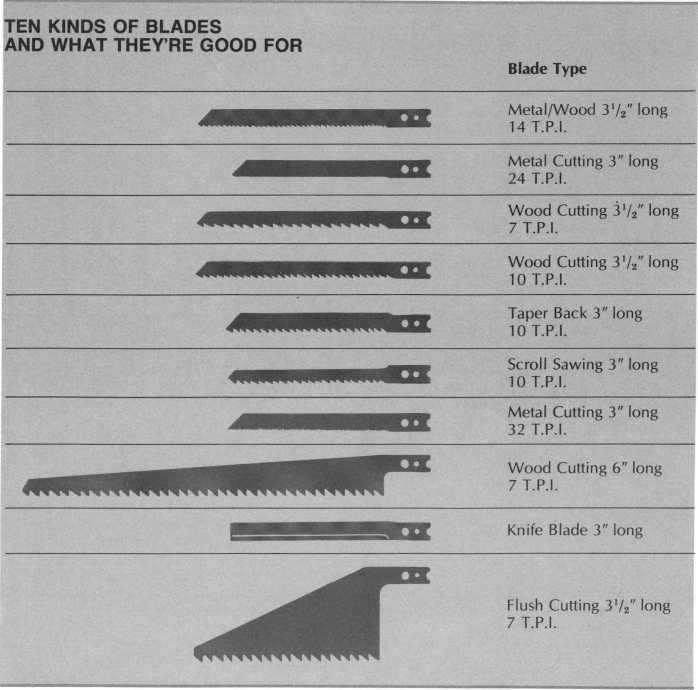

	Blade Type
	Metal/Wood 3½" long 14 T.P.I.
	Metal Cutting 3" long 24 T.P.I.
	Wood Cutting 3½" long 7 T.P.I.
	Wood Cutting 3½" long 10 T.P.I.
	Taper Back 3" long 10 T.P.I.
	Scroll Sawing 3" long 10 T.P.I.
	Metal Cutting 3" long 32 T.P.I.
	Wood Cutting 6" long 7 T.P.I.
	Knife Blade 3" long
	Flush Cutting 3½" long 7 T.P.I.

MANUFACTURERS

Black & Decker, Rockwell, Skil, Wen, Electro, and Millers Falls are home-use manufacturers. Stanley and Milwaukee make professional power tools only, but only the price need stop you from buying them. Sears, Wards, and J. C. Penney sell tools made for them by manufacturers.

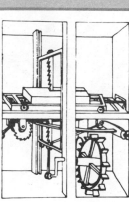

17.

RECIP SAWS

The two-speed Sawzall operates at 2400 or 1700 spm. Unlike most other recips, Sawzall refers to itself as a hacksaw. That's because when it first appeared on the market it wanted to distinguish itself from a jigsaw. Weight is 7 lbs., 11 blades are included.

This big muscle-saver was first introduced in 1953 by the Milwaukee Electric Tool Company. It previously had made reciprocating saw mechanisms for $1/4$" drills. It called its new tool a Sawzall, and that's exactly what it does. It saws all. Since that time a number of manufacturers have begun making them and they go by the generic name of reciprocal, recipro, or simply recip saws.

The recip is a portable tool that can get in where a circular saw or a jigsaw can't. It's not as smooth as either of those tools, and it's harder to handle, but it does jobs for which you'd probably otherwise have to use a handsaw. It's like a handsaw in that it imitates the back-and-forth motion on a more or less horizontal plane. It differs from a handsaw in that it cuts on its backward or return stroke.

Plumbers use a recip saw to cut holes and notches for pipes. Electricians use it to cut holes for outlet boxes. Carpenters use it for rough remodeling tasks. Heating contractors use it to install duct work. Though widely used in the building trades, the recip saw nevertheless comes in inexpensive models that are well within the reach of the do-it-yourselfer.

You'll use a recip saw for everything a tradesman does, and probably for cutting branches and firewood as well, though its speed is no match for the chain saw. Nor is it an accurate or precise tool. It tends to vibrate, chatter, and wander, so if you don't strong-arm it as it rips into material you may find it hard to follow an exact line.

But it's excellent for other things, like plunge cuts into walls, floor, or roof. You just rest the saw on its sole plate and pivot the blade into the work. The Millers Falls recip has a special rocker type shoe to facilitate this operation.

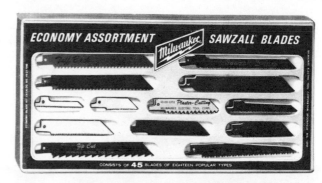

An economy assortment of 45 blades, including the 18 most popular blade types for woods and metals. Made by Sawzall, but they fit most makes of recips.

WHAT TO LOOK FOR

Recip saws may have one speed, two speeds, or variable speed. Sawzall's single-speed model has 2250 strokes per minute, its two-speed saw has 1700 and 2400, and its variable speed can be dialed from 1100 through 2550 spm.

A two-speed recip has a decided advantage over a one-speed. With two speeds, you can use the fast speed for wood, composition board, and other soft materials, and the slow speed for metals. The stroke length of a recip may be from $5/8''$ to $1\frac{1}{4}''$, with 1" about the average.

Most blades range from 6" to 12" in length. Usually, you can mount blades to cut up, down, or horizontally, and flush with an adjoining surface. Shopmate offers three blade positions, Skil four, and Stanley six.

The sole plates on some recips can be angled up to 45° for bevel cutting. By moving the shoe in or out, a different section of blade can be brought to bear on the work, so that you don't waste any of the blade. Some recips blow sawdust off the work area, which is handy in following a line.

In relation to cost, consider speed range, power, weight, number of blade positions, vibration and noise, sawdust disposal, length of cord, electrical safety, and brush accessibility. Because a saw may have a color housing, do not assume automatically that it is plastic. Wen housing, for example, is painted die-cast aluminum.

How long does the saw run after you take your finger off the trigger? It's both a safety and convenience factor. How many blades are provided with the tool? Shopmate gives you one. Sears gives you three. Sawzall offers eleven. Basic blade types include 12" general purpose, 6" smooth cutting, 6" flush cutting, 5" metal cutting, and $4\frac{1}{2}''$ sheet-metal cutting.

You may want to check on comparative cord length. It varies from $5\frac{1}{2}'$ to $9\frac{1}{2}'$. Having extra cord reduces the number of times you must get out an extension cord.

The Stanley all-purpose saw model 90459 has six blade positions for multi-directional cutting. Variable speed—0 to 2300 spm. Five-position handle.

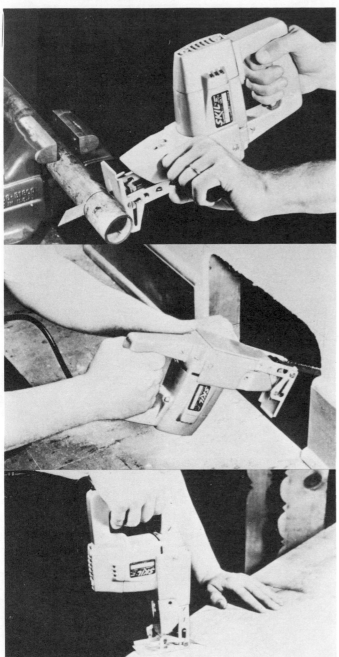

The two-speed Skil 577 has a $^3/_4$" stroke and a blade which adjusts to 4 positions. Either jig or recip blades can be used. Double reduction gears and "canted" blade allow you to do fast cutting in tough materials.

Olson's saw machine had true recip action.

The single-speed Millers Falls "Super Saw" has an aluminum housing and a plastic handle. It is double insulated—no grounding required. Features rocker shoe for easy entry cuts. Similar two-speed and variable-speed models are also available.

The recip has helped take the muscle out of sawing.

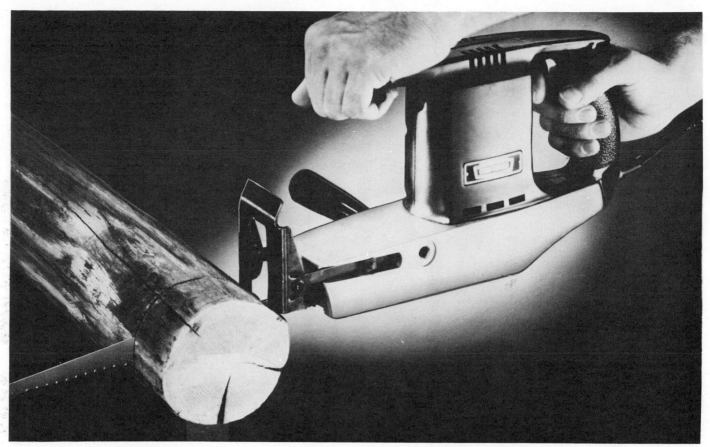

Double-insulated reciprocating saw by Sears has 1¼" blade stroke, variable speed from 0 to 2000 strokes per minute. Will cut wood to 12", aluminum to 2" and cast iron to 1" thick. Blade clamp rotates.

Rockwell double-insulated single-speed "Tiger Saw" 4392 has a pivoting guide shoe. Its housing and handle are both of plastic. Blade does 2400 spm, and stroke length is 1".

MANUFACTURERS

Makers include Milwaukee, Skil, Stanley, Rockwell, Black & Decker, Shopmate, Wen, and Millers Falls. Sears, Ward, and Penney sell recips made for them by other manufacturers.

Use the right TOOL!

18.

ROUTERS

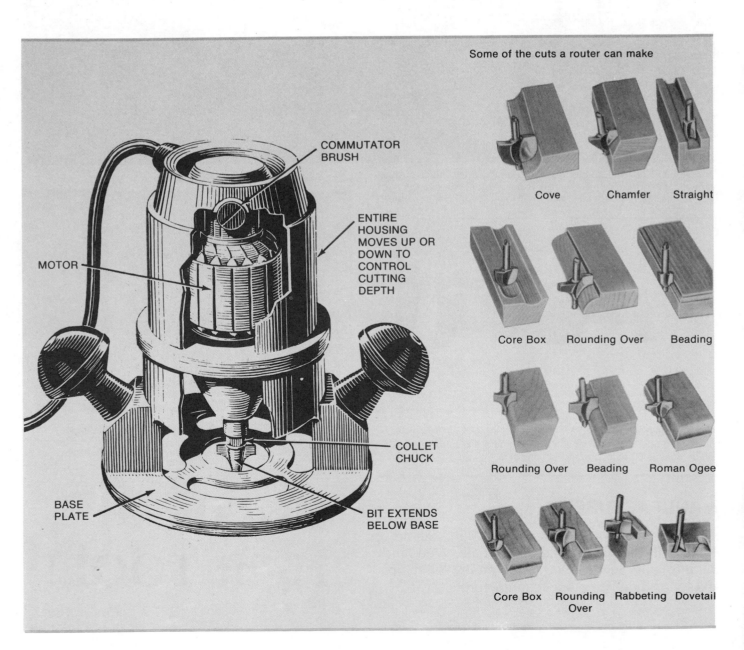

Some of the cuts a router can make

COMMUTATOR BRUSH

ENTIRE HOUSING MOVES UP OR DOWN TO CONTROL CUTTING DEPTH

MOTOR

COLLET CHUCK

BASE PLATE

BIT EXTENDS BELOW BASE

Cove   Chamfer   Straight

Core Box   Rounding Over   Beading

Rounding Over   Beading   Roman Ogee

Core Box   Rounding Over   Rabbeting   Dovetail

During World War I, an ingenious young patternmaker, R. L. Carter, in the little town of Phoenix, New York, looked for an easy way of doing a laborious routing job. He took a motor out of some electric barber clippers and improvised a tool for the purpose. With it, he did the job in three hours instead of the seven days it normally would have taken. He called the power tool he had made a hand shaper, but it was really a router.

Carter knew he had a good thing. When the war was over, he began selling power routers, improved now with a collet to take a variety of bits. Within ten years he had sold 100,000 of them.

The router is a tool that separates the pro from the amateur. Anyone who is serious about woodworking needs one. It enables you to achieve professional touches such as decorative edges, dovetail joints, intricate contours, dropleaf table joints, chamfers, rabbets, relief panels, and inlays. In addition, it can be used to trim the edges of plastic laminates.

Basically, a router is a high-speed motor supported vertically in a base. The motor holds a variety of cutting bits in its collet, and can be raised up or down in the base to adjust the depth of cut. In a sense—as R. L. Carter felt—it is a portable shaper. But it differs from a stationary shaper in two important ways. First, instead of passing the work over the machine, the machine is passed over the work. And second, where a stationary shaper spindle may revolve at 10,000 rpm, a router whizzes at 18,000 to 27,000 or more rpms.

The more power a router has, the quicker it can do its job. It may make a cut in one pass instead of two or three. Skil, as an example, makes routers with $1/2$, $3/4$, 1, and $1^3/4$ hp, but only the first two are recommended for home use.

The classic Stanley router has been around for more than a generation in essentially this form. It is still a favorite. Its motor and base are of polished aluminum. It has a $1/4$" collet-type chuck and push-button lock for changing bits. Available in $1/4$ hp and $7/8$ hp models.

Dovetail joints are easy with the dovetail fixture made by Stanley for some of its routers. It handles wood 12" wide and $7/16$" to 1" thick. Kit includes fixture, template guides and bit.

This kit has both a router and a powerful jointer plane, powered by one motor. Kit includes 1 hp motor, router base, straight/circular guide, plane attachment, arbor, router bit, plane cutter, and carrying case.

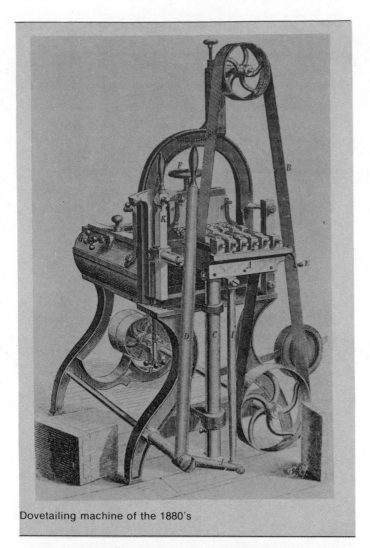

Dovetailing machine of the 1880's

A router is not more expensive than most other power tools, but accessories and bits can quickly multiply the price many times. It's like the old cowboy song about a $10 horse and a $50 saddle. In this case, the router may cost $50, and the accessories $100 upward. With a special attachment, you can convert a router to a power plane. With a table you can convert it to a shaper. For about $65 you can get an accessory that converts a router into a lathe. If you want to make dovetail joints, you need fixtures that cost from $35 to $70, depending on whether you want to make $1/4''$ or $1/2''$ dovetails. Most routers come without bits. Bits generally range from $10 to $30, though there are a number that sell for less.

As with most portable power tools, double-insulated plastic designs are replacing metal. Even metal routers are now part plastic. It's lighter and safer.

A good choice for the serious woodworker is the Black & Decker model 7610—a $3/4$ hp router. A manual with complete easy-to-follow instructions is included.

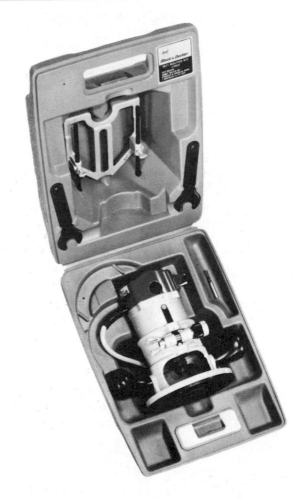

The Black & Decker 7610 router kit includes all the basics: a straight/circular guide, 2 flute bits, 2 wrenches, and custom-fitted plastic carrying case.

The Skil 548 is a lightweight, economical router for home use. It has a $1/2$ hp motor which operates at 27,000 rpm. Also available in a kit including straight bit, edge guide and plastic carrying case.

Green high-impact plastic housing, capacity of 28,000 rpm, and all ball-and-bearing construction are features of the 6 lb. Rockwell model 4620. It comes with a straight bit and edge guide. Double insulated, $5/8$ hp.

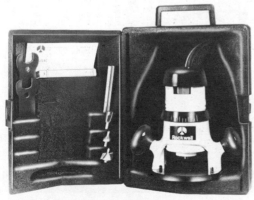

A colorful yellow and black housing distinguishes this double-insulated $1/2$ hp router, the Rockwell 4600. It weighs just $53/4$ lbs., comes in "Tool Toter" case with edge guide, wrenches, and three bits—straight, V-groove and corner-round.

This table, which accepts the Skil 548 router, makes it easy to shape and joint small pieces that otherwise might be difficult to handle. Good for making picture frames, plaques, and adding decorative touches to moldings.

This Sears table has a die-cast aluminum top. Ridges collect sawdust to avoid build-up under work. Hinged guard provides protection as you cut. Also accommodates Sears jigsaws.

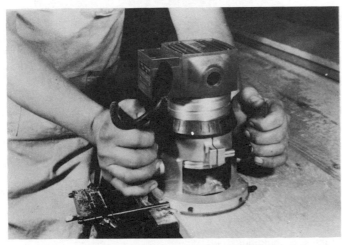

Professional routers with 1 or $1\frac{1}{2}$ hp motors. Milwaukee calls these the most powerful 1 and $1\frac{1}{2}$ hp routers on the market because they have the highest amp ratings of any routers in their class. They have a no-load speed of 23,000 rpm. The 5620 1 hp model will take $\frac{1}{4}$" to $\frac{3}{8}$" bits, and the 5660 $1\frac{1}{2}$ hp model will take $\frac{1}{4}$", $\frac{3}{8}$", and $\frac{1}{2}$" bits.

Sears best router features a zero-reset on depth gauge for identical depth on repeat cuts. Flat top is handy when you turn router over to change bits. Develops 1 hp on initial surge.

A special plunge base on the super-duty Stanley allows vertical plunge of the bit into work. There's an adjustable depth stop up to 2". No wrench is needed to change bits; just turn top knob. $\frac{1}{2}$" chuck. 2 hp and $2\frac{1}{2}$ hp models.

Stanley 93005 sash/door holder holds woodwork up to 3" thick, automatically releases when work is lifted out. Here, router is used with plane attachment.

"Router-Crafter" converts a router into a lathe. For use with routers of more than 1/2 hp that accommodate 1/4" shank bits. Mounts work stock up to 3" square and 36" long. A 6-piece bit set is also available. Sears.

MANUFACTURERS

Stanley acquired R. L. Carter's company in 1929 and is tops in the field. Others include Skil, Rockwell, Millers Falls, Shopmate, and Milwaukee.

Much of the skill and dexterity that old-time cabinetmakers learned only after years of work are within easy reach of anyone with a router. But there is a difference. The craftsman's work is human, touched by minor error, irregularity and flaw. A router's work is precise and machine-perfect.

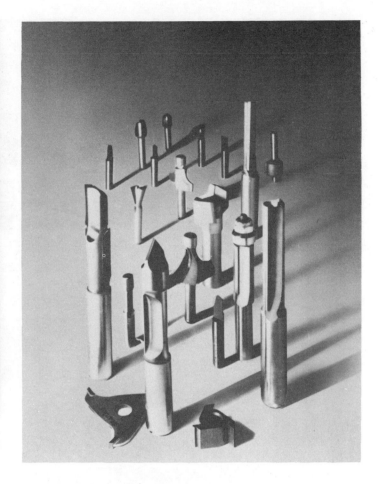

Stanley offers four varieties of bits—high-speed steel, carbide-tipped, solid-carbide, and super-sharp. Bits that stay sharp longer mean faster cuts, smoother cuts, less breakage.

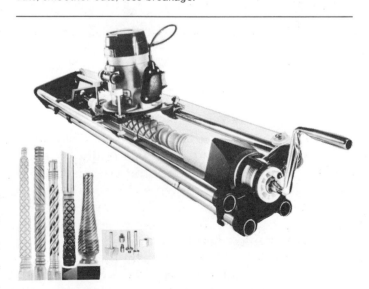

There are two ways to trim plastic laminates. One way is to use a veneer trimming kit to convert your router for the operation. The other way is with a router designed especially for the purpose, like this Stanley 91263. It's faster (30,000 rpms) and more versatile than the converted router.

19. PORTABLE SANDERS

Ancient Egyptians knew about the abrasive action of sand.

Nineteenth-century finishing methods

Primitive people used dried sharkskin as an abrasive—if they had it. It was really rough. In 1678, people—no longer primitive—used scouring rush, commonly known as horsetail or Dutch rush, to smooth wood. By 1772, however, emery paper was known, and an advertisement in the *Boston Gazette*, dated September 10, 1764, offered it for sale, along with sandpaper.

There was another kind of smoothing material before long—a do-it-yourself kind. A guide published in 1829 told how to make "glass paper." You did it by spreading glue on a kind of pasteboard used in making cartridges. You then sprinkled crushed glass on it.

Skip 100 years and you come to another important milestone. In 1929 Black & Decker introduced a portable belt sander. Then in 1952 they brought out a finishing sander. That's how new these two important power tools are, and they are important.

Sanding is a vital step in most woodworking. It is essential in accurate fitting and joining. It is indispensable in smoothing surfaces before applying finish, and often for smoothing between coats. It is also used for removing paint and varnish, smoothing the edges of glass, feathering painted edges, and even slicking drawer runners so they slide easier.

FINISHING SANDERS

By hand, you can sand about 375 strokes per minute. Finishing sanders do from 9000 to 12,000 strokes per minute, which is about 30 times faster and a million times better. These wonderful sanding machines are of two varieties—straight line and orbital. A few machines combine the actions of both these varieties, switching from one to the other at the shift of a lever.

The pad of a straight-line sander moves exclusively forward and back, so you can keep it unerringly with the grain. The orbital sander, on the other hand, describes a slightly elliptical path as it shuttles back and forth. It's a difference of only $1/8''$ to $3/16''$ between one stroke and another, not enough to create swirl marks, but enough to remove wood faster. Technically, half of each cycle is against the grain, that's why the faster removal.

If you are a purist, and rigidly adhere to the never-against-the-grain dictum of woodworking, the straight-line sander is for you. If you are a pragmatist, and flexible, the orbital fills the bill. A middle of the road choice is the dual-action sander. You can then do the preliminary sanding in the orbital mode, and switch to straight sanding for the finish.

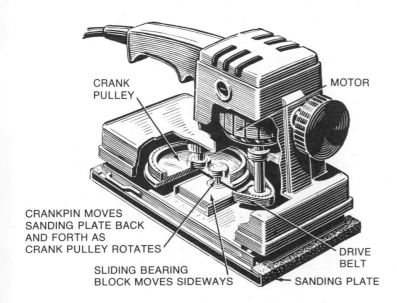

CRANK PULLEY

MOTOR

CRANKPIN MOVES SANDING PLATE BACK AND FORTH AS CRANK PULLEY ROTATES

SLIDING BEARING BLOCK MOVES SIDEWAYS

DRIVE BELT

SANDING PLATE

Finishing sander

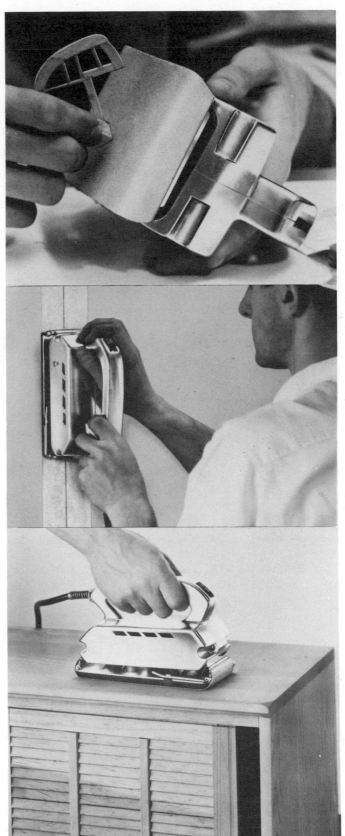

The inexpensive Wen straight-line sander has aluminum housing and takes $1/3$ of a standard sandpaper sheet. Its electro-magnetic motor provides 7200 strokes a minute, each $3/16''$ long.

Stanley says its model 90501 is the fastest sander in its class. It takes a full $1/2$ sheet of sandpaper and does 10,000 orbits per minute. Orbits are only $1/8$". It is double-insulated, quiet, and runs smoothly. Motor hum is well under 90 decibels. The integral vacuum system of super-duty model 90502 (shown at right) improves sanding efficiency. This model also has all the same good features of model 90501.

Rockwell model 4420 features 12,000 orbits a minute and all ball-bearing construction. It has a break-proof housing and flush side design for sanding in corners. Model 4400, which does 10,000 opm, costs a little less.

Milwaukee model 6005 takes $1/2$ sheet of sandpaper. It has direct drive; no gears or belts. Similar models 6000 and 6002 take $1/2$ sheet and do 10,000 opm.

Stanley's disc sander 90368 is for big jobs. It has a 7" molded rubber backing pad and does 6000 rpm. Powerful air exhaust cooling system. Can be converted to grinding wheel with guard.

DISC SANDERS

Basically, these are like a drill with a sanding disc, except that sanding is not a sideline with them. They are designed for sanding. With a lambs' wool bonnet, they may also do polishing. With a proper guard and wheel, they may even do grinding.

Disc sanders are for big jobs, like refinishing cars or boats, or smoothing welding seams. With tungsten carbide discs, they do an excellent job of removing paint and rust.

Typically, disc sanders have a 6", 7", or 9" diameter flexible pad, and may travel at 2000 to 4000 rpm. Some sanders have two speeds—2000 for polishing and 2500 rpm for sanding.

WHAT TO LOOK FOR

There are two other factors in speedy sanding. The more powerful motor a sander has, and the larger its pad, the faster it will do a job. Sanders may use $\frac{1}{2}$ of a 9"-by-11" sheet, $\frac{1}{3}$, $\frac{1}{4}$, $\frac{1}{5}$, or even less. A typical sander, if there is one, has a pad $3\frac{1}{2}$" by 7", and requires exactly $\frac{1}{3}$ sheet, or a piece $3\frac{2}{3}$" by 9", allowing for tucking in. Its effective sanding surface is about 25 square inches.

The pad on a sander may be of felt, which does a good job on flat surfaces, or neoprene, which is better for contours. Neoprene has the further advantage of being amenable to use in wet sanding.

As for power, is the motor $\frac{1}{6}$, $\frac{1}{5}$, $\frac{1}{4}$, or $\frac{1}{3}$ horsepower? If you want to make an informative study of how two sanders compare in power, bear down on each until it stalls, and you'll have your answer. In normal sanding, of course, only the weight of the tool and of your hands provides the required pressure.

Does the sander have one- or two-handed control, and with which do you feel the more comfortable? Does it permit three-sided flush sanding? Most do. Is it all plastic, or part metal, not that it makes a significant difference as long as the tool is double insulated.

How about the ease of inserting and tensioning sandpaper? One sander may be easier for insertion and another may do a better tensioning job, perhaps even requiring a screwdriver. The choice is a personal one.

Does it have provision for dust collecting? That can be important. How about comparative price? That, too, can be important.

The Rockwell 4480 has all ball-bearing construction with direct motor-to-pad drive. Offset pad permits flush sanding on four sides.

The Black & Decker 7404 orbital sander holds six pieces of paper for fast changing. It does 10,000 opm and is double insulated. With accessories, it does polishing (top) and dustless sanding.

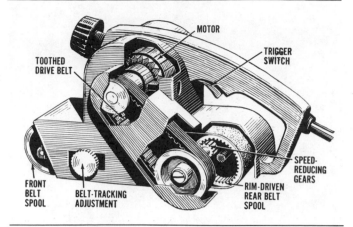

The Stanley 90031 will stand upside down on a bench for stationary use. It is powered for industrial use; its 3" × 24" belt does 1600 SFPM. Easy belt-changing system. For dust collection, it can be attached to any vacuum cleaner hose.

Two views of Milwaukee's heavy-duty belt sander, model 5900. At right, the vacuum attachment is in use. It has a 24" belt, available in 3" and 4" widths. 1700 SFPM.

BELT SANDERS

Though a finishing sander, with a coarse grit paper, may take wood off in a hurry, it is simply no match for the speed of a belt sander. These are made for rougher work. They can flatten cupped boards, renew a scarred and battered table or desktop, or churn away layers of paint and varnish with refreshing alacrity.

Important factors to consider in selecting this tool, in relation to price, are the belt size and horsepower. Also, how many surface feet per minute (SFPM) does it sand? Typically, this may range from 900 sfpm to 1300 sfpm. At 1300 sfpm, a sanding belt is traveling one-fourth mile per minute.

Belt sanders these days are double insulated, which means they can be used in relative safety without being grounded. It may have a gear housing of aluminum, with the motor housing and handles of plastic. Or everything may be plastic. If you are doubtful about the durability of plastic, remember that it is the material of which hard hats and crash helmets are made.

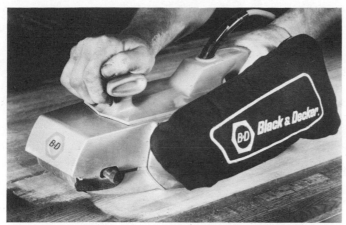

The motor is between the pulleys in this Black & Decker model 7450, giving it a low center of gravity that minimizes tilting and gouging. Its 3" x 24" belt does 1200 SFPM. Dust-collector attachment is available.

ABRASIVES

Flint is quartz, a natural mineral lacking in hardness and toughness. Paper made with it is suitable only for light hand sanding on wood. It is not suitable for use on hand power tools. There are six kinds of mineral abrasives that are.

1. Garnet is a reddish natural abrasive. It is hard and tough and especially good for the final sanding of cabinetwork.
2. Aluminum oxide is garnet's synthetic, brownish equivalent, though a little coarser. It can be used like garnet and is tough enough to tackle metals.
3. Emery cloth is used for polishing metals and removing rust.
4. Crocus cloth employs an iron oxide and is for polishing metal.
5. Silicon carbide is about as hard as a diamond, but fractures under pressure. Use it only where significant pressure is not required.
6. Tungsten carbide is bonded to thin steel, which will give you an idea how tough it is. It is extremely abrasive and long lasting.

The grit numbers on the back of abrasives refer to the number of openings in a 1-inch square of screen mesh through which the grit particles will pass. The bigger the number, the finer the grit, and the number may range from 12 to 600.

Abrasive coating may be open or closed. It's closed when the grit covers all the surface of the backing. It's open when only 50 to 70 percent of the surface is covered.

Tricks you should know

When two pieces of wood join, with grain running in two directions, cover one part with tape while the other is sanded.

For fastest hand sanding, use a block with no padding.

When sanding open-grained wood, like oak or ash, sand at a slight angle to the grain to avoid enlarging pores.

To divide a sheet of sandpaper, fold grit side in, crease along the fold, then open and tear carefully.

To detect irregularities when fine sanding, hold the workpiece below eye level and obliquely to a light source.

20.
TABLE SAWS

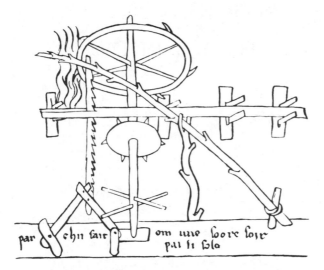

In 1245, an architect named Villard sketched this "automatic" saw.

ROWLEY & HERMANCE'S SELF-FEEDING RIP SAW TABLE.

A year after the American Revolution a different kind of revolution took place in England. On August 7, 1777, Samuel Miller of Southhampton patented a circular saw. Sawyers—people who made their living by sawing—didn't like it. They saw it as a threat to their occupation.

About 1814, Benjamin Cummins in Bentonville, New York, made the first circular saw in the United States. It took a while to catch on, but around 1850 sawmills began to use this strange new device. In the next fifty years a variety of what might be called table saws came on the market. They were hand or foot powered, or a combination of both. While you cranked or treadled, a heavy flywheel sustained momentum and evened the speed.

As a motorized shop tool, the table saw did not become a favorite until after World War II. Before that it ranked behind the scroll saw and the band saw in popularity. There wasn't so much need for making long, straight cuts, at which it excelled. That need accelerated with the increasing use of plywood and panel materials.

Today, the table saw holds stage-center in the shop, sometimes teamed with a jointer and both run by the same motor. It's more than just a saw. With a dado head, it can make dado cuts. With an accessory molding cutterhead and knives it can produce moldings in a variety of styles. Other accessories and attachments equip it for tenoning and sanding.

Toolkraft's model 100K 10" table saw is shipped complete with built-in 1$\frac{1}{8}$ hp motor. Its 17"×20" table is cast iron with two sliding steel extensions. Depth of cut at 90° is 3$\frac{1}{2}$", rip capacity with extension is 24".

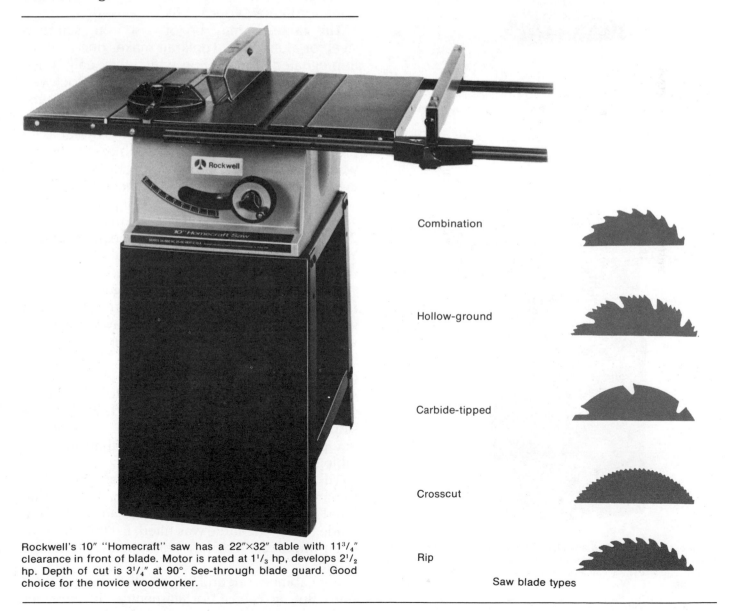

Rockwell's 10" "Homecraft" saw has a 22"×32" table with 11$\frac{3}{4}$" clearance in front of blade. Motor is rated at 1$\frac{1}{3}$ hp, develops 2$\frac{1}{2}$ hp. Depth of cut is 3$\frac{1}{4}$" at 90°. See-through blade guard. Good choice for the novice woodworker.

Combination

Hollow-ground

Carbide-tipped

Crosscut

Rip

Saw blade types

Rockwell's most popular table saw is the 10" model 34-345. It has a 40"×27" precision-ground aluminum alloy table with stamped-steel extension wings. There is 16" space in front of blade, so it will handle large material.

For the professional and advanced home craftsman. This 9" "Contractor's" saw by Rockwell is designed for prolonged use and accuracy. Table size is 22"×30" and rip capacity is 24" to the right and left of blade.

VITAL STATISTICS

Size. Saw size is measured by blade diameter, and though these may range from $5\frac{1}{2}$" to 12" or more, it's with the 9" and 10" models that most of the action lies.

Quality. Some saws are made for amateurs, others for professionals. There are good, inexpensive models for the average person who doesn't use a saw in business or every day. They can provide reliable accuracy for paneling a room or putting on an addition.

Then there are heavy-duty saws made for continuous, demanding operation. They're nice to have, but they may cost twice as much. So it's important to know your needs.

The table. It may be of cast iron, stamped steel, or aluminum. Toolkraft makes one of iron-impregnated composition which they call Ferrolon. It's lightweight and won't rust. Rockwell makes stamped steel tables for average users, machined iron tables for pros.

Rigidity can be built into a lightweight table by proper design. Like a massive table, it may not warp. But a massive table has another advantage—weight. Rockwell's 10-inch Homecraft with a built-in motor ships at 110 pounds. Their 10-inch contractor saw, without a motor, ships at 220 pounds. That extra weight means stability. You don't have to think about bolting the tool down. It also means less vibration.

Table size is important. A larger table can mean greater convenience, greater safety, and greater capacity for work. Not all saws of a given size have the same size table. Sprunger's 8" saw has a table 14" x 18", but a Sear's 8" saw has a table only $10\frac{1}{2}$" x 13". Toolkraft's standard 10" saw has a table 17" x 20", but their top-of-the-line 10" saw has a 20" x 27" table which with extensions becomes 40" x 27". Most saws come equipped with extension wings that increase table size, or they are offered as accessories.

Tilt. The saw blade can be raised or lowered to handle varying thickness of material. It can be tilted for bevel cuts. In earlier days, instead of the blade tilting, the table was tilted. Except for European imports, these have disappeared from the scene.

For cabinetwork and joinery, the tilting table is fine. But it is not for carpentry. It becomes awkward when big boards or panels must be handled.

Cut-off capacity. On spec sheets this is indicated by the distance in front of the blade at 1" depth of cut. The greater the distance in front of the blade, the greater the cut-off capacity and work support. Less space in front of the blade is a limiting factor and can even be a safety factor.

Sears makes an 8" saw with only 5" in front of the blade. Sprunger makes an 8" saw with $10\frac{1}{8}$" in front, and another 8" with $12\frac{1}{8}$". A Toolkraft 10" saw has $16\frac{1}{2}$".

Rip capacity. It's nice to be able to cut to the middle of a 4' panel. Some 9" saws will. Others may be able to rip 15" or less. A Craftsman 9" rips up to $14\frac{1}{2}$" wide on the left side, $13\frac{1}{2}$" on the right.

Depth of cut. Almost everyone wants enough capacity to cut through a 2 x 4 at a 45° angle. With the 2 x 4 lying flat, that's $1\frac{5}{8}$". Some 9" saws barely make it. Others will cut 2" on a bevel, and that's a comfortable margin. At 90° these saws cut to a depth of 2" and $2\frac{3}{4}$" respectively. The depth of cut at 90° on typical 10" saws ranges from $3\frac{1}{8}$" to $3\frac{5}{8}$". A typical 12" saw will cut $4\frac{1}{8}$".

Rockwell manufactures a combination saw and jointer, both powered by one motor. The 9" saw features 24" rip capacity, $2\frac{3}{4}$" cross-cut capacity. The 4" jointer features a double-tilt fence with positive stops at 45° and 90°.

Sears 9" table saw is relatively inexpensive. Table of cast aluminum measures 17"×20". Rips up to $14\frac{1}{2}$"-wide workpieces on left, up to $13\frac{1}{2}$" on right. Extensions included measure 10"×20" each.

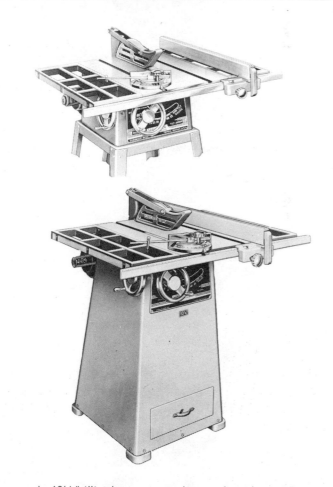

Sprunger's $10\frac{1}{4}$" tilt-arbor saw can be purchased as a floor or bench model. It meets the rigid requirements of professional crafts-people but has a price that makes it attractive for home workshops. Well-ribbed gray iron table (including two extensions) measures 35" x 24". A 1 or $1\frac{1}{2}$ hp motor is recommended.

The Powermatic 66 is made of cast iron, ribbed and cross-ribbed for absolute stability. With extension sections and 72" rails, it will cut 49" to the right of saw blade. Designed for use with motors from $1\frac{1}{2}$ to 3 hp. Controls work smoothly and are vernier-accurate. With motor, it weighs about 500 lbs.

Build your own floor saw with a kit. Gil-Bilt (Gillion Mfg. Inc.) provides all necessary parts and materials to build this 10" tilt-arbor saw, except for blade, motor, and wood parts. Table size is 27"×29", with $13\frac{1}{2}$" in front of blade. Table and cabinet are of wood.

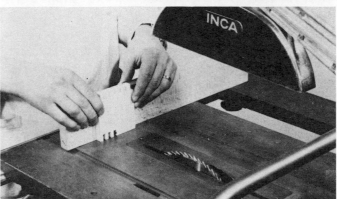

Inca saws have accessories for special operations. Shown are a molding setup (top) and setup for corner lock joints. An abrasive disc or drum sander can be used with the table. There is also a mortise table (not shown).

SAGER'S ICE CUTTING MACHINE.

The Toolkraft 9" saw has a table made of "Ferrolon," a material that is lighter in weight and less expensive than iron. Saw comes completely assembled, ready to plug in and operate. Table is 17"×20", with 9³/₄" ahead of blade. With accessory extension it will rip to center of a 48" panel. Weighs only 49 lbs.

Two quality Swiss-made saws offer unusual features. The 7" "Modelmaker's" (top) and 10" "Cabinetmaker's" saws have tilt tables, 16¹/₂"×22¹/₂" and 20⁵/₈"×33³/₄" respectively. Both have a special device for cutting tenons and grooves and an effective protecting device for safe, accurate grooving and shaping with molding cutters. They also offer an optional mortise drill. Available from Garrett Wade and Anson Industries.

Using a wobble washer, up to ¹/₂" dado cuts can be made with Inca's 10" saw blade, or up to ⁷/₁₆" cuts on the 7" blade. For professional use, 4⁷/₈" (122 mm) dado blades are available in 3, 4, 5, 6, 8 and 10 mm widths.

Width of cut can be varied from ¹/₄" to ¹³/₁₆" on Rockwell's wobbler-type dado head without removing it from the saw. Two cams in the center of the blade are rotated in dial fashion to determine the wobble of the blade, which regulates the width of cut. Maximum depth of cut is ³/₄". Teeth are carbide-tipped.

"Powr-Kraft" blade set consists of two outside blades each ¹/₈" thick, four ¹/₈"-thick chippers, and one ¹/₁₆"-thick chipper. Available in 6" or 8" diameters. Wards.

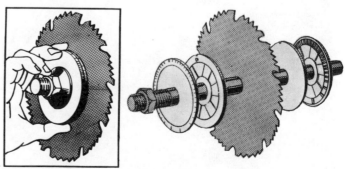

Dado saw washers mount on the shaft with your present blade. There are 40 calibrations; they adjust to cut any desired width. Models for ¹/₂", ⁵/₈", and ³/₄" shafts. Brookstone.

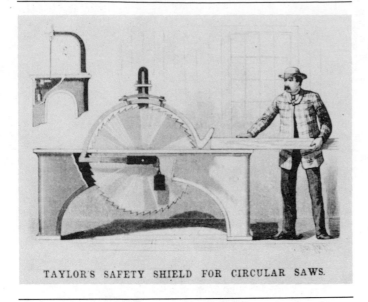

TAYLOR'S SAFETY SHIELD FOR CIRCULAR SAWS.

With a cutter head and any of these knives, you can do a wide variety of trimming, joining, and molding operations. Wards.

The Shopsmith miter gauge makes sawing safer. Any saw with table slots to accommodate a ³/₈″×³/₄″ bar can benefit from added accuracy, convenience, and capabilities with this superior miter gauge. Pistol-grip handle clamps keep hands away from blade.

SAFETY RULES

All power tools are dangerous, but the table saw is particularly so. One reason is that when the blade is spinning its edge is invisible. A cardinal rule is never to reach across it. When work is less than 3 inches wide, feed it with a push stick.

Before using the table saw, understand it and all its requirements. Always be alert, always respectful of its power.

Besides the standard safety rules for all tools, detailed in the chapter on safety, here are additional ones for circular saws, suggested by Rockwell.

1. *Always* use guard, splitter, and antikickback fingers on all "thru-sawing" operations. Thru-sawing is when the blade cuts completely through the work piece.

2. *Always* hold the work firmly against the miter gauge or fence.

3. *Always* use a push stick for ripping narrow stock.

4. *Never* perform any operation free-hand. Always use either the fence or the miter gauge to position and guide the work.

5. *Never* stand or have any part of your body in line with the path of the saw blade.

6. *Never* reach behind or over the cutting tool with either hand for any reason.

7. *Always* move the rip fence out of the way when crosscutting.

8. *Never* run stock between the fence and the molding cutterhead when cutting moldings.

9. *Always* feed work into a blade or cutter against the direction or rotation of the blade or cutter.

10. *Never* use the fence as a cut-off gauge when crosscutting.

11. *Never* attempt to free a stalled saw blade without first turning off the saw.

12. *Always* provide support to the rear and sides of the saw table for wide or long workpieces.

13. *Never* use a dull blade.

14. *Never* rip work that does not have a straight edge to guide along the fence, or release work before it is pushed all the way past the saw blade.

15. *Always* avoid awkward operations and hand positions where a sudden slip could cause your hand to move into the cutting tool.

An early blade-sharpening device

WHAT TO LOOK FOR

Whatever the size, you want sturdy, precision construction. Most of it is visually apparent. Try the action on lowering and tilting the blade. Are the handwheel controls large and easy to grasp?

Test the ease and firmness with which the rip fence locks. Does it square and lock both front and rear from a single handle up front? Is the scale on the fence bar easy to read? Is the fence removable at any point on the saw?

How easy is it to change blades? A large insert plate makes blade changing easier. Is the saw switch lockable?

Don't be confused about horsepower. Manufacturers have two ways of indicating it. One way is to give you a high figure, which is the horsepower a motor develops on its initial surge. A lower figure is the rated horsepower. A motor which develops $1\frac{1}{2}$ hp may be rated at only $\frac{3}{4}$ hp.

What does the price include? On some saws, stand, table extensions, motor, long bar, even the saw guard may be extras.

To sharpen blades like an expert, set this jig to the desired pitch and angle—and file. Handles almost any blade. Clamps to bench or table top. Brookstone.

MANUFACTURERS

Table saw manufacturers include Rockwell, Toolkraft, Sprunger, American Machine & Tool, and Shopmaster.

Shopmaster, Amco, Toolkraft, and Rockwell saws are available from U.S. General Supply. Rockwell saws are also available from J.C. Penney and Silvo Hardware.

Inca is a leading import from Switzerland, distributed by Garrett Wade on the East Coast and Anson Industries on the West Coast. Sears Craftsman saws are made by Emerson Electric Co.

Gilt-Bilt saws are made from build-it-yourself kits manufactured and sold by Gilliom Mfg. Inc.

For saw blade maintenance—the jointer makes all teeth the same distance from the blade center for smoother cutting. Setter provides proper tooth angle to prevent binding in cuts. Brookstone.

21.
RADIAL SAWS

The first radial-arm saw was built in 1922 by Raymond E. DeWalt. Early models were known as the "Wonder Worker." It was an apt description, and still applies.

A radial saw is like an oversize portable saw that moves on an overhead track. The track can be raised or lowered, or swung to various angles. The saw itself can be rotated and tilted. It is thus adaptable to a wide variety of cutting jobs and is capable of performing a whole bagful of tricks.

Unlike the table saw, which requires clearance on all sides, the radial saw can be located against a wall—for example, in a garage. Its table can be extended on either side to provide long benches that support the work. It's also fairly easy to move to a project location.

If you could have just one power tool in your shop, a wise choice might be the radial saw. It does the work of many single-purpose machines. It thus can save you floor space and money.

A radial saw is quickly set up for dadoing, rabbeting, mortising, routing, tongue-and-grooving, scalloping, fluting, and raising and sinking panels. With attachments, it can become a horizontal drill, a plane, a metal cutter, buffer, polisher, surfacer, jig (or saber) saw, a disc and drum sander, a jointer, and a shaper.

For shaping, you can get knives for making such cuts as bead and cove, nosing, quarter round, screen mold, window sash, glue, dropleaf table joint, and others.

For mitering, you just swing the saw arm over to the desired angle. You may not even have to do that. For its 10" contractor's radial saw, DeWalt has a "Magic-Miter Table Top." With it you can make crosscuts, and right and left miter cuts without moving the saw arm.

In ripping, a radial saw's action is comparable to that of a table saw. You push the work into the rotating blade. But in crosscutting, or dadoing, the work is kept stationary and you pull the blade through it. This is a decided advantage. The saw blade rotates down and away from you, so the work is held to the table and the rear fence. It's highly unlikely ever to get thrown back at you.

You're cutting from the topside, so you always know where the blade is. It's not hidden beneath stock. The blade is well-shielded, and you can complete cuts without your hands coming anywhere near it.

Sawdust is directed away by a directional spout. It doesn't fly up in your face. As an accessory, you can get a sawdust collector. It may chute the sawdust to a box or bag, or you can attach a vacuum hose.

On many models, a brake automatically stops the blade almost the instant you switch off the motor. On others, you can do it manually. Even for these, an electronic brake can be bought as an accessory. Coasting blades are a prime hazard.

Black & Decker's DeWalt 740 (top) includes 10" blade, steel stand and instruction manual. The "Deluxe" DeWalt 770 (middle) has an automatic brake stop in addition. By mail order from J.C. Penney.

The classic 8" DeWalt (bottom) is easy to transport because it weighs only 58 lbs. without stand. Flakeboard table is 22" x 32". Blade stops instantly when saw is turned off. From Wards.

CAPABILITIES OF THE RADIAL-ARM SAW

The radial saw performs six basic cuts with accuracy: crosscut, rip, miter, bevel crosscut, bevel rip, and compound. With accessories, you can dado, shape, plane, drill, rout, and more.

Crosscut

Bevel crosscut

Rip

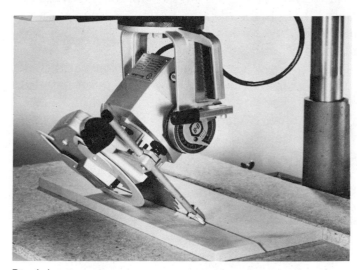

Bevel rip

Miter

Compound

Dado

Route

Rotary plane

Surface cut

Shape

Sand

Wards Powr-Kraft cuts deeper than most other 10″ saws. It cuts through 3⁵⁄₈″ stock and rips up to 25¹⁄₂″. Key-locking pistol-grip switch for one-hand work. Safety clutch helps guard against kickbacks and motor burnout. Dust collector, extra, can be used with any vacuum. Shipped semi-assembled.

Sears best 10″ radial saw is model 2310. It has a more powerful motor and sturdier construction than their less expensive models. Automatic blade brake. Maximum depth of cut is 3″ at 90°.

CHECK THESE POINTS

Weight: This is often an indication of ruggedness of construction and durability. Three typical 10″ saws with stand weigh 157, 232, and 305 pounds.

Accessories: Which come with the saw, and which are available in case you want them?

Controls: Are they rear or front mounted? Front is preferable, both for convenience and safety.

Motor: Does it have a brake, and is the brake automatic or manual? Does it have a safety clutch? This means if the blade jams, the motor can keep turning. It can prevent motor damage. Does the motor have a double-end shaft for mounting of accessories?

Stand: Is it included? Does it have shelves, drawers, leg levelers, casters?

Warranty: Most offer a one-year warranty covering faulty material and workmanship. DeWalt sets no time limit on its warranty.

WHAT TO LOOK FOR

DeWalt, Rockwell, Ward's Powr-Kraft, and Sears Craftsman are the makes generally available. Compare all four before you buy, noting such items as rated horsepower and motor amperage. You'll find these on the plate attached to the motor.

Saw size is determined by the size of blade used. The 10″ size is the favorite for the home shop, but there is an 8″ available. There are 12″, 16″, and 18″ saws for commercial use, and some of these may require 3-phase electrical power or 230 volts.

Not all 10″ saws have equal capability. The depth of cut on a Powr-Kraft is 3⁵⁄₈″, on the Sears Craftsman only 3″. The most expensive 10″ saw may cost $200 more than the cheapest. What are you getting for the extra investment?

The Rockwell 10″ saw features a double overarm that allows the blade to rotate 360° over table for a full-table capacity on right and left miters. Controls are in front. Mechanical blade brake and dual-shaft motor. Available with or without stand.

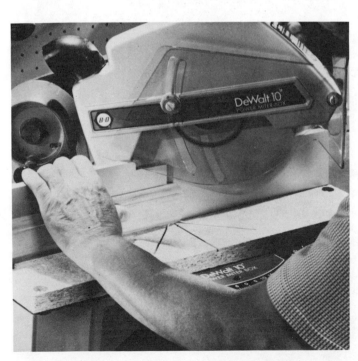

DeWalt 10″ power miter box is tops at trim work. Cuts wood, plastics, compositions, lightweight aluminum. Automatic blade brake. Table size: 4″ x 21¼″.

Rockwell offers a 9″ power miter box. It is an excellent tool for trim work and fast, accurate square cuts or miters in various materials. Push-button blade brake. Table size: 4″ x 17″.

22.

BAND SAWS

"Back to the drawing board!" was the cry when the circular band saw was invented at the beginning of the 19th century. The pesky things just wouldn't work. The blades kept breaking. They didn't have enough tensile strength or elasticity, and the know-how to make better blades didn't exist.

Of course there were reciprocating band saws at the time. They had straight blades and worked fine. So people continued to use them, though they knew that having a circular band saw would increase sawing speed many times. Then, about 1885, finer grades of steel with greater tensile strength came along, and the circular band saw was, at long last, a success. Soon there were circular band saws run by water power, steam, foot treadle, and handcrank. It had become *the* band saw.

Basically, a band saw is a continuous blade that runs on two rubber-tired wheels. The blade has teeth on one edge, and it cuts with a never-ending downward motion. It's not as smooth a cut as that obtained with a circular saw, but the thinness of its blade means much less kerf waste. That's important to sawmills. It also means it can cut curves as well as straight.

The size of a band saw is determined by its "throat depth," the distance from the blade to the back support. Most band saws have a depth of 10", 12", and 14".

Blades usually range in width from $3/8$" to $3/4$". The narrower the blade is, the tighter the curve it can cut. When you're not cutting a curve, however, it's best to use the widest blade the saw will accommodate. Wide blades are less subject to breakage. Some blades are plastic coated. They slide easier and the plastic is a protection against rust.

A typical band saw may cut stock 6 inches thick. Cut a cylinder out of a 6 x 6 block and you can use it as a blank to turn on a lathe. Cut the 6 x 6 into a pattern, and you can then slice it into many separate pieces, each with the identical pattern. Or you can make a 6" pad of twenty-four pieces of $1/4$" plywood and duplicate a pattern twenty-four times with a single cut.

The band saw's ability to make many duplicate pieces is why it is so popular for turning out boat ribs, furniture parts, toys, and other items anyone might want to mass-produce.

Sawing stock from two or more sides is called compound cutting. The band saw excells at it. An

BRAZING BAND SAWS.

A correspondent of the *English Mechanic*, gives the following directions for brazing band saws: 1. Make a splice with a file on flat way of saw, the length of two teeth. 2. Get a

piece of flat iron, and bend it into the same shape as in the diagram, and with some small binding wire bind the saw perfectly straight and firm to the flat iron, so that the splice may come directly over the curve. 3. Wet the splice with clean water and rub on some powdered borax. 4. Make a stiff paste with spelter and borax mixed with water. Take a piece the size of a small nut and lay on top of splice. Put the splice between two pieces of charcoal and with a blow-pipe direct a steady flame from a gas-jet on the paste.

At first, broken blades were a common problem.

Frame-to-blade capacity on this Rockwell 10" model 28-120 is $9^{5}/_{8}$". Thickness of cut is $6^{1}/_{4}$"; blade length $71^{3}/_{4}$". Table size: 10" x 11". Option of $1/3$ or $1/2$ hp motor. Shipping weight 100 pounds.

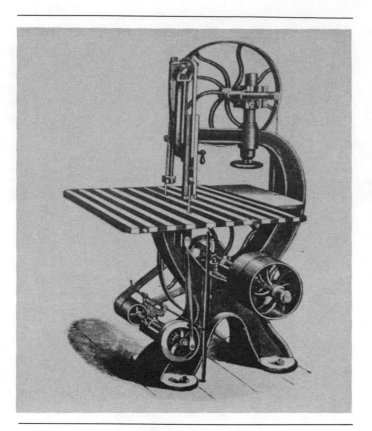

example of compound cutting is a curved, tapering cabriole furniture leg.

A band saw can be used for making straight cuts, but these cuts aren't as smooth as those made on a table or radial saw. They have a washboard texture. Cutting thick boards into thinner ones is known as resawing, and it's a popular application of the band saw. The washboard texture of resawn lumber can provide a highly desirable character.

Some band saws are designed for cutting wood, others metal, and a few will cut both. A typical metal band saw can slice as thin as $1/_{64}$th inch, accurate to .002 inch, and will cut all shapes—round, flat, square, and odd.

For cutting steel, a band saw is best run at 75 to 100 feet per minute, for nonferrous metal at 250 to 350 fpm, and for wood at 2000 to 3000 fpm. If your band saw doesn't have variable speed, you can get special drives that will provide it.

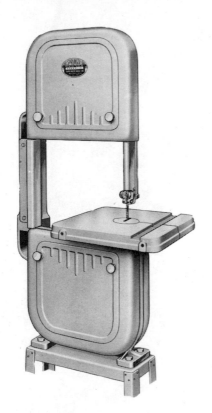

Sprunger 10" band saw has a 10" x 10" smooth-ground table that is supported at two points to keep it rigid when level or tilted. Throat capacity of saw is 10$^1/_8$" and it will rip or resaw thick stock to 6". Table is drilled for fence, grooved for miter gauge.

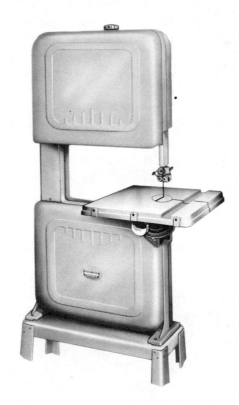

Sprunger 14" model will cut to center of a 28" circle. Table is 14" x 14", throat capacity 14", blade length 94". It will cut to depth of 6$^1/_2$". Rugged one-piece cast frame is ribbed to withstand rigors of home workshop or production use.

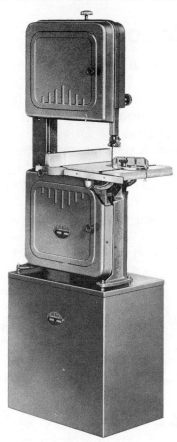

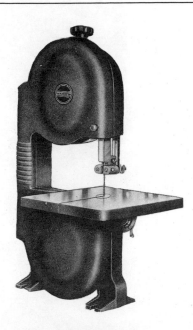

Toolkraft 9$^1/_2$" saw (model 500B) cuts to center of a 19" circle. The 11" x 10" table tilts 45°. Handles stock up to 4$^1/_2$" thick. Blade is 60" long, $^1/_8$" to $^1/_2$" wide. Rigid one-piece cast frame. All working parts except cutting edge are fully enclosed.

Sprunger 14" metal-cutting saw has a gear box and step pulleys enclosed in its stand so that it can be operated at eight speeds. Range is 46 sfm to 836 sfm (surface feet per minute).

Popular makes of 10", 12", and 14" band saws can readily be converted to metal cutting with the Sprunger BDM band saw drive base. Belts and pulleys are included for Sprunger 14" saw, but dealer can substitute others if needed.

Blade-changing is easy on the Shopsmith 11" band saw. It is designed for use with the multi-purpose Shopsmith, can be converted to individual stand operation with special accessories that are available directly from manufacturer. Tool has 11$^3/_4$" × 12" tilting table, handles up to 6" stock. It takes blades from $^1/_8$" to $^1/_2$". Blade tracking is automatic.

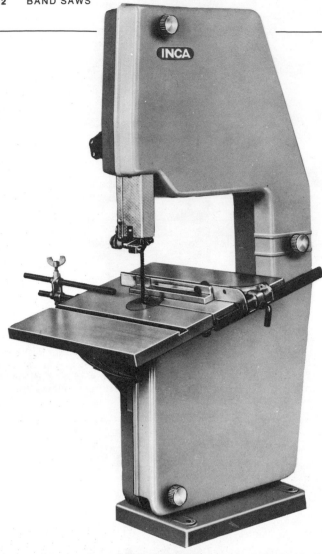

A home shop band saw with professional features. Swiss-made Inca 10" model 310 has a movable brush to remove sawdust from lower band wheel. Table is dovetail-slotted for optional miter guide. Band wheels are precision balanced. Maximum cutting space under guides is 6¼".

WHAT TO LOOK FOR

Shop comparatively. Take the cover off and see what's inside. Look at the castings, fittings, bandwheels. You'll find differences in quality, generally in proportion to the price you pay.

What is included? Does the price include a motor? Stand? Rip fence and miter guard? The latter two are usually optional, but the saw must be equipped to accept them. Is it? Does its table have a slot for a miter guide? If it has a slot, is it dovetailed so the guide won't tip when extended?

A rip fence helps cutting accuracy. Is the table drilled to accept one? Most band saw tables tilt 45° to the right. If it also tilts 10° to the left, that's a plus. Blade tension is usually adjusted by moving the upper bandwheel up or down. Having a blade tension indicator is a good feature. You can then easily get the best tension for each blade width.

MANUFACTURERS

Band saw makers include Rockwell, Toolkraft, Sprunger, and Shopmaster. Sears has Craftsman and Wards has Powr-Kraft. Inca is a Swiss import available from Garrett Wade and Anson Industries.

Silvo, U.S. General Supply, Wards, Sears, and J.C. Penney are mail-order sources. Penney pays shipping costs to their store nearest you.

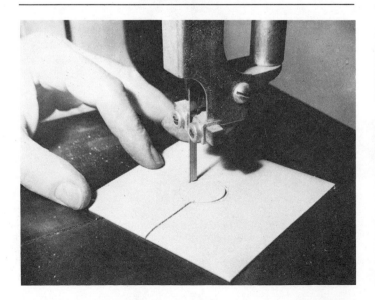

HOW TO AVOID A TRANSFUSION

Pushing a band saw's upper guide high may improve visibility, but it also means exposing more of the blade. This is cause for concern. If the blade is dull, and you're exerting pressure on the stock, what happens when you hit a soft spot in the wood and it moves forward into the blade unexpectedly and rapidly?

Play it safe, and keep the guide bar no more than about ⅛" above the material being cut.

Here's another safety tip. Stop the machine before removing scrap pieces from the table.

FOUR POWERMATIC MODELS

14″ wood-cutting model 141 has a 15″ x 15″ cast-iron table. Measures 14″ from blade to column. Offers 6½″ cutting depth with blade speed of 3000 sfm. Weight with stand and motor is 355 lbs.

If you're a pro, you may pick this one. Model 81 is a 20″ wood-cutting saw with a 12″ maximum depth of cut. Fully enclosed motor and drive assures longer motor life. Ball-bearing guides top and bottom increase blade life, adjust to fit any type of blade. Weight, crated with motor: 895 lbs.

Model 143 is rugged; it will cut even stainless steel with accuracy. It's the ultimate for production needs, but is also bought by many hobbyists. Just one of its good features: eye-level blade-tension scale shows correct tension for different blade widths.

Powermatic model 87 cuts all types of ferrous and non-ferrous metals. You can dial any speed from 47 sfm to 5200 sfm. Depth of cut: 12″. Table size: 24″ × 24″—and it's 3″ thick!

Craftsman 12″ model is a band saw and sander. Cuts wood up to 6″ thick, 12″ wide. Sanding belt provides smooth finish even in tight crevices. Built-in light.

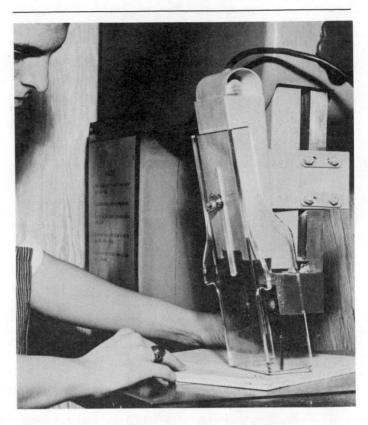

Plexiglas safety shield with a built-in 60 watt bulb makes any band saw safer and better illuminated. Easy to install. Brett-Hauer.

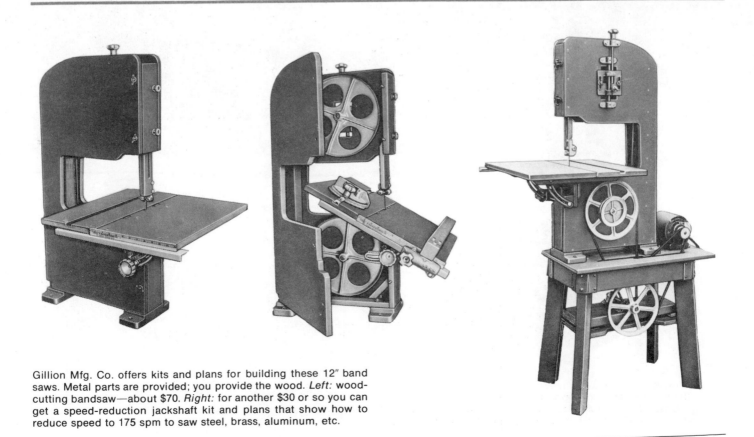

Gillion Mfg. Co. offers kits and plans for building these 12″ band saws. Metal parts are provided; you provide the wood. *Left:* wood-cutting bandsaw—about $70. *Right:* for another $30 or so you can get a speed-reduction jackshaft kit and plans that show how to reduce speed to 175 spm to saw steel, brass, aluminum, etc.

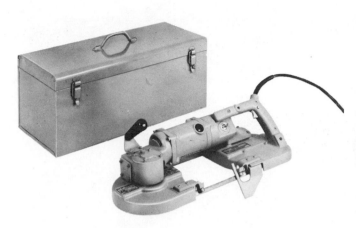

Millers Falls portable band saw weighs only 24 lbs. It has a high speed of 275 sfm and a low of 235. With Tuf-Flex blade it will cut mild steels, tubing, angle, etc. With Jet-Band blade it will cut stainless steel and other tough alloys.

A 17 lb. portable band saw that cuts almost anything. Use it to cut large cable, pipe, or round stock up to about 3½″ in diameter. Two speeds: 200 and 250 sfm. Milwaukee.

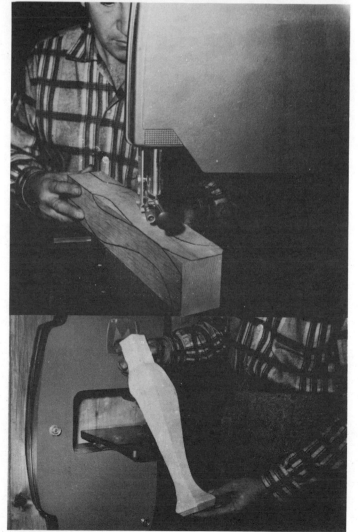

Metal-cutting band saw incorporates a grinding machine. Four-speed Sprunger saw has speeds ranging from 65 to 280 sfm; saw capacity is 4½″ x 6″. Swing the table to a vertical position and you have a vertical bandsaw. The grinding wheel can also be used in this position.

A band saw can make the compound cuts required in roughing-out a cabriole leg for a Queen Anne chair.

23.

JIGSAWS

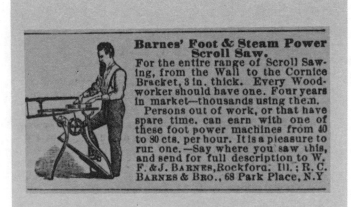

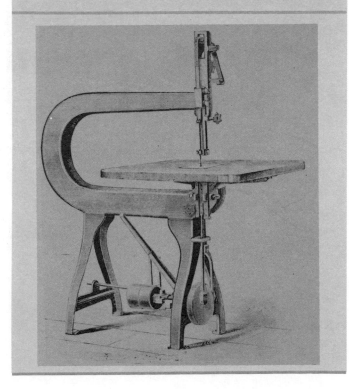

What was the first home workshop stationary power tool? It was the jigsaw. A Milwaukee mechanic named Herbert E. Tautz motorized a jigsaw in 1925, and started the whole "light power tools" industry. That industry today accounts for $200 million a year in sales.

Once, the stationary electric jigsaw was the tool every craftsperson wanted above all others. Today, it holds only a minor place among power tools. The band saw and the portable electric jigsaw, especially when used in combination with an accessory table, have taken over most of its operations. But they're not quite the same. It still does work these two tools can't match.

The jigsaw (or scroll saw) has very special characteristics. It does what the band saw and portable jigsaw do, but on a much smaller, finer scale. It is without question the best tool for cutting elaborate curves in thin material. It cuts wood, paper, leather, cloth, plastics, and thin-gauge metals. It is also the safest tool. Even a child can be turned loose on it.

Where the band saw goes round and round, the stationary jigsaw's movement is up and down. Unlike the portable jigsaw or saber saw, its blade is fastened at both ends. A slim blade, often called a "jeweler's blade," fits in a lower and upper chuck. A spring or cam provides tension. The blade is moved by a mechanism like a car's crankshaft.

You can make interior cuts by drilling holes in each area where stock is to be removed, then slipping the work over the blade. All kinds of fancy fretwork can be made by this piercing technique. It is the perfect tool for jigsaw puzzles, cut-out letters in signs, and inlaying. With an abrasive sleeve, it can be used to smooth concave and convex surfaces. With a file, it can shape and smooth metal.

The House scroll saw—"light enough for a lady to lift around."

MANUFACTURERS

Dremel, Powermatic, and Sprunger all make jigsaws. Sears and Wards offer private label jigsaws by mail order. Dremel jigsaws are available by mail order from Silvo Hardware.

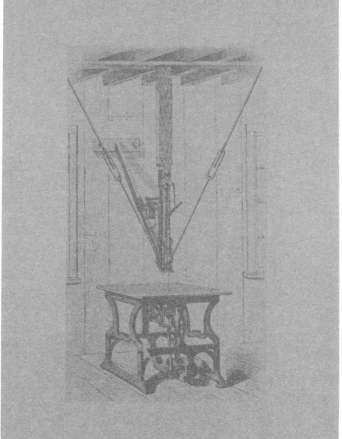

Scroll saw, 1870. Elaborate devices were designed to assure uniform tension at all points of the stroke.

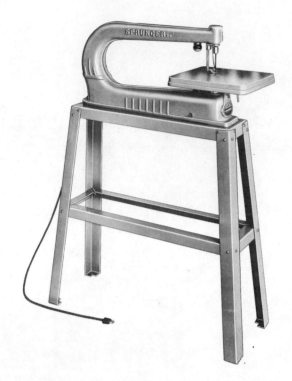

Sprunger 20" jigsaw cuts 2"-thick wood. It has a 12" x 12" table that tilts to right and left. Blade length is 5" and speed is 2575 sfm (surface feet per minute). Weighs about 60 lbs.

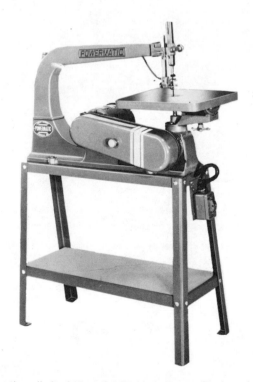

Powermatic calls its 24" model 95 a scroll saw. Choice of variable-speed or 4-speed; constructed of cast-iron and steel, with 1³/₄" thickness of cut. Weight, crated, with stand and motor is 220 lbs., so you know it's hefty. Uses either jig or saber blades.

FOUR MODELS

Jigsaw size is measured by clearance from blade to back support. Four sizes, five models, are commonly available. Dremel makes a 12", a 15", and a 15" deluxe, which is the same as the regular 15" but with more accessories. Sprunger makes a 20", Powermatic a 24".

The Dremel 15" is run by a built-in 3450 rpm motor. The manufacturer describes it as a "card-table-size" workshop. It sets up on any surface 8" x 18" or larger, stores in 2 square feet of space.

The Dremel saw's lockable 8" x 9¹/₂" table tilts 45° right or left for angle and bevel cutting. It is marked with a ¹/₂-inch grid. A "3-way" blade holder permits facing the saw teeth in any direction. Cam action keeps the blade taut. It can be changed without tools. An ingenious blade guard also serves as a hold-down. When the blade gets dull at one spot, the table can be adjusted to an unused section of teeth.

Dremel has added something new to the original jigsaw design. It is a power takeoff. With an arbor adapter, this takeoff can be used for sanding and buffing. With a 30" flexible shaft, it can be used for drilling, grinding, routing, wire-brushing, and carving, and a wide variety of accessories is offered for these uses. Dremel calls the whole setup a "Moto-Shop."

Sprunger's 20" jigsaw is larger and heavier than the Dremel designs. Dremel's 12" weighs 9 pounds, the 15" about 15 pounds. The Sprunger motorized 20" weighs about 64 pounds.

The Sprunger jigsaw has a 12" x 12" table that tilts 45° to the right, 30° to the left, with the tilt angle indicated on a protractor scale. Like other jigsaws, it has an automotive-type drive mechanism. Bearings at both ends of the drive shaft help provide smooth, vibrationless operation.

A coil spring holds the blade. A spring-steel pressure foot holds work against the table. During sawing, a steady stream of air close to the work keeps layout lines clear, and saw speed is 2575 sawing feet a minute.

The saw comes in a motorized model, or with a 2" pulley for belt drive. A ¹/₃ hp 1750 rpm motor and a 2¹/₂" motor pulley are recommended. A stand and light are available as accessories.

Dremel model 550 Moto-Saw is lightweight, portable—and inexpensive. It weighs in at 9 pounds. At 3450 rpm it cuts wood up to $1\frac{1}{2}''$, thin-gauge metals and plastics. 12″ throat.

Whether you call it jigsaw, scroll saw, fret saw, or "Moto-Saw," it's the safest power tool.

Moto-Shop by Dremel; model 572. This "rocker-action" jigsaw has a power takeoff, and includes flexible shaft and 12-piece accessory set for drilling, routing, grinding and buffing. Cuts wood $1\frac{3}{4}''$ thick. 15″ throat. Weighs 17 pounds.

24. JOINTERS

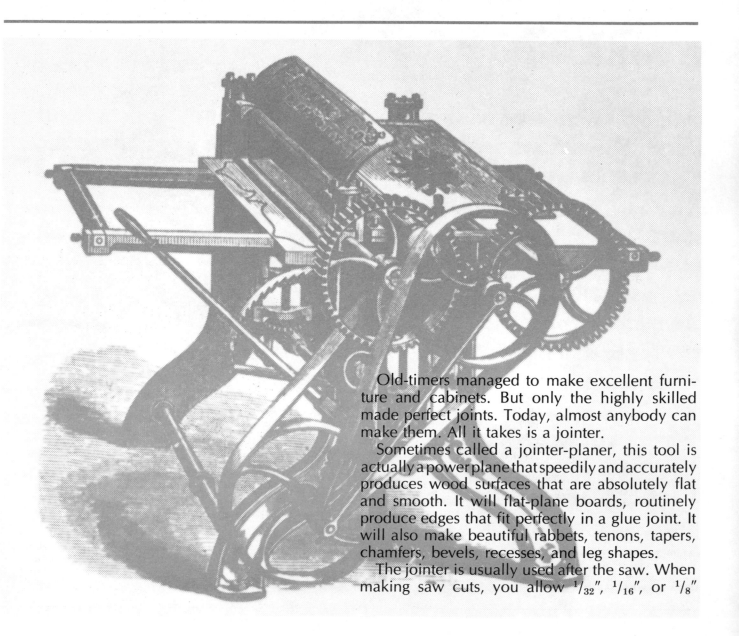

Old-timers managed to make excellent furniture and cabinets. But only the highly skilled made perfect joints. Today, almost anybody can make them. All it takes is a jointer.

Sometimes called a jointer-planer, this tool is actually a power plane that speedily and accurately produces wood surfaces that are absolutely flat and smooth. It will flat-plane boards, routinely produce edges that fit perfectly in a glue joint. It will also make beautiful rabbets, tenons, tapers, chamfers, bevels, recesses, and leg shapes.

The jointer is usually used after the saw. When making saw cuts, you allow $1/32''$, $1/16''$, or $1/8''$

extra to be cut off by the jointer. Saw and jointer are such a good team, they are often paired and run by the same motor.

The cutterhead on a jointer is located between a front and rear table, the rear one set fractionally higher. The amount of wood removed is equal to the difference in elevation of the two tables. The cutterhead, protected by a guard, usually has three knives. Wood is run along a fence past these revolving knives.

The width of the cutter knives determines the size of the jointer. Some currently available sizes are 4", $4^1/_8$", $4^1/_2$", 6", $6^1/_8$", and $8^5/_8$".

On some jointers, both the front (or infeed) and the back (or outfeed) tables are adjustable. In others, only the front table is adjustable. A typical fence tilts up to 45° both ways for bevel cuts.

The average hobbyist will buy a jointer in the 4"–$4^1/_2$" range. Study the specifications. Things that are important are:

Table size. The longer and wider the table is, the more support you have for your work. Toolkraft table length is $22^3/_4$ for their 4" jointer. Rockwell's is $27^1/_4$". So there are significant differences. But this is only one factor. You want to consider all factors in the overall picture, including price.

Fence height. Naturally, a 3" fence gives you more support than a 2" one.

Depth of cut. This is especially important in dadoing. The greater the depth of cut, the better.

Weight. This is a good indicator of a tool's stability and durability. Greater weight usually means less vibration.

What's included? Figure the total price, including motor, table, dust chute, and whatever else you may want or need.

Sprunger 4" jointer is made with the same quality workmanship as other Sprunger jointers. It is less expensive only because its cutting width (4") and rabbet-cutting depth ($^5/_{16}$") are limited. Overall table length is only $20^1/_4$".

Sprunger $4^1/_2$" jointer has a 31" working surface so that work is easier to handle. It uses the same $^1/_3$ hp motor as the 4" model. All Sprunger tools are test-run before leaving factory.

Table of Sprunger 6" jointer is 43" long. The tool weighs about 80 lbs. more than the $4^1/_2$" model, and it requires a bigger motor—$^1/_2$ hp. It runs faster, too; about 5000 rpm as compared to 4300 rpm for the $4^1/_2$" model.

Toolkraft offers 4¹/₈″ and 6¹/₈″ models. Both jointers have a built-in motor and are ready to plug in and operate. Table lengths are 22³/₄″ and 35³/₄″ and widths are 6¹/₂″ and 10″. On the bigger tool you can plane lumber up to 6″ wide.

Rockwell offers a variety of options. You can select either a 4″ or 6″-capacity jointer, with or without stand, and either a ¹/₂ hp standard or heavy-duty motor. Both tools feature adjustable front and rear tables and tilting fence with positive stops at 45° and 90°.

LOOK THEM OVER

Here are some facts about the most commonly available and desirable jointers:

Rockwell offers 4″ and 6″ jointers with both front and rear tables adjustable. Table size for the 4″ is 5¹/₄″ x 27¹/₄″, and the fence is 3¹/₄″ high. It has a maximum cut of ¹/₄″. The 6″ jointer has a table 6¹/₈″ x 35¹/₂″, and a fence 4¹/₄″ high. Its maximum cut is ³/₈″. Both size jointers have ground aluminum alloy tables.

Sprunger offers 4″, 4¹/₂″, and 6″ jointers. Their base, rear table, and front table are made of close-grain gray iron, accurately machined, then assembled and finished-ground to provide exact alignment. Table lengths of the three tools are 19″, 31″, and 43″ respectively. Fence heights are 2″, 2¹/₂″, and 3¹/₂″.

Depth of cut is ⁵/₁₆″ for the 4″ and 4¹/₂″ jointers and ¹/₂″ for the 6″ jointer.

The 6″ requires a ¹/₂ hp, 3450 rpm motor, which will turn the cutting head at 4500 to 5000 rpm. The other sizes require a ¹/₃ or ¹/₂ hp motor.

Toolkraft has a 4¹/₈″ jointer with a table 6¹/₂″ x 22³/₄″, and a 6¹/₈″ jointer with a table 7¹/₈″ x 39″. Fence heights are 2¹/₂″ and 4″ respectively. Depths of cut are ³/₈″ and ¹/₂″.

Both jointers have built-in motors. They are ready to plug in and operate. Tables are ground cast iron.

Amco (American Machine & Tool) makes an inexpensive 4¹/₈″ jointer. Its table is 4″ x 22″, and depth of cut ¹/₈″. Its fence is adjustable to any angle from 0° to 50°. It weighs 19 lbs. Sears has one like it.

Shopmaster's 4″ jointer has a 4″ x 25″ table, ³/₈″ depth of cut, and comes complete with a ¹/₂ hp capacitor ball bearing motor, pulley, and floor-stand (138 lbs.). Or you can get the jointer only (45 lbs.). They also have a 6″ model.

Inca, a Swiss import, is an 8⁵/₈″ jointer with a 8³/₄″ x 30″ table and a fence 3³/₄″ high. It has two cutters, and a ¹/₅″ depth of cut.

It has a thicknesser attachment available as an accessory. With it you can surface a board, perhaps one that is cupped, and then run it through for desired thickness.

Inca also has a 10¹/₄″ combined jointer-planer/automatic feed thicknesser which has two rates of automatic feeds, a fast speed for soft wood and a slow one for hard wood. It has cutters so tough they can handle very hard woods like rosewood and teak, or pecan which contains silica.

Wards sells jointers similar to Toolkraft's.

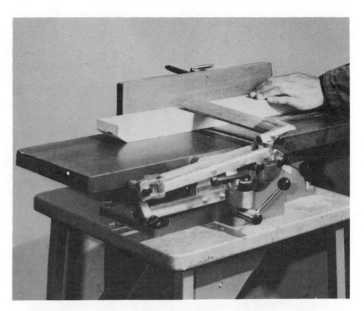

Inca Swiss-made jointer-planer can plane 8$\frac{1}{2}$"-wide boards in one pass. The head has only two cutters but it is 8$\frac{5}{8}$" wide. Table of die-cast aluminum is 30" long. Requires a 1 hp motor. As an option, you can get an attachment for thicknessing boards.

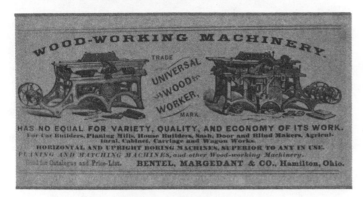

Powermatic 6" jointer, model 50, is a superior machine. Even the design, free of dust-catching corners and crevices, is planned to save clean-up time and make your work a joy. Table is 7" x 48". Motor is $\frac{3}{4}$ hp. Weight is 290 lbs.

Craftsman 6$\frac{1}{8}$" jointer-planer can plane boards up to 6" wide in one pass. It weighs only 178 lbs., complete with stand and motor. If you wish, you can buy it without stand, or without stand and motor.

Combined jointer-planer/automatic-feed thicknesser, made by Inca. Its two-cutter head, 10$\frac{1}{4}$" wide, turns at 6000 rpm, which means 12,000 cuts per minute. To switch from planing to thicknessing, you remove fixed rear jointing table, reducing table length from 31$\frac{1}{2}$" to 15$\frac{3}{4}$", then attach chip guard. Depth of cut is adjusted by hand wheel. Two rates of automatic feed—one for soft wood, one for hard.

Precision device for adjusting cutters can be used with most planers. Exact adjustment makes work more accurate and cutters last longer. Accurate to within 0.00039″. Device is 11¼″ long. Inca.

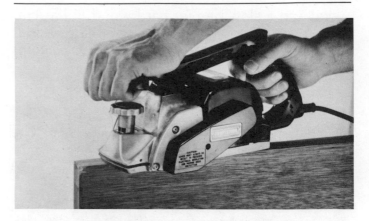

Craftsman power planer can plane the broad side of a 2 x 4 in one pass. It has razor-sharp blades that spin at 15,000 rpm. Dial can be set for thick or thin shavings.

Wood stand with motor platform for use with Inca jointer-planer.

Rockwell model 4690 is a power block plane that weighs only 6 lbs. Its cutting capacity is only 1¹³/₁₆″, but that's enough to smooth 2″ dressed stock. Motor speed is 21,000 rpm. Depth of cut ¹/₆₄″.

Powermatic 12″ model 100 is a small planer for the small professional shop. It has a 12″ x 24″ bed to provide the in-feed and out-feed support needed for accurate gap-free surfacing. Has many of the same features as larger planers.

The Rockwell 16″ Porta Plane is especially recommended for planing glue-bonded doors and panels. The 7 amp motor turns at 25,000 rpm. Width of cut is 2¹³/₁₆″, depth ³/₃₂″. It has a 60° bevel planing range, from −15″ to +45°.

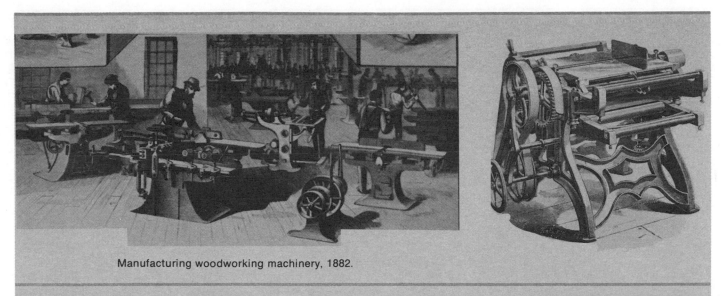

Manufacturing woodworking machinery, 1882.

In addition to the safety rules that apply to all power tools, Rockwell recommends these additional rules for a jointer:

1. Keep cutterhead sharp and free of all rust and pitch.

2. Always use a push block when jointing stock too small to allow a reasonable distance of safety for your hands.

3. Don't pass hands directly over cutterhead.

4. Always make sure exposed cutterhead behind the fence is guarded, especially when jointing near the edge.

5. Do not perform jointing operations on material shorter than 6", narrower than $3/4$", or less than $1/4$" thick.

6. Do not perform planing operations on material shorter than 6", narrower than $3/4$", thinner than $1/2$".

7. Maintain the proper relationship of the infeed and outfeed table surfaces with the cutterhead knife path.

8. Support the workpiece adequately at all times during the operation; maintain control of the work at all times.

9. Do not back the workpiece toward the infeed table.

10. Do not attempt to perform an unusual or little-used operation without study and the use of adequate hold-down/push blocks, jigs, fixture, stops, etc.

Staying Out Of Hot Water

25.

SHAPERS

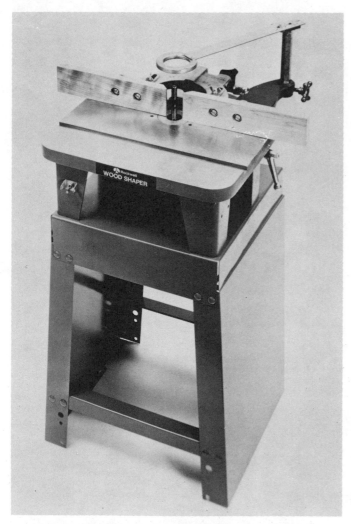

Rockwell $^1/_2$ hp wood shaper handles $^1/_2$" hole, standard 3-lip shaper cutters and cope cutters using $^1/_2$" stub spindle accessory. Table 15$^1/_2$" x 18". Speed 9000 rpm.

You don't have to have a shaper. If you have only occasional need for a shaper, shaping can be done with a drill press, table or radial-arm saw, or with a router mounted under a table. But if you are a dedicated homecrafter, or do shaping operations with some consistency, you need a tool designed for the purpose. The shaper is designed to do one specific job—shape—and it does it easier, faster, and more accurately than any other tool.

A shaper cuts all the classic molding forms, on curved or irregular surfaces. It can provide decorative finishing touches on cabinets, tables, chairs, and other furniture.

It does nondecorative jobs too, like cabinet door lips and tongue-and-groove joints. It can be used to raise panels, make dowels, and at reduced speed, to sand rough surfaces. It also performs routing tasks.

The heart of the shaper is a spindle, usually $^1/_2$" in diameter, with 3-lip shaper cutters or 3-knife cutterhead. It extends up through a hole in a table and can be raised or lowered, typically $^7/_8$", and locked in place at any point.

A split fence may be used to guide work through. The front, or in-feed fence, controls depth of cut. The out-feed fence supports work after it has passed the cutters. To do freehand work you don't use the fence.

Freehand work is done against collars, mounted on the spindle, which control depth of cut. They provide bearing surface above and below the cutters for the part not to be shaped. A starting pin is used as a support when starting the cut. Without it, work would be kicked back. Collars are also used to fill up the part of the spindle not occupied by the cutters.

A shaper is better than a drill press with a shaper attachment because it has no column at the rear or obstructions above to interfere with work. Further, the spindle is specifically designed to take the pressure of work thrust against it. Most shapers operate at speeds from 9,000 rpm to 18,000 rpm.

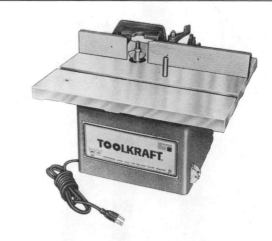

"Delivers sanded-smooth cuts on first pass." Toolkraft motorized shaper, model 255, has an 18" x 15 1/4" table and a spindle speed of 18,000 rpm. Manufacturer says that speed never drops below 14,000 even when cutting oak, maple, or birch.

THE SHAPE OF AN OBJECT CAN BE IMPORTANT

Shape is one of the most important elements of design. It can be decorative or functional—or both.

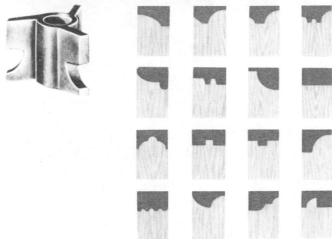

These Wards steel alloy cutters may be used in combination for almost unlimited patterns. Can also be used on any radial arm saw or drill press that has a 1/2" arbor adapter.

Wards super-fast motorized shaper has direct drive. There are no belts, pulleys or gears to slip or decrease power on this 18,000 rpm Powr-Kraft shaper. Hold-down spring holds work in place.

Cutterhead of Sears shaper revolves at 9000 rpm. Cast-iron table measures 19″ x 27″, has groove for miter gauge (not included). Each half fence is individually adjustable from left to right, front to rear. Motor and guard for contour shaping are included; light not included.

A shaper cuts all the classic molding forms and can provide a great variety of decorative finishing touches.

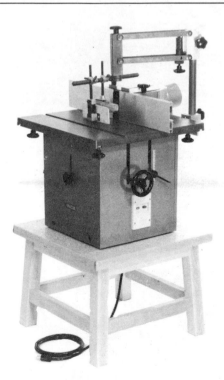

Inca shaper is available in floor (right) or bench models. Spindle turns at 4000, 6000, or 8000 rpm. Spring-loaded hold-down and pressure unit is standard safety feature. Table is 20$\frac{1}{2}$″ x 20$\frac{1}{2}$″ with optional extension rails 39″ x 20$\frac{1}{2}$″. Slot for miter guide.

Powermatic universal spindle shaper is a professional tool for high-quality work. It accommodates four interchangeable spindles and a 1″ solid spindle for extra heavy duty work. Spindle adjusts 3″ vertically. Cast-iron table, 28″ x 29½″, and cast-iron fence faced with hardwood blocks. 7000 to 10,000 rpm.

WHAT TO LOOK FOR

The best shaper for you depends on how much you are going to use it, and how much your budget allows. If you are going to give it considerable use, you want a sturdy machine.

You can buy the shaper alone, or with stand and motor. Typically, the motor will be ½ hp. The power switch should be easily accessible, and preferably lockable. The quality of bearing construction is important.

Faster speed, under load, usually means faster, smoother cutting. Slower speeds mean it will take two or three passes to complete some cuts instead of one. Remember that a speed given as 18,000 rpm may become 14,000 rpm under load, especially when cutting oak, maple, or birch.

Look for a fence with both halves independently adjustable. Also, do you have to buy a ring guard as an accessory, or is it included? A ring guard is for use when doing curved and circular edge-shaping operations. You'll also want spring hold-downs. They hold work firmly against fence and table.

Stay out of trouble. Understand the machine before you try to operate it.

MANUFACTURERS

Rockwell and Toolkraft are leading manufacturers. Wards has a private-label shaper closely resembling the Toolkraft model. Sears also offers a private-label shaper. Amco sells a low-cost shaper kit. Powermatic makes professional shapers, as does Inca.

26.
STATIONARY SANDERS

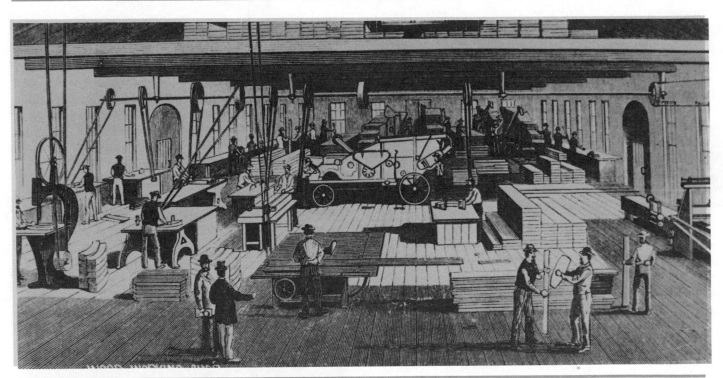

Sanding isn't sanding any more. It's still called sanding, but materials far superior to sand are used as abrasives . . . like aluminum oxide.

The success of a project often depends on the quality of its sanding and the resulting finish. The variety of tools available for sanding is a tribute to the importance of the operation. You can sand with portable tools, attachments on tools, or with special stationary tools designed specifically for the purpose.

BELT SANDERS

These stationary tools are very much like portable belt sanders except that they are bigger and more versatile. They also offer more control. This is because it is easier to apply work to a machine than to apply a machine to work.

A typical belt sander consists of a belt which rotates on two drums, one of which is powered. Usually, it is operated vertically or horizontally—vertically for end sanding, horizontally for surfacing and long edges. The nonsupported backside of the belt can be used for sanding convex surfaces.

A typical belt is 4" x 36". The size of the belt, however, doesn't limit the width of material that can be worked. With wide stock, you merely make repeated passes.

Compact, rugged 4" Toolkraft belt sander has a 4½" x 12" table and a cast-iron stop fence. Uses 4" x 36" belts. Sander alone weighs only 19 lbs.

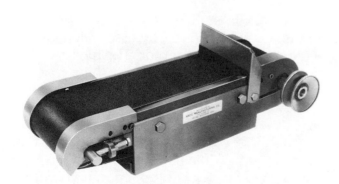

Arco horizontal sander uses 4" x 36" belts. With the correct belt you can grind, polish, and deburr all materials from wood to diamonds. Made for bolting to bench or pedestal. Requires ⅓ hp motor.

Arco's 6" sander can be used horizontally or vertically. Belts come in coarse (80 grit) for deburring, medium (120 grit) for sharpening, fine (220 grit) for polishing. Apply blackboard chalk to belt and soft materials like aluminum and copper won't clog it.

A disc sander is especially good for smoothing end grain.

DISC SANDERS

These have a flat steel or aluminum plate on which you fasten a circular sheet. A disc sander is not for with-the-grain sanding. It will leave cross-grain marks. It's for end grain, miter cuts, outside curves, and for breaking edges.

The $8\frac{1}{2}''$ Rockwell is typical of disc sanders. It has a table that tilts 35° toward and 45° away from the disc. Its speed is 1080, using a standard pulley and a 1725 rpm motor. The manufacturer recommends 40-grit coarse and 80-grit medium garnet sanding discs. The tool has a $\frac{1}{2}''$ outboard accessory shaft.

Powermatic offers individual belt and disc sanders. The belt model (right) uses a 6" x 48" belt and has a miter-slotted 7" x 17$\frac{1}{4}$" tilting table. The disc model uses a 12" disc and also has a miter-slotted tilting table.

FIVE WAYS TO SAVE MONEY

1. Shop around. You'll regularly find that prices for the same tool vary as much as 100%.

2. Assemble it yourself. Tools that come all put together inevitably cost more than those that come unassembled or partly assembled.

3. Supply your own motor. The motor you salvage from an old dishwasher, washing machine, or vacuum cleaner may be perfect for powering your new tool.

4. Buy multi-purpose tools. A combined disc and belt sander costs less than two separate tools.

5. Buy the tool that fits your needs. Don't get a tool designed for heavy production if you need it only for occasional or light duty.

COMBOS

Combination belt disc sanders are justifiably popular for they offer complete versatility. Typically, they come with a tilting table that can be used with either the belt or disc.

A 9″ disc and a 6″ x 48″ belt adds up to many square inches of sanding surface. Besides being used on wood, belt and disc sanders can also be used for finishing metal and plastics. Aluminum oxide belts and discs use the same abrasives that are in grinding wheels, so they are tough. You can sharpen power-mower blades, precision-grind lathe tool chisels and hollow-grind plane blades and wood chisels.

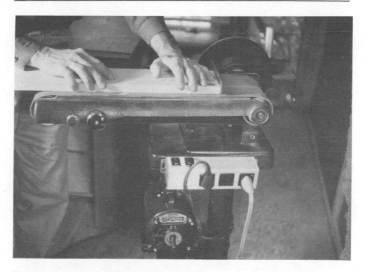

Belt is used horizontally for surfacing.

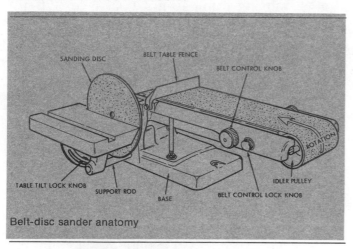

Belt-disc sander anatomy

The 6″ x 48″ belt on this Toolkraft model operates horizontally or vertically. Table tilts 45°, can be used with either belt or disc. Table size is 6¼″ x 12″.

Powermatic belt-disc sander has its own dust collection system. It uses a 6″ x 48″ belt and a 12″ sanding disc. Tilting table is 7″ x 14¼″. Rugged cast-iron construction virtually eliminates vibration. Belt's end guard is removable for contour sanding.

Sears combination has a 9″ disc and a 6″ x 48″ belt. The 6¼″ x 12″ cast-iron table tilts 45° for bevel sanding, can be used with either disc or belt. It has a miter gauge groove, but miter gauge isn't included.

Sand, grind, deburr, sharpen, contour, or finish. Rockwell's ¹/₂ hp sander/grinder can be used on wood, metal, plastics, ceramics, etc. Abrasive belts may be ¹/₈" to 1" wide, and 40", 42" or 44" long. The 7" x 8" table tilts 10° in, 90° out. Speed: 4000 sfpm.

STRIP SANDERS

These are also known as sanders/grinders and vertical belt sanders. Typically, they use an abrasive belt 1" x 42" and have a tilt table that supports work at the desired angle. A typical table, 7" x 8", tilts 10° in and 90° out.

A strip sander is ideal for wood, metal, leather, rubber, ceramics, composition, or plastics, and can be used for such jobs as sharpening, polishing, grinding, and sanding. It grinds inside and out.

For use on strip sanders, aluminum oxide abrasive belts with cloth backing are available in 7 grits, ranging from 40-grit coarse to 320-grit extra fine.

"Quik-Sand" won't sink your budget; Arco's 1" vertical sander-grinder is one of the least expensive models. You supply the motor, which can be almost any ¹/₄ hp deal, so long as it has ¹/₂" shaft, 1720 rpm. Suction feet hold tool to any smooth surface. Silvo Hardware.

Arco's sander-grinder sells for less because you assemble it yourself, using your own ¹/₃ hp motor with ⁵/₈" shaft. Horizontally or vertically, suction feet hold it tightly to any smooth surface. Takes a 2" x 48" belt.

HELPFUL HINTS

Don't throw away your old sander-grinder belts. Turn them inside out, apply jeweler's rouge liberally, and use them as hones. This hint from Arco.

Another hint: To sharpen circular saw blades, use a 120-grit belt and sharpen every other tooth, holding the work just above the platen. Make a complete circle, then turn blade over and sharpen the other teeth.

SOMEBODY COULD GET HURT

Two things need protection in all grinding operations—you and the motor.

1. *You.* Wear goggles during all operations.

2. *The motor.* It should be protected, especially from metal dust which may cause shorts.

MANUFACTURERS

BELT: Toolkraft, Arco, Powermatic.
DISC: Rockwell, Powermatic.
COMBO: Toolkraft, Sears, Amco, Powermatic.
STRIP: Rockwell, Shopmaster, Arco, Sears.

27. DRILL PRESSES

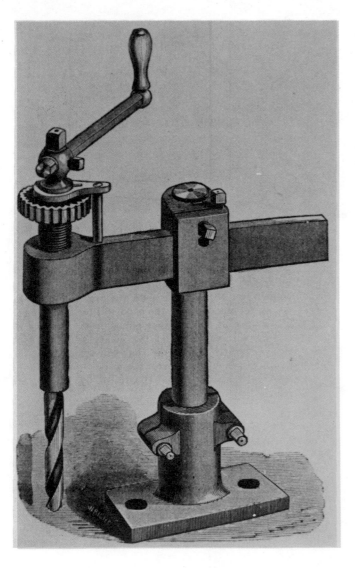

Through the ages, people have been drilling holes. But they haven't always been straight or true. Even with modern hand tools, control is often difficult. The ultimate in precision hole drilling is offered by the drill press. It will drill holes with absolute accuracy of almost any depth, at any angle, from pinhole size up to 8" in diameter. It can even drill square holes.

But it is more than a driller of holes. It can also be adapted for use as a planer, sander, and shaper. It can make dovetails, do routing, tapping, wire brushing, honing, paintmixing, and even damaskeening. Damaskeening is the technique of producing wavy lines on steel.

A spindle, with a chuck at its end, is turned by a motor inside a hollow sleeve known as a quill. The chuck holds a twist drill or other tool. By means of a feed handle, the chuck is moved down and the drill contacts the work.

To adjust distance between work and drill, the power head can be moved up and down on a column to which it is fastened. Or a table, fastened to the column, can be moved. The table may also tilt, for angle drilling.

There are also "radial" drill presses. The head on a radial drill press swivels 360° around the column. It tilts more than 90° right or left, and does jobs that are impossible on conventional type drill presses.

In a drill press you can use twist drills, spur bits, auger bits, hole saws, expansive bits, and fly cutters.

The size of a drill press is twice the distance from the center of the chuck to the column. For example, if this distance is 7″, it is a 14″ drill press and it will drill to the center of a 14″ panel. This is a popular size for the home shop. A typical radial drill press will drill to the center of a 32″ panel.

Other important measures of capacity are chuck to table distance, chuck to base distance, and quill travel.

The vertical distance from chuck to table at its lowest position determines the maximum thickness of work you can handle. Larger work-pieces can sometimes be handled by swiveling the table to the rear and placing the work on the drill's base. The distance the quill travels determines the maximum depth of hole that can be drilled without shifting the work table.

Drill press tables aren't large. Typically, one may be 8$\frac{1}{2}$″ x 9″ or 10″ x 10″, but auxiliary tables made of chipboard are available which will increase an 8$\frac{1}{2}$″ x 9″ table to 23$\frac{7}{8}$″ x 15$\frac{7}{8}$″.

Slow spindle speeds are best for metal and large holes in wood. High speeds are best for routing, shaping, and carving.

With a 1725 rpm motor, you may have speeds of 700, 1250, 2400, and 4700 rpm. The four speeds are usually achieved through step pulleys. Some drill presses have variable speed control, and in these cases you don't have to shift the belt to adjust the speed.

Toolkraft 4-speed 12″ model 350G has several accessories, including a mortising attachment for drilling square holes and a 3″ drum for sanding. Six-spline spindle travels 3″. Table to chuck 9$\frac{11}{16}$″, base to chuck 12$\frac{1}{2}$″. Table size 7$\frac{1}{2}$″ x 8$\frac{1}{2}$″. For safety, V-belt and machine pulley are enclosed in head. Column diameter 1$\frac{5}{8}$″. Complete with $\frac{1}{3}$ hp motor. Silvo.

Low-cost $\frac{3}{8}$″-chuck Shopmate has a built-in variable speed motor that "senses" power requirements. Drills to depth of 2$\frac{9}{16}$″. Capacity in steel $\frac{3}{8}$″, in wood $\frac{3}{4}$″. Throat 4$\frac{7}{8}$″. Column height 18″. Table 7″ x 10″. Weight 12$\frac{1}{4}$ lbs. Ward's.

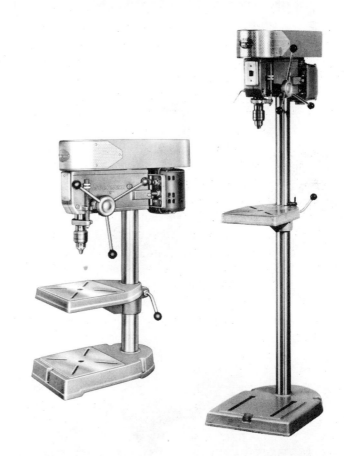

Sprunger 15″ bench model (left) and floor model. Both have a husky quill that travels 4$\frac{1}{8}$″, lockable in any position. Floor model takes a $\frac{1}{2}$ hp motor; bench model a $\frac{1}{3}$ hp motor. Both have 9 speeds between 600 and 5200 rpm. Table travels 41$\frac{3}{4}$″ on the floor model, 13$\frac{3}{4}$″ on the bench model. Table size for both 9″ x 9″; floor model has a larger base.

Powermatic 15″ has a full 6″ stroke; comes in bench or floor models. Five speeds, or variable-speed. A control lets you choose speeds instantly while machine is running. Many optional accessories. Capacity in steel $^1/_2$″. Bench model height 42″, floor model height 66″.

PORTABLE DRILLING MACHINE.

Rockwell 11″ drill press with stand has four speeds, 700, 1250, 2400 and 4700, for drilling a wide range of materials and for buffing, sanding, and grinding with optional accessories. Capacity is $^3/_8$″ in steel, $^1/_2$″ in cast iron. Quill travels $3^5/_8$″. Self-ejecting chuck key. A $^1/_3$ hp motor is recommended.

Table size of Rockwell 4-speed 15″ floor model is 10″ x 10$^1/_2$″; base size, 8$^1/_2$″ x 12″. Quill travels 4$^7/_{16}$″. Table has side ledges and slots for clamping work. Mount plate of motor pivots for easy belt tensioning and quick speed change. With $^1/_2$ hp motor.

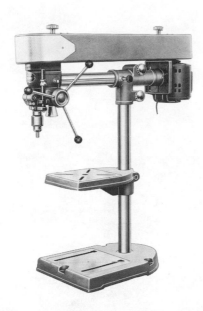

Sprunger radial arm drill press (RD 33) does angle operations with ease, both right and left, and it can drill to the center of a 33″ circle. Its head can be moved in and out, tilted, or rotated completely around the column. A $1/2$ hp motor is recommended.

Rockwell 32″ radial drill press with stand. Drills to center of a 32″ circle, performs horizontal and angular drilling, multiple and series hole drilling. Quill travels $3^5/_8$″. Auxiliary chipboard table is $23^7/_8$″ x $15^7/_8$″. Sold with or without motor.

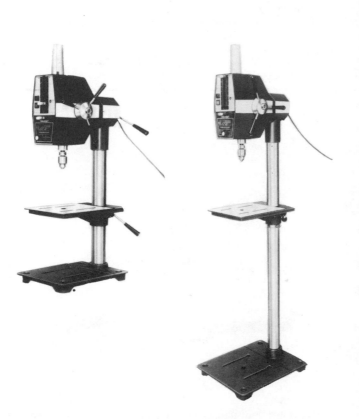

Toolkraft bench (left) and floor drill-routers have no belts. All moving parts are sealed in one gear-driven unit. Drills to 6″ depth in one operation. Speeds from 600 to 18,000 rpm. Table size 12″ x 14″; column size a husky 3″. Drill capacity 17″, router capacity 20″.

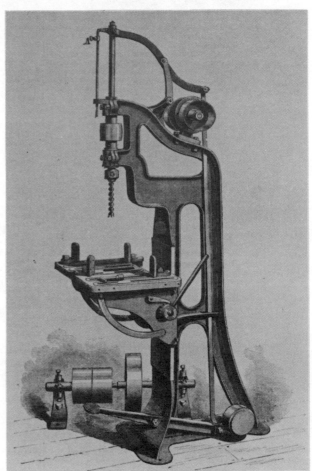

An outstanding boring machine of the 1870's.

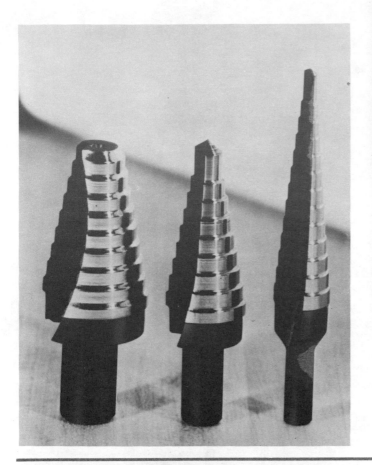

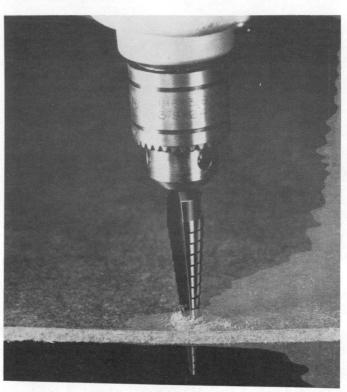

Unibit drills 13 different-sized holes from $1/8''$ to $1/2''$ in $1/32''$ increments. For wood, sheet metal, or plastic up to $1/8''$ thick, or up to $1/4''$ thick if both sides of the material can be drilled. Can be used in any 3-jawed $1/4''$ or larger drill press, lathe, and/or electric drill. Medium Unibit drills 9 holes to $3/4''$ and large Unibit drills 8 holes to $1''$. Brookstone.

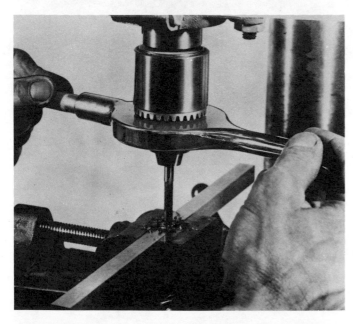

Useful tool lets you hand-rotate drill press chuck and spindle. Almost eliminates breaking of taps and reamers, insures accuracy. Solid aluminum body is 19″ overall. Steel shaft locks into chuck keyhole. Brookstone.

Vise is just 9″ overall, clamps to drill press table. Jaws can be set at any angle from 0° to 90°. There is one smooth jaw plate, one that is grooved horizontally and vertically for holding round or tapered pieces. Jaw width is $2^1/2''$, depth $1^1/2''$, maximum opening $2^1/2''$. Weight, 9 lbs. Brookstone.

WHAT TO LOOK FOR

Size, capacity, and power are of primary importance. So is speed choice. The more speeds, the greater the tool's potential versatility.

Look for factors of convenience. Does the table have ledges and slots for easy clamping of work? Is the power switch lockable? Do quills return quickly and easily when you ease up on the feed handle? Is there a work light? Do light and power switches work independently?

You can get a drill press for mounting on a bench, table, or stand. Or you can get one free-standing on its own base. Choice is a matter of personal preference, and how you plan to locate and use the tool.

What kind of accessories are offered? You can get a rotary planer that mounts on the spindle in place of the chuck. It will surface-plane wood or true-up and finish rough or warped lumber.

For safety, is there an effective belt guard? How conveniently located is the on-off switch? Also for safety, the chuck key should be self-ejecting so that it cannot be left in the chuck. Leaving a chuck key in the chuck can be very hazardous. Start the motor and it will go flying. You can buy a self-ejecting safety chuck key if your drill press does not come equipped with one.

Any drill from 1/8″ to 1/2″ can be sharpened to perfection at exactly the right angle in this Eclipse drill sharpener. Just tighten the drill in place and roll the tool back and forth on the abrasive surface provided. It's as simple as sharpening a pencil.

MANUFACTURERS

Sprunger, Rockwell, Toolkraft, Powermatic, Shopmate, and Milwaukee make drill presses. Mail-order sources include Sears, Silvo, U.S. General Supply, J.C. Penney.

SIZE AND WEIGHT ARE IMPORTANT

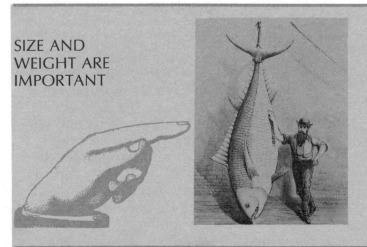

Physical dimensions and weight are important factors to be considered in judging drill presses as well as other stationary power tools.

Physical dimensions are an indication of capacity and sometimes durability. Weight often indicates ruggedness and stability. Good engineering and design, however, can sometimes lend strength and stability where sheer bulk and weight may merely mean clumsiness.

28. LATHES

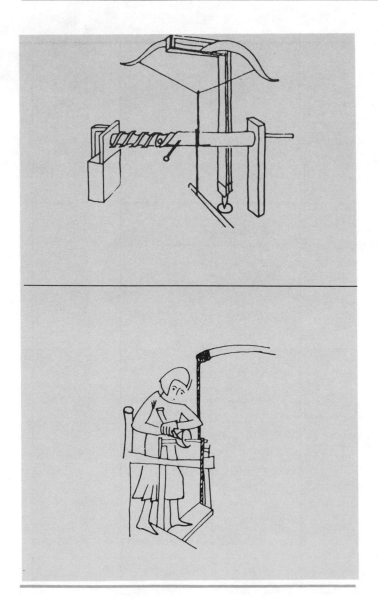

Leonardo da Vinci designed a lathe, but he wasn't the first. The Egyptians had one as early as 300 BC. It was a natural progression from the potter's wheel, except that it took two men to operate. The spindle being turned was held vertically between two supports. One man passed a cord around it and made it rotate by pulling. The second man did the cutting.

The horizontal lathe came much later. One variety, known as the pole lathe, was turned by a foot-treadle and flexible-pole combination. The pole bent down with pressure on the foot treadle, sprang up with release of pressure. The trouble was that it didn't revolve continuously, but back and forth. The worker had to take his chisel away at every backward twirl. Then someone got the idea of using a flywheel to get continuous motion.

Today, lathes are enjoying a resurgence after years of being regarded as an old-fashioned machine. Lathes were very popular when furniture had fancy legs and balustrades had fancy spindles. When they went into eclipse, so did the lathe. Now, people are finding out how much creative fun they are.

Besides making fancy furniture legs and spindles, they are discovering you can turn out candlesticks, lamp bases, posts, bannisters, doorknobs, rosettes, finials, chess pieces, chandelier parts, wooden bowls, and round boxes with fitted covers. You can even make baseball bats and salt and pepper grinders. By addition of a lap wheel, you can use a lathe for stone and glass cutting.

The tool consists of a bed, and a fixed head stock and a moveable tail stock between which you clamp a block or length of wood. There is a moveable tool rest to steady your hand and chisel. While the tool rotates the wood, you carve it with chisels. It's fun, and relatively easy.

The distance between the head-stock and tail-stock centers determines how long a spindle you can turn. The maximum length is usually 36″ or 37″. In practice, however, you can join separate turnings to make any length spindle you require—a porch post, for example.

Also to be considered is the clearance between the turning spindle and the tool bed. This "swing measurement" determines lathe size. Typically, it may be 12″ or 14″. Actually, this maximum turning capacity is less over the tool rest than over the bed.

You support work at two ends for spindle turning (for chair and table legs, lamp stems, etc.). You support it at one end for face-plate turning (making bowls, trays, ship's wheels, etc.). Some lathes have a "gap bed." In this design, the bed dips down to provide greater capacity at the face plate. For large work, on some lathes, a special face plate can be attached on the outside of the head stock, or outboard.

A typical lathe has four speeds. Rockwell, for example, offers 990, 1475, 2220, and 3250 rpms. The various speeds are achieved by shifting a belt to various pulley combinations. There are also solid-state variable-speed controls on some lathes which offer almost unlimited choice of speeds between zero and top capacity.

In practice, slow speeds are used for large, hard, or rough work, high speeds for small, soft, or fine work.

Rockwell's 10″ wood lathe, model 46-011, is specifically designed for the home craftsman. It has four speeds to handle all operations from initial roughing to final finishing. Distance of 36″ between centers; optional 1/3 hp motor available. Silvo.

Rockwell 46-150 4-speed lathe for woods, plastics, metals. Special bed gap allows turning of stock up to 14″ x 3″ on face plate. You can turn stock of 11″ diameter, 36″ length over bed. Built-in indexing mechanism. Includes stand, 4-step pulley, drive and cup centers, 3″ face plate, 6″ offset, 4″ and 12″ tool rests.

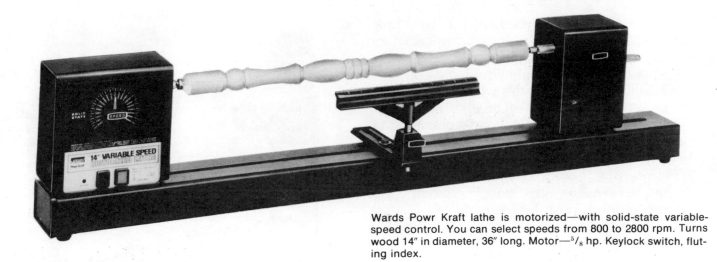

Wards Powr Kraft lathe is motorized—with solid-state variable-speed control. You can select speeds from 800 to 2800 rpm. Turns wood 14″ in diameter, 36″ long. Motor—$^5/_8$ hp. Keylock switch, fluting index.

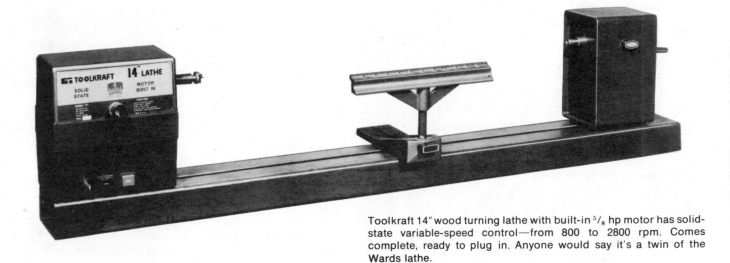

Toolkraft 14″ wood turning lathe with built-in $^5/_8$ hp motor has solid-state variable-speed control—from 800 to 2800 rpm. Comes complete, ready to plug in. Anyone would say it's a twin of the Wards lathe.

Build-it-yourself lathe-drill press combo. All parts are included for a three-speed lathe except wood and pipes, motor and switch. There are 31″ between centers; clearance for 12″ diameter workpieces. Converts to a drill press. Gilliom.

CHISELS

A basic set consists of eight chisels. Typically, these may be a $1/4''$ gouge, $1/2''$ skew, spear point, $1/2''$ gouge, parting tool, round nose, $3/4''$ gouge, and $1''$ skew.

You can get a special four-piece set of chisels for making bowls, plates, etc. These may be half-round, full-round, right skew, and left skew.

Some chisels have carbide tips. These chisels keep their edge longer. Chisels with tungsten alloy tips can be used for cutting any material, including steel, at woodworking speeds.

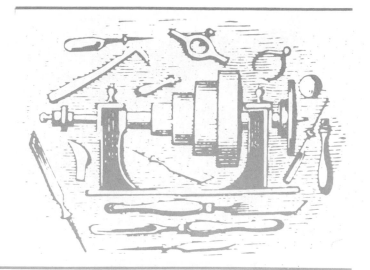

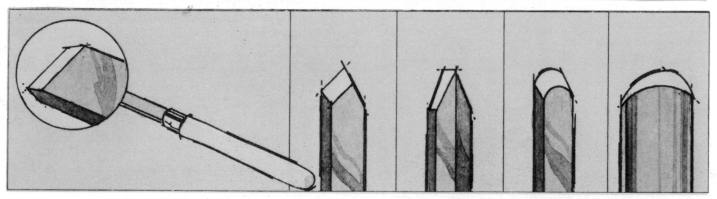

Wood turning tools, from left—skew cut, parting tool, skew cut, round nose, gouge cut.

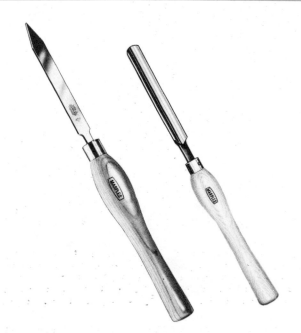

Turning gouge and parting tool are typical of Marples line, made of fine Sheffield steel.

Standard size chisels with an overall length of $16^{1}/_{2}''$. Set of 8 standard Marples chisels in box.

Inca 9" lathe is for woodworking—with accessories for metalworking. There are 39½" between centers. Four spindle speeds with back and forward drive, ½ hp motor. Wide range of accessories. Especially designed for schools and advanced woodworkers. Detailed operating manual.

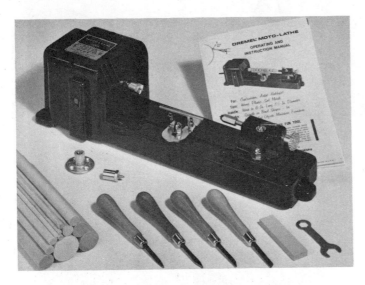

This miniature Moto-Lathe measures just 6" between centers. It will turn round stock of up to 1½" diameter. Its overall size is 15⅝" long, 6" wide, and 4¼" high. Excellent for doll house furniture, beads, chess pieces, models and miniatures of all kinds. Complete as shown for under $60. Dremel.

WHAT TO LOOK FOR

It takes strength and rigidity to provide precision and accuracy. Better lathes are made of fine-grade cast iron and have quality bearings. Avoid unknown makes. You want to buy from a manufacturer who will stay in business and provide replacement parts when you need them in the future.

Vibration can be a problem. It's less with a heavy, substantially made lathe. In any case, you may find you have to bolt the lathe bench or stand to the floor. How does this fit into your plans? In considering the size, remember the base of the tool rest cuts into the theoretical maximum diameter you can turn.

What does the lathe include? A motor? Stand? Accessories? What variety of accessories is available? How many tool rests are included? Typically, a lathe may include a 4", 6", and 12" rest. Can you get a tool rest for outboard lathe turning, if the lathe permits this?

Safety shield for wood-turning lathes protects worker and bystanders from broken work pieces, flying tools, chips. Available in 36" and 42" lengths. A duplicator attachment for identical wood turnings is also available. Toolmark.

ACCESSORIES

There are outside, inside, and hermaphrodite calipers. These are for measuring diameters. For spacing out designs, dividers are useful.

There are inboard or outboard screw-on arbors for attaching wire, fiber, and buffing wheels. Don't try to use a grinding wheel on a lathe. It's dangerous.

Some lathes can be equipped for turning metals. They should be rugged machines, with good bearings. Special metal-turning accessories are required, and speed must be reduced. With a countershaft, a lathe may be converted to 16 speeds instead of four, including such speeds as 340, 475, 525, 675, and 900 rpm.

Rockwell makes a ruggedly designed machine which, with a compound slide rest and other metalworking accessories, can turn nonferrous metals such as aluminum, brass, and copper.

Some lathes have an indexing mechanism. Typically, this is a special pin in the head stock which permits making equally spaced flutes on furniture legs, divisions on ship's wheels, etc.

MANUFACTURERS AND RETAILERS

They include American Machine and Tool, Gilliam, Wards, Powermatic, Rockwell, Sears, Sprunger, and ToolKraft.

Silvo, U.S. General, and J.C. Penney are other catalog sources.

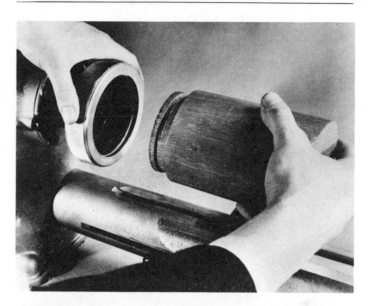

Coil-grip chuck will hold end-grain work such as vases and goblets. Designed especially for Rockwell 11" and 12" lathes. Woodcraft.

THEN—AND NOW!

Engraving (left) shows how a bowstring was used to power a lathe centuries ago. Photo recently taken in Morocco illustrates how little the equipment and technique have changed in some areas of the world.

29.
MULTIPURPOSE TOOLS

The Shopsmith Mark V, as it is today

An inventor named Hans Goldschmidt was the guiding genius behind the Shopsmith, introduced to the world in 1946. It became the glamour tool of the era that followed, and played a major role in the post-war do-it-yourself boom.

Though radial-arm saws and some other tools qualify as multipurpose, the Shopsmith remains unique. It is five woodworking tools in one: a 10" table saw, a 12" disc sander, a horizontal boring machine, a $16\frac{1}{2}$" vertical drill press, and a 34" lathe.

With accessories, it can also become a 4" jointer, a 6" belt sander, an 18" variable-speed jigsaw, and an 11" bandsaw. No other single tool can lay claim to so much. It can be bought directly from the factory.

The Basic Shopsmith

A 10″ table saw

A 12″ disc sander

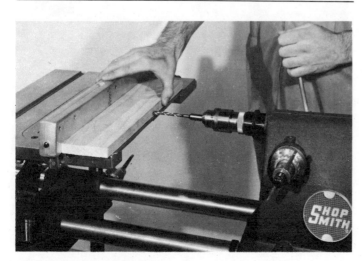

A horizontal boring machine

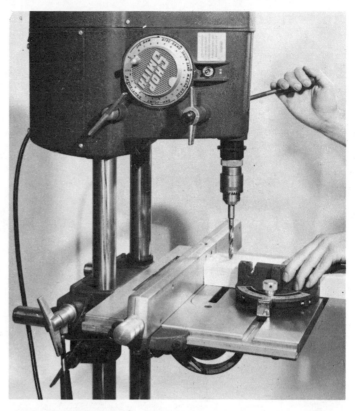

A 16½″ drill press

A 34″ lathe

Add-on Tools for the Basic Shopsmith

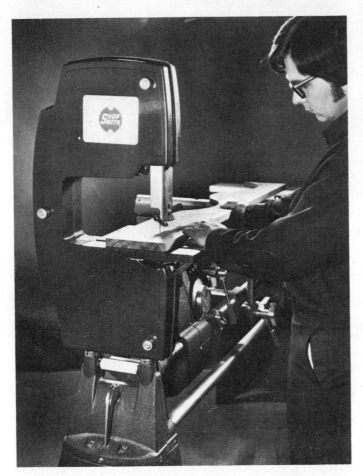

Bandsaw

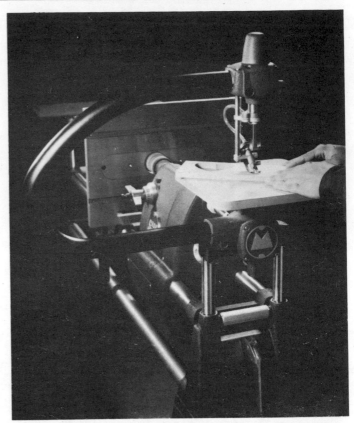

Jigsaw

4" jointer

6" belt sander

PART II

PAINTING/ DECORATING TOOLS AND EQUIPMENT

30.
SCRAPERS AND OTHER PAINTING ACCESSORIES

The Egyptians used paint as early as 8000 B.C. They made reds and yellows by mixing colored clay with water; green, blue, and black by grinding up pottery for pigments. In 1000 B.C., they developed varnish, making gum arabic from the sap of the acacia tree, and using beeswax as a varnish vehicle.

The Romans carried on where the Egyptians left off. They devised pencils for application of wall decoration and knew how to stain and paint floors. They imported iron oxide and vermillion from Spain and began the manufacture of white lead. They mixed pigments with wax to conceal imperfect marble. Good marble was certified "sine cere," without wax, the origin of our modern English word, sincere.

In early America, ordinary people did not paint their houses; they left them to weather. Painting a house was a symbol of social prestige and position, and only the rich could afford it. With American independence came the belief that if all men were created equal, all should enjoy an equal right to paint their homes.

In the early 1700s, Thomas Child of Boston imported a paint mill for grinding pigments, but before 1867 there were few ready-mixed paints available. Paints were made locally. Do-it-yourselfers mixed water with lime to make whitewash. They made other colors from earth pigments and buttermilk.

Prehistoric men

SCRAPERS

In the good old prehistoric days, early man used scrapers, made of bone and stone, for scraping skins to make leather. Today, scrapers are important for removing old paint, blisters, scale, rust, accumulated grime. There are three distinct styles.

1. **Hook.** All hook scrapers are characterized by blades that turn at a right angle to the handle. Some blades are multi-position. Four-position blades, typically, have two serrated edges for rough scraping, and two straight ones for fine finishing. The blade is rotated and tightened in position, usually by a wingnut.

There are flip-over hook scrapers with double-sided blades, one side for coarse, the other for fine work. One type of hook scraper has a knob for gripping. It helps in applying pressure.

Early "reversible" wall scraper. Sharpened edge was for scraping straight walls, blunt edge for use on irregular surfaces.

Razor Scrapers

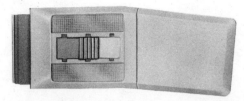

Red Devil molded-plastic scraper has a contoured handle, 3-position retractable blade. Two blades in storage compartment.

Hyde retractable blade scraper has push-button control to lock single-edge razor blade in cutting or scraping position. Comes with five blades.

Hyde 7½" scraper opens like jacknife, locks in three positions. With five single-edge blades.

Scraper with 7" polypropylene handle that holds a 2½" double-edge high carbon steel blade is a popular size, good for corner work. Also comes in smaller sizes with 1" and 1½" blades.

It's five painting tools in one. Sharp forward edge is a scraper, putty remover, and spreader. Half-round cutout removes paint from roller coater. Sharp point is to open cracks for patching. Blade is one piece through to end of nylon handle.

2. **Razor blade.** One morning, in 1895, while King Gillette was shaving, the idea for the safety razor dawned on him. Nowadays, razor blades are used in some exceptionally good scrapers. For safety, some of these scrapers have retractable blades. Others close up like a jackknife.

In comparison shopping, note the number of blades that come with the scraper. Some come with only one, others with as many as five. You may find a scraper in which you can use your own old razor blades, but most have their own special type.

3. **Wall scrapers.** Essentially, these are like putty knives, except that their blades are 3"–4" wide, instead of 1¼"–2". The blades, which have a beveled chisel edge, can be flexible or stiff. On some jobs a stiff blade seems to work better, on others, flexible, and it's a good idea to have both.

In buying a flexible-blade knife, check its resilience. In buying either a flexible or stiff knife, check its finish. A durable, high-finish steel is not just better-looking. It's easier to clean and will be slower to discolor and rust. Better scraper blades are of high-carbon steel, cheaper ones of spring steel.

The handle, and the way it is attached, is important too. It may be of metal, plastic, or wood. Whatever the material, it should be solvent-resistant. In better scrapers, blades are of one-piece steel from the tip through the end of the handle. One kind of scraper has a handle capped with metal so that it can be used for setting nails.

Over 100 years ago, Issac Perkins Hyde made knives and scrapers and delivered them himself by horse and buggy. Today, Hyde is still a big name in the business.

Flexible, Stiff, and Chisel Blades

Inexpensive heavy-duty wall scraper has 3″ flexible blade, red polypropylene handle with 3 brass grommets. Handle is impervious to paint and lacquer thinners.

Dig-zum opens paint-stuck windows. Insert it into paint-covered crevices using sawing action to cut paint film. Saw tooth blade is stainless steel. Tool is 9″ long, with blue plastic grip. Hyde.

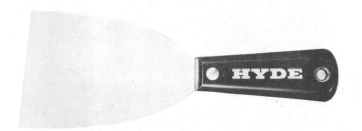

Heavy-duty paint scraper has a rugged 3″ wide stiff steel blade bent at a 20° angle for easy paint removal.

Mini-trowel for patching and pointing. Its polished steel blade measures only 4″ x 2″. Securely staked in natural hardwood handle.

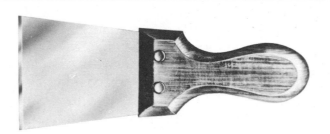

Stanley heavy-duty wall scraper is a favorite with painters and paper hangers. It has a high quality tempered steel blade, 3¹/₂″ wide, with an accurately ground beveled edge.

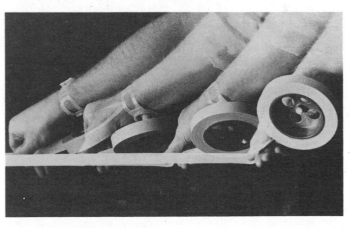

"Quicker Sticker" tape dispenser slips on the wrist. It's lightweight and comfortable, and it makes the job of applying masking tape easier. One thing's sure—you always know where the tape is.

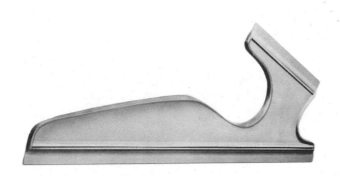

"Dual Trim Guard" has two trimming edges. The short edge is for hard-to-get-at corners, the long one for larger areas. Contoured for easy gripping. Red Devil.

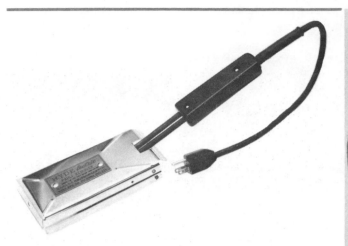

"Lectric" paint remover softens paint for easy removal by scraper. Removes old alligatoring no matter how many coats. Tool measures 13³/₄" long; handle is plastic. Not recommended for removing varnish. Hyde.

Roto-chipper removes thick paint. Fifteen hardened steel-tooth cutters rotate to chip away paint, scale, rust from metal, rock, concrete. Also for rough wood with heavily built-up paint. Use with any ¹/₄" or larger electric drill or sander polisher. Brookstone.

Disston Abraders do the same jobs as sandpaper, but last longer and cost less. The finishing surface is a stainless steel sheet etched with hundreds of sharp-edged pillars. The tool comes in five different models for a variety of applications. Some models offer coarse grit only, others have fine or coarse surfaces.

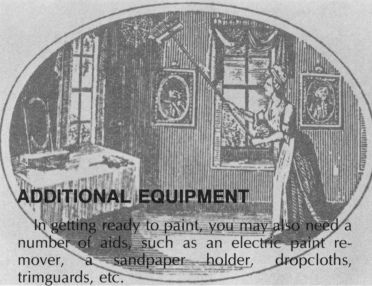

ADDITIONAL EQUIPMENT

In getting ready to paint, you may also need a number of aids, such as an electric paint remover, a sandpaper holder, dropcloths, trimguards, etc.

Electric paint removers. They soften up the paint film so you can scrape it away. It's often the only treatment for a badly blistered or scaly surface. Typically, removers have a 100-watt range-type element. A wire stand supports the hot unit when you want to set it down.

Sandpaper holders. Sanding is usually an inescapable part of preparation. Sandpaper can merely be wrapped around a dowel, stick, or wood block, and used that way, but a manufactured holder is often better. Mosh holders accept a quarter sheet, 4¹/₂" x 5", and are either of plastic block or steel. For use on curved surfaces, they may have a rubber pad.

Some holders will accept both regular sandpaper and "Dragon Skin," a steel sandpaper.

Trimguards are to protect adjoining surfaces as you paint. They may be of metal or plastic. You want one that is light, but sturdy, and which will get into tight corners. You can also protect adjoining surfaces with masking tape. A holder for masking tape called "quicker sticker" makes applying the tape a one-hand operation.

Dropcloths or tarpaulins. Indoors, you need them to protect floors, furniture. Outdoors, to protect shrubs and walks. Typically, they are 9' x 12'. Many are of plastic to which paint doesn't stick readily and which wipe fairly clean with a cloth. Lightest weight is ¹/₂ mil gauge, middleweight 1 mil, and heavyweight 1.75 mil. Low in cost are 9' x 12' dropcloths made of paper.

Et cetera. There are many other items which you may find useful in getting ready to paint, some of which are shown in the illustrations. Ladders and scaffolds are covered in Chapter 41.

Plastic pour ring for gallon cans makes paint easier to pour and keeps paint from covering up the can label. It also provides a handy rest for the paint brush. Tracy Engineering Co.

CHECKLIST

These are tools and equipment you may wish to have before starting to paint:

1. Scraper
2. Putty knife
3. Wire brush
4. Sandpaper holder
5. Caulking gun
6. Drop cloths
7. Mixing pails
8. Paddles
9. Ladder hook
10. Trim guard
11. Electric paint remover
12. Tack clothes

Surface "prep" tool removes loose and flakey paint, dirt, dust, cobwebs. Dulls the surface for paint application. Replaceable pad is 8$\frac{1}{2}$" x 4". Use on any threaded extension pole. Padco.

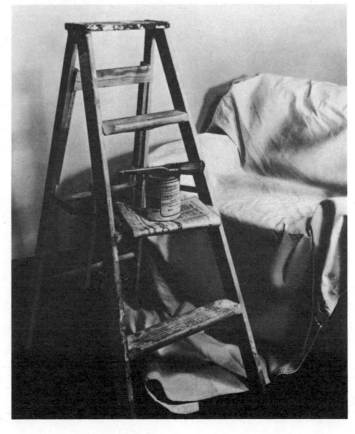

31.

BRUSHES

Early man used sticks and tufts of grass as paintbrushes. Stone Age artists used brushes made of feathers, bristles, leaves, pieces of fur, or frayed pieces of wood. Today, most paintbrushes have bristles made of synthetics—nylon and polyester, replacing hog bristles which, up until 1939, were the prime brush material.

Most hog bristles come from China, though the Soviet Union is also a producer. Typically, they consist of the hairs that grow along the hog's back. These bristles have qualities that suit them ideally for painting. They taper, which gives them stiffness at the metal collar or ferrule which attaches them to the handle, and flexibility at the application end. They are also characterized by split ends or "flags." These flags are like little fingers, increasing the bristle's capacity to carry paint. If you have 2000 hairs in a 3" brush and each filament has three flags, it means you have 6000 points of application.

High on the hog is where you find the best bristles for making paint brushes. This old sketch is from the collection of PPG Industries.

After the hog gave up his bristles, the people of China bundled them as shown in this drawing from the PPG collection.

When evaluating a brush, check on the quantity of bristles and the flagging of each bristle end.

Varnish and enamel brushes, 1" to 4", in this Thomas collection of 100 percent natural bristle, are stained ox-color. All have glossy walnut handles with brass-plated ferrules, except 4" brush at left. It has walnut lacquered round-grip handle, nickel ferrule.

Flax grows 12 to 24 inches high and has flowers with five petals that are blue, white or pale pink in color. Every household used to have a small garden patch to grow flax for making its own linen. Around 1800, the processing of linseed oil from flax seeds was begun in the U.S. To this day, linseed oil remains an important paint ingredient.

Someone took this picture of PPG sales and warehouse employees, in the days when you could buy a good brush for as little as 25¢.

For all paints, varnish and stain—EZ Paintr 100% polyester brushes with hang-up slots. They come in handy storage pouches.

THE NYLON BREAKTHROUGH

When DuPont first developed nylon filament, it appeared to be an excellent material for brushes. It was flexible, durable, and relatively inexpensive. The only trouble was that the paint rolled right off the filaments. American ingenuity went to work. It was found that by holding the ends of the filaments against a sanding machine they could be frayed or flagged, just like natural bristles.

Not all nylon filaments are alike. Some are straight, with the same diameter from the butt end to the tip. Others are tapered, just like natural bristles. Smaller at the tip, they are easier to flag. Pull a filament out of a nylon brush and hold it up to the light. You can then see just what the flags are all about.

Nylon also varies in quality. Press the bristles against the palm of your hand. There should be a nice "spring." If the nylon is too fine, the action will be floppy. Under pressure, they'll bend all the way back to the ferrule. If they're too coarse, they won't spread paint smoothly.

Good nylon bristle brushes are not inexpensive, but they cost less than natural bristle, and they last longer, paint better, and are easier to clean. You should not use natural bristle brushes in water-emulsion paint. The bristles will absorb the water and become limp. Nylon, however, takes to water like a duck. Since water-based paints are the most widely used, nylon brushes have a very important place.

Nylon, however, is not used successfully in oil-based finishes, lacquer, or anything that tends to disintegrate its filaments. That is where the new filament, polyester, made by DuPont and some of the French, shows its superiority. Polyster can be used in all paints and finishes, including varnishes, lacquers, and shellac without wilting or disintegrating.

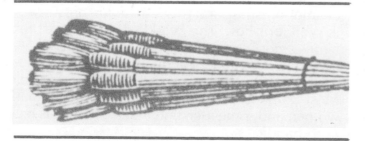

Small brushes for varnish and enamel. From bottom, 1" brush with orange plastic handle, 1" and 1½" brushes with glossy black plastic handles. Thomas.

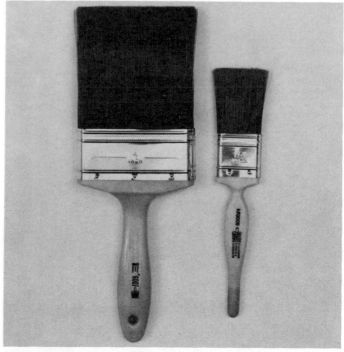

Polyester bristle can be used with any kind of finish. Shown here are two fine Baltimore brushes with tapered "Orel" bristles. Orel is DuPont's variety of polyester.

Paint brush with an angle is ideal for doing sash and similar work. Rubberset ''Versa Pro'' has a round grip, satin-clear wood handle, chisel trim. Sash brushes usually run from 1'' to 3''.

THE CHISEL END

When you wield a brush, you naturally hold it at an angle to the surface. That's one reason why good brushes usually have a chisel end. The V-conformation makes for easier, smoother application. It makes it easier to get into corners and cracks.

Most brushes have a simple straight V-chisel. Others are ''cup chiseled.'' In manufacture, the brush filaments are assembled by means of a tool shaped like an eyecup. This produces a taper that is widest at the center, curving to nothing at either side, a sort of half-moon effect.

FERRULES

A metal band joins the bristles to the handle. This is a ferrule. Most are made of tin, which is plated with nickel, copper, or ''gold,'' as it is known in the trade. It's really brass. Best is the seamless ferrule which is a stainless steel. It's more expensive, but it won't rust or deteriorate.

Hidden by the ferrule is the joint where bristles meet handle. At this point, bristles used to be set in rubber. Now almost all bristles are set in epoxy, and there is far less shedding.

Good hardwood for handles has become increasingly scarce and expensive. It's one reason why the trend is toward plastic in handles. This isn't all bad. Plastic isn't bothered by water and so it actually stands up better with water-based coatings.

KINDS OF BRUSHES

Four kinds of brushes are in general use: wall brushes; sash and trim brushes; varnish and enamel brushes; and miscellaneous brushes.

Wall brushes. The workhorses of the brush family, most come in widths of 3'' to 6''. They're designed to hold a great quantity of paint and for covering large flat areas as quickly as possible. Most painters prefer the 4'' size, though many women and some men find that a 3'' brush is easier to handle.

Sash and trim brushes. These come in square, angular, and round or oval styles. The square variety is for woodwork, paneling, trim, and so forth. It's ideal for use with a roller, picking up where the roller leaves off. It's available in sizes from 1″ to 3″ wide, with the 2″ or 2½″ size the most popular.

The angular brush is for use near surfaces you don't want painted, since it literally leans away from the work. It's good for painting around window glass or finishing the area where wall meets ceiling.

Round or oval brushes are designed for chair rungs, pipes, railings, and irregular or curved surfaces of all kinds. They are good for straight striping.

Some sash brushes are made with a mixture of China (hog) bristle and oxhair. The hair, which comes from the ear of the ox, is extremely fine and soft. Brushes with 20% to 30% oxhair are used for fine enameling, varnishing, and lacquering. It can produce a very smooth surface, like that on a piano, for example. Oxhair is very expensive.

Fitch brushes are a variety of oval sash brush that is popular in the Philadelphia area.

Varnish and enameling brushes. Available in 2″, 2½″, and 3″ sizes. Brushes intended for enameling tend to have a somewhat finer bristle and to be fuller than those used for varnishing. Most have a chiseled or beveled edge, which makes it easier to get into corners and tight spots.

Miscellaneous brushes. Many kinds of brushes are available for specific uses. There are special brushes for painting stucco, shakes, and shingles, and for applying calcimine. There are *dusters* for sweeping off surfaces prior to applying finish. There are *radiator brushes* with long handles and some with angled brushes. *Industrial brushes* are designed for rough maintenance work, such as painting bridges, telephone poles, concrete blocks, etc. Most combine bristle and horsehair. For the application of creosote and other preservatives there are industrial brushes that combine synthetic, horsehair, nd bristle.

Makers. Baker, Wooster, Thomas, and Linzer are a few of the top manufacturers.

Boar's hair sash brush has a removable spring-loaded brass guide that follows any straight or gently curved contour, corner or edge. Ideal for butting two colors on a flat surface. Brookstone.

32.

ROLLERS

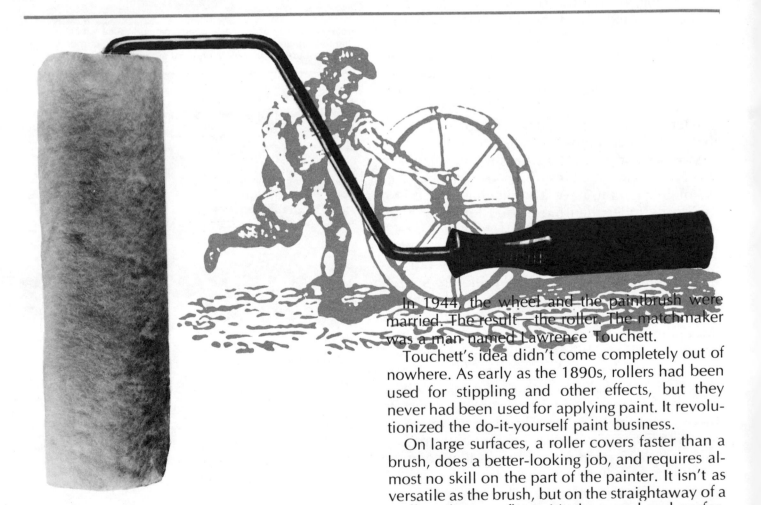

In 1944, the wheel and the paintbrush were married. The result—the roller. The matchmaker was a man named Lawrence Touchett.

Touchett's idea didn't come completely out of nowhere. As early as the 1890s, rollers had been used for stippling and other effects, but they never had been used for applying paint. It revolutionized the do-it-yourself paint business.

On large surfaces, a roller covers faster than a brush, does a better-looking job, and requires almost no skill on the part of the painter. It isn't as versatile as the brush, but on the straightaway of a wall, ceiling, or floor, it's the speed and performance champ. In no time at all it killed the business for brush sizes larger than 4".

There are two parts to a roller—a frame and a sleeve.

THE FRAME

There are several styles. One consists of a rotating cage mounted on a handle. The cage is made of four or five springy steel rods. When a sleeve is slipped onto the cage, it's held firmly, but it isn't difficult to remove either.

Another, and less expensive, style usually has two semicircular pieces of sheet metal on which you slip the roller. It's harder to clean and there's more surface on which the paint can harden and hold the sleeve fast.

Least expensive is a "rod and nut" frame. The sleeve is held by plastic end-caps and a wingnut.

There are also special frames for wood-core sleeves, used by professionals.

The steel shafts supporting the rotating mechanism, and on which the handle is mounted, is usually made of $1/4''$ rod. Lower-quality frames have only $3/16''$ rod. For heavy-duty use, you can get frames made with $5/16''$ rod. Even with abuse, these are unlikely to bend.

Most handles these days are plastic rather than wood. Wood has a tendency to split and crack. Plastic may be damaged by some solvents, but water isn't one of them, so it has a special advantage over wood for water-based paints.

Whether the handle is wood or plastic, it's a good idea to get one that's threaded for an extension pole. Poles may be of wood or aluminum. Wood has the advantage of being shockproof. Aluminum has the advantage of being lightweight. You can get threaded wooden poles 12″, 48″, 60″, and 72″ long. You can also get a 3-piece hardwood handle with an overall length of $42^3/_4''$. Each section is $15^1/_4''$, and by using one, two, or three sections, you can suit almost any need.

You can get anodyzed aluminum handles that are telescopic. Red Devil makes a 4' handle that extends to 8', and a 6' handle that extends to 12'. Baker makes "hand-lock" extension poles that extend from 4' to 8', 4' to 12', and 8' to 16'. However, unless you are an expert, you may find anything exceeding 10' rather unwieldy.

You can get frames in sizes to fit 7″, 9″, 12″, 16″, and 18″ sleeves. The most popular size is 9″. Baker makes one frame that's adjustable to fit any size sleeve from 12″ to 16″.

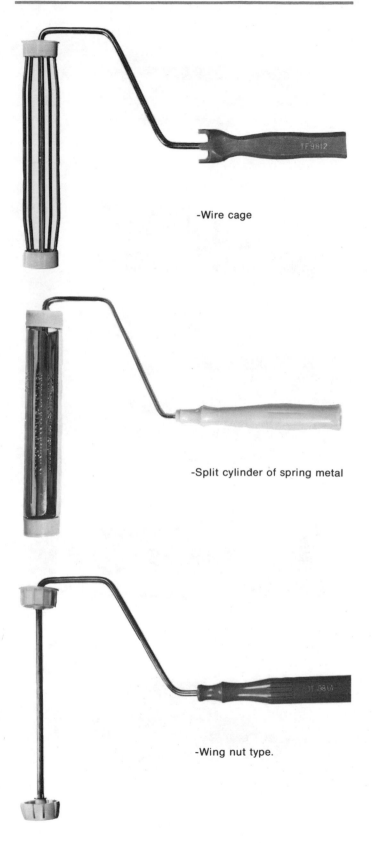

—Wire cage

—Split cylinder of spring metal

—Wing nut type.

The three frame types. All have polyethylene unbreakable handle, threaded for use with extension pole. Thomas Industries.

A short nap is for smooth surfaces, longer naps for rougher surfaces. Enamel performs better with a short nap, latex paint works better with a long nap.

THE SLEEVE

Read the label and you'll know what kind of sleeve to buy. The wrapper on most roller sleeves tells you what kind of paint it's for, and on what texture surface it works best. Sometimes, too, the label on a can of paint will recommend the kind of sleeve to use.

In the past, sleeves made of synthetic fibers, such as Dynel and Orlon, were recommended for latex and water-based paints. Sleeves made of mohair and lambswool were recommended for oil. Now, polyesters and blends of polyesters have taken over for just about everything. Dynel is no longer manufactured. Lambskin and mohair, never satisfactory in latex, are also being superseded in oils, though pros still cling to them because of tradition. They are still recommended, however, for very high solvents, such as epoxy and fiberglass. Being natural skins, with each filament growing out of the hide and firmly attached, lambskin and mohair are the most lint-free of rollers.

Polyester, for the present, is king—used on the least as well as the most expensive rollers. But there is polyester and there is polyester. There are many different types, blends, filament sizes, and configurations, and that's where quality and price enter the picture. Usually, you'll get what you pay for.

At the bottom of the quality scale is rayon. It's very poor, but cheap. It looks good, but it absorbs water. It's usually a roller you use once and throw away.

Some sleeves are made for special uses. Sleeves made of carpeting are for texture effects. Foam is recommended for use on sprayed-on acoustical ceilings.

Sleeves come with varying nap to suit varying surfaces. The rougher the surface you're painting, the longer the nap should be. Naps range from $3/8''$ for smooth, $1/2''$ for medium, $3/4''$ for medium rough, 1" for rough, to $1\,1/4''$ for extra-rough surfaces. For best results, select the sleeve or cover with the shortest nap that will do the job.

Originally, the roller core was made of wire. It's good, but expensive. Very few are made of it today. Most are of phenolic—paper impregnated with resin and baked. A few are of plastic, though manufacturers find trouble adhering covers to that material. Cheapest cores are just plain card-board. They're made to use and throw away.

Standard sleeves are 1$\frac{1}{4}$ inches in diameter. There are jumbo sleeves, 2$\frac{1}{4}$ inches in diameter, which fit on a special jumbo frame. They hold more paint than the standard sleeve.

Lambskin costs less in the long run because it can be cleaned and used again and again. For this reason it is preferred by professionals. For best results, use with oil base paints only.

Throw it away! If you find cleaning a bore, get disposable sleeves or covers. They're recommended for quick, non-fussy jobs.

This sleeve is a solid sheet of synthetic foam rubber. It's designed for use on smooth surfaces. Another type has a "waffle-cut" and greater flexibility; it's recommended for acoustical ceilings.

TRAYS

Trays are usually of bright metal or plastic and have lock-legs for gripping a ladder. You can get a 9" x 14" tray for a 7" roller, or a 10" x 15" one that will accommodate either 7" or 9" rollers.

Some trays have deep wells that hold more paint than others. Two- or 3-quart capacities are not unusual. For really big jobs, you can get an industrial tray that holds 3 gallons.

To ease cleanup, there are special plastic tray liners, or you can line the tray with aluminum foil.

The chevron or other design on the bottom of the tray is to help in rolling out excess paint. There's a little diamond-grid mat, however, that snaps onto the tray that does a better job. Even better are metal grids.

Economy tip. You can often save by buying a paint roller kit. Besides tray, roller frame, and cover, it may include an extension handle, a roller cleaning tool, and a trim brush.

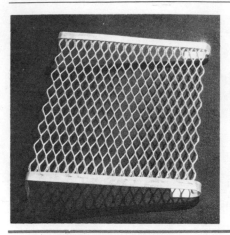

Left: A grid like this (by Thomas) helps prevent excessive paint build-up. You just run a roller over it to squeeze away excess. Fits paint tray or five-gallon bucket. *Center and right:* Plastic paint trays by Baltimore.

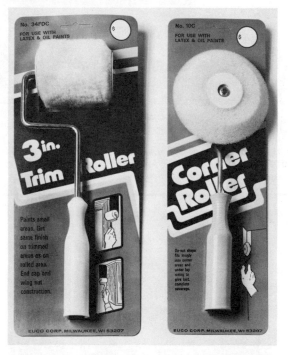

Indispensible aids in roller painting are a trim roller, like this three-incher, and a corner roller. Corner rollers can also be used under lap siding.

SPECIAL ROLLERS

There are few jobs you can complete with a standard roller. It just can't be maneuvered in restricted spaces. You can use a brush to get at tight spots, but it won't produce the same finish as a rolled area. For this purpose, there are special aids.

The *trim roller* is 1" to 3" wide and is used mostly for trim and sash painting. Typically, they are of end-cap and wingnut construction, though the sleeves are removable and replaceable.

The *corner roller* is donut-shaped and beveled. Usually made of foam, it's for doing inside corners. A somewhat similar roller that's cone-shaped is good for fine-line trimming.

The *painter's mitt* is designed for covering pipes, grilles, radiators, and contoured surfaces that are otherwise a problem. It's made of lambskin and has a thumb. You put it on your hand, dip it in the paint, and go to work.

Three accessories that come in handy. *Left:* For cleaning roller sleeves, this is the tool. It literally squeegees sleeves clean. *Middle:* Screen painter won't clog perforations. *Right:* An economical 3" trimmer with wire handle.

MANUFACTURERS

Today, there are about forty manufacturers in the business. Almost everyone who makes brushes makes rollers, just as almost everyone who makes rollers makes brushes.

EZ Paintr, the company that inventor Touchett started, is still the leader. Wooster Brush Company is probably second, and the Tip Top division of Beatrice Foods third. But you'll find excellent rollers made by all major brush companies. There are very few imports.

"No-spray" roller has a built-in shield that protects you from spatter and spray. The jumbo roller is only 6³/₈" wide, yet it holds more paint than a standard diameter 9" roller. The handle is threaded for an extension pole.

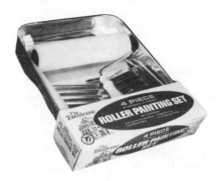

You save by buying a four or six-piece set. Sets above are by Thomas. Set at right by EZ Paintr.

A three-piece extension handle that extends to 42³/₄" is a good accessory for painting ceilings. It fits paint rollers and pad applicators with threaded handles. Why climb a ladder?

A painter's mitt can get around pipes, columns, radiators, and into a variety of tight places a roller can't reach. Mitt is plastic lined and cleanable. Just place it on your hand, dip in paint, and spread evenly. Red Devil.

33.

SPRAYERS

The first paint sprayer was made by the DeVilbiss Company in Toledo, Ohio, in 1909. Based on a medical atomizer invented by a doctor named Allen DeVilbiss, it speeded up painting enormously, and became a very important painting tool. A paint sprayer has certain advantages and drawbacks.

First, the drawbacks. A sprayer is difficult to control. It lofts paint everyplace, a problem called overspray. That means you have to take precautions, like masking glass and hardware, and working in a booth if you're indoors. If you're going to paint a house exterior, you must cover the bushes and everything else you don't want covered with paint, and wait for a windless day. There's also a tendency to breathe the mist, so a mask is recommended. After painting, or when changing colors, cleanup can be messy and time consuming. Unless you have a sizable job to do, it may not pay to get out the sprayer.

Now, for the advantages. A sprayer is incredibly fast, five, even ten times as fast as some brush jobs. Things with many surfaces, like fences, shutters, radiators, and wicker or metal furniture, can be done in short order. It takes a little practice to catch on to its use, but actually it's easier to become an expert with a spray gun than it is with a brush. Perhaps most important of all, it produces a smooth, uniform coating almost nothing else can match. It's ideal for painting auto bodies, machinery, appliances, and other demanding work.

Dr. Allen DeVilbiss

Economy-priced lightweight pressure feed gun, model 212, handles house and barn paints, flat alkyd enamels, screen enamel, water-mixed paints, stains, varnishes and wood sealers. Paint is mixed internally. W.R. Brown.

Powerful spray outfit with diaphragm compressor that delivers 2¹/₂ cu. ft. per minute at 35 lbs. pressure. Diaphragm guaranteed for 1000 hours of operation. Multi-purpose gun, model 312, sprays all paints, lacquers and enamels, plus garden and household liquids. Internal or external mix operation. W.R. Brown.

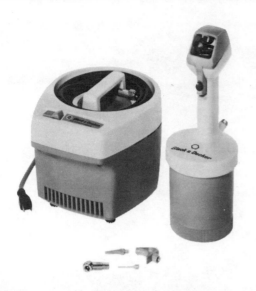

As a bonus, the compressor used with a spray gun can be used for other jobs, such as inflating tires, applying caulking, sand blasting, and powering a variety of other air tools.

Most spray equipment consists of a compressor, a spray gun, and a connecting hose. The compressor supplies air under pressure which sucks or blows paint or other material through a nozzle which converts it into a spray mist. Some sprayers are airless, and the material they apply is driven through the nozzle by centrifugal force or vibration. Many of these can handle only very light materials and are useful for only the smallest jobs. It takes power to spray paint, and the thicker and heavier the paint the more power it takes. Air guns with more powerful motors are likely to be heavy (nearly 4 pounds unfilled) and tiring to use.

Versatile spray outfit of unusual design (model 7761) comes with inexpensive throw-away nozzles for easy cleanup. Hose nests in top of piston-driven compressor. With accessories it can spray water-base and oil paints, inflate bicycle tires and toys, apply caulking compound or spray insecticides. Black & Decker.

Speedy Sprayer compressor delivers 2 cu. ft. of air per minute at 30-40 lbs. pressure. Use with any $1/4$ or $1/3$ hp, 1750 rpm motor. Internal mix, bleeder-type gun handles all materials. W.R. Brown.

"Sprayit" is an economical spray outfit by Thomas. Diaphragm compressor, external mix spray gun, and hose are included. Available in $1/4$, $1/3$ and $1/2$ hp models.

SPRAY GUNS

The *bleeder gun* is called that because it constantly "bleeds" air. It's used with a continuously running compressor, and air flows through the gun nozzle even when you're not pulling the trigger to make the paint flow.

The *non-bleeder* gun operates off a tank fed by the compressor. The trigger controls the flow of air and paint.

Guns may be *pressure fed* or *siphon fed*. In pressure-feed guns, air fed directly into the paint cup forces the paint up a fluid tube to the nozzle. In the siphon gun, the air supply is directed across the opening of the fluid tube. This creates a vacuum, and atmospheric pressure, entering through a vent, pushes the paint up into the gun.

The pressure-feed gun is best for heavy materials, like latex paint, and for fast spraying. The siphon gun produces finer atomization and is best when an extra-fine finish is desired. It is a slower gun than the pressure feed.

Twin diaphragm-type compressors mounted on a steel base that is ready to accept your own ½ hp motor or gasoline engine. It comes with multi-purpose model 331 spray gun. W.R. Brown.

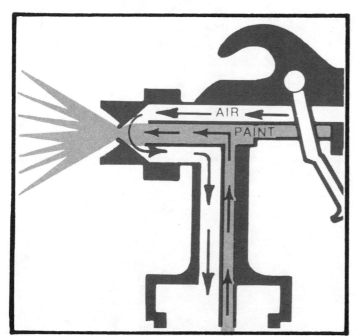

PRESSURE

![SIPHON diagram with AIR and PAINT labels]

SIPHON

Air or Airless?

The most commonly used type of spray equipment uses compressed air to atomize the paint at the nozzle and feed the paint under pressure from the supply. It's the most versatile spray equipment, more easily controlled, and it is the kind most widely used. The airless sprayer atomizes fluid without the use of air jets. Using liquid pressures as high as 3200 PSI, it forces paint through a very small opening in the spray cap. Its advantage is that it covers large surfaces very quickly with a minimum of overspray mist. Extra care is required to avoid excessive coverage. It is for specialized, professional and commercial use.

Five Models by W.R. Brown

Model 331 works three ways. Use it as an internal mix pressure feed, external mix pressure feed, or external mix syphon feed. It has built-in air valve for "bleeder" or "non-bleeder" operation.

Model 112 is an internal-mix "bleeder" type gun. It comes with round, fan and angle nozzles.

Model 212 is an internal mix "bleeder" type, with round and fan nozzles. Not convertible to use with paint tank.

Model 107, an external mix syphon-feed production spray gun with clamp-type cover.

Model 145 is an inexpensive external mix, syphon-feed gun that produces a round spray pattern. For small jobs, super-fine finish.

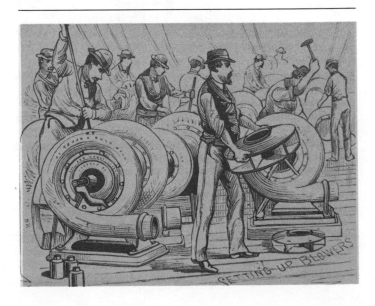

Four by DeVilbiss

Type QGB. General-purpose home-type spray gun with one quart aluminum cup. Suitable for use with $1/4$ and $1/3$ hp compressor. Pressure-feed design enables heavy-bodied paints to be sprayed with low air use.

Type JBA. High production gun and drip-free suction cup. Controls at back of gun adjust fan, pattern, size and fluid flow.

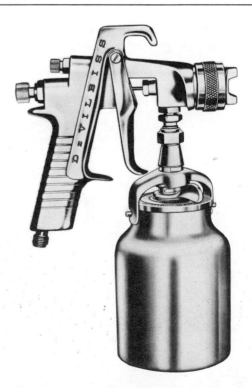

Type MGB. High production external mix gun and cup with quick-clamp cover. For all conventional materials.

Type EGA. For spraying small areas and intricate work. Operates like an artist's air brush, with index-finger trigger. For shading, stenciling and sign work.

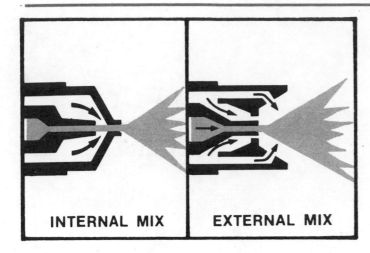

INTERNAL MIX   EXTERNAL MIX

NOZZLES

Spray-gun nozzles are of two kinds.

The *internal nozzle* mixes air and paint inside the nozzle. It's best for heavy-bodied paints and liquids.

The *external nozzle* mixes air and paint just as they leave the nozzle. It's best suited for fast-drying finishes like latex and lacquers.

In the past, you needed two guns to handle all types of finishes. You needed a pressure-feed internal-mix nozzle for regular paints. You needed a siphon-feed external-mix nozzle for lightweight fast-drying lacquers You couldn't spray latex at all because it was so heavy and so rapid-drying. Now, you can spray all types of finishes, including latex, with one gun. These multi-purpose spray guns work three ways: 1. As an internal-mix pressure feed for heavy-duty spraying of house and barn paints, stains, flat wall finishes, and so forth. 2. As an external-mix pressure-feed gun for fast-drying latex paints. 3. As an external-mix siphon-feed gun for finest finishes with lacquers and enamels. Some even have a built-in air valve for "bleeder" or "non-bleeder" operation.

Most spray guns have screws that adjust the rate of flow and degree of spread.

Internal mix

Fan air cap.

External mix, pressure feed

Multiple jet air cap

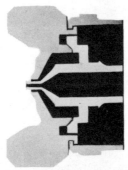

External mix, suction feed

Round orifice air cap

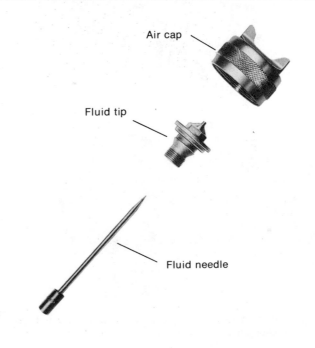

Air cap

Fluid tip

Fluid needle

COMPRESSORS

There are two types commonly used:

The *diaphragm compressor* provides air by flexing of a diaphragm. It requires no lubrication, and its capacity suits it ideally for most home and shop use.

The *piston compressor* develops pressure by means of a reciprocating piston. It requires lubrication with oil, and is generally for heavy-duty use in conjunction with a storage tank.

Compressors are rated by their air flow, measured in SCFM, or Standard Cubic Feet per Minute. They are also rated by the air pressure delivered at their nozzle. It's measured in PSI, Pounds per Square Inch. A higher PSI permits thicker paints to be used, which means less thinning required. It also means quicker coverage and it permits a wider range of spray-gun adjustments.

The higher the SCFM rating, the more paint can be moved and the greater the speed of its movement. A typical diaphragm compressor may deliver air at 2 or 2.5 SCFM at 35, 40, or 45 PSI. Piston compressors are larger, and typically deliver between 3 and 7 SCFM at a pressure of 100 PSI or more. The largest compressors may have twin pistons.

Large compressors deliver enough power to operate most air tools, including large nailers, staplers, tackers, sand blasters, and caulk guns. They let you operate two spray guns simultaneously.

Typical air storage tanks are 12, 20, 30, and 80 gallon sizes. A typical air hose is 15 feet long, but you can also get them 25 and 50 feet.

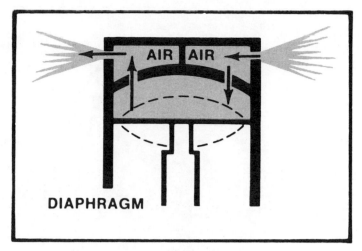

DIAPHRAGM

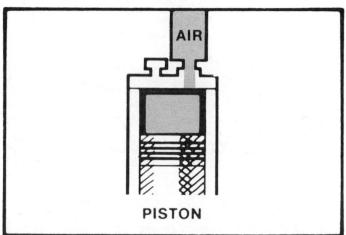

PISTON

Diaphragm or Piston?

In a diaphragm compressor, a flexible membrane is moved back and forth to bring air to the compressor and then force it out through the air hose. In a piston compressor, a piston moves up and down inside a cylinder, drawing air in on the downstroke, then forcing it out through the air hose on the upstroke. Both units deliver comparable air volume as measured in cubic feet per minute, but piston units provide higher pressure in pounds per square inch.

"Porto Tank" paint sprayer. A $\frac{1}{3}$ hp motor operates compressor that sits atop a five-gallon welded steel air storage tank. Delivers 2 CFM of air at 35 PSI. W.R. Brown.

Low-priced diaphragm-type compressor is for farm or semi-commercial use. It delivers $2\frac{1}{2}$ CFM at 35 PSI. Integral $\frac{1}{2}$ hp motor, 12-gallon air storage tank. Multi-purpose gun for internal or external mixing. Uses quart cup or $2\frac{1}{2}$-gallon paint tank. W.R. Brown.

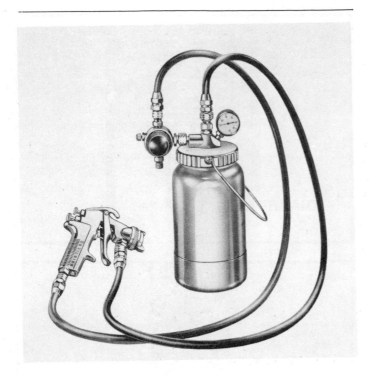

One or two-quart pressure feed cup attaches to any model spray gun with short hose lengths. Adjustable air and fluid pressure; equipped with regulator, gauge, valves. Uses 45″ air hose, 48″ fluid hose. DeVilbiss.

Steel 2½-gallon tank speeds up big jobs—one filling lasts several hours. Also holds standard one-gallon paint can. Aluminum cover has handle for carrying or ladder-hanging. Comes with 10′ air and paint hoses. W.R. Brown.

Pressurized outfit for roller or sprayer—Sprayit two-in-one kit uses gallon paint can in which paint is purchased. Three clamps lock top and bottom discs in place. Fingertip control determines paint flow to roller or spray. 15′ hose. Accessories include 42″ extension handle and spray head. Use with almost any air compressor. Thomas.

WHICH TO BUY?

A question to ask yourself is: How fast do you want to work? Most spray equipment will do a good job. The bigger units will do a good job faster.

Cheaper units will handle only paint. The more expensive will handle a much wider variety of finishing materials.

Some spray guns can be taken apart and used with a pressure-fed paint tank for large jobs. If you're going to spray a barn, a quart of paint is sprayed out very rapidly. You have to stop often to refill a 1-quart cup. With a pressure-fed tank, you can use as much as 2½ gallons at one time without stopping. Some guns can be used in this fashion. Some cannot. The cheaper guns cannot.

Match gun and compressor. A gun must match the available supply of air. If a compressor puts out 2 cubic feet a minute, get a gun that operates within that range. Don't get one that needs 2½ SCFM.

W.R. Brown's model 450 is for commercial or professional use. It has a ½ hp motor that drives a 4 cu. ft. capacity twin-diaphragm compressor. Furnished with model 331 multi-purpose gun. Use with 2½-gallon paint tank for maximum speed and coverage.

High pressure portable air compressor for airless or conventional spray painting. Ten-gallon air supply tank. DeVilbiss.

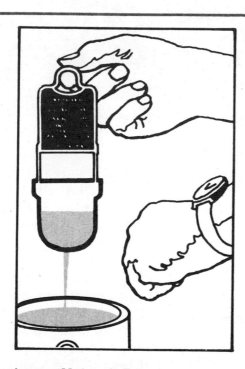

A Viscosimeter Makes It Easy

Having paint at the right consistency is critically important in the proper operation of a sprayer. A viscosimeter takes the guesswork out of it. You merely tip the cup of the device in the material to be sprayed, lift it out, and time its flow until the stream breaks for the first time. You then compare this time with a chart on the top of the viscosimeter's handle to see if you have the right consistency.

Accessories for spray equipment.
At left: Airline filter keeps oil, water, etc., out of regulator and spray gun. *Right:* Air-pressure regulator maintains uniform working pressures from 0 to 140 lbs. Also available for 0 to 50 lb. pressures. Both by Speedy.

34.

PADS

The use of pads for the wide-area application of paint began in the early 1960s. Before that, there were small, flat, mohair applicators used as trimmer-edgers, specifically for touching up areas that rollers couldn't reach. Then a man named Robert I. Janssen got the idea of using a pad for large areas. But there was a problem.

The problem was, using mohair as a pad, paint squeezed out at the sides when he applied pressure. Mohair just wasn't suitable for applying paint in a wholesale way. So he developed a process of embedding nylon fibers directly in urethane foam, and using it as a pad. It worked! Paint no longer was squeezed out at the sides, and Janssen was on his way to success. His company became Padco, the largest in the field, and a supplier to the industry at large.

Here's how pads fit into the paint application scene.

Paintbrushes are the *most* versatile. They can do anything—cover broad areas, get into corners, even draw pictures. They are also the *slowest* and require the *most* skill.

Rollers are at the other end of the spectrum from brushes. They are the *least* versatile. It's difficult to use them for anything except covering wide areas. But they are *fastest,* and produce the most uniform finish. Also, no skill is required to use them effectively.

The pad fits right in the middle. It is not as fast as a roller, or as versatile as a brush, but it has a little of the qualities of each. If you could have only a single paint tool, it would be the pad. But you really have need for all three. In doing the ceiling, you'll want a roller. It has the speed. In doing cabinets, you'll want a brush. It has the versatility. In doing wide areas, involving considerable trimming around doors, windows, and cabinets, you'll want the pad.

The pad is replacing large brushes. Rollers have already substantially taken over the work of all brushes larger than 4". Now, pads are taking over the niche occupied by the 4" brush. It's safe to predict that eventually most brushes will be 3" or less. A 7" pad is about twice as fast as a 4" brush. It's slower than the 7" roller, but more versatile.

It's called a "Shake Painter," but it can be used on the inside of the house as well. Comes in 6", 8" and 10" widths. Use it anywhere you might use a large brush or paint roller. Padco.

It's a nylon fiber pad 1¼" thick, especially for acrylic latex paints.

Wand-type paint pad for small areas and touch-ups has a 1⅛" x 1¾" applicator. Pad is easily replaced—just push the button to pop it off, then snap on a replacement. Padco.

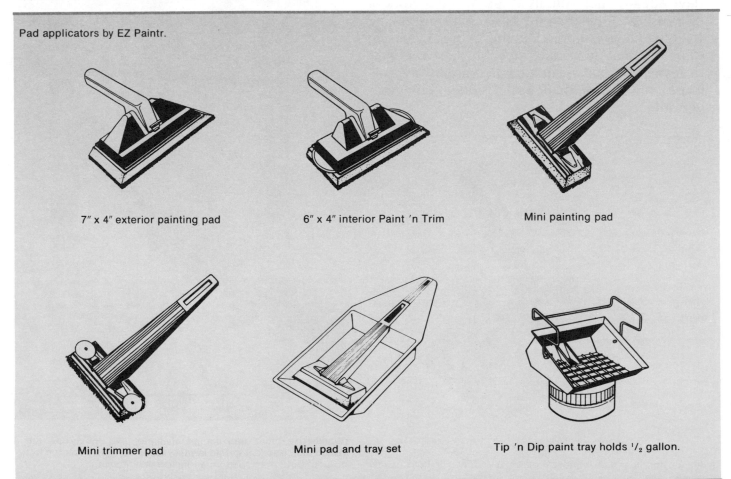

Lambswool pad is preferred by many painters for applying stain because it holds more of the thin-bodied material than other applicators. Lambswool is bonded to urethane foam. Padco.

VITAL STATISTICS

Pads are made in sizes ranging from 5" to 11" and can be used inside and out, on walls, ceilings, floors, woodwork, exterior shakes and shingles, siding, soffits, fences, shutters, and boats. A typical pad consists of a nylon-foam applicator and a handled holder. Pads are removable, so you can switch them for quick color changes. They are also replaceable when they wear out. They don't last as long as brushes, but one may be sufficient for two or three bedrooms, and two for doing a small house. Most have wheels or projections, as guides for trimming around windows, doors, and moldings. These ride along any straight adjoining surface, like a window frame, producing a straighter, cleaner edge than a brush. But you must keep the guides clean, or they will mark the adjoining surface. And you don't want wheel guides to become clogged with paint. It can stop them from turning, and contributes to drip.

Pad applicators by EZ Paintr.

7" x 4" exterior painting pad

6" x 4" interior Paint 'n Trim

Mini painting pad

Mini trimmer pad

Mini pad and tray set

Tip 'n Dip paint tray holds ½ gallon.

SPECIAL VARIETIES

The most popular pads are the 7" x 3½" or 7" x 4" size, but there are also 5", 9", and 11" widths. There are special pads for painting exteriors and applying stain, and special interior models with beveled foam pads for painting close to cabinets, moldings, and corners. Some painters prefer a lambswool pad for stain application. It holds more stain.

There are mini-trimmer pads, 3" x 1", with wheel guides to help make trimming around obstructions fast and easy. There is a paint wand with a 1⅛" x 1¾" pad for trimming, touch-up, and small objects. A special pad is for inside corners.

For use with pads, Padco makes a "paint bucket" which holds up to one gallon of paint and can be hung on a ladder. EZ Paintr makes a "Tip 'n' Dip" paint tray which holds ½ gallon. It can be hung on a ladder and also be used for rollers.

Pad Painter system from Tip Top includes everything needed for pad painting. Dispenser wheel, which snaps on to tray, applies paint to entire pad surface, minimizing mess, spatter, drip. Besides tray, wheel and 7" pad, 4" trimmer edger and 1" sash painter are included.

A SPECIAL TECHNIQUE

A pad can't be handled like a brush or a roller. If you douse it in a pan of paint and then try to use it, it's sure to drip. To avoid dripping, dip only the upper half of the pad, and slightly angle the pad to the wall as you spread the paint in long, smooth strokes. Go over an area only once. Don't use a scrubbing motion or you'll drip.

EZ Paintr, a leading manufacturer, has pads with a switch action handle. The handle locks for painting overhead areas and for use with oil paints. Locked, the pad stays flat on the surface to the end of each stroke. Unlocked, for use with latex, it becomes more flexible. It lifts up off the surface at the end of each stroke. EZ Paintr's advertising slogan is, "Stroke of Genius."

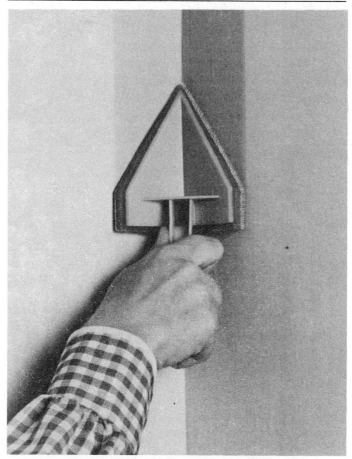

You can use Padco's corner paint pad anywhere wall meets wall or wall meets ceiling, door, or window frame. It paints inside corners faster and more neatly than any other tool.

35. WALLCOVERING TOOLS

The Chinese invented paper making. This Oriental art was introduced into Europe about the time Columbus was setting sail for the New World, and the canny Europeans developed wallpaper soon after. Up until that time the accepted coverings for walls were tapestry, painted cloth, leather, and wood paneling. Wallpaper imitated these materials—at greatly reduced cost.

In the United States, there is record that wallpaper was manufactured in 1739 by Plunket Fleeson of Philadelphia. He used wooden blocks to stamp the design on sheets of paper, and filled in the colors by brush. At that time, Fleeson advertised in the *Philadelphia Gazette* the sale of "Bedticks, choice live geese feathers, blankets, as well as paper hangings."

Today, plastics have joined paper as a means for decorating interior surfaces and the term wallcoverings is used to include them.

Space saving is a feature of this Padco wallcoverings tool kit for pre-pasted and contact wallcoverings. Fitted into the handle of a wallcoverings smoother are a razor blade knife, spare blades, plumb line and chalk.

This 1¹/₄″ flat maple roller can be used in two positions. By removing the roller and refastening it to the opposite side of the frame, it's perfect for corners. Hyde.

Trimmer holds a single-edge razor blade, cuts double and single layers of all types and weights of wallcoverings, including vinyl, cloth-backed and waterproofed materials. Hyde.

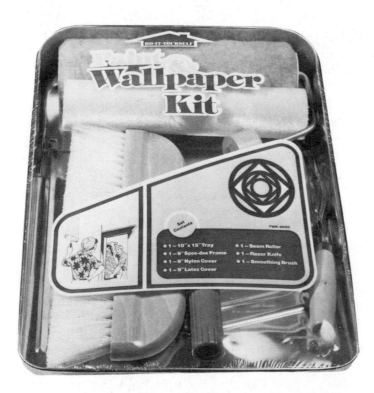

Thomas paint and wallpaper kit includes a roller with a special cover for applying paste, a tray which you can use for either paint or paste, a seam roller, a razor knife, and a smoothing brush.

Popular among professionals, this trimmer has fingertip blade control for instant positioning against the side of a straight edge. Very sharp. Extra blades available.

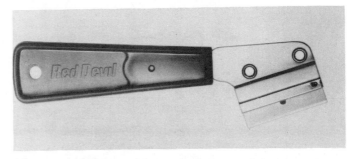

Razor knife is set at a good angle for trimming wall covering. Also does countless other jobs.

Wallpaper shaver holds a 3¼" super-sharp blade at an angle. Head is of die-cast metal; handle is of tubular steel with bright blue plastic grip. Overall length is 11". Hyde.

This wallpaper scraper is especially made for shaving off or stripping old wallpaper that has been softened with a chemical wallpaper remover. Steel 4½" blade has rounded edges.

If you rent a pasting table to make your paper hanging easier, it may be like this one from Hyde. It's 24" wide and 33½" high; equipped with rests for straightedge.

TOOLS OF THE TRADE

The tools needed for hanging wallpaper or wallcoverings are few and simple. You can buy them all in an inexpensive kit, or you can rent what you need.

For successful installation, a good sound surface is required. Loose paper should be removed, by soaking, scraping, or steam, and cracks repaired. Steamers can be rented. Even when paper is sound, if it's over three layers thick, it's recommended that it be removed.

New walls require a coat of sizing. This not only assures good adherence of paper, but makes it easier to remove the paper in the future. If you don't size unpainted plasterboard (a coat of oil-based paint is recommended), paper will be impossible to remove in the future. Bare plaster is usually sealed with glue size. The sizing seals in stains and keeps the plaster from drying water out of the paste too rapidly.

Worktable. You can rent a professional-type table, or improvise one for yourself. You need a surface at least 2' wide and 6' or 8' long. You can make it by placing two or three boards or a piece of plywood on sawhorses or on a pair of card tables. Most lumberyards will sell you half a sheet of 4' x 8' plywood, and this will give you an excellent 2' x 8' working surface.

Straightedge. There are professional straightedges, 6' or 7' long, of magnesium or brass-bound aluminum. You can make your own by cutting a 4" strip from a 4' x 8' panel of ¼" plywood.

Stepladder. You will need at least one 5' ladder. For ceiling work, you will want a scaffold of planks, and a second ladder comes in handy for easy support, but you can improvise with a table for a second support.

Bucket. This is to hold paste. Tie a string across its top for use in scraping off excess paste. You can also use it to rest your brush.

Paste brush. Typically, these are 6" wide. Synthetic bristles are easier to keep clean. Instead of a brush, a paint roller can be used for applying paste. A pad, like that used for painting, may also be used.

Smoothing brush. The typical brush is 12" long and has two rows of bristles. A brush for hanging vinyl wallcoverings has shorter, stiffer bristles than one for paperhanging.

Seam rollers. To get good adhesion at seams, these are invaluable, if not indispensable. A 1" flat roller is standard.

Shears. You want one with a good long cut, and a 12" shear is best for the purpose.

Knives. A razor-type knife with replaceable blades does a good job, but sometimes tears paper. Wheel cutters are better. Ones with a 1/2" to 2" blade are especially good around windows and baseboards. The blade edge may be smooth or V-toothed.

Water box. This is used for wetting prepasted wallcoverings and is usually of plastic-coated cardboard.

Manufacturers. Tools for hanging wallpaper and wallcoverings are made by Red Devil, Warner, Hyde.

The success of the whole job depends on having the first strip straight. This goes for the walls as well as the ceiling. Self-chalking line by Hyde is also a plumb bob.

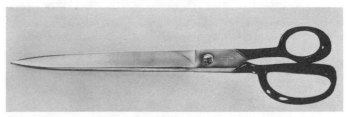

The best shears for cutting paper carry the name "I.P. Hyde," and their full length is 12", with a 6 1/2" length of cut.

A bristle brush is usually used for smoothing wallcoverings. This smoother, though, is of a sponge-like plastic foam. It won't mark even delicate foils and flocks. Padco.

36.
TOOLS FOR CERAMIC TILE

Eighteenth century French tiling equipment

Banner of the "Tilers of Paris"

Tile has been used for centuries. It was among the first building materials mankind developed. It is simply clay, fired at high temperature to make it waterproof, fireproof, and durable. Until recently, tile was installed almost exclusively with mortar, and that required skill. Now it can be installed with easy-to-use mastic adhesives and it is a do-it-yourself operation.

The special tools required are few. The only expensive one is a tile cutter, and it can be rented where you buy tile. For small jobs, you can get along without it and trim tile with a heavy-duty glass cutter and nippers. The tile cutter is for larger tiles, $4^1/_4''$ x $4^1/_4''$. Small mosaic tiles are cut with nippers.

Trowels. The typical trowel for the application of adhesive is $10^1/_2''$ x $4^1/_2''$ and has U-shaped notches $3/_{16}''$ x $3/_{16}''$ on $5/_8''$ centers. But follow the recommendations of the adhesive manufacturer as to the kind of trowel and its notching. He may recommend a V-notched type. If installing quarry tile, an unglazed floor variety, and using a cement mortar, you may want a trowel with $^1/_4''$ notches, spaced $^1/_4''$ apart, with teeth $^3/_8''$ high. The best trowels are of tempered spring steel. Less expensive trowels are of cold rolled steel.

Tile cutters. An ordinary glass cutter can be used for cutting tile, but it is difficult and the cutter won't last long. Special heavy-duty cutters designed specifically for tile are better. Red Devil makes a tile cutter that looks like a pair of pliers. The lower jaw accepts a 3-wheel carbon-steel turret head or a $^1/_2''$ carbide wheel. The wheel does the scoring. The upper jaw has a breaker bar to complete the cut. Turret heads and carbide wheels are replaceable.

Professional ceramic tile cutters work on the same principle as the pliers, but are designed to take much of the muscle out of the operation. As with the pliers, the cutting turret has three carbon-steel wheels, which can be replaced with a $^1/_2''$ carbide wheel for extra-long life.

For cutting curves and other shapes, you can use a rod saw. The rod has thousands of super-sharp tungsten-carbide cutting edges. It cuts in any direction. They come in sizes to fit 10" or 12" hacksaw frames.

Tile nippers. Nippers, made especially for gnawing and for cutting 1" x 1" mosaics, have handle stops that prevent the jaws from biting completely together. A return spring opens the jaws. Typical nippers are 8" with $^1/_2''$ or $^5/_8''$ offset jaws. Jaws may be of plain steel, but carbide-tipped are recommended.

Rub bricks. To smooth and dress tile (also marble, granite, and concrete), there are tile setter's rub bricks. Made of silicon carbide, often 6" x 2" x 1", they come in a variety of grits from fine to coarse.

Rubber-surface trowel. This is the tool to use for forcing grout into the spaces between tiles. A good grout float is of nonporous hard synthetic rubber mounted on aluminum, with a wood handle. It not only forces material deep into the tile joints, but can be used to squeegee away excess material.

Manufacturers. When you think of tools for installing ceramic tile, Goldblatt and Red Devil are two good names to remember.

The simplest tile cutter is essentially a heavy-duty glass cutter. A wheel scores the cutting line; wheel unit is replaceable. Exclusive handle design is said to produce considerably more pressure than regular models.

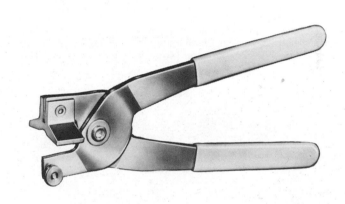

A handy tile cutter. You score the tile with wheel on the lower jaw; upper jaw has breaker bar for crisp cuts. Accommodates a 3-wheel carbon steel turret head or accessory $^1/_2''$ carbide wheel for extra durability. Red Devil.

Diamalloy tile nippers have durable carbide cutters. Jaws are offset and handle stops prevent jaws from meeting. Yellow plastic handles have springs between them. Diamond.

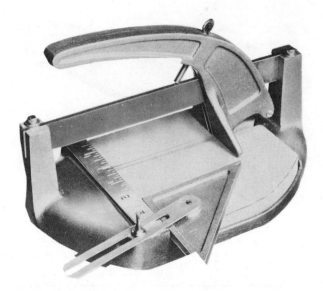

Tile cutting machine of cast aluminum and steel features a turret head cutter with three wheels. For longer life, it can be replaced with a 1/2" carbide wheel. Junior model, shown here, takes tile up to 6" x 6". There's a "Senior Cutter" for all sizes. Red Devil.

Cutter with 6-wheel turret scores and breaks wall tile, bull nose, shoe base, thin vitreous and quarry tile in one operation without moving tile. Works on tile up to 7/8" thick. Goldblatt.

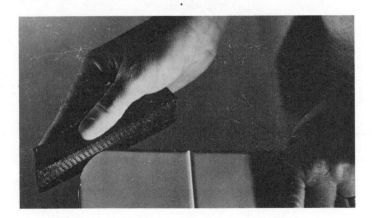

Non-clogging tough edges on Surform pocket plane do a good job of smoothing cut tile. Overall size, 1⅝" x 5½". Stanley.

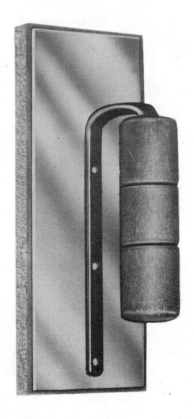

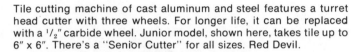

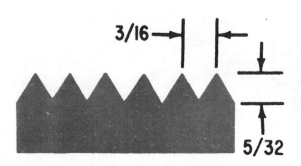

For spreading ceramic tile adhesive, a 5/32" notched trowel is a typical recommendation. Red Devil and others make "throw away" spreaders for one-time use.

Ceramic tile grouting float forces grout into tile joints and squeegees off excess. Especially made for the do-it-yourself tile setter. It's 3" wide, 7½" long and ⅜" thick. Easco.

Trimming dry tiles into hexagonal shape before glazing and firing in eighteenth century France. *At right:* Laying tile in a new palace.

37.
FLOOR COVERING TOOLS

ALLEN'S CARPET FASTENER.   WINTER'S CARPET STRETCHER.

Resilent tile and sheet vinyl are relatively new to the scene. The installation of any or all of them is simple and requires only a few tools not found in a standard collection.

RESILIENT FLOORS

They're new, but not so new that changes haven't been made. Linoleum, the original sheet material, is no longer around. It used to break; especially when cold. Vinyl sheet, which has taken its place, can take all kinds of bending and twisting without damage. Asphalt tile is also gone, replaced by vinyl asbestos. Sizes are different too. No more 9" x $\frac{3}{4}$" tiles. They are 12" x 13" now. And there are many new adhesives and application aids. You have to be an engineer to understand them all. One is a solvent to weld sheets together at seams.

Tile and sheet material, applied with an adhesive, call for a brush, roller, or notched trowel. You will also need a chalk line, rule, knife, 6' straightedge, scriber, heavy shears, and a pry bar—the last, for prying off moldings. Two kinds of knives are handy. One is the hooked linoleum knife, or banana knife as it's called in the trade. It's good for sheet materials, but you may find a straight-blade utility knife better for scoring or cutting tiles. A propane torch is useful in softening vinyl asbestos tile as an aid in cutting.

For one-time use, brush, roller, or trowel can be the throw-away kind. They offer pleasurable relief from the clean-up chore. You can buy an installation kit that includes a linoleum knife, adhesive spreader, scratch awl for scribing, and chalk line with chalk.

Another tool you may find useful is a three-corner file for notching. It's like the file you would use for sharpening a saw. Pros use a special notching tool. They also use an "underscriber." It will scribe sheet material with another sheet lapped on top of it.

A heavy roller, 100 pounds or more, is useful in gaining adhesion between resilient flooring and the subsurface. You can get away with using a rolling pin, but a heavy roller is better. You may be able to borrow or rent one where you buy your tile. A lawn roller is awkward and clumsy to use, but you may want to try it.

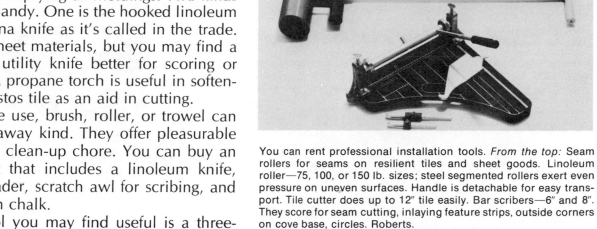

You can rent professional installation tools. *From the top:* Seam rollers for seams on resilient tiles and sheet goods. Linoleum roller—75, 100, or 150 lb. sizes; steel segmented rollers exert even pressure on uneven surfaces. Handle is detachable for easy transport. Tile cutter does up to 12" tile easily. Bar scribers—6" and 8". They score for seam cutting, inlaying feature strips, outside corners on cove base, circles. Roberts.

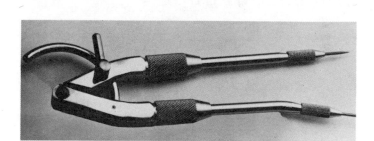

These dividers feature a bent tracing leg for straight or pattern scribing. They use a standard replaceable pin and Esterbrook pen for marking rotovinyls.

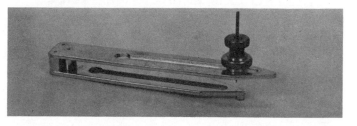

Recess scribing tool for underscribing seams and certain types of metal edgings. Adjusts to thickness of material. Uses same kind of pin as dividers.

Roberts straightedges for precision marking. *At left:* Straightedge that adjusts from 19³/₄" to 36¹/₂" to fit almost any doorway. *From top:* Angled edge model comes in 75" and 48" lengths, each 2⁷/₈" wide. Aluminum straightedge is 2" wide, comes in two lengths: 36" and 75". Blue clock-spring steel unit is flexible, for use in tight places, like closets and doorways. T-square is 75" long, 2¹/₂" wide, with a 14" cross arm.

If the area is too wide for an ordinary pair of dividers, you can use the Armstrong steel scribing tool. It's 18" long and accurately scribes any width from 2" to 16".

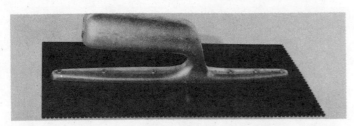

Notched steel trowel has angled front edge for easy spreading along walls and fixtures. Notches are $^1/_{16}''$ deep and $^1/_{16}''$ wide, spaced $^3/_{32}''$ on one side and end. On other side they are $^1/_{32}''$ deep, $^1/_{16}''$ wide, spaced $^5/_{64}''$. Armstrong.

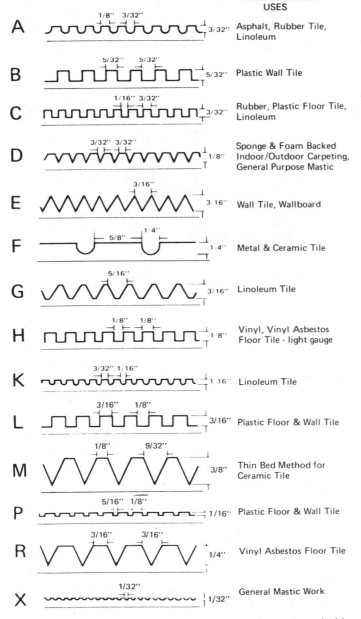

		RECOMMENDED USES
A	1/8'' 3/32'' 3/32''	Asphalt, Rubber Tile, Linoleum
B	5/32'' 5/32'' 5/32''	Plastic Wall Tile
C	1/16'' 3/32'' 3/32''	Rubber, Plastic Floor Tile, Linoleum
D	3/32'' 3/32'' 1/8''	Sponge & Foam Backed Indoor/Outdoor Carpeting, General Purpose Mastic
E	3/16'' 3/16''	Wall Tile, Wallboard
F	5/8'' 1/4'' 1/4''	Metal & Ceramic Tile
G	5/16'' 3/16''	Linoleum Tile
H	1/8'' 1/8'' 1/8''	Vinyl, Vinyl Asbestos Floor Tile - light gauge
K	3/32'' 1/16'' 1/16''	Linoleum Tile
L	3/16'' 1/8'' 3/16''	Plastic Floor & Wall Tile
M	1/8'' 9/32'' 3/8''	Thin Bed Method for Ceramic Tile
P	5/16'' 1/8'' 1/16''	Plastic Floor & Wall Tile
R	3/16'' 3/16'' 1/4''	Vinyl Asbestos Floor Tile
X	1/32'' 1/32''	General Mastic Work

For proper spread and adhesion, it's important to have a trowel with the right tooth shape, size and spacing. Shown are the most common configurations. In general, it's best to follow the recommendations given on the adhesive can.

Floor tile cutter's dimensions are $17^1/_2'' \times 11^5/_8'' \times 7^1/_2''$. It will cut all resilient floor tile and even a 12'' wide sheet of aluminum, or brass up to .030'' thick. Powerful leverage action. Ruled squaring edge for exact cutting. J.M.J. Industries.

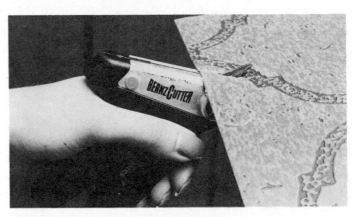

BernzCutter spring-action tool cuts everything from asbestos to galvanized metal, and is useful for making special tile cutouts.

Edge trimmer to trim the factory edge of non-pattern sheet materials. It slides on the subfloor so material doesn't have to be lifted for cutting. Armstrong.

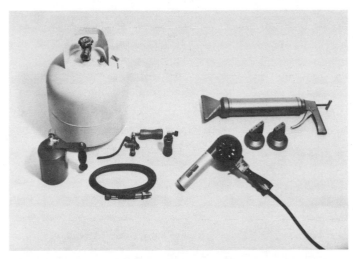

Spot nailer and mallet for driving staples into Masonite type underlayment. You can staple as fast as you can swing the mallet. Holds up to 200 chisel-pointed $7/8''$ staples. Armstrong.

Sometimes heat helps. For small jobs, you can use a propane torch. For bigger jobs, you may want to use professional equipment. Small dark cylinder at left can be refilled by means of hose from 20 lb. capacity storage cylinder. Above hose is a trigger valve, which has a pilot flame to save fuel and eliminate need to re-light frequently. Shown with it are tips that spread heat quickly. Device that looks like a hairdryer is a heat gun. It delivers the ideal heat (550°-750°) for working all kinds of resilient floor coverings and plastic laminates. Above it is adhesive applicator gun with nozzles, an easy way to apply cove base to wall surfaces. Roberts.

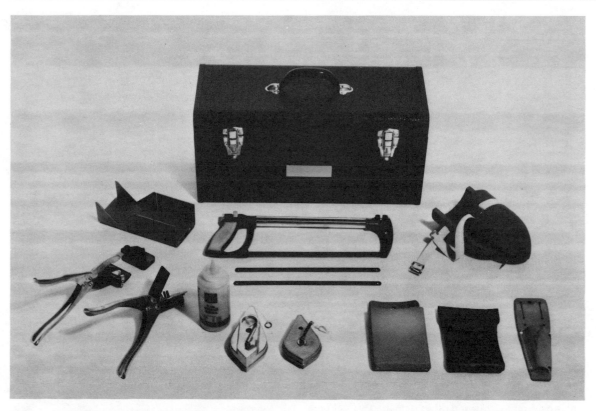

Professional installer's tool box is black crackle metal with a lift-out tray and measures 20" or 24". **Installer's tools** in top-bottom order *from left:* Miter box for accurate left or right 45° angles. Miter handle and dies for mitering, notching, trimming and nibbling metals, asphalt tile, or plastic laminates. Just slip in the die, squeeze the handle and you've made a clean and accurate cut. Hacksaw with 12" blades. Chalk wheels and chalk. Knee pads of foam rubber with adjustable strap. Three tool pouches for carrying knives and other small tools. All by Roberts.

CARPETS

Two special tools are useful in laying carpeting. One is an offset cutter. It's a special knife for trimming near a wall. It has an angled handle and built-in guide. The other is a kicker. It is used to stretch carpeting at the edges where it's impossible to exert much pull by hand. It can usually be rented where you buy the carpet.

Manufacturers. Armstrong, GAF, and other flooring makers offer installation tools, adhesives, accessories, and allied products.

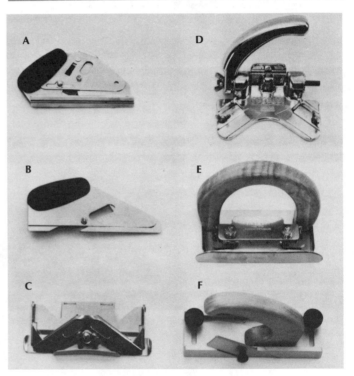

Trimmers and cutters by Roberts. A. Cutter for loop pile carpets. B. Cutter for cushion-back carpets. C. Device to convert conventional carpet trimmer to cushion-back trimmer. D. Wall trimmer that cuts into corners and hard-to-get-at places. E. Wall trimmer for conventional carpets. F. Double cutter for seaming and repairing sheet goods and cushion-back carpets.

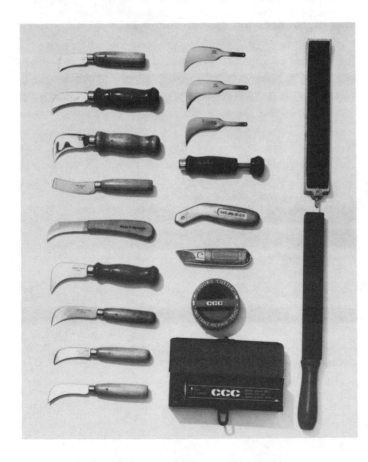

Knives, stones, carpet repair tools. There's a knife for every use and to suit every taste. Most have $2^{1}/_{2}$" or 3" blades and are easy to stone-sharpen. Round device marked "CCC" is a "Cookie Cutter." It's for repairing cigarette burns and other damaged carpet areas up to 3" in diameter. Below it is case containing a "CCC instant repair tool" which cuts circles up to 12" in carpet for making virtually invisible repairs. At right is stone and holder, for sharpening knives and shears. Holder protects stone without interfering with sharpening. Roberts.

Wiss rug shears for cutting hooked and candlewick rugs. Hot drop-forged, nickel-plated blades; offset black handles. Double sharp points. Length $7^{1}/_{2}$"; cut $2^{7}/_{8}$".

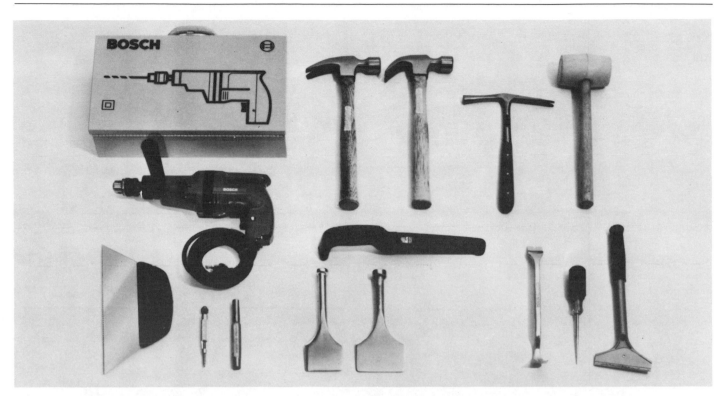

From a carpet installer's tool box, in top-bottom order *from left:* A Bosch $^3/_8$" hammer drill for anchoring tackless strip and metal moldings in concrete, terrazo and similar hard floors. A fan-shaped carpet spreader for tucking carpet over gripper used in power stretching. Ankorite tool for tacking down carpet edges without leaving tack marks. Hexagonal magnetic nail set for starting and driving nails in hard-to-reach places. Three hammers designed specifically for the carpet installer. Under the hammers, a "Gold Touch" nail driving bar for nailing under radiators, toe-spaces, overhangs and next to glass doors or easily damaged structures. Stair tools with blades to drive carpet into crotch on stair installation, $1^3/_4$" and $3^1/_2$" wide. White rubber mallet for installing metal moldings without leaving marks. Base molding lifter. Awl with cushion-grip. Floor/wall scraper with 4" angled replaceable blade. Roberts.

Electric cutters for every type of carpet or padding. Roberts.

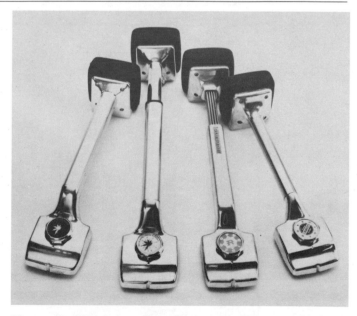

It's usually difficult to pull a carpet up snugly to a wall. With a kicker, you engage teeth of head in carpet edge and butt padded end with your knee. Dial shows how deep teeth are penetrating into carpet. Most kickers are about 17" long, but some extend a few inches more. Roberts.

38.
TOOLS FOR PLASTERBOARD

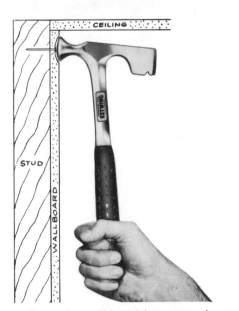

Estwing hammer, of one-piece solid steel, has crowned scored face to make nailing easy and prevent damage to wallboard. Angled blade provides good ceiling clearance. Available from Goldblatt.

Plasterboard, commonly known as gypsum wallboard, has been in use since 1915, but it didn't take off until the housing boom following World War II. It took wall finishing out of the hands of professionals and made it an operation an amateur could tackle.

The right tools are half the battle. Some are standard shop tools—like a utility knife for scoring panels and cutting them apart after they have been folded to break their core.

A saw is used only for irregular cuts, or where a scorebreak is impossible. A coarse-toothed saw, like one used for pruning, is best for long cuts, a pointed utility or keyhole saw for others.

A T-square is essential for quick, accurate scoring. A knife will dig into one made of wood. If you don't want to buy one, you can improvise one by using aluminum bar stock, $1/4''$ x $1''$ x $6'$. The top of the T should be approximately $22^1/_2''$. Rivet the stem to the top so that it extends exactly $47^7/_8''$.

Panels are heavy and difficult to lift, when flat against the wall, without a foot lift. You can improvise one for jacking up a panel by wiring a flat chisel or a tire iron to a pipe nipple. The nipple acts as a fulcrum. You can also use a brick hammer as a "rocker arm" in raising a panel.

You can get by with an ordinary hammer, but a drywall hammer is better. It has a crown face that dimples nails, setting them just below the surface for covering with compound. Its flat end can be used for prying panels into place, and it has a slot for pulling out misdirected nails.

You need a scaffold for installing ceiling panels. With a scaffold at just the right height, you can use your head as a "third hand" to help support a ceiling panel while it is being nailed. Cleats, tacked to sidewalls, can also assist.

Good taping knives are indispensable. Two good ones to have are a 5" flexible taping knife, and a 10" taping knife.

Without a special tool that's designed especially for the purpose, you'll find it almost impossible to get a smooth finish on both sides of a taped inside corner. When you get one side smooth, you're apt to mess it while doing the other side. The secret is to finish one side at a time and let it dry, before doing the other side. Having the right tool, however, makes it all much more convenient.

When joint work isn't perfect, texture, stipple, or sand float paints can hide faults.

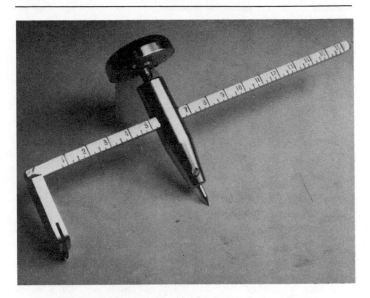

Wal-Board circle cutter cuts circles up to 32" in diameter. It has a cast alumimum body and steel shaft. Heat-treated cutter wheel and center pin remain sharp indefinitely.

This tool punches holes for electric outlets quickly and cleanly in ³/₈" and ¹/₂" wallboard. No patchwork necessary. Far better than sawing holes by hand. Made of cadmium-plated steel. Goldblatt.

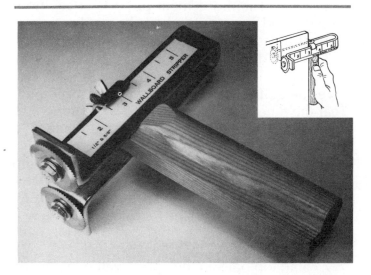

For narrow hard-to-make cuts, tool has toothed wheels that cut both sides of a panel simultaneously. Adjusts to any size 4¹/₂" or smaller. The piece can be snapped off neatly with no paper tearing. Wal-Board.

Top: This 15" drywall saw has only five teeth per inch, and an exceptionally stiff blade. It's so stiff you can punch it through plasterboard by hitting the handle with the palm of your hand. *Bottom:* The original drywall saw. Its 6" blade doesn't readily bend or flex and it will penetrate the thickest wallboard. Sharp point really digs in. Wal-Board.

Drywall screwdriver is especially engineered for fast, easy fastening of wallboard, acoustical tile, and other drywall materials. It drives screws flush, or dimple sinks them with uniformity without marring panels. Reversible $1/4$ hp motor.

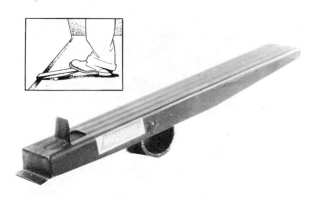

Dolly for lifting panels into place. Weighted nose keeps it in ready position. Roller-wheel moves it forward as pressure is applied to raised panel. Vertical lip lets you guide it into place with your toe.

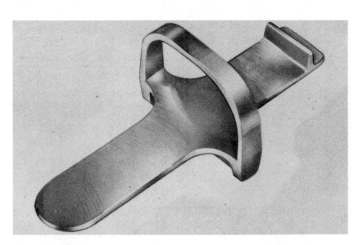

This Goldblatt tool for drywall lifting is of one-piece aluminum casting. Drop it, kick it, or throw it, and it always lands right side up, ready to use.

"TRADE SECRETS" OF A PROFESSIONAL PLASTERBOARD APPLICATOR

1. Reduce the number of joints to an absolute minimum by using the largest possible panel size—you can get them up to 14" long. Where corners are tight, don't cut an unwieldy panel. Score it on its back and break the core. Then fold it for easier maneuvering into place. Plan the fold line to fall on a stud.

2. Put end joints under windows. Light is poorest here, and joints easiest to hide. Put joints above doors, but never at door corners. Continuous door slamming will crack open corner joints.

3. Use wood the same thickness as plasterboard for a narrow strip under register, or wherever plasterboard would have no backing. Also use wood for casing untrimmed wall openings. Taped, primed, and painted, wood can't be told from plasterboard.

4. Nail metal beading on all outside corners, around uncased openings, on columns and beam edges. Metal reinforcement protects edges from damage and is concealed by the application of cement, just as if it were paper tape.

5. If you don't have a tape dispenser, unwind an entire roll of tape, let it drape across floor. It saves time. It is easier than to unroll it as you go. Tear the tape at the end of a run by pinning it to the panel with a knife and using the blade as a cutting edge.

6. Never depend on nails to draw panels up snug to framing. Push the panel against the framing as each nail is driven. If the panel doesn't make firm contact with the framing, vibration will work nails loose. Use threaded drywall nails only.

7. Start top nails in the upper wall panel while it is resting on the floor, then raise the panel and drive them home. Don't nail closer than 8" from the top. "Floating joint" helps prevent cracks.

8. Avoid a corner joint by scoring the back of the panel, breaking the core, and then bending the panel, with the unbroken face paper around the corner.

9. Stagger joints so they don't fall on adjoining panels.

10. Don't cut openings for outlets or ducts before erecting a panel. Instead, indicate their location on adjoining panels, use marks as a guide for punching through to the center of the opening, sawing out to sides and around.

11. On walls, erect upper panels first and work down.

12. Tape blisters are caused by not enough adhesive. Open them up to let air out, then reseal. No tape should be visible after final finishing coat.

13. Put all plasterboard up with minimum nailing, go back and complete nailing afterwards. It's faster.

14. Store panels flat to avoid warping, but stand them on edge for easy cutting.

15. Where fit is tight, trim edge at an angle, undercutting the panel back. Undercut will help lock in joint cement.

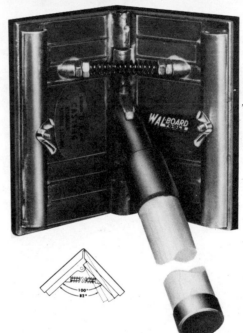

Try to keep sanding to a minimum, but when you must, these hand sanders will help. *Top:* Cast aluminum sander, with a base plate measuring 3¹/₄″ x 9¹/₄″. *Bottom:* Universal angle sander has a coil spring that automatically adjusts for corners and angles over or under 90°.

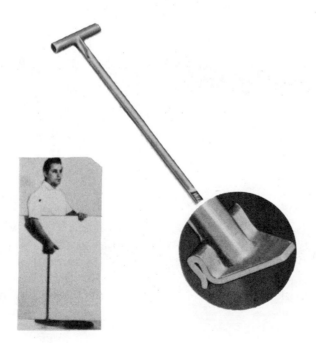

A panel of plasterboard is too wide to get your arm around, but with this 26″ tool, made of tubular steel, you can handle the big sheets easily and safely. Wal-Board.

Tool for corner compounding and taping features a 4″ wide flexible one-piece stainless steel blade that will not tear tape. It has a 103° angle to flex tightly into all corners. Lacquered wood handle has pitch to provide knuckle room.

Drywall joint knife comes with tempered steel blades 8", 10", or 12" wide. Paintbrush-style handle is for maximum comfort. Also available—blade widths to 24" and blades of stainless steel.

Flexible lightweight trowel with aluminum mounting has a curved blade, ideal for finishing drywall joints. Comes in 11" x 4¹/₂" and 14" x 4¹/₂" sizes. Marshalltown.

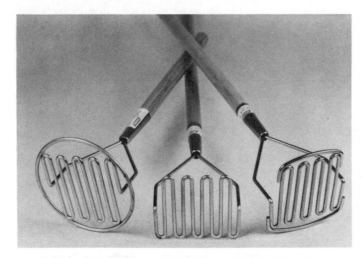

Potato-masher mud mixers are made of heavy gauge wire, cad-plated so they won't rust. Square heads measure 5", and round ones about 7". Over-all length varies from about 2 to 3 feet.

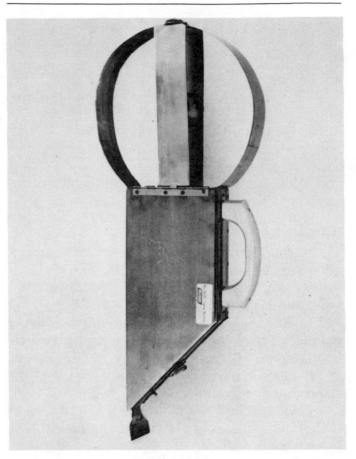

In the trade, adhesive compound for plasterboard tape is known as "mud." Banjo stainless steel taping machine holds a 500' roll of tape; feed controls amount of mud as tape is run out. Saw-tooth cut-off blade cuts tape. 25¹/₂" long x 10" high.

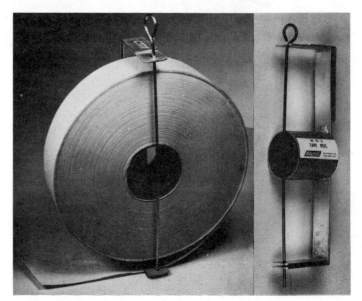

Tape reel is a great timesaver; holds a 500' roll. Tapes thread through lower slot for quick unrolling and tear-off. Handy belt clip. Length is 10¹/₄". Wal-Board.

Each leg of workbench adjusts separately at two-inch intervals from 18″ to 32″. Aluminum with 9$\frac{1}{2}$″ x 48″ Masonite top. Entire trestle folds up compactly and locks shut. Wal-Board.

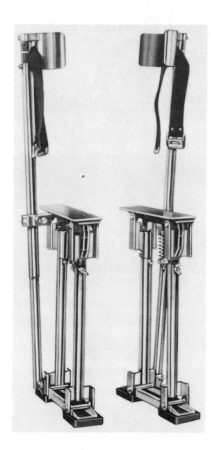

Walking scaffolds are a favorite of professional installers. Made of aluminum, with rubber soles that help prevent slipping. Heights are adjustable every two inches by means of a squeeze tab. Shoes are fastened with bolt mechanism or straps. Wal-Board.

39.
TOOLS FOR GLASS

Egyptians were glazing beads around 4000 B.C. They were making small solid-glass objects about 2500 B.C., and glass vessels around 1500 B.C. The technique of blowing glass, however, wasn't developed until nearly the beginning of the Christian era. The Syrians probably did it.

THE FIRST WINDOWS

Glass was not used for windows until the 12th Century. Before then, windows were merely openings in the wall. If the weather was bad, you boarded up the opening. The first window glass was stained glass, used in churches to keep out the hot sun. Later, mirrors were made by backing glass with shiny tin.

Glass was difficult to cut, and for centuries that restricted its use. It could be cut with a diamond, but that was expensive. Some tried to cut it by drawing a heated rod along the line of the desired cut, and then snapping the glass apart. It produced shark's teeth. The breakthrough came in the mid-1800s.

In 1868, O. M. Pike of Leveritt, Massachusetts, found he could use a beveled steel rod under pressure, instead of a diamond, in scoring glass. By revolving the glass as he scored, it worked even better, but for that he needed a machine. So Pike went to a machine shop to have one made. An employee in the shop, Samuel Monce, wondered why a revolving wheel wouldn't work better than a rod. Six months after Pike patented his "Magic Diamond" rod cutter, Monce patented his "Excelsior" wheel cutter. Pike never got anywhere. Monce's company is now the Fletcher-Terry Company, the leader in the field.

CUTTING GLASS

Some people follow all the rules, but still can't cut glass. Part of the problem is they don't understand what a glass cutter should do. Actually, of course, it doesn't cut the glass. But it shouldn't scratch the glass or gouge a furrow either. What it should do is make a shallow crack or fissure in the glass. That's why it's important when scoring to make only a single pass. If you go over the score line a second time, you destroy the crack and create an irregular furrow filled with glass chips and dust.

When you score glass, it should appear as only a clean, barely perceptible line. If you bear down too hard, you will get a gritty score line—a gouge instead of a fissure.

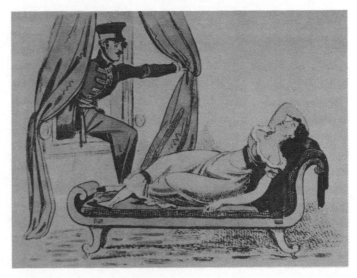

Windows were just openings.

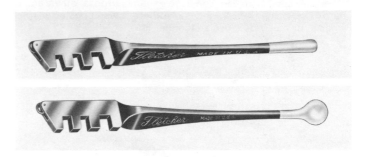

General purpose glass cutter comes with either a straight or ball end, and individual pouch. Best for general cutting of domestic window glass, single and double strength. The tip is gold. Fletcher.

Turret cutter has six wheels. By loosening a small screw and slightly turning the turret, a new wheel is brought into cutting position. Turret is replaceable. Handle is of wood. Red Devil.

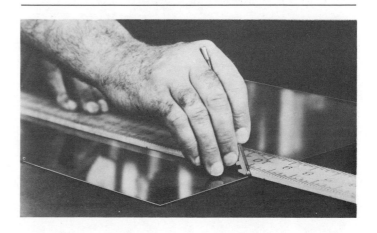

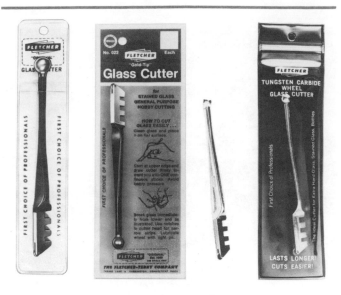

Read the information on the package in selecting a glass cutter to meet your specific needs. Some are general purpose, others are for hard and stained glass, and still others have tungsten carbide wheels for heavy-duty use and longer life.

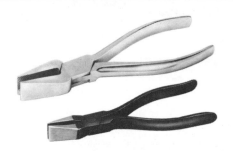

Glass pliers for breaking out narrow strips. *Top:* 8″ nipping pliers have box joint and are chrome plated. Flaring serrated jaws are ⁷/₈″ wide. *Bottom:* 6″ nipping pliers with wide jaw. Fletcher.

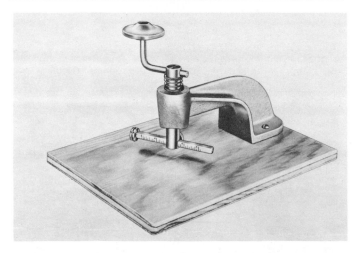

Small lens cutter. Adjust the graduated rod to cut circles from ¹/₂″ diameter to 5″ diameter. Turret head contains three wheels. A slight turn of a screw brings a new wheel into position.

A fast, uniform speed is important. You should cut at a minimum rate of 12 inches per second. Slower than that won't produce enough of a fissure, and varying speed will make a fissure of uneven depth. The cutting wheel must roll freely. Anything that makes it skid will mean an interrupted fissure. It also hurts the cutter. Then you have to throw it away and get a new one, because if a wheel is chipped it will cause skidding.

To make sure the wheel turns freely, it must be lubricated, cleaned, and must not lean sideways. If you lean it sideways, it will rub against the sides of the cutter slot and skid. Lean the top of the cutter about 5° in the direction of the cut. Kerosene can be used in lubricating, but a mixture of half kerosene and half very light oil is better. Turpentine should never be used.

Often, cutting failure is due to glass that is not clean. It must be free of film, gum or dirt.

In making a score line, start about ¹/₈″ from the edge and run off the edge of the sheet at the end of the score. This is where the "break-out" or deepening of the fissure into a full fracture is made. Breaking is started by bending the glass at the end of the score line. A bend of only 2°–3° is needed. Once you start the break-out fracture, it will propagate itself along the entire score line. With thick glass, you can help start the break-out by tapping the underside of the score line about 1″ from its end.

A score line starts to heal as soon as it has been made, so complete the break immediately after scoring. If you wait, the cut will get "cold." If you make a bad score, turn the glass over and score it on the opposite side exactly above the old score. If you go over the same score line twice, it not only ruins your wheel, but makes the glass almost impossible to break clean.

Always wear gloves when handling glass, when cleaning or wiping it, especially when breaking out a score.

By adjusting the graduated measuring bar, you can cut circles from 3″ to 23″ in radius. All metal, nickel-plated, with heavy base. Comes with three extra refills. Accessory extension bar cuts circles up to 72″ in diameter. Acme.

Spear point, tungsten-carbide-tipped, will make holes in sheets, plate, mirrors, bottles, and in many glass-like materials. Comes in $1/8″$, $3/16″$, $1/4″$, $5/16″$, $3/8″$, and $1/2″$ diameters. Brookstone.

Glazer's chisel has a tough plastic handle. Blade and shank, forged in one piece, meet shank of steel cap. Blade is 2″ x 3¼″.

ANATOMY OF A GLASS CUTTER

The essential parts are a wheel and a body. The body usually consists of a notched cutter head and a stem. The notches in the cutter head are for engaging and breaking off narrow strips. The stem may be plain-end or ball-end. The ball-end is used in tapping a score to start a break-out. Some find the straight stem cutter easier to use. A ball can interfere with the proper holding position.

A few cutters have wood handles. Some have slotted heads to accommodate refills. When a cutter wheel becomes worn, you don't throw the tool away. You stick in another wheel. Other cutters have "turret heads." It may include as many as six wheels. By loosening a small screw, and slightly turning the turret, a new wheel is brought into cutting position.

Though most glass cutters look alike, there are important differences that may not show up at a casual glance. "General-purpose" glass cutters are for general use. "Hard glass" cutters are for hard glass, glass with decorative pattern (cathedral glass) and stained glass. Wheels for either type may be steel or tungsten carbide. The latter lasts much longer.

There are cutters especially designed for pattern cutting. They have a smaller wheel ($5/32″$ instead of $7/32″$), making it easier to turn corners and produce clean cuts on curved edges. There is a hobbyist carbide-wheel cutter especially designed for working stained glass.

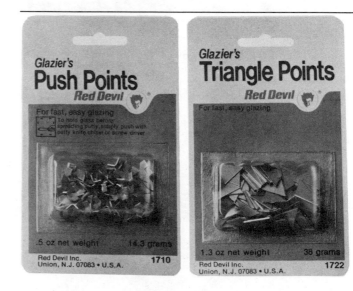

Push points (left) are designed so they can be readily pushed in with putty knife, chisel, or screwdriver. Conventional triangle points (right) like push points are zinc-coated.

Putty Knives With Stiff or Flexible Blades

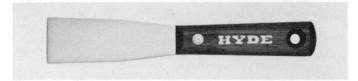

1¼" flexible putty knife with rosewood handle. Also available with stiff or flexible blades in 1½" and 2½" sizes.

2" flexible putty knife with black nylon handle.

1½" low-cost flexible putty knife. Handle is red polypropylene with brass grommets.

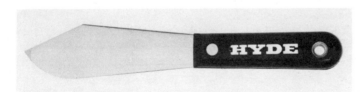

English style putty knife with blade 4⅝" long, 1½" wide at its widest point. One piece of steel from point of blade through nylon handle.

Vacuum-cup glass holder. Its 5" rubber discs are actuated by channel-type vacuum levers. Also available in styles with one or two cups.

Lens cutters are used by many dealers to convert scrap glass into profitable flashlight and clock lenses. A typical cutter will cut circles as small as ½" and as large as 5". It is equipped with a three-wheel turret, which makes wheel-changing simple.

Circle cutters are for cutting circles from 3" to 23" and more.

Gauge cutters cut glass tubes used as gauge glasses.

Bottle cutters are available in kit form, for use in cutting bottles to make lamp bases, terrariums, aquariums, and other containers.

Carbide drills make clean, accurate holes in all kinds of glass and ceramic materials. They're usually recommended for use in a drill press and have a spear point. They're useful in converting jugs and bottles into lamps, making picture frames, glass shelves, mounting mirrors, etc. They come in sizes from ⅛" to ½" diameter, and can be resharpened. Drilling must be done slowly.

Plastic cutting tools are for scribing and breaking acrylic plastic sheets.

PLIERS

Three kinds of pliers assist in glass cutting.

Cut-running pliers have jaws with a half-round pressure point on one jaw. This point of pressure is designed to start the break-out fracture at the edge of the sheet where the score line ends.

Nipping pliers have wide, flat-surface jaws. They are for breaking off narrow strips that have been scored near the edge of the sheet.

Grozing pliers are used for nibbling and shaping a sheet of glass at its edges and corners.

GLASS INSTALLATION

Installing window glass is a big part of working with glass. In a window sash, glass is traditionally held by glaziers' points, which are then covered by putty or glazing compound. Putty is made of mineral clays mixed with linseed oil. Glazing compound is an elastic material that is better than putty for holding glass, and has largely replaced it for this use.

To remove old and crumbling putty or compound it may be necessary to soften it. An electric soldering iron can sometimes be used, but you must be careful to avoid damage to the frame.

Electric putty softeners are inexpensive tools that take the work out of removing putty and eliminate the danger of damage to the sash or glass. Typically, a softener has two heating edges, one about 11″ long and one about 6″ long.

Points. There are triangle points and push points. They may be inserted with putty knife, chisel, or screwdriver. Professionals use automatic point drivers, which drive diamond-shaped points into the hardest wood. In effect, they are a specialized kind of stapling gun. Diamond points are cemented together in columns of 100.

Points are also used for glazing small picture frames and installing mirrors.

MANUFACTURERS

Fletcher-Terry is the big name in cutters in the United States. They date back to 1869. But they are not the oldest in the business. Shaw and Son, an English firm, have been making glass-cutting tools since 1815. They were in business when diamonds were used for cutting. Red Devil is also big in glass-cutting and installing equipment.

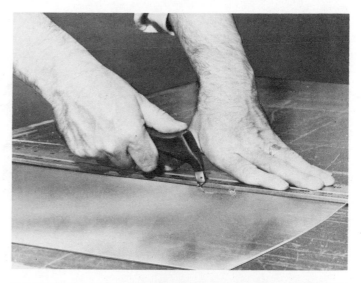

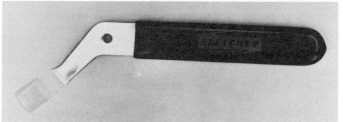

Some plastic is worked like glass. *Top:* Acrylic sheet is scored with special plastic cutter. *Bottom:* Homeowner's double-edge plastic cutters come with protective tip, are good for cutting acrylic, other plastics, soft sheet metals.

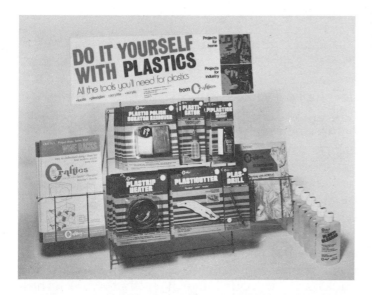

What do you need? Plastic sheets offer an opportunity to the do-it-yourselfer to make such items as trays, plant stands, bookcases, wine racks and photo frames. Many hardware stores offer everything needed—tools, accessories and project sheets.

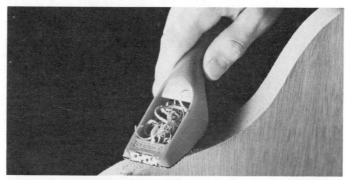

Some plastic can be worked like wood. Stanley Surform Shaver, typically used on wood (as above), here is used to smooth edge of acrylic plastic sheet. This one-handed tool works on pull stroke.

40.
TOOLS FOR PLASTIC LAMINATES

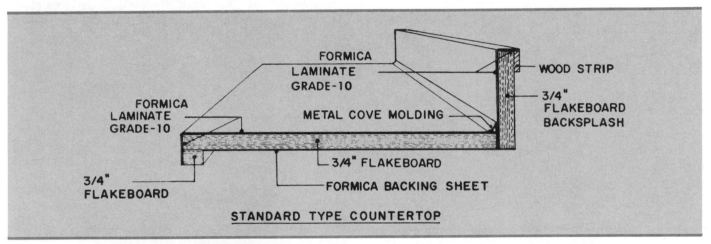

FORMICA LAMINATE GRADE-10

WOOD STRIP

3/4" FLAKEBOARD BACKSPLASH

FORMICA LAMINATE GRADE-10

METAL COVE MOLDING

3/4" FLAKEBOARD

FORMICA BACKING SHEET

3/4" FLAKEBOARD

STANDARD TYPE COUNTERTOP

Tungsten carbide cutter for plastic laminates. With this tool, you score material by drawing tool toward you several times against a straightedge. Like glass, material will break cleanly along scored line as you lift up. Also cuts acrylic plastics, floor tile, even thin sheet material, such as roof flashing. Available from Brookstone.

Removable handle can be placed over cutter tip to protect it when not in use. Similar in method of use to cutter shown above and made by the same manufacturer—Cintride.

Mica is a mineral that separates into thin, tough sheets. Often it is transparent and flexible. Researchers, looking for a substitute "for mica," developed Formica. This plastic laminate was the forerunner of a host of other laminates that are highly chemical-proof and heat-proof, and which are now widely used for covering countertops and furniture.

As far back as 2000 B.C. veneering was widely practiced to economize on more valuable woods. Cheap woods were covered with thin layers of expensive woods. Plastic laminates employ photography and other modern technology to take veneering a giant step forward (or backward, if you look at it that way). They reproduce wood's appearance and texture with remarkable accuracy—in almost indestructable plastic. Most plastic laminates are made from layers of resin-impregnated paper which is bonded, under high temperature and pressure, into rigid sheets. These are usually $\frac{1}{32}$″ or $\frac{1}{16}$″ in thickness. The material should be cut with a fine-toothed saw, on the decorated side. Or it may be cut by first scoring with a special cutter and then snapped apart like glass. Material should be cut slightly oversize to allow for a final trimming.

Laminates are usually cemented in place with contact cement. The edges then can be finished using a file, but a router with a special bit is much the better and faster way. Carbide-tipped trimming bits will finish the edge either flush or on a bevel. Best and most economical for the nonprofessional is a combination flush and bevel trim bit.

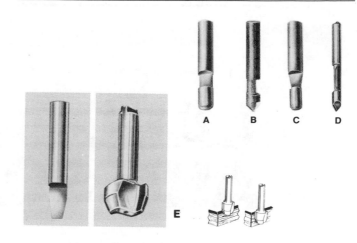

Router bits for laminate trimming. You can trim laminates with almost any router. You must use either carbide-tipped or solid carbide bits. Bit **A** is for flush trimming. Bit **B** gives flush cuts but will also drill through a piece of laminate where a sink or other cutout exists. Bit **C** trims at a $7\frac{1}{2}°$ bevel. Unlike these three solid carbide bits, bit **D** is carbide tipped and has greater length. Not shown is a bit which has a ball bearing at its bottom to act as pilot. It has a cutting edge as long as 1″, which means long life, for it can be raised or lowered to make use of different parts of the cutting edge. Combination bits **E** can be used to make either bevel or flush cuts, depending on the depth at which they are set. The lower part of the bit produces the bevel, the upper a flush cut. These bits must be used with a special laminate trim kit provided as an accessory by the router manufacturer.

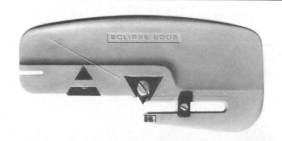

Plastic laminate trimmer incorporates all the necessary features for scribing and trimming plastic laminates to size on straight, round, or contoured profiles. It also produces the parallel strips used for edging. Woodcraft.

Though almost any router can be used for laminate trimming, some are especially designed for the purpose. Rockwell trimmer is compact, double insulated and includes many bits.

Powerful plastic laminate shears can cut any length of high-pressure plastic laminate, including Formica. There is a locking device for safety. Red Devil.

Stanley trimmer has a tilting base that allows it to trim in tight corners (left). Ledge guide attachment (right) is used to trim laminate mounted on $\frac{3}{4}$″ plywood, attached to wall as a backsplash.

41.
LADDERS AND SCAFFOLDS

The cliff dwellings of the ancient Hopi Indians would not have been possible without ladders. Neither would the Tower of Babel. It's obvious that the history of ladders is a long one.

Rungs are no longer tied on with thongs, but essentially ladders have not changed through the years. Modern technology has merely made them lighter, stronger, more rigid, more stable, and more durable. Those, incidentally, are five qualities for which to look when buying a ladder.

STEPLADDERS

Wood ladders are cheaper than aluminum ones, but they are about 40% heavier. Six-foot stepladders of aluminum typically weigh from $10\frac{1}{2}$ to 15 pounds. Wooden ones of that size weigh from 14 to $19\frac{1}{2}$ pounds. Metal 24' extension ladders usually weigh from 24 to 30 pounds. If they are wood, they may weigh in at about 50 pounds. When you continually have to move a ladder, that extra weight makes a big difference.

Heavier weight, however, usually means greater stability. A wooden ladder isn't as likely to blow over in the wind as a metal one.

Wood is usually less durable than metal. If you store a ladder outdoors, weather can affect it, as can rot and termites. A wooden rung or tread can become hazardous almost before you are aware of it. Metal ladders, on the other hand, can be hazardous if you're working around electric wires. Wood ones are hazardous around electric wires only if the wood is wet. If you work regularly around electric wires you may want to choose a fiberglass ladder. These usually have metal treads, but they're generally nonconductive.

As for capacity, stepladders fall into three categories. Type I ladders, meant for industrial use, have a 250-pound rated capacity. Type II models, for commercial use, have a 225-pound rated capacity. Type III ladders, for household use, have a 200-pound capacity.

In all cases, a safety factor is assumed of at least four times a metal ladder's rated capacity, and five times a wooden ladder's rated capacity. That means a 200-pound rated ladder will actually sustain a maximum load of at least 800 pounds if it is metal and 1000 pounds if it is wood. Wood requires a higher safety factor because you can't be as sure of its strength as you can of metal.

Stepladder paint shelves are designed to take a 50-pound load. Obviously, they are not meant for standing.

How much a ladder will hold isn't really a matter of its breaking under your weight. It's more a matter of rigidity, and the sense of security and balance it gives when you're on it. A ladder should be rigid enough to prevent excessive

Two wooden models by Griffith. *Top:* The "36 Heavy Step" is a Type II commercial ladder with 1" thick grooved steps supported by 12 gauge truss rods. This 8' ladder weighs about 24 lbs. *Bottom:* General purpose step stool is 2' high, weighs 7 lbs. Each step is supported and grooved.

"Painter's Stepladder," model 49, comes in 3' to 8' sizes, weighs about 3½ lbs. per foot. Griffith.

Ladders were an important military tool in the fifteenth century. Da Vinci invented a device to overturn them.

swaying. If it isn't, and it twists as you climb it, it not only will give you an uneasy feeling, its rear legs may move in relation to the front ones and "walk." In order to steady the ladder, you then have to reset the legs. This is a nuisance. Aluminum stepladders are more likely to walk than wooden ones.

Aluminum ladders usually have footpads that function as floor protectors. Wooden ones don't, but then they don't need them as much.

Household stepladders are usually available in 4', 5' and 6' heights. Commercial stepladders usually range from 3' to 8'. Industrial ladders go up to 10'. In addition to wooden and metal stepladders, you can get heavy-duty 4', 6', 8', and 10' stepladders with fiberglass siderails (1⅛" x 3¼"), and grooved 3" metal steps riveted into the rails.

When buying a ladder, check metal for sharp edges, and wood for knots or cracks that may spell weakness.

Griffith's "61 Mechanic's" is a Type I industrial ladder available with or without locking paint shelf in sizes from 3' to 12'. Weighs about 4 lbs. per foot.

An excellent 6′ household ladder, ruggedly built, with 3″ ribbed steps. Light, strong, with roomy paint shelf. Slip-resistant feet; extra bracing at stress points. Werner, model 366.

Industrial quality at a household price. Spartan Type I industrial 4′ ladder by Scranton has 3″ treads and 3″ side rails. It weighs only 9 lbs., but its second tread and top tread are tested to hold 1000 lbs. This qualifies it to hold a recommended load of 250 lbs. total weight (test load divided by 4). *Insert:* Scranton's 8′ Super Rocket has similar construction, weighs 25³/₄ lbs.

CHOOSE THE RIGHT SIZE LADDER

1. MEASURE FROM GROUND TO EAVES
2. CHECK CHART FOR CORRECT SIZE

Height to Resting Point	Buy this length* Ext. Ladder	Max Working Length
to 9½' Max.	16'	13'
From 9½' to 13½'	20'	17'
From 13½' to 17½'	24'	21'
From 17½' to 21½'	28'	25'
From 21½' to 25'	32'	29'
From 25' to 29'	36'	33'
From 29' to 32'	40'	36'

* THIS LENGTH SELECTION ALLOWS FOR THE
PROPER OVERLAP AND A 3' EXTENSION
OF THE LADDER ABOVE THE EAVES AS
REQUIRED BY MINIMUM SAFETY CODES.

HOW TO SET UP YOUR LADDER PROPERLY

SUPPORT POINT MUST BE AT LEAST 24"

Height to Gutter Line or Bearing Point "V"	Horiz. Distance Resting Point to Ladder Base - "H"
9½'	2½'
13½'	3½'
17½'	4½'
21½'	5½'
25'	6½'
29'	7½'
32'	8½'

SET UP SINGLE OR MULTI SECTION LADDERS AT 75½° BY
PLACING BOTTOM OF LADDER ¼ OF THE LENGTH BEING
USED, OUT FROM VERTICAL RESTING POINT.

EXTENSION LADDERS

Like stepladders, extension ladders are available in metal, wood and fiberglass, and in Type I (Industrial), Type II (Commercial) and Type III (Household). For average household use, there is no reason why you need a heavier ladder than Type III.

Extension ladders consist of a lower, or base, section, and an upper, or fly, section. By means of a rope and pulley, the fly can be raised to any desired height and locked there by means of a rung-lock mechanism.

It used to be that the fly section was in front of the base section. This made it awkward in stepping from one section to the next. Now, the fly section is usually in back, closer to the wall. This makes the transition from section to section easier. It's also a convenience in hoisting and lowering.

Household extension ladders start at extended sizes of 16' and go up at 4' increments to 32'. The 24' ladder is most popular, but you must remember it gives you a maximum of only 21' of working length. This is because the top and bottom sections overlap. Also, you lose another foot in height because of the tilt of the ladder. The correct tilt is 75°.

Just as extension ladders have a maximum usable height, they also have a minimum usable height. This is the lowest height that can safely be reached. At low levels, the tilt of the ladder takes you beyond reach of the wall against which it's set. A 16' ladder may reach a maximum height of 9' and have a minimum usable height of 5'. A 20' ladder may reach 10' to 13', and have a minimum usable height of 7'.

Get a ladder that will safely take you to the highest point you'll ever want to reach. A ladder should extend 3' beyond the eaves. This will allow you to get from the ladder onto the roof safely.

For electrical safety, Werner extension ladder with nonconductive fiberglass rails. It meets standards of American National Standards Institute (ANSI) and Occupational Safety and Health Act (OSHA). If you must work around electrical wiring, this kind of ladder gives maximum protection.

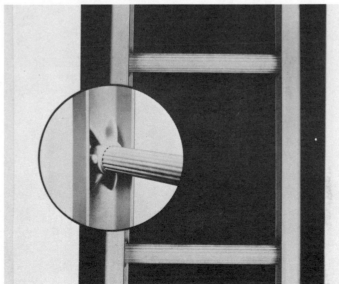

Flat steps provide sure footing. When ladder is properly positioned at a 75° angle, its 1³/₄" flat steps are horizontal. Smooth rung-lock operation, polypropylene rope. Household extension ladder, D1100 series. Werner.

Industrial Ladder Company makes a complete line of ladders with both rungs and rails of fiberglass. (Some fiberglass ladders have wood or metal rungs.) A special patented connection system joins parts. Available in a wide variety of lengths and types.

Ladder jacks can be used with expanding scaffold planks to create a working platform. Both accessories available from Sears.

Ladder stabilizer or "stand-off bracket" is a useful accessory for extension ladders. Unit is 48" wide; spans gutter pipes, windows, and other obstacles. A.W. Flint.

WHAT TO LOOK FOR

Look for a ladder that's rigid. You don't want it to be unstable, and twist and sway excessively as you climb. Look for a capacity label. The greater its rated capacity, the greater its stability.

How wide are the ladder's top and bottom sections? A 19" width gives good stability.

Compare the rung-lock mechanisms. Some work easier than others. Rung locks that are hard to set, and bind and drag over the base section rungs, make height adjustment difficult. Check the extension mechanism. Does the rope move easily on the pulley, or might it tend to jam between the pulley and its bracket, or rub and fray? Is the rope plastic or cotton? If the rope is plastic, it won't rot.

Rollers at the top of the fly section make height adjustments easy. Some ladders have a single roller on each rail, others have two on each side. This helps minimize slippage and side-sway.

Newer metal ladder designs have flat rungs, which provide more comfortable footing. Most wooden ladders come only with round rungs.

Ladder stabilizers. If you lean an extension ladder against rain gutters, it can damage them. If a window is exactly where you want to rest the top of the ladder, what can you do? The answer to both of these problems is a sturdy rectangular-shaped aluminum stabilizer that spreads 48" to span windows and other obstructions, and that holds the ladder away from wall and gutters on protective rubber bumpers.

Ladder jacks. Steel jacks enable you to support a plank between two heavy-duty extension ladders. For the purpose, you can get a 12"-wide extension plank that extends from 6' to 12'. working from a plank can be much easier than working from a ladder and constantly having to reset it.

Manufacturers. Werner, Scranton, White Metal, Howard, A.W. Flint, Lincoln, Larson, Griffith, American, Alproco, Ballymore, COB Industries, and H.K. Metalcraft are just some of the firms that make ladders. You can buy ladders by mail order from J.C. Penney, Wards, and Sears.

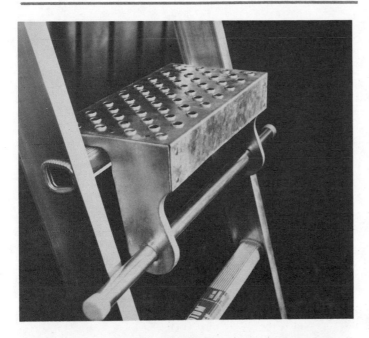

"Comfort Step" slips over rung of ladder to provide comfortable standing during long jobs. Wide, non-slip surface. Sears.

When you can't use a straight, rigid ladder, Peerless roll-away ladder, made by H.K. Metalcraft, is easy to carry and rolls up for storage. Hardwood rungs are supported by chain.

Fold-up 19-lb. rig can be set outside a window from inside. It has safety chain and gate, supports over 1,000 lbs. Port-a-Skaf.

Wal-Board midget rolling scaffold is fast, easy to use, and safe. Rolls on 4" casters. Available 2' wide x 4' long x 4' high, and 2' wide x 6' long x 6' high.

Feel safe on any surface. Alproco levelers, made of heavy extruded aluminum, bolt to ladder. Adjustable to 9″ in ¼″ increments. Non-skid neoprene feet. Inner extrusion becomes pick for use on icy or slick ground.

Ladderite braces can be quickly and permanently attached without tools to any 6′, 8′, or 10′ ladder. They can then be swung out to stabilize the ladder, even on irregular or multi-level surfaces. An adjustable "hold bar" which extends up to 30″ above the top of the ladder is an added safety feature. Henry Stewart Co.

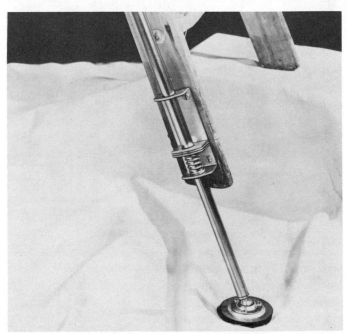

Adjustable leg attaches to metal or wooden ladders, extends up to 15″, locks at any point. Ribbed, round neoprene foot swivels on ball joint to adjust to uneven surfaces. Plated steel. Brookstone.

PLUMBING TOOLS

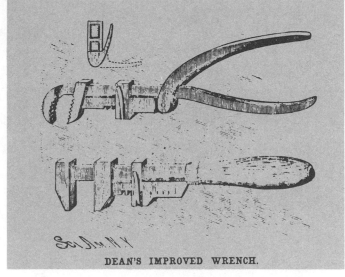

DEAN'S IMPROVED WRENCH.

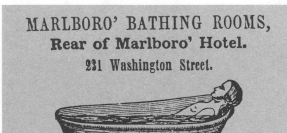

42.
PIPE VISES

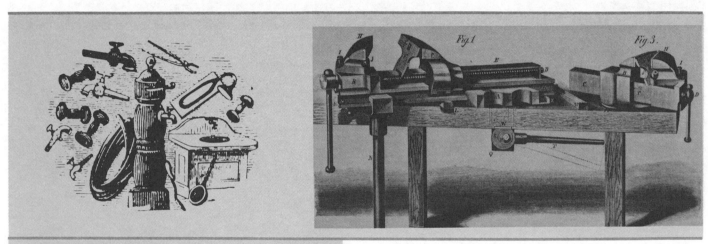

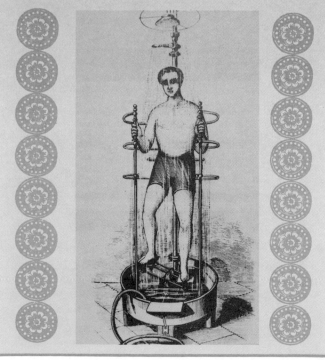

The vise is a basic plumbing tool. To work pipe, you must first be able to hold it securely. The vise does that. Typically, it has two jaws which are brought together or separated by means of a screw. The screw is its key element. It can exert tremendous pressure, and won't relax its hold unless you want it to.

An ordinary machinist vise may include both regular and pipe jaws. In a typical combination vise of this kind, pipe jaws may securely grip pipe or rounds as small as $1/_8$" diameter, or as large as 6".

The vise base may be stationary, or it may swivel. A turn device on the base permits securing it anywhere within its 360° rotation.

Bench yolk vise. This is a vise specifically designed for holding pipe, and it is handy and efficient. Unlike the machinist bench vise, which screws on a horizontal plane, this one operates vertically. By turning the screw you come down on the pipe, which is held in a lower jaw. An extension of the base acts as a pipe rest and bender. Most bench yolk vises hold pipe as small as $\frac{1}{8}''$, and its capacity upward may be anywhere from $1\frac{1}{4}''$ to 6".

A variation of the bench yolk vise is a portable yolk vise. By means of an auxiliary screw it can be attached to a plank or post up to 4" in thickness, or to a workbench. It can be attached horizontally as well as vertically.

Open side vise. With a yoke vise, the pipe must be fed through its center. When swing space is limited, this may be awkward. To make clamping long pipe lengths quick and easy, there is the open side pipe vise. It is made for bolting to a bench. Typically, its maximum capacity is $2\frac{1}{2}''$ or $4\frac{1}{4}''$.

Stand yoke vise. If you're working on plumbing in a kitchen or a bathroom, it's convenient to have your vise right there, not on your shop bench. The stand yoke vise is designed for such portability. It is easily carried from place to place. To set it up, you merely insert four pipe legs and a connecting horizontal pipe section. One stand yoke vise, made by Ridgid, is equipped with a pipe bender and a tray for holding oil can, dope, pot and tools. Typical capacity od this kind of vise is $2\frac{1}{2}''$ or $3\frac{1}{2}''$.

Another portable type of yolk vise quickly and easily attaches by means of a chain fastener to any post. You don't need any tools to make the attachment.

Chain vise. Another means of holding pipe is with a chain which is tightened by cranking a handle. This vise can be attached permanently to a bench top. It also may be portable, and equipped with legs and connecting pipe. Or it may be attached to a post by means of a second chain.

The tristand. This is a portable type of vise especially popular with plumbers and other professionals. It has three integral legs, braced by a tray. Legs and tray fold in for easy carrying, and it's easy to set up. The vise itself may be a yoke or chain type.

Manufacturers. Top vise manufacturers include Ridgid, Reed, Wilton, Columbian (Warren), and Littlestown.

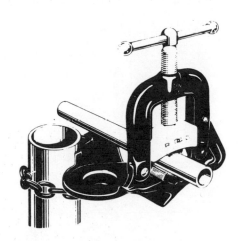

Yoke vise fastens to a pipe or post by means of a chain. Red yoke, hardened tool-steel jaws. Includes pipe rest, bender, and holder for dope pot and oilcan. Holds $\frac{1}{8}''$ to $2\frac{1}{2}''$ pipes. Weighs $24\frac{1}{2}$ lbs.

This yoke vise fastens to bench or other support, has a useful pipe rest and bender. Yoke is red; base is of malleable iron. Available in eight sizes. The smallest handles $\frac{1}{8}''$ through $1\frac{1}{4}''$ pipes, weighs 4 lbs. Largest handles up to 6" pipes and weighs 65 lbs.

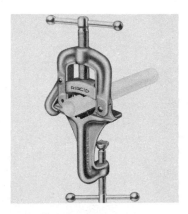

Portable yoke vise clamps quickly in any position, attaches to plank, workbench or post up to 4" thick. Yoke is red. Available in three capacities up to $2\frac{1}{2}''$. Integral pipe rest.

For fast work on long pipe, open-side pipe vise makes it easy to clamp long pipe lengths. Available in model with top capacity of $2\frac{1}{2}''$, weight $3\frac{3}{4}$ lbs, and larger model with top capacity of $4\frac{1}{2}''$, weight $26\frac{3}{4}$ lbs.

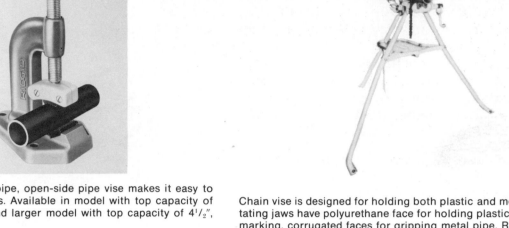

Chain vise is designed for holding both plastic and metal pipe. Rotating jaws have polyurethane face for holding plastic pipe without marking, corrugated faces for gripping metal pipe. Reed.

Legs of portable tristand yoke vise fold for easy carrying. Integral steel tray adds rigidity when set up. Vise base overhangs front legs to give clearance when you're using threader. Capacity through $2\frac{1}{2}''$, weighs $48\frac{1}{2}$ lbs. Ridgid.

Top-screw bench chain vise. The crank handle on this easy-to-operate chain vise is anchored to the base so it can't fall out. Seven models are available with capacities through 8″, two of them for plastic pipe. These have neoprene-coated jaws without teeth to prevent scarring of pipe. Ridgid.

Tristand top-screw chain vise with crank handle that tightens the chain on top so you don't have to grope to find it or stoop to turn it. Has all the features of conventional tristand yoke vise, such as base overhanging front legs to give ample room for tool swing. Capacity through 5″, weighs $45\frac{1}{2}$ lbs. Ridgid.

42-7

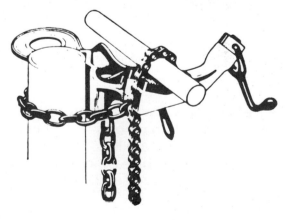

Top-screw post chain vise. Similar to the Ridgid bench chain vise (above) except that it is designed to fasten to a post by means of a chain. Model 640 has capacity of $\frac{1}{8}''$ through 5″, weighs $3\frac{1}{2}$ lbs.

Stand-style chain vise is similar to other chain vises except that it is designed to attach to legs. Legs and connecting pipe are not furnished. Capacity $^{1}/_{8}$" through 5". Weighs 25$^{3}/_{4}$ lbs.

Ridgid combination pipe and machinists' vise comes in three sizes. The 3$^{1}/_{2}$" jaw width holds pipe to 2$^{1}/_{2}$". The 4$^{1}/_{2}$" jaw width holds pipe to 4". The 6" jaw width holds pipe to 6".

Home vise features large anvil and built-in pipe jaws. Available in jaw widths from 3$^{1}/_{2}$" to 5" to handle up to 1$^{1}/_{2}$" pipes. Locking swivel base. Wilton.

New Flip-Grip II swings 90° left or right for long workpieces. Includes separate 4" smooth jaws for wood, 4" metal-working jaws, and built-in pipe jaws with $^{3}/_{8}$" to 1$^{3}/_{8}$" capacity at any angle. Wilton.

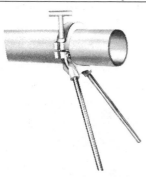

Bipod vise for plastic pipe. This novel stand uses the pipe you're working on as the third leg of the stand. Weighs only 8$^{1}/_{2}$ lbs., making it easily portable. It holds 3", 4" and 6" pipe, but does not adjust to intermediate sizes.

Powr-Kraft pipe vise stand holds either self-locking vise or chain vise. Either one takes pipe to 2". Stand's legs fold for easy storing and transport. Wards.

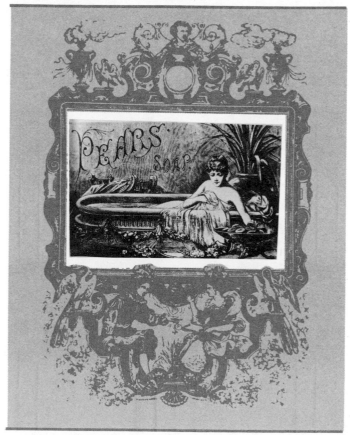

43.
CUTTERS AND REAMERS

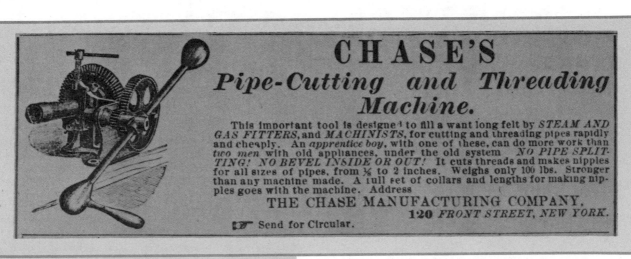

CHASE'S
Pipe-Cutting and Threading Machine.

This important tool is designed to fill a want long felt by *STEAM AND GAS FITTERS*, and *MACHINISTS*, for cutting and threading pipes rapidly and cheaply. An *apprentice boy*, with one of these, can do more work than *two men* with old appliances, under the old system. *NO PIPE SPLITTING! NO BEVEL INSIDE OR OUT!* It cuts threads and makes nipples for all sizes of pipes, from ⅛ to 2 inches. Weighs only 100 lbs. Stronger than any machine made. A full set of collars and lengths for making nipples goes with the machine. Address

THE CHASE MANUFACTURING COMPANY,
120 *FRONT STREET, NEW YORK.*

☞ Send for Circular.

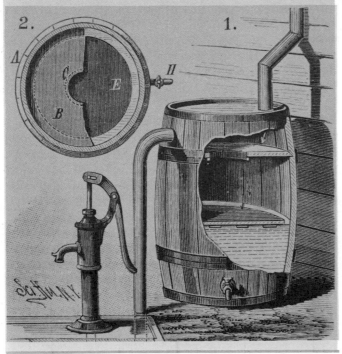

Some inventions are older than you expect. The self-winding watch goes back to the eighteenth century. So does the toilet. In fact, it was 1778 that Bramak invented the first water closet.

Plumbing itself goes back much further than that. The first plumbing, as we know it, employed lead pipe. *Plumbum* is the Latin word for lead, and so roots of it all are quite clear.

Many simple plumbing jobs require cutting pipe. You will have occasion to cut pipe if you install a clotheswasher, dishwasher, icemaker, or water softener. You will also have to cut pipe if you install a new hosecock, or replace a pipe that springs a leak.

The tools you need for working with pipe, and that includes cutting, depend on whether the pipe is galvanized steel, copper, or plastic.

Copper tubing may be cut with a hacksaw, but pipe and tubing cutters are faster and better. You don't have to be an expert to get a square cut.

HOW A CUTTER WORKS

Most pipe and tubing cutters have two rollers and one cutting wheel. The pipe fits between these three points, and the revolving wheel is adjustable. To make a cut, you turn the handle counterclockwise until the opening between wheel and rollers is large enough to insert the pipe. Then you tighten the wheel until it begins to bite. You begin revolving the cutter about the pipe, gradually tightening the wheel on the pipe as it cuts. In short order it will have cut all the way through. You do have to avoid the temptation to cut too fast. If you do, you'll raise a lip on the outside of the pipe. You then have to file it off.

Most tubing cutters will cut copper, brass, aluminum, and thin-wall conduit. Special wheels are available for cutting thin PVC, flexible plastic, and poly-type tubing. Wheels for cutting plastic are usually coated with Teflon-S, DuPont's registered trademark for its nonstick finish.

Small, relatively inexpensive tubing cutters have a capacity from $1/8$″ through 1″ or $1 1/8$″ O.D. (Outside Diameter), but you can get them with capacities through $2 1/8$″, $3 1/8$″ and $4 1/8$″. If you're doing whole-house plumbing, or adding a bathroom and doing drainage work, you will need one of these larger capacities.

All small cutters are not alike. Compare a cheap cutter with a good one, and you'll immediately note obvious differences of sturdiness, capability, and quality. Better cutters are easy to line up with cutting marks and have wheels that are easily changed. Usually, their wheels are thinner, so they cut more smoothly, leave less burr.

TUBE CUTTERS

You may get annoyed spending the time loosening and tightening a cutter on tubing. If you're that kind, you can get quick-acting cutters that open and close instantaneously. Instead of having to screw the cutter all the way, you merely push the handle to snug it up against the tubing. Then, when the cut is complete, you press a release nut and the cutter wheel slides away. Some cutters have four rollers instead of two.

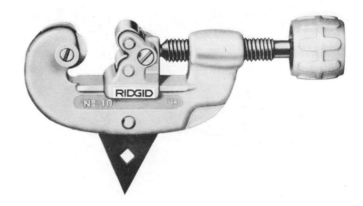

Cutter for copper tubing also handles brass, aluminum and thin-wall conduit. Available with heavy-duty wheel for steel cutting and a special wheel for plastic. Comes in six sizes. Shown is No. 10 for cutting $1/8$″ through 1″ O.D. (outside diameter) tubing.

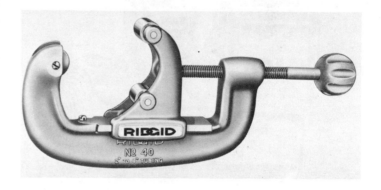

Cutting drain or vent pipe? Ridgid No. 40 cuts 2″ to 4″ tubing. Available in model 40-P for cutting plastic.

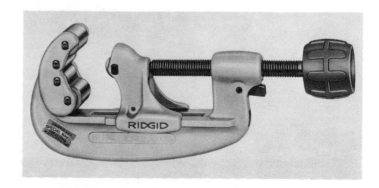

Quick-acting tubing cutter. To close it, push handle. To open it, press release nut. No tedious tightening and loosening from work. Equipped with special wheel for cutting plastic pipe and tubing $1/4$″ to $2 5/8$″ O.D. Other models cut 1″ through 6″ sizes.

Here's the answer to cutting in close quarters on small size hard and soft copper, aluminum, brass, and plastic tubing. Cutter is 2$^1/_8$" long, cuts up to $^5/_8$" O.D. (outside diameter) tubing. A cutter 2$^9/_{16}$" long cuts up to $^{15}/_{16}$" O.D.

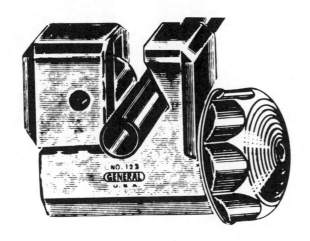

For hard-to-get-at places—this tiny cutter needs only 1$^1/_4$" clearance. It cuts $^1/_8$" to $^1/_2$" O.D. tubing, weighs only three ounces.

Model 102 internal tubing cutter for internal cutting of $^1/_2$" and $^3/_4$" I.D. copper water tube. Preset adjustable stop collar for length of tubing to be cut ($^5/_{16}$" through 4$^1/_2$"). Knurled feed knob controls cutting action. Ratchet handle means minimum clearance is required when cutting.

Others have two wheels. The advantage of a two-wheeled cutter is that it requires no more than a 90° swing. You can cut a pipe even when it is against a wall or joist.

One type of cutter has groved rollers for making cuts close to a flared end. Often it means saving the tubing. If you couldn't make the cut, you'd have to throw the piece away and start with a new piece.

Another cutter type is for cutting tubing in extremely close quarters. One of these midget tubing cutters with a capacity of $^5/_6$" O.D. has a length of only 2$^1/_8$" and a turning radius of only 1$^5/_{16}$" maximum. One with a $^{15}/_{16}$" O.D. capacity is only 2$^9/_{16}$" long with a 1$^{11}/_{16}$" maximum turning radius.

It's usually best to hand-hold copper tubing while you cut it. If you put it in a vise, you're likely to crush it. If you have to hold copper in a vise, do it at a distance from the end, so the end won't be pushed out-of-round. The best way to insure a square cut, if you use a hacksaw, is with a miter box. Use a hacksaw with 24 teeth to the inch.

Sometimes, you may want to cut tubing that is out of reach. For this, you can often use an internal tubing cutter. You insert this special kind of cutter inside the tubing to the point at which you wish the cut to be made. One kind, for internal cuts of $^1/_2$" and $^3/_4$" O.D. copper water tube, can be adjusted to cut at any point from $^5/_{16}$" to 4$^1/_2$". The tool has a reamer-like end. This enables it to get into tubes that are out-of-round. Another style is designed for 2" or 3" copper and plastic tubing.

An internal pipe cutter is an easy answer to the problem of trimming extending ends of closet bowl and shower waste lines which are below the level of their flange.

STEEL-PIPE CUTTERS

Steel pipe comes in galvanized, for plumbing, and black iron, for gas lines. Its size is its inside diameter. It's usually sold in 10' and 21' lengths, and a variety of shorter lengths cut to size and threaded. Though you can hand-hold copper tubing while you cut it, steel pipe has to be held by a vise or other means.

For cutting steel and iron, you need a tough blade-cutter wheel. Some steel pipe cutters have one cutter wheel, but others have three or four. One type has a second handle so it can be used in making two-man cuts on large pipe sizes. Most of these cutters are designed for use with power drives.

If you want to try power cutting, you can usually rent a power drive at a local rental shop. Typically, it holds the pipe between three vise jaws and rotates it slowly. All you do is turn the cutter handle to move the cutting wheel against the pipe. When cutting steel pipe, use thread-cutting oil.

It is important to smooth burrs caused by cutting pipe. Burrs can cause clogging. Copper tubing cutters usually have their own attached reamer. For steel and cast-iron pipes you usually have a separate reamer. Most popular types work on a ratchet. A power drive can be used in conjunction with a reamer.

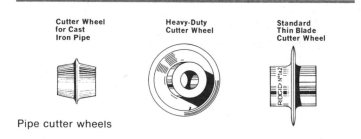

Pipe cutter wheels

Two handles mean extra leverage. Ridgid model 4-S cutter takes 2" through 4" pipe, weighs 18¼ lbs. There is also a model 3-S which takes 1" through 3" pipe, weighs 15 lbs., and model 6-S, which takes 4" through 6" pipe and weighs 24 lbs.

Extra-long handle makes adjustment easy. Ridgid's heavy-duty pipe cutter comes in model 1-A for cutting pipe up to 1¼" and model 2-A for pipe through 2". Can be converted to a three-wheel cutter by replacing rollers with cutter wheels.

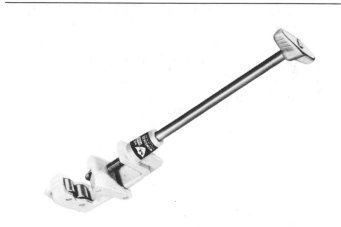

Milwaukee do-it-yourself pipe cutter is similar to one sold by Wards. It comes in two sizes. No. 1 cuts up to 1" pipe, No. 2 cuts up to 2" pipe.

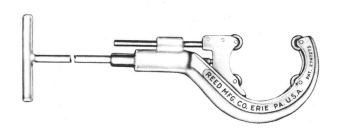

Cutter for soil pipe has four wheels so you can work in close quarters. With this heavy-duty tool you can score soil pipe and snap it off in short order. Cutter wheels are made of extra hard, shock-resistant steel.

Light, compact soil-pipe cutter cuts 2″ through 6″ cast iron, clay, asbestos and cement pipe. Because ratchet action parallels direction of pipe, trench can be minimum width. Pumping of handle tightens chain until pipe is cut apart. Hand guard protects knuckles.

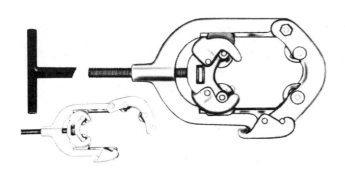

Hinged cutter that handles up to 12″ pipe. Most multiple-wheel cutters are hard to track, but this four-wheel cutter has special guide fingers to force perfect alignment. Easy to use in close quarters or in a ditch. Reed.

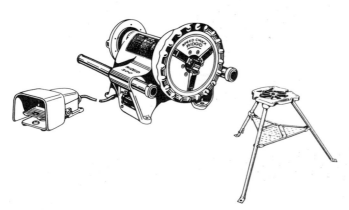

Power for threading, cutting, or reaming. Its ½ hp motor turns pipe, rod, or conduit for hand-threaders, cutters, reamers. Foot switch control, It can be mounted on a stand like the one shown, or on a bench or truck.

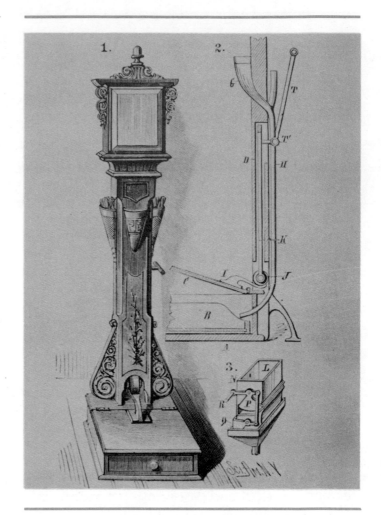

CAST-IRON PIPE CUTTERS

Service-weight cast-iron pipe can be cut by a method similar to that used in cutting glass. You score the pipe, producing a weak line along which the break is made when pressure is exerted. Scoring can be done with a hacksaw or with a chisel. Cut all the way around the pipe to a depth of about $1/16$″. Then place the pipe over the edge of a 2 x 4 and tap it with a hammer until it comes apart.

You can also cut cast iron with a soil-pipe cutter. One type, made by Reed, looks like other pipe cutters, but has a nominal capacity of $1\frac{1}{2}$″ to 4″. Another type, made by Ridgid, uses a chain, which is tightened by ratchet action. It will cut cast iron, clay, cement pipe, etc., from 2″ to 6″. Getting a square cut helps make vertical drain/vent lines or stacks more stable, especially when gaskets are used.

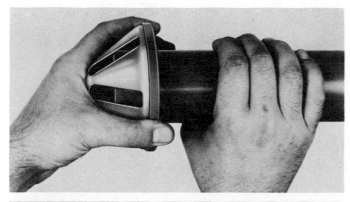

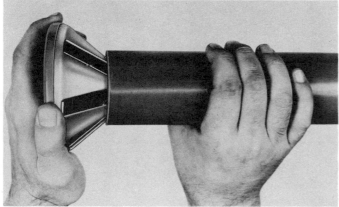

This tool removes inside burrs and outside ridges from all types of plastic pipe and tubing; essential for preparing plastic for solvent or threaded joint. All you do is apply tool and twist. Vinyl-cushion handgrip. Ridgid.

BENDING

If you try to bend soft copper or aluminum tube, you'll kink it, especially in short-radius bends. For a smooth bend, the thing to use is a spring-type tube bender. They are made of spring wire in a variety of tube diameters, and come in lengths of 10″ to 12″.

For heavy-wall steel tube (up to $\frac{1}{8}$″ wall thickness), stainless-steel tube, and hard copper water tube, a lever-type tube bender is the best choice. It will produce distortion-free bends up to 180° and you don't have to pre-heat the tube. It works by ratchet action and comes in sizes for $\frac{5}{8}$″, $\frac{3}{4}$″, and $\frac{7}{8}$″ O.D. tube. There are also lever-type tube benders without the ratchet.

Self-feeding ratchet pipe reamer has spiral design to make hand-reaming faster and easier. You can use it for enlarging any kind of hole. For $\frac{1}{8}$″ through 2″ pipe. Weighs $7\frac{1}{4}$ lbs.

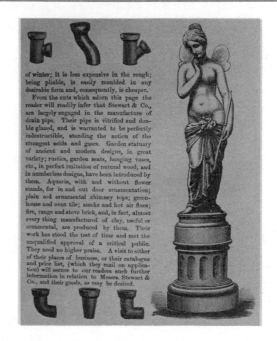

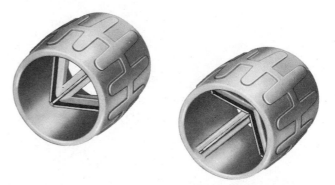

Inner-outer reamer for inside reaming or outside beveling on $\frac{1}{4}$″ through $1\frac{1}{2}$″ copper, aluminum, brass and other types of tubing. Made of plastic, with alloy-steel blades. Ridgid.

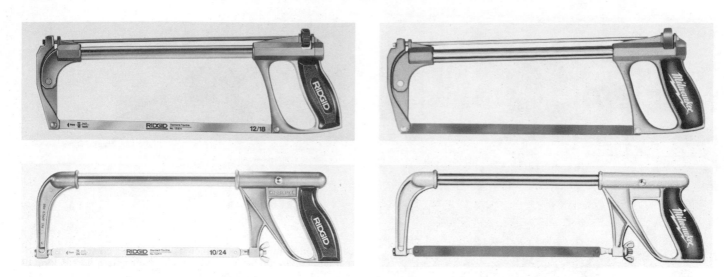

What's in a name? Often it's the features rather than the brand name that count. At top are 12″ saws with tension-wheel control. Below, 10″-12″ models with wingnut adjustment. Bearing private labels, both frame styles are essentially the same as those manufactured by Columbia.

Jab saw for hard-to-get-at jobs uses any size blade, even broken blades. Blade can be extended for deep cuts, flexed for flush cuts. Handle is cast aluminum.

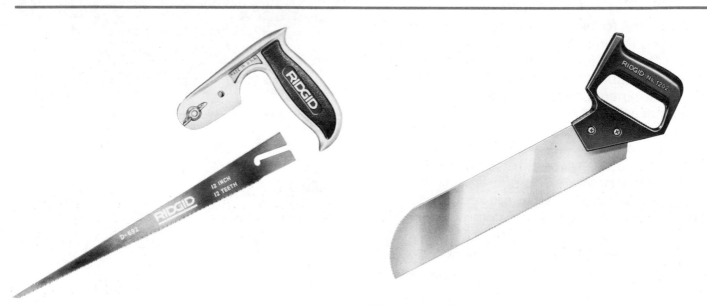

Seven different blade types are available for this compass saw handle. Two are metal-cutting blades. Of the metal cutters, one has 10 teeth per inch, the other 24. Both are 12″ long.

Ridgid model 1202 universal saw is useful for cutting plastic pipe. It also cuts laminates, plywood and veneers. Works well in a miter box. The 12½″ blade has 14 teeth per inch; special toothing on curved back edge cuts slots.

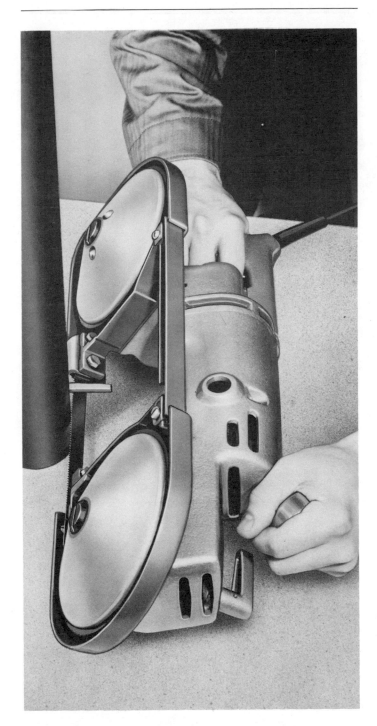

"Whizz-Disc" cuts tubing and pipe. Its silicon-carbide cutting wheel, distributed by Arco, fits any electric drill, flexible shaft. The 7" disc also cuts brick, ceramic tile, and plastics. In addition, it's a sanding disc for removing rust and paint, as well as smoothing, shaping and sharpening.

MANUFACTURERS

Ridgid, General, and Reed are three big names on the pipe-cutting scene.

Ridgid portable metal-cutting band saw easily handles most ferrous and non-ferrous metals, operates at any angle, can be bench-mounted. Single-speed, two-speed and variable-speed models.

Water system plan for Canterbury, thirteenth century

44.

PIPE WRENCHES

Eskimo wrench used on wood or bone

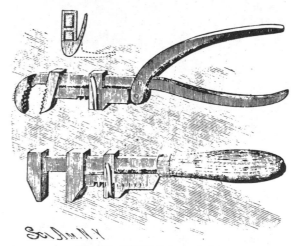

DEAN'S IMPROVED WRENCH.

The first application of a screw to a wrench was in the eighteenth century. An early "screw" wrench was adjusted by turning its handle. The monkey wrench came along at the beginning of the 1800s, but it had no teeth and was not suitable for gripping pipe and other rounds.

A GALLERY OF WRENCHES OF THE 1880's

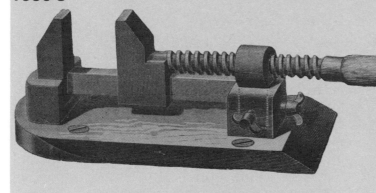

LOVE'S COMBINED WRENCH AND VISE.

Established in 1839.

Registered, March 31, 1874.

L. COES & COMPANY,
MANUFACTURERS OF SCREW WRENCHES,
Worcester, Mass.

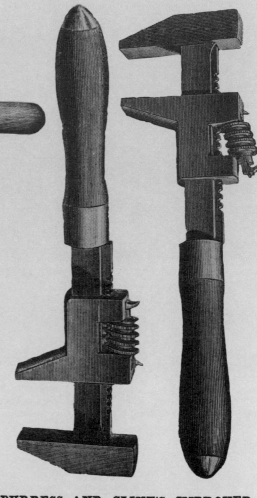

BURRESS AND CLINE'S IMPROVED
SCREW WRENCH.

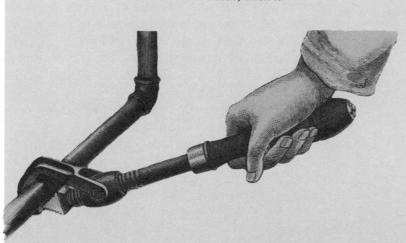

TAYLOR'S ADJUSTABLE PIPE WRENCH

MORRISON'S IMPROVED PIPE WRENCH.

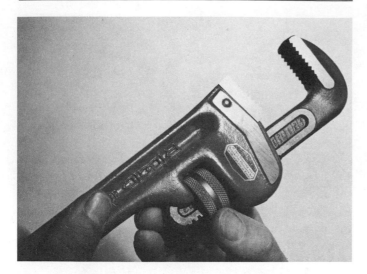

An excellent heavy-duty straight pipe wrench. Its floating hook jaw gives instant grip, quick release. Handy pipe scale and easy to turn adjusting nut make setting to fit pipe a one-hand operation. Ten sizes—6″ through 60″.

Milwaukee pipe wrenches are imported. Standard heavy-duty model comes in sizes from 10″ (for 1″ pipe) to 24″ (for 2½″ pipe), and the deluxe heavy-duty model in sizes from 8″ (for ¾″ pipe) to 36″ (for 4½″ pipe).

THE STILLSON TYPE

Inventing a wrench that could grip a pipe remained an unsolved problem until an early American maker of wrenches, Stillson, came up with an ingenious solution—a fixed lower jaw and a loose upper one that is free to pivot in a retaining collar. It gets a real bite on round objects. The harder it is pressed, the tighter it holds, for its milled teeth are pitched. Pull back on the handle and it lets go. It's more than just a plumbing tool. In woodworking shops it can be used for gripping and turning dowels, worn nuts, etc.

Today, Stillson-type pipe wrenches come in several varieties. Besides the classic Stillson, there is the heavy-duty pipe wrench. It differs from the Stillson in that the retaining collar for its upper jaw is not on a pivot but is forged as an integral part of the lower jaw and handle. This makes it more rugged, but also more expensive. It comes in at least 10 sizes, from 6″, with a ¾″ pipe capacity, to 60″, with an 8″ capacity. These weigh from ½ pound to over 50 pounds.

There are also end pipe wrenches and offset pipe wrenches (see photos). These are good for working in tight quarters, such as near a wall or on closely-spaced parallel lines. There is a wrench (10″ size only) designed for occasional hammering, and one with hex-jaws designed to give a multi-sided secure grip on all hex, square nuts, unions, valve packing nuts and flat-head gas cocks. They have smooth jaws and won't hurt plated-finished nuts.

Most pipe wrenches have malleable iron handles, but there are aluminum-handle varieties that are 40–50% lighter in weight. Instead of $1\frac{3}{4}$ pounds, a 10″ wrench weighs just 1 pound. It comes in 6 sizes, 10″ through 48″. Only the handle is aluminum. The jaws and other parts are of steel—identical to those on other pipe wrenches.

Two Stillson or pipe wrenches are needed for most jobs. One holds the pipe while the other does the turning. A 10″ Stillson, which takes pipe up to 1″, and an 18″ size, which takes pipe up to 2″, are a good pair for the home shop.

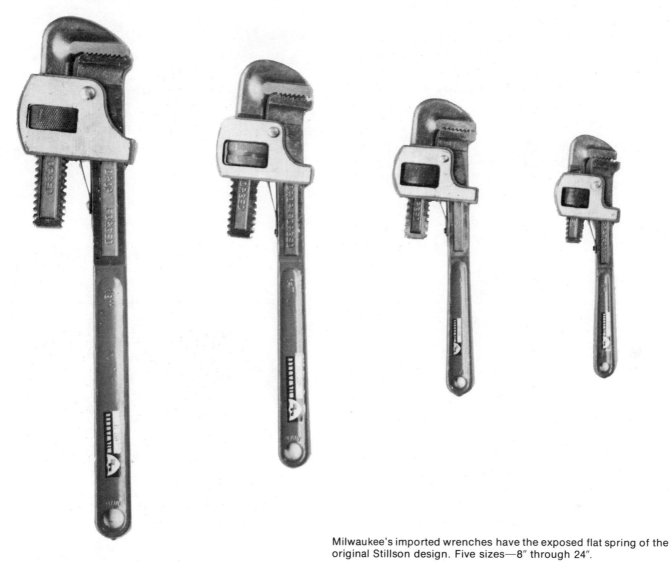

Milwaukee's imported wrenches have the exposed flat spring of the original Stillson design. Five sizes—8″ through 24″.

Ridgid wrench bears this guarantee seal: "If this housing ever breaks or distorts we will replace it free." Only the handle is aluminum, but that makes it 40% lighter than regular models. Jaws and other parts are like those of other Ridgid pipe wrenches. 10″ through 48″ sizes.

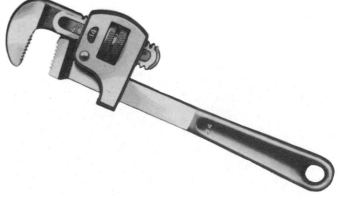

Ridgid improved Stillson wrench is better than the original because instead of an exposed flat spring for the hook jaw there's a cone-coil safety spring located in the frame. Seven sizes, 8″ through 24″.

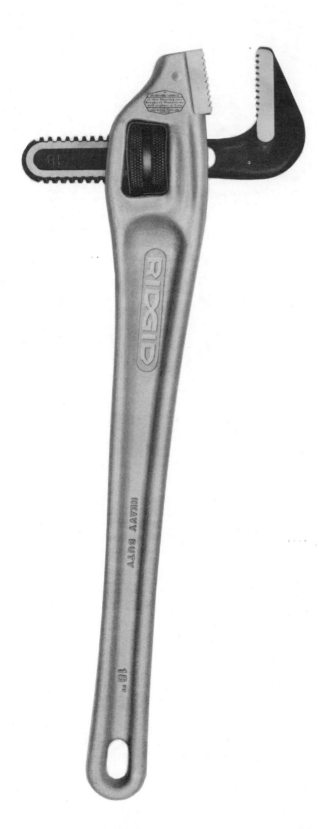

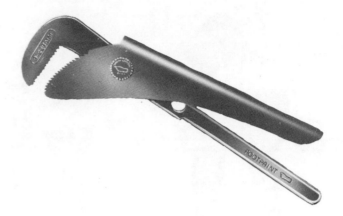

Adjustable pipe wrench made by Footprint Tools Ltd. in Sheffield, England. It comes in five sizes from 6″ to 14″, with maximum jaw openings from 1¹/₂″ to 3″.

Vertical pipe wrench. Note the square slot on the housing—it attaches at right angles to a ¹/₂″ square rod or a socket wrench extension handle. A set screw tightens the connection. Pipe capacity through 2″.

Offset wrench with aluminum handle is just as strong as all-iron wrenches of the same size, and almost 50% lighter. Lightweight and forward-facing jaw make it ideal for overhead or tight-quarter work. Three sizes: 14″, 18″ and 24″.

"Rap wrench" is so called because its hook jaw housing is deeper and broader than that of other models, creating a smooth flat surface that can be used for occasional hammering. Otherwise, it's like other Ridgid heavy-duty wrenches.

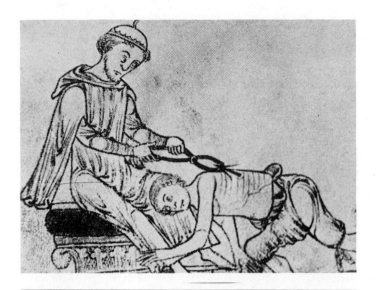

The first adjustable wrench was designed by Da Vinci. It utilized the newly invented bolt.

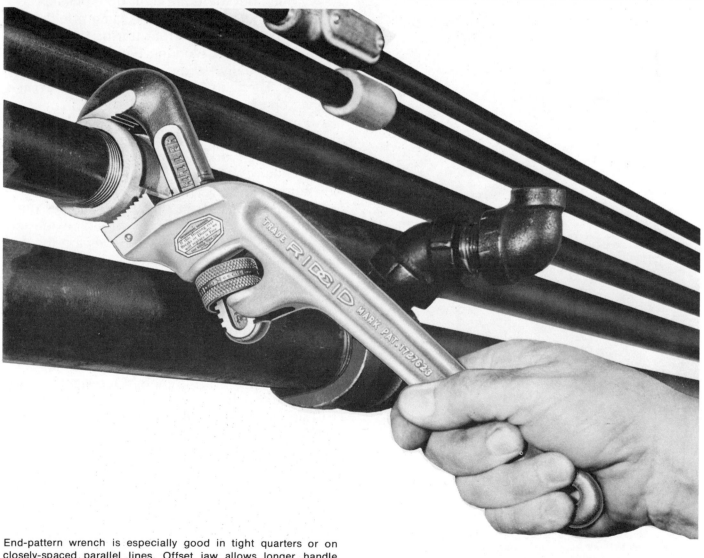

End-pattern wrench is especially good in tight quarters or on closely-spaced parallel lines. Offset jaw allows longer handle swing. Eight sizes: 6″ through 36″.

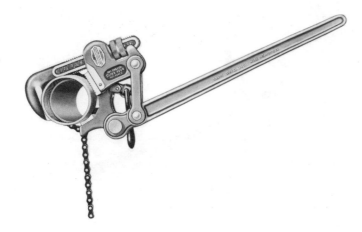

Compound leverage multiplies turning force, so one man can do the work of two. Superb at freeing frozen joints even in tight quarters. Four sizes: 2″ through 8″. Ridgid.

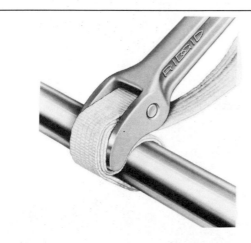

Woven nylon strap takes a tight grip but won't mar finish of polished pipe. Strap is easily replaced. Comes in five sizes; smallest with a capacity of up to 2″, largest up to 5″.

Lightweight chain wrench has a flexible chain that slips through narrowest clearances to provide grip. Gets a tight hold on all shapes without crushing them. Grab ring is for locking and releasing; gives ratchet-like action in either direction. Chain is 15³/₄″ long. Wrench has a rated pipe capacity of 2″, and an actual O.D. capacity of 4″. Ridgid.

OTHER PIPE WRENCHES

Besides Stillson-type wrenches, there are chain, strap, compound leverage, vertical, internal, and basin wrenches.

Chain wrenches use a chain, instead of tooth jaws, to get a tight grip. They can get into extra-close quarters that shut out ordinary wrenches, and have ratchet action in either direction. They fit regularly shaped objects as well as pipe and conduit. Typically, jaws are made of hardened alloy steel and are replaceable.

Chain wrenches usually have a rated pipe capacity of 2″ to 4¹/₂″ and an actual outside diameter (O. D.) capacity of 5″ to 7¹/₂″. Chain length runs from about 18¹/₂″ to 29″. Most models are heavy-duty, but there are light-duty ones too.

Strap wrenches work on the same principle as a chain, but they won't mar finish. They are the thing to use when working with polished pipe. The strap, usually sturdy, woven nylon, is easily replaced. There are special polyurethane-coated straps to prevent marring of plastic pipe.

Compound leverage wrenches are cleverly designed to double your strength. They let one person do the work of two. They are the answer to frozen joints. Ridgid offers 4 sizes with capacities from 2″ to 8″.

Vertical wrenches attach at right angles on a ¹/₂″ square rod, or on a socket wrench extension handle. These useful pipe wrenches are the answer to some especially difficult-to-get-at locations that you often find in water wells, sprinkler systems, and gasoline station pits.

Internal wrenches are handy for installing or pulling short nipples out of fittings. If you use an ordinary wrench, you damage the threads. Internal wrenches will also hold closet spuds and bath, basin and sink strainers. One size handles pipe ³/₄″ through 2″.

Basin wrenches, as their name implies, are for getting up behind wash basins. Excellent for attaching or disconnecting faucets or water pipes, they have use in many other tight spots as well. Jaws, typically, are spring-loaded to grip nuts, so you get fast, one-hand ratcheting action. The jaw flips over for reversing direction.

One type of basin wrench is a solid shank, usually about 10″ long. Another has a telescopic shank that adjusts to four lengths from 10″ through 17″.

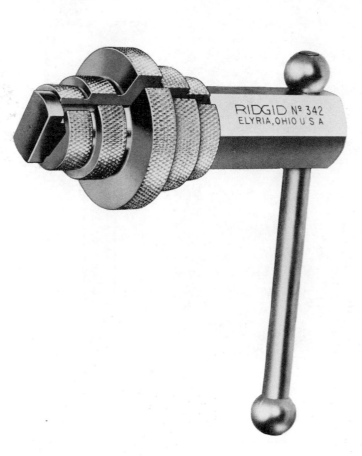

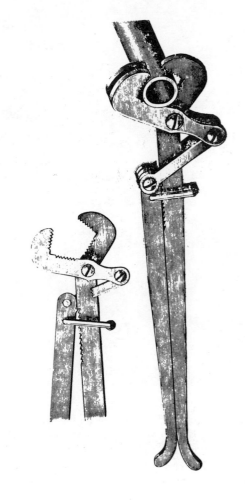

Internal wrench holds closet spuds and bath, basin or sink strainers from ³/₄″ through 2″. Jaws expand by eccentric action. Sliding reversible handle is handy in close-quarter work.

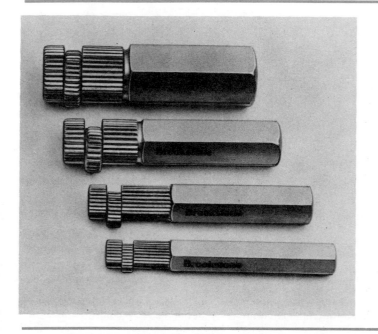

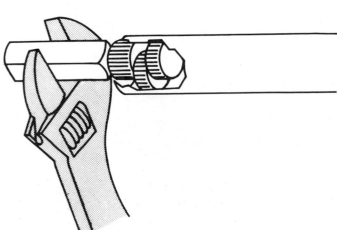

Knurled eccentric cam of internal wrench automatically grips wall of pipe. Tightens or removes fittings, short or broken pipe. Can't damage chrome plating or threads. About 3³/₄″ long. Four-piece set fits ³/₄″, ¹/₂″, ³/₄″, and 1″ pipe.

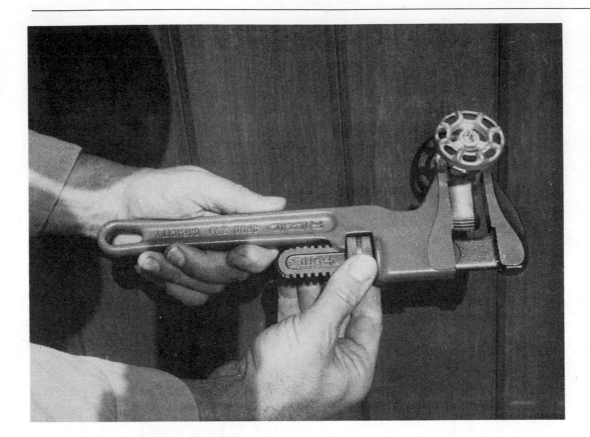

This 12″ spud wrench has $2^5/_8$″ capacity. It's like an oldtime monkey wrench, but better. Narrow jaws fit into tight quarters. Hook jaw is drop forged and heat treated. Weighs $2^1/_2$ lbs.

Offset hex wrench is the tool for getting a good grip on sink and tub drain nuts. Its thin, smooth jaws slip into the tightest places. It can handle up through $1^1/_2$″ drain nuts.

Small 10″ basin wrench has solid shank. Larger wrench has telescopic shank that extends from 10″ through 17″. Both have a capacity of $^3/_8$″ through $1^1/_4$″. There's also a larger telescopic wrench (not shown) that handles nuts $^1/_4$″ through $2^1/_2$″. Ridgid.

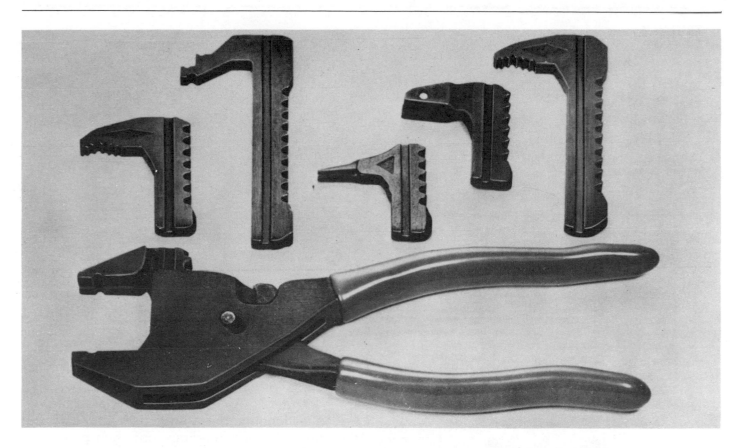

Multi-purpose plier-wrench has six interchangeable jaws to do a variety of jobs. Set includes standard flat jaws with 1¹/₂″ capacity, small pipe jaws for holding round objects, wire jaw specially grooved for holding and bending wire, tube-cutting jaw, internal-external grabber, and side cutter for wire. Brookstone.

Wards is a good mail order source for plumbing tools. Shown here are heavy-duty pipe wrench (10″, 14″, 18″, 24″, 36″), Stillson wrench (10″, 14″, 18″), and basin wrench.

Celtic monument to Vulcan, god of metalworking

45.
THREADING AND FLARING TOOLS

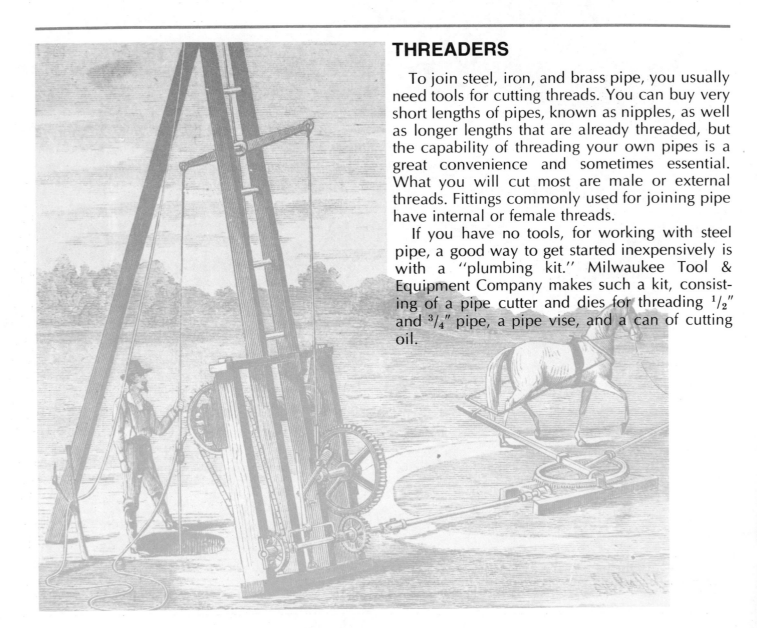

THREADERS

To join steel, iron, and brass pipe, you usually need tools for cutting threads. You can buy very short lengths of pipes, known as nipples, as well as longer lengths that are already threaded, but the capability of threading your own pipes is a great convenience and sometimes essential. What you will cut most are male or external threads. Fittings commonly used for joining pipe have internal or female threads.

If you have no tools, for working with steel pipe, a good way to get started inexpensively is with a "plumbing kit." Milwaukee Tool & Equipment Company makes such a kit, consisting of a pipe cutter and dies for threading $1/2''$ and $3/4''$ pipe, a pipe vise, and a can of cutting oil.

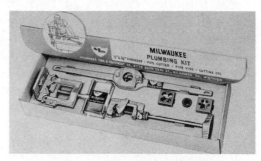

Kit for the occasional plumber includes pipe vise, threader with dies for $\frac{1}{2}$" and $\frac{3}{4}$" pipe, Saunders type pipe cutter to cut $\frac{1}{8}$" to 1" pipe, and a can of pipe thread cutting oil.

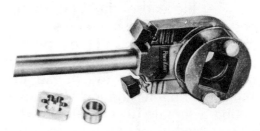

Wards offers this inexpensive double-action, reversible ratchet threader with $2\frac{1}{2}$" × $2\frac{1}{2}$" Japanese-made block dies for $\frac{1}{2}$", $\frac{3}{4}$", 1" and $1\frac{1}{4}$" pipe. Heavy-duty model is also available with 4" × 4" dies for $1\frac{1}{4}$", $1\frac{1}{2}$" and 2" pipe.

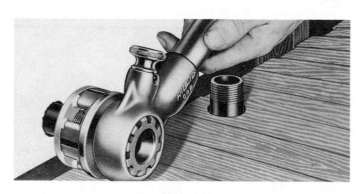

Light duty drop-head threader with exposed ratchet for pipe through 1". Die heads lock into ratchet and handle assembly. Dies can be reversed for close-to-wall threading. Also available in models with capacities through $1\frac{1}{4}$" and 2".

This sturdy two-handled threader is instantly ready to cut any of three popular sizes of threads. One model cuts $\frac{3}{8}$", $\frac{1}{2}$", and $\frac{3}{4}$". Another cuts $\frac{1}{2}$", $\frac{3}{4}$" and 1".

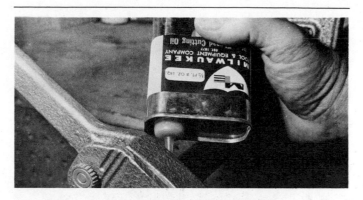

Rugged, low-cost pipe threader is the same as one shown in Milwaukee kit at left. This set includes two steel block dies for $\frac{1}{2}$" and $\frac{3}{4}$" pipe, a guide for $\frac{1}{2}$" die, and cutting oil. The pipe stock itself forms a guide for the $\frac{3}{4}$" die.

A convenient carrier comes with this assortment of drop-head dies that fit the exposed ratchet threaders described above. Die heads lock into ratchet and handle assembly when reversible ratchet knob is pulled out.

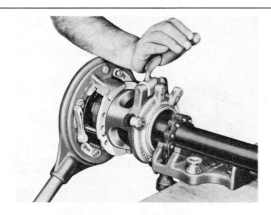

Ridgid model 65R-TC ratchet threader threads 1", $1\frac{1}{4}$", $1\frac{1}{2}$" and 2" pipe with one set of dies. Flip of lever tightens all three jaws together to correct size almost instantly. It's jam-proof—kicks out automatically after thread is cut. Threader is shown with model BC-2A bottom-screw bench chain vise.

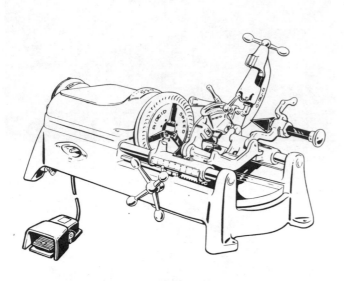

Ridgid model 535 is designed for bench or stand mounting. It cuts, reams and threads $1/8$" through 2" pipe and $1/4$" through 2" bolts. All tools operate independently, swinging away when not in use. Pump recirculates and cleans thread cutting oil. Motor is $1/2$ hp. Integral foot switch.

A typical threader consists of two parts—a stock and a die. The stock is a handled holder with an opening into which you put the die, which does the actual thread cutting. On the other side is a guide or bushing, so you get the threads straight. Simple cutters have two handles extending out from the die on a straight line. Better cutters have ratchet action and are one-handled. You can use either type with a "power drive," a motor-driven device that turns pipe, rod, or conduit for cutters and reamers as well as hand threaders.

Pipe threads are unlike bolt threads in that they are tapered. At the end of the pipe, the threads are deepest and the pipe diameter is smallest. The threads become shallower and the pipe diameter bigger as you move away from the end. As a result, the more you turn the thread into the female fitting, the tighter the joint becomes.

For cutting a female or interior thread, a tool called a tap is used. It looks like tapered bolt with slots running lengthwise across its threads. It is generally available for cutting threads for pipe $1/8$" to 2". The smaller the pipe, the more threads per inch.

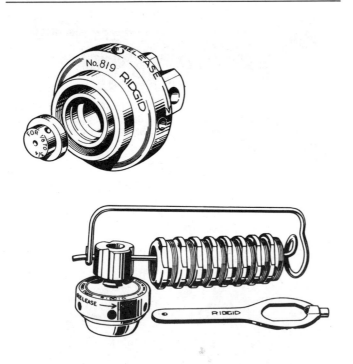
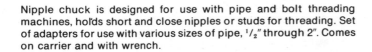

Nipple chuck is designed for use with pipe and bolt threading machines, holds short and close nipples or studs for threading. Set of adapters for use with various sizes of pipe, $1/2$" through 2". Comes on carrier and with wrench.

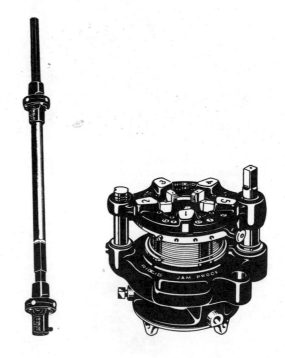

By means of a telescoping drive shaft, threading machines and power drives can be used with geared threaders, such as this No. 141 Ridgid threader for $2 1/2$", 3", $3 1/2$" and 4" pipe and conduit. Also available is No. 161 for 4", $4 1/2$", 5", and 6" sizes.

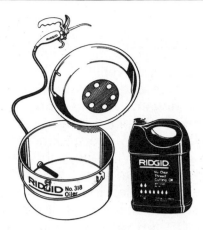

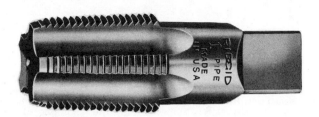

Hand operated oiler. Drip pan catches oil runoff, chips and scraps. Oil is double-screened and recirculated. It stops oil waste, and you can keep dies flooded for easy threading and lengthened life.

To cut interior threads, you need a "tap." Taps like one shown are made of carbon steel and are for right-hand threads only. The number of threads per inch depends upon the size of the tap. Available in nine sizes from $1/8$" through 2".

Here is a No. 535 pipe threading machine being used as a power drive to operate a No. 141 threader by means of a universal drive shaft. Worker is using hand-operated oiler. The pipe threading machine is mounted on an enclosed wheel stand. Open wheel stands and leg stands are also available.

Hammer-type flaring tools come in eight sizes for all $3/8$" through 2" water tube. Long nose helps center tool to produce smooth, uniform flares. Construction is hollow to allow the full impact of each hammer blow to be transmitted to the tube and reduce number of blows needed. Ridgid.

Flaring tool for copper, brass and aluminum tubing. Hook-on self-centering yoke. Cone swivels on ball bearing, producing 45° flares on $3/16$", $1/4$", $5/16$", $3/8$", $7/16$", $1/2$" and $5/8$" O. D. tubing.

Unique flaring tool has one opening that holds all tube sizes—$3/16$" to $5/8$" (4.7mm to 16mm) O. D. Design is more compact and easier to use than multi-opening flaring bars. Produces 45° flare and original wall thickness is maintained at base of flare. Slip-on yoke permits use in tight quarters. Wards.

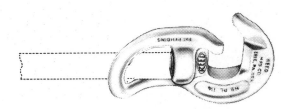

Screw a convenient length of 1" pipe into the tap socket and this pipe puller is ready for use. It takes hold the moment lifting or pulling pressure is applied. Each puller is designed for only one pipe size, and sizes from $3^1/4$" through 2" are available. Reed.

FLARING TOOLS

Slip a flanged nut over the end of a pipe and then flare the pipe end and you have the means of attaching fittings of various kinds. Flare joints can be made in copper tubing, brass, stainless steel, and plastic pipe, and all kinds of flare fittings are available. With the right fittings, flare pipe can be coupled to screw threads.

Some plumbing codes don't allow flare fittings, and they cost more than sweat or thread fittings, but they have advantages. You make them without heat or big, heavy tools and they come apart easily.

Good workmanship is essential in making a water-tight flare. That means pipe ends must be cut perfectly square, and internal burrs and external ridges removed, and the flaring tools be perfectly clean.

Flaring tools are screw-type or hammer-type.

A screw-type flaring tool consists of a vise and a ram. The tube is clamped firmly in the vise, its end flush with the surface. The ram is fitted over the tube end and screwed down slowly and carefully to produce a flare. A single tool may handle from five to seven different pipe sizes ranging from $1/8$" to 1". Some screw-type flaring tools are recommended for aluminum and soft copper only. Others will flare steel, stainless steel, hard copper, and brass.

Hammer-type flaring tools are commonly available in eight sizes, from $3/8$" through 2". Typically, the tool has a diameter stop so flares won't be over- or undersized, and will make a tight seal with the fitting. If the tube being flared is distorted, a long-nose guide will smooth it out.

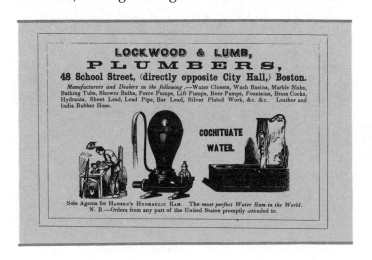

Making and installing a water fountain.

Pipe extractors to remove broken threaded ends of pipe, pipe plugs, fittings, etc. Each extractor is marked with drill size required when solid ends of plugs and fittings must be drilled to receive extractor. Set shown will remove ¹/₈″ through 1¹/₈″ pipe. Sizes through 2″ available.

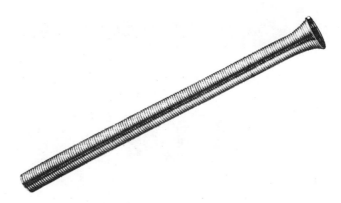

Tube bender spring is applied externally to bend ¹/₂″ soft copper or aluminum tubing. Helps prevent kinking. Seven additional sizes available. Ridgid.

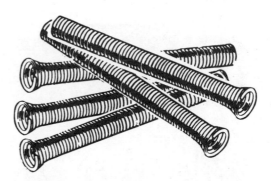

Five-piece tube bender set—external springs for bending soft copper or aluminum tube in sizes from ¹/₄″ to ⁵/₈″. Plumbcraft.

COMBINED FAUCET AND TOY.

46.

TORCHES

Gasoline blow torches are still made, though largely replaced by propane torches. This one is model T-15-C by Cleanweld Turner.

Ever since Prometheus stole fire from Olympus and gave it to mankind, we have been using it for good and ill. One of the better uses is the torch. In New York Harbor, a statue holds it aloft as a beacon of hope. The torch, at a less lofty level, has helped provide drinking water and sanitary facilities for mankind through its role as a plumbing tool. It heats copper pipe and fittings so that they can be joined with solder, an operation known as "sweating." Torches come in several varieties.

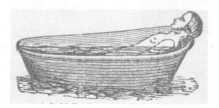

PROPANE TORCH

Up until the early 1950s, blowtorches, usually fueled by gasoline, were used in sweating joints. They were cumbersome and hazardous. Then a lightweight, disposable steel cylinder was developed that could be filled under high pressure with propane, a colorless gas that occurs in petroleum and natural gas, and the two-piece propane torch was born! Give Sidney Reich, then president of BernzOmatic, the credit. The torch opened a new era in do-it-yourself plumbing.

The little propane torch, with its pencil flame burner, will burn up to fifteen hours on a tank that contains just 14.1 ounces of propane. For producing solder joints, especially on larger sizes of copper pipe, you need a burner head with a bigger, hotter flame. These may use up the disposable cylinder in eight hours or less. It's BTU delivery that counts. That's why, incidentally, you can't use a soldering iron for doing plumbing. It just can't give out enough BTUs.

Torches have other uses besides soldering copper pipes. A flame can be used for loosening up rusted nuts and bolts, removing paint, window putty, or ice. It can be used for removing resilient floor tile, or softening a tile to help make it conform to slightly uneven surfaces. It can be used for raising grain in wood, thawing frozen pipes, and making charcoal burn.

Torches may be sold with several accessories or in a kit. The kit may include a pencil flame burner, blowtorch head, flame spreader, soldering tip, spark lighter, and a metal storage case. The soldering tip is handy for soldering wires where electricity for a soldering iron or gun isn't available. The flame spreader is good for removing paint.

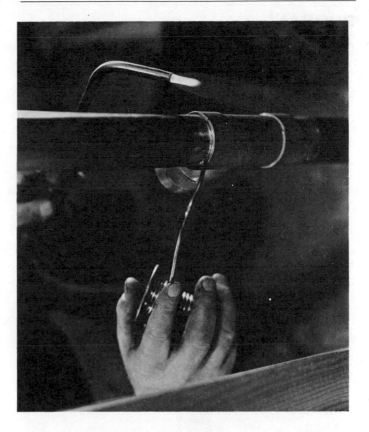

Early propane torch looks much like its present-day counterpart

PROPANE TORCHES

Model JT-10 has "pencil flame" burner and is for ordinary use.

JT-11M "Maxi" jet torch provides more heat over a larger area.

TX-65 has pushbutton to control size of flame, from pilot light to a blow torch big enough to sweat 4″ copper fittings. Up to 8 hours burning time.

Hose extension gives model TX-610 added versatility.

UL 100 "Blow Torch" burner on standard 14.1 oz. fuel cylinder.

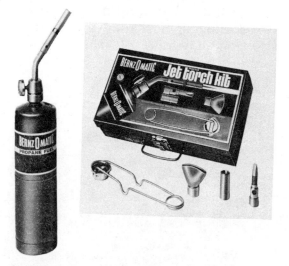

Kit includes pencil flame burner, blow torch head, soldering tip, flame spreader, spark lighter, propane cylinder and storage chest.

MAPP GAS TORCH

The word MAPP stands for methylacedylene propadiene, a gas that produces a hotter flame than propane. Its temperature may reach 3700°F, which is about 500°F more than most propane torch flames.

MAPP, like propane, is available in disposable cylinders. Though the same size as a propane cylinder, they contain 13% more fuel—a full 16 ounces.

MAPP gas can be used for sweating plumbing joints, and it does it faster than propane. Most important, it can sweat joints when propane is ineffective. This is when water is in the line. It is im-

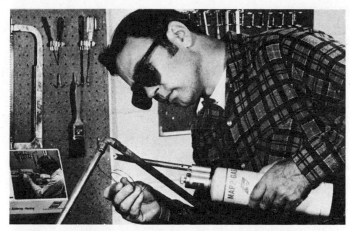

MAPP gas comes in a small steel cylinder, just like propane, but it contains 14% more fuel. Its higher heat makes possible phos-copper brazing of pipe and tubing without the need for a flux.

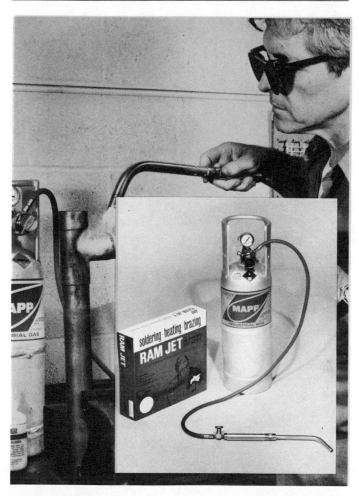

Professional style "Ram-Jet" outfit is especially designed for plumbing, air conditioning, refrigeration, and general maintenance. Outfit is designed for use with 7½ lb. gas cylinder, and includes regulator, hose, aluminum torch with valve, and a high-velocity tip. A 10-foot hose provides additional flexibility. The aluminum torch is lighter, less tiring, and easier to handle than a one-lb. disposable cylinder. MAPP Products.

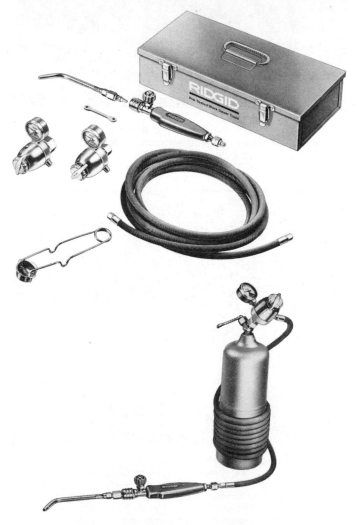

Air acetylene torch kit delivers flame nearly twice as hot as propane. Ideal for soldering or light brazing. Available with choice of five burner assemblies (fine to extra heavy) and two regulator assemblies—for "B" tank or "MC".

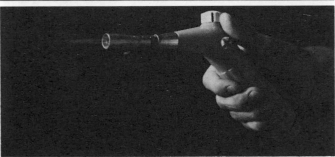

Propane/MAPP torch works without cylinder attached. You fill the "Liberty Torch" from standard propane or MAPP gas cylinders. Supply lasts from 10 to 30 minutes and is conveniently small and light—weighs only 11 ounces. With detachable stand. Turner.

Paul Revere and copper plumbing. Copper is the most widely used of plumbing materials. It was Paul Revere, famous for his midnight ride and as a Revolutionary War patriot, who introduced it to the United States as a native industry. In 1792 he began working with copper, and in 1801 he wrote to a friend: "It is the universal belief that no one in this country could make copper so malleable as to hammer it hot. I have further found it a Secret that lay in very few breasts in England. I determined, if possible, to find the Secret and have pleasure to say that after a great many trials and much expense, I gained it."

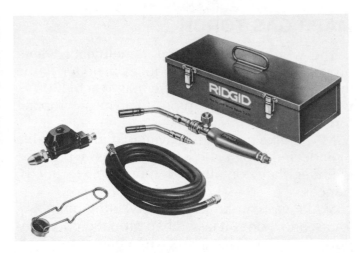

Ridgid No. 70 propane torch kit is recommended for general plumbing, heating, air conditioning, refrigeration, electrical and automotive work. Soft-solders copper, stainless steel, galvanized steel, brass tubing and fittings and electrical cable connectors. Silver-solders copper and other material. Kit includes regulator assembly, two burner assemblies, hose, flint-spark lighter, and steel carrying case.

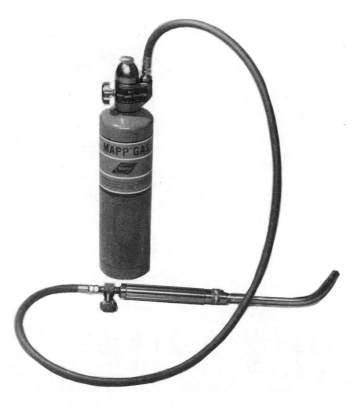

Accessory allows use of a torch handle with a Braze-Pak. Hose fitting adapts the regulator for use with a $3^1/_2$" hose to which a lightweight aluminum torch is attached. Any desired size of tip can then be screwed into the torch.

possible to sweat a joint with propane unless it is completely dry, and there are occasions when achieving this is extremely difficult or inconvenient. With MAPP gas you can actually produce a flame and work under water.

MAPP gas produces a temperature high enough for brazing or hard soldering, silver soldering and aluminum welding, but it won't weld or cut steel. For that, you need oxyacetylene equipment, or a torch that combines oxygen with either propane or MAPP gas.

In ordinary soldering, a tin lead alloy is used. For making electrical joints, or assembling copper pipe, it's strong enough. In brazing, a much harder solder is used, commonly a bronze alloy—from which the term brazing is derived. A silver alloy base can also be used. Previously, the usual way to braze was by means of an acetylene torch.

One secret of the MAPP torch is its special burner tip. Gas leaves it at such high velocity, it can put two to three times as much heat on the work. The torches also include a built-in pressure regulator, so the torch can be used in an upside-down position, and its flame won't blow out in the wind.

MANUFACTURERS

BernzOmatic, Cleanweld Turner, and Ridgid are leading makers of propane torches and equipment. MAPP equipment makers include MAPP Products, BernzOmatic, and Cleanweld Turner.

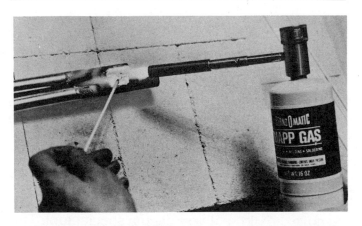

This torch features a spiraling-flame "Cyclone Jet" burner that, manufacturer says, doubles the BTU output of previous MAPP gas torches. BernzOmatic.

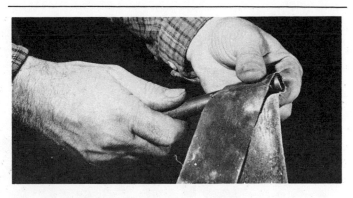

Emery abrasive cloth is specially processed for cleaning copper tube and fittings. It's 1½" wide, and comes in rolls 15' and 75' long. 3/0-120 grit.

Copper cleaning tool is made of washable rubber impregnated with abrasive. Cleans outside of tubing as well as the end and inside of fittings. To use, simply squeeze the tool.

Fitting and tubing cleaner cleans ½" and ⅝" tubing, ⅜" to ⅝" fittings. All metal, with steel wire bristles and protective cap.

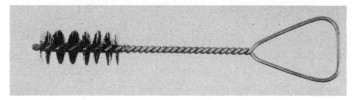

Cleaning brush for cleaning inside of copper fittings in preparation for soldering. Bristles are made of fine wire. Plumbcraft.

47.
MISCELLANEOUS PLUMBING TOOLS

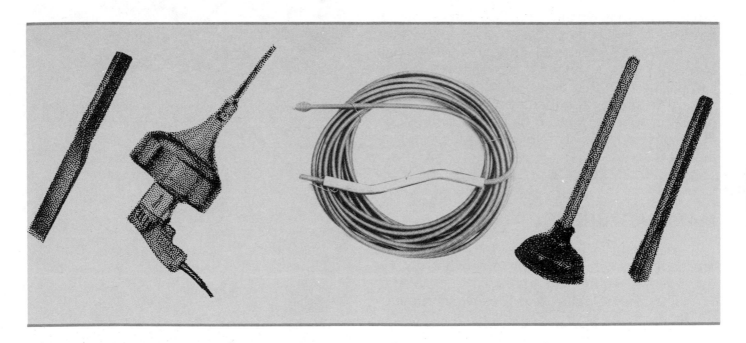

The ancient Chinese used dripping water as a means of torture. The drip-drip-drip of a faucet can be torture, too, and it wastes an incredible amount of water in the course of even one day. Sometimes all a dripping faucet needs is a washer. At other times, a little surgery may be required as well.

Valve-seat dressers. Often, a new washer is insufficient to stop a drip, or if it does it may do so for only a short time, because the seat on which it makes contact is rough. A simple faucet seat dresser can be used to smooth the metal and solve the problem.

There are two types of dressers. One type uses the cap nut of the faucet as a guide and holder.

For faucets that have no cap nut, or can't otherwise accommodate this tool, there is a second type which comes with a "guide cone." Both types are usually sold in a kit which consists of cutters for three sizes of faucets, washers, brass screws, and packing. Packing is used to stop leaks around the faucet cap nut.

Valve-seat replacement tool. Some faucets of conventional washer seat design have removable and replaceable seats. Installing a new brass seat is usually better than resurfacing an old one. To remove the old seat you need a special tool. This tool comes in both a straight and an "L" pattern and will fit seats with either a square or octagonal hole. A significant difference is that with a straight seat tool you must use a wrench or pliers. No wrench or pliers is required for the L-shaped seat tool.

There are twenty-four different sizes of faucet seats. Get a new seat by the make and model number of the faucet, or by taking the old seat as a sample to your plumbing parts supplier. For some faucets that have no removable seat, you can get a tool that will tap threads into the faucet seat hole. You can then install a new brass seat.

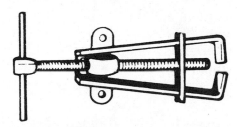

This tool by Kirkhill easily removes all common faucet handles.

"Drip-Fixer" is for smoothing faucet seats. Set includes two cutting heads with coarse and fine files for $\frac{1}{4}$", $\frac{3}{8}$", $\frac{1}{2}$" and $\frac{5}{8}$" faucet seats, T-handle, and four replacement washers. Wrightway.

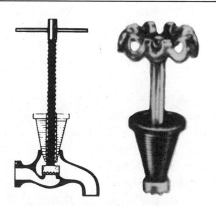

Some faucets are designed so that you can use a seat dresser or reamer only if you have a cone guide. *Left:* Plumbcraft cone guide comes in kit with four faucet washers, three brass bib screws, faucet packing and three cutters for various sizes of faucets. *Right:* Wards seat dresser comes with $\frac{1}{2}$", $\frac{5}{8}$" and $\frac{3}{4}$" cutter wheels.

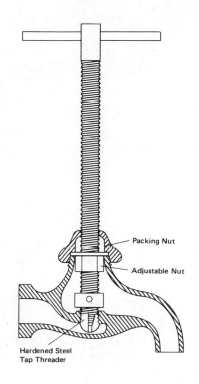

You can use this tool to tap threads in a seat, then screw in an O'Malley brass "Nu-Seat" with your screwdriver. It's a big help in stopping drips.

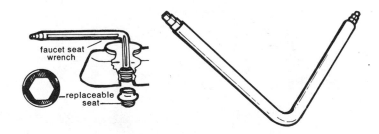

To remove or install a replaceable seat, you need a wrench. This Kirkhill step-type wrench is designed to fit various seat sizes.

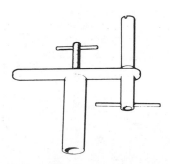

Moen is one of the most popular single lever faucets. This tool by Kirkhill will pull the entire cartridge or remove stem only, so you can make repairs or replacements.

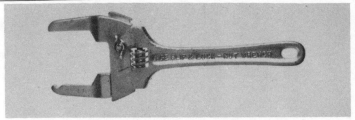

Above left: Combination closet spud wrench adjusts to 3". *Above right:* Waste and water connection wrench fits faucet, vanity, sink and toilet connections. Hancock-Gross.

Wards offers this low-priced 25" drain cleaner made of highly tensile $3/8$" spring wire. It has a one-piece boring head and a twist-adjustable handle.

Flat steel sewer rod, made of oil-tempered spring steel. Available $1/16$" or $1/8$" thick, $1/2$" or $3/4$" wide, and 50' to 150' long. Includes frame, slide handle and revolving head. Wards.

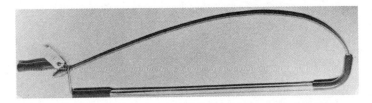

Toilet auger, made of highly tensile wire, has a protective sleeve and bowl guard so it won't mar bowl. Plumbcraft.

Force pump. Also called a plunger or a "plumber's friend," this is good for minor clogging. A typical model has a rubber vacuum cup 4" to 6" in diameter, and a handle from 9" to 24" long.

Another type of force pump is a hemisphere with a flexible tube extension which can be folded back. This type is especially good for toilets.

A third type has a bell-shaped chamber, rather than a hemispherical one, and it provides somewhat more pressure.

Pressure pump. This works on the same principle as the tire pump. It has a tapered rubber end which fits various size drain openings. With every stroke, you send a surge of water through the drain. Usually, one or two strokes are enough to clear an obstruction.

Sears has an English-made power cleaner which discharges a blast of air from a carbon dioxide bulb. It works on pipes up to 2" in diameter, and one bulb is usually sufficient for one blockage.

Drain King is a hose attachment for clearing clogged drains. The force of the water stream clears the blockage. It fits in 3" to 6" pipes, and you can insert it in a roof vent near the clogged area.

Snake. Also called an auger, this is usually made of flat steel, or steel wire wound in a tight spring, and has a spiral gimlet head. It comes in a variety of sizes, generally ranging from $1/4$" x 6' to $1/2$" x 50'. Some are fitted with a steel slide handle or a twist-crank adjustable handle to help them move through traps and around bends. A variation of the simple auger is one that is self-storing in a steel cannister. You feed out the wire for use, crank it back in when finished. Generally, it has $1/4$" wire and it is 15' to 25' long.

Other augers are adaptable to variable-speed portable drills, which give them spin action. Still others are specifically designed for use with $\frac{1}{4}''$, $\frac{1}{2}''$, or $\frac{3}{4}''$ drills. They can drill through packed deposits without any need to remove trap or crossbars.

Sewer rods. When a blockage occurs in a 5″ sewer pipe or in a run of 25′ or more, you can rent a rod and motor to clear it. You will need heavy leather gloves to protect your hands. Sewer rods are actually a group of flexible rods joined together, with their ends shaped to serve as cutters. They can cut away roots, a frequent cause of blockage.

Closet auger. This is a short snake especially made for the trap that is part of a toilet. The best ones are unkinkable and in 3′ or 6′ lengths. They are made of plated wire, have a wood handle and a vinyl bowlguard.

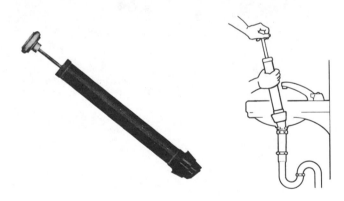

Drain opener pressure pump. A few strokes of the pump handle send a surge of water suddenly and swiftly to clear wasteline stoppages. Tapered rubber end fits various sized drain openings in sink, basin or tub. Hancock-Gross.

"Drain King" attaches to hose, transmits powerful pulses of water to loosen and clear drain blockage. One model is for drains 1″ to 2½″. Another is for 3″ to 6″ pipes. G. T. Water Products.

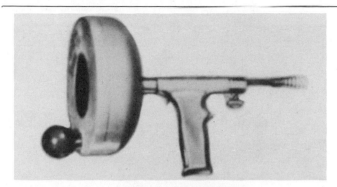

Self-storing auger is made of $\frac{1}{4}''$ highly tensile wire. It comes 15′ and 25′ lengths. Spin action snakes wire through traps and around bends. Wards.

Pipe and drain cleaner operates as easily as an electric drill. Merely loosen chuck, pull a length of cable from the drum, tighten the chuck and squeeze the trigger. You can feed bulb auger into the line past crossbars and trap. Cable is 25′ long. Variable speed reversing motor—0 to 500 RPM. Ridgid.

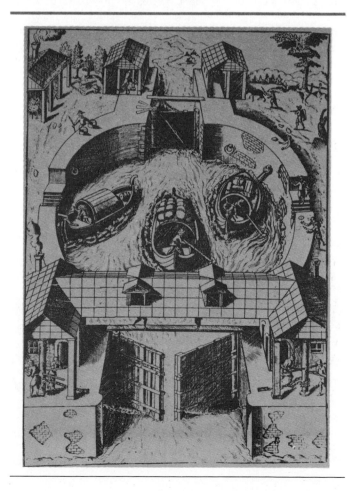

Professional drain cleaning machine. Ridgid's Kollmann K-50 comes in eight different package combinations to solve any $3/4$" through 3" line cleaning problem. It spins 25' of $5/16$", 35' of $3/8$", or 100' of $5/8$" sectional cables.

Caulking tools. Cast-iron pipes are frequently joined with lead caulking, and a variety of special tools is needed for the job. A straight end of pipe fits into a bell end and the space around it is packed with okum, a fiber that was traditionally used for caulking the seams of wooden ships. To pack in the okum, yarning irons are needed.

After the okum is packed in tightly, the joint is filled with molten lead. To melt the lead, a furnace, a cast-iron lead pot, and a ladle are needed. To keep the lead from running out on a horizontal run of pipe, a joint runner is used. After the lead has cooled somewhat, it is further compacted with special caulking irons. All this equipment is shown in accompanying illustrations.

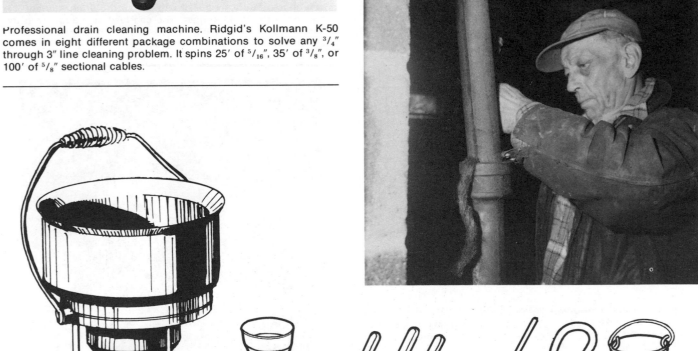

Tools for working with cast iron pipe. *From left:* Gasoline furnace, offset yarning iron, caulking irons, pouring ladle, asbestos joint runner, and cast-iron lead-melting pot.

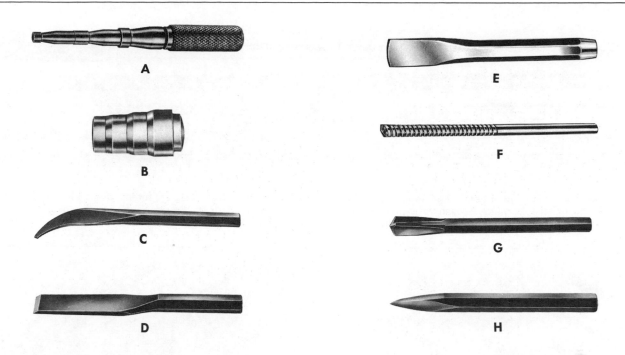

A variety of plumbing aids. A. Small tubing expander swages $3/8''$, $1/2''$, $5/8''$ and $3/4''$ copper tubing. **B.** Large tubing expander expands $1^1/4''$, $1^3/8''$ and $1^1/2''$ tubing. **C.** Lead picking tool has 2" blade length, 9" overall length. **D.** Floor chisels come in $5/8''$, $3/4''$, 1" and $1^3/16''$ widths. **E.** Soil pipe chisels have $5/8''$, $3/4''$ or $7/8''$ widths. **F.** Power masonry drills have tungsten carbide cutters, come in sizes from $3/16''$ to $1/2''$. **G.** Star drills cut holes in concrete and masonry from $1/4''$ to $1^1/8''$ in diameter. **H.** Concrete gads for breaking holes in concrete and masonry. All are by Proto.

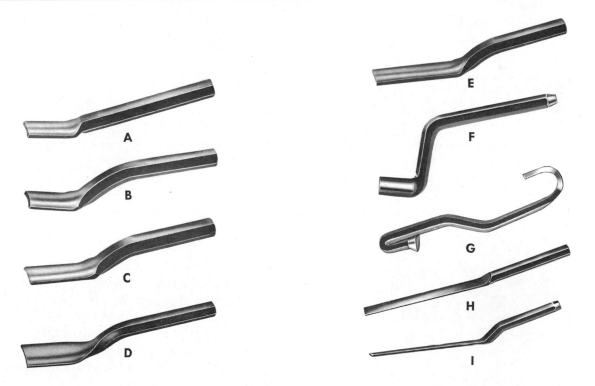

Caulkers and yarning irons. A. Long caulkers—inside and outside. **B.** Offset caulkers—inside and outside. **C.** Water main caulker. **D.** Broad curved-nosed caulker. **E.** Long gasket caulkers. **F.** Left and right caulkers. **G.** Ceiling caulker. **H.** Spring yarning iron. **I.** Offset yarning irons. Foregoing tools mentioned in the plural come in more than one size. All by Proto.

Extra long bits for plumbers are 24″ long, made of premium quality carbon steel. Designed for fast drilling in wood, plastic, metal, lath, plaster—even through nails. Square shank can be cut off for chucks requiring round shanks. $^1/_4$″ for $^1/_4$″ drill, $^3/_8$″ for $^3/_8$″ drill and $^1/_2$″, $^5/_8$″ and $^3/_4$″ sizes for $^1/_2$″ drill. Brookstone.

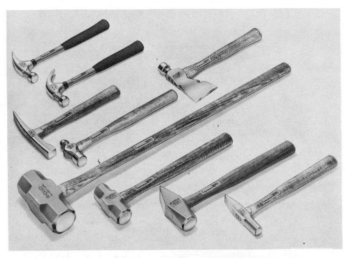

These hammers are not exclusively for plumbing use; other trades use them as well. But they are nine kinds of striking tools a plumber has occasion to use. From left top, ripping, claw, brick, ball peen, long handled sledge, short handled sledge, engineer's and riveting hammers. Half hatchet at right. Ridgid.

High-speed hole saws. These are deep-cut models ($1^7/_8$″ depth) for cutting through joists and studs. Available in diameters from $^7/_8$″ to $3^3/_8$″. Larger saw arbor is for $^1/_2$″ chuck, smaller one for $^1/_4$″ or $^3/_8$″.

Plumber's hole saw kit includes six saws, sizes from $^7/_8$″ to $2^5/_8$″. Also, two arbors and metal carrying case. Ridgid.

Other plumbing tools. Hole saws are used for a variety of purposes, but for plumbing they are almost indispensable. Sometimes you can run pipe or tubing below joists or in front of studs, but often you have to go through the structural members. A hefty $^1/_2$″ drill and an assortment of hole saw sizes is the answer.

Plumbers, along with electricians, frequently share the need for extra long bits to reach farther and drill deeper. They come in diameters from $^1/_4$″ to $^3/_4$″, and the latter is just right for $^1/_2$″ tubing.

Plumbers aren't supposed to be carpenters or masons, but that doesn't stop them from frequently needing a variety of hammers, and, of course, a hatchet. An accompanying illustration shows an assortment of such tools.

PART IV

CONCRETE/ MASONRY TOOLS

48.
TOOLS FOR MIXING AND PLACING CONCRETE

Cement sticks things together. The cement used in concrete and masonry work is a gray powder called portland cement. It's called portland because its inventor thought it looked like the color of stone on the Isle of Portland, off the British coast. The inventor was Joseph Aspidin, an English bricklayer who, in 1824, made the first manufactured cement by burning clay and limestone in his kitchen stove and then grinding the resulting clinker.

Before Aspidin's time, natural cements were used. The Egyptians used lime and gypsum mortar in building pyramids. The Romans made cement mortar out of lime and volcanic ash. Today, limestone, clay, cement, rock, gypsum, and other materials go into the manufacture of portland cement. It's so fine a powder, most of it will go through a screen with 40,000 openings per square inch. Thomas Edison had a hand in making cement what it is today. In 1902, he invented the rotary kiln which revolutionized its manufacture.

Cement, then, is powder that holds the mix together. The sand, gravel, or other materials in the mix that the cement sticks together are known as *aggregates*. Cement, mixed with sand as the aggregate, produces *mortar,* which is used in the laying of brick and stone. Cement mixed with sand and gravel produces *concrete*. Concrete is not a new invention. The Romans used concrete in making the foundations of the Forum.

Concrete is usually laid on a smooth, well-drained base. In preparing that, you'll need shovels, picks, and other excavating tools. You may have use for a tamp and a roller.

If your concrete is to be poured into forms, you'll need a variety of carpentry tools—saw, hammer, and certainly a level.

Concrete is frequently reinforced. This may be with rods or mesh. Reinforcing rods are cut with a hacksaw, oxyacetylene torch, or hammer and chisel. Rods are wired together where they cross, and for this you will need heavy pliers.

To bend rods, you can use a piece of pipe as a lever. To save cutting, have rods cut to the specific lengths you want when you buy them. Rod suppliers have special heavy-duty cutters for this purpose. Welded wire fabric can be cut with a hacksaw or a pair of heavy cutters.

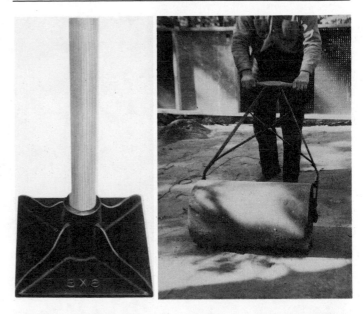

To provide a firm, solid base—cast iron tampers by Easco are available in 8" x 8" (11 lb.) and 10" x 10" (14 lb.) sizes. Shaped hardwood handle is 44" long.

This 36" lawn roller, used for preparing base, weighs 82 lbs. empty, 450 lbs. filled with water. 18" diameter. Jackson Mfg. Company is a leading roller manufacturer.

A variety of levels is shown in Chapter 11. This 2' model by Stanley works almost as well as a 4' model if you provide a bridge to span the distance between forms.

Basic tools for small concrete and masonry jobs include wheelbarrow, hoe, shovel, brick trowel, cement finishing trowel, wood float and mortar board.

Length of this mahogany mason's level is an aid to accurate reading—it's 48" long. It has six matched vials (two double plumb and one double level). Stanley.

Wire reinforcement gives concrete tensile strength it otherwise lacks. Popular 14″ utility cutter transforms 50 lb. hand pressure on handles to 4000 lb. pressure on cutting edge of jaws. H. K. Porter is a leading manufacturer of these tools.

Poly cover protects wire fabric against rust.

These cutting nippers are especially designed for easy cutting of large nails, small spikes, and the tie wires on concrete forms. Drop forged. Polished head and enameled "T" handles. Available 10″ and 14″ long. Channellock.

A hack saw blade with 18 teeth per inch does an acceptable job of cutting reinforcing rods.

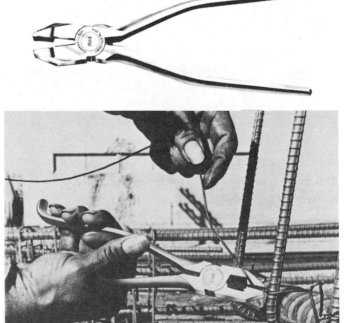

Concrete reinforcing bars must be tied with wire wherever they cross. Here are the pliers for this job. Balanced tension coiled spring eases jaw opening and closing, and long handles provide extra leverage. Channellock.

TOOLS FOR MIXING CONCRETE

For mixing concrete you need a container in which to do the mixing, a hoe, a shovel, and a bucket. A wheelbarrow is a satisfactory container for mixing a small quantity. For larger quantities, you can buy a metal "boat," or make your own boat, using 2 x 10s as the sides, and making ends and bottom of exterior plywood or tongue-and-groove boards. Ends should be slanted at about a 45° angle.

For mixing a small quantity of concrete, you can get by with using a garden hoe. For any significant mixing, you should have a concrete hoe. A concrete hoe is larger than a garden hoe, and has a pair of holes to aid the blending process. A shovel is useful both in measuring materials and placing the concrete.

For large projects or regular use, you can buy or rent a power mixer. It may be run by either an electric motor or a gas engine. If you need a cubic yard or more of concrete, you'll probably find it better to skip mixing it yourself and have it delivered by a ready-mix truck.

Steel mortar box is leakproof, and its smooth interior makes mixing or cleaning easy. In cold weather, you can put it over a fire to heat mortar or cement. Rolled outside edges strengthen box, make handling easy. Shown is 9.2 cubic foot box. Six and 16 cubic foot sizes also available. Goldblatt.

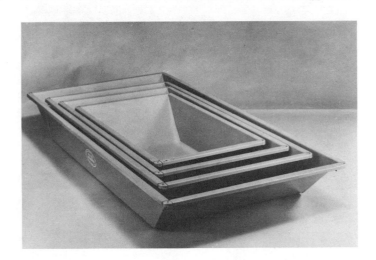

Steel mixing boxes by Jackson with sides and bottom formed from a single sheet of steel. Corners are lapped and electric welded with pressed steel reinforcements. Sizes range from 1" x 28" x 51½" to 11" x 40" x 75½". Maximum capacities range from 6 to 16 cu. ft.

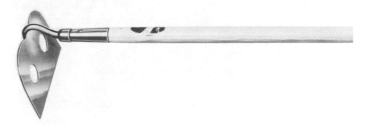

The right tool for hand mixing—two-hole mortar hoe with 10" blade, 5½' handle. Goldblatt.

Thomas Edison invented the rotary kiln, which revolutionized cement manufacture.

English-made Roll-A-Mix produces 100 lbs. of concrete in two minutes. No engine. Push it along the ground and the polyethylene barrel revolves. J. C. Penney.

All-purpose Foote mixers. Besides concrete, mortar, and stucco, you can use them for mixing animal feed, fertilizer, soil, resin, or for industrial tumbling. Both models can be run by a $1/2$ hp electric motor or a 3 hp engine with 6-to-1 gear reduction. *Top:* This model has semi-pneumatic tires for easy hand-portability. Can be loaded or emptied from either side. *Bottom:* This trailer portable model has moderate-speed towing capabilities. Both models have a capacity of $3^1/_2$ cu. ft. dry and $2^1/_2$ cu. ft. wet. That amounts to half a bag of cement plus aggregates per load.

TOOLS FOR PLACING CONCRETE

The best wheelbarrow for handling and moving concrete is a deep-tray contractor's buggy. It holds over twice as much as an ordinary wheelbarrow. It also has a pneumatic tire that makes pushing the barrow easier and gives the concrete a smoother ride so that its ingredients stay mixed and don't segregate.

A garden rake is a good tool for tamping concrete, eliminating air pockets, and bringing fine pastelike material, or "fat," to the surface. This makes for easier finishing, and by pushing larger aggregates down into the slab you give it greater strength. For professional use, there are special concrete rakes of lightweight magnesium or steel. They have wide, flat teeth on one side, which are strong enough to lift reinforcing mesh set in the concrete. The other side is a smooth edge for screeding or floating, preliminary leveling-off.

Some professionals prefer concrete placers or Kumalongs to shovels or rakes. These have no teeth. Typically, they have steel blades 20″ by 4″, and a 54″ handle. One type has a hook attached to the top of the blade for lifting reinforcing wire.

There are also tools especially designed for tamping concrete. A typical one, made by Marshalltown, has a tamping surface 48″ by 6½″, made of reinforced round-hole grill.

Ready mixed concrete can sometimes be chuted to where you want it, but often you have to wheel it. Most home barrows have a capacity of only 2 cu. ft. Big concrete barrows hold 4 cu. ft.—or 6 cu. ft. if you heap it.

Large gear ratio means slower turning, which is the secret of a good batch. It's also the reason why you can use a ⅓ or ½ hp motor to run most small mixers.

Twelfth-century wheelbarrow is here compared to an earlier mode of conveyance.

Three Jackson Wheelbarrows

Jackson is the largest manufacturer of wheelbarrows, carts, etc. Shown here are some of their models.
Steel-handled wheelbarrow takes vinyl handgrips. Available in 4½ and 5 cu. ft. capacities. Double disc steel wheel, 4.00 x 8" two-ply tubeless pneumatic tire. Self lubricating bearings.

Press-formed 16 gallon steel tray has a 5 cu. ft. capacity. Special "Glide Ring" lets shovel or hoe glide over bolt heads. One-piece steel handles. Steel braces support front slant of tray.

Large capacity (8 cu. ft.) concrete cart will take full batch from small mixers. Rocker feature makes dumping easy. 4.00 x 18" pneumatic tires, 26" O.D.

When concrete has been poured in a slab, it is leveled off with a screed or straightedge. A 2 x 4 or 2 x 6 is the usual "tool" for this operation, but professionals use magnesium screeds. They come in 1 x 4, 2 x 4, and 2 x 5 in a variety of lengths. There is also a power screed. It takes boards up to 16' long and its 3 hp engine gives it the muscle to strike off, compact, and float a slab in one pass, leaving it as a semifinished surface. It is now ready for troweling and other finishing operations.

If a concrete surface is so large you can't reach it from the edge, you can erect a wooden bridge across the slab, using planks, or you can use a darby. A darby is a variety of long float. Most floats are around 4" wide and 8" or 16" long. Darbies are from about 28" to 60" long. They taper from point to rear, typically from about 2½" to 3½".

Largest are bull floats. These are usually 42" to 60" long and have center-attached handles 4' to 6' long. With a handle 6' long you can have a forward reach of 8' or more. For a still longer reach, you can attach a magnesium extension handle. All these long-arm tools are designed to float large, wide slabs without putting down planks. If you're worried about tangling with overhead electric wires, you can get insulated extension handles that are nonconductive.

Troweling and final finishing begin when concrete has begun to stiffen and has lost its sheen. Depending on the weather, this may be anywhere from twenty minutes to eight or ten hours. When surface water has completely disappeared and a trowel can be arced over the surface without digging in, the time has arrived.

Eighteenth century French gypsum mine. Gypsum is a prime ingredient of cement.

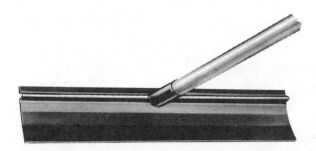

Place concrete with a "concrete placer." Goldblatt says it works better than a shovel or rake. Made of 14 gauge steel, size is 19$\frac{1}{2}$" by 4". Weighs 3$\frac{1}{2}$ lbs. 54" handle.

Tamping with a "Jitterbug" brings fine material to the surface, settles larger aggregate. In 36", 46", and 48" sizes and three grill styles—round hole, expanded steel, and big diamond. Goldblatt.

Ordinary garden rake with tines turned upward is a good tool for pushing concrete mix around.

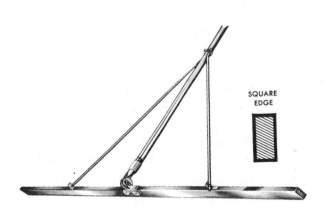

How do you know when concrete's level? A 10' or 12' pavers' straightedge makes it a snap. These straightedges are one-piece hollow extruded aluminum that's lightweight and die-straight. Flat bottom and square sharp edges make inspection easy. Goldblatt.

This lightweight concrete rake is made of magnesium. Concrete won't cling to it. The 19$\frac{1}{2}$" size is 4" deep with $\frac{3}{4}$" wide teeth on 1$\frac{1}{2}$" centers. Also available 24" wide. 54" handle. Goldblatt.

49.
TOOLS FOR FINISHING CONCRETE

Edging tools. After the forms have been removed, the edges of concrete are rounded with an edger tool. A low-cost edger is 3″ by 6″, made of steel with both ends turned up. It has a softwood handle which helps minimize blisters for the occasional worker. Better edgers are made of rivet-free stainless steel or of one-piece bronze. Width may vary from 2″ to 6″ and length from 6″ to 10″. A popular size is 6″ long and 3″ wide; it produces a rounded edge with a $1/2$″ radius. The radius may be anywhere from $1/8$″ to $3/4$″ for sidewalk edgers. For highways, the radius may be as much as $1\,1/2$″.

Though the edger is used as a first step in the finishing, edging is usually repeated after each subsequent finishing operation.

Groovers. Grooves are cut in sidewalks and driveways to control checking and cracking.

They can also help provide a safer, nonskid surface.

Most groovers are made of stainless steel, bronze, or cast iron. Bronze groovers cost more than cast iron, but are superior. On big jobs, professionals use long-handled walking groovers. They are a back saver.

Deep-bit groovers may cut 1", 1½", or 2" deep, and provide effective crack-control joints. Other groovers, known as "cheaters," may cut as shallow as ⅛" and are largely decorative.

To provide safe footing, ¼" grooves are customary. A driveway safety groover cuts six ½" grooves at a time on ¾" centers. A safety step edger cuts four grooves while edging the step.

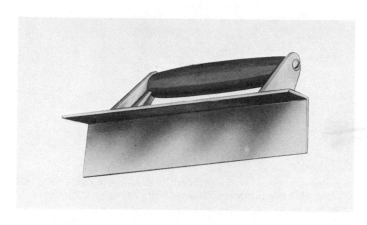

This cast iron tool by Easco puts a beautiful edge on steps. It is 8" long; useful for finishing any outside corner. There's a matching tool for finishing inside corners.

Stainless steel sidewalk edgers are 6" long and come either straight or with curved ends. Many cement finishers find edgers with curved ends are easier to work with.

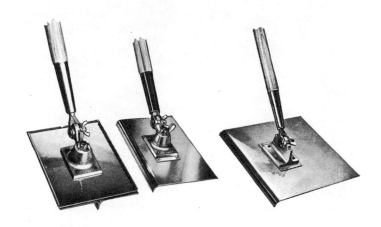

Walking edgers and groovers save your back. Goldblatt's stainless steel tools have 10" long blades, with 5' wood handle. Handles adjust to any position.

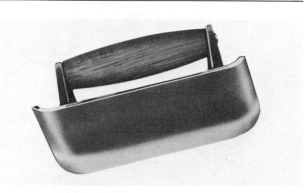

Easco edger of durable cast iron for rounding exposed concrete edges and seams. Curved ends. Measures 5½" x 2¾" with choice of ⅜" or ½" radius.

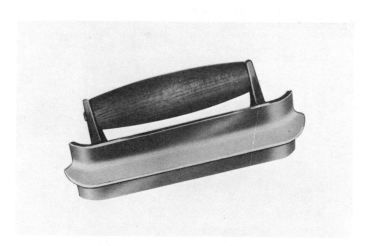

Groover by Easco has a ½" cast-iron bit that is smooth and durable. Body is 6" by 2½"; ends are curved. Another model by Easco has one curved end, one straight. A long model, 9" by 2½", also has one straight end.

Stainless steel groover by Goldblatt is available in models that cut 1", 1¹/₂" or 2" deep grooves. Groover bodies are 6" x 6" and have ¹/₈" wide bits on ¹/₄" radius.

Floats. Hand floating is usually the next step in finishing. Better floats are made of mahogany or magnesium. Floats are also made of teak, laminated popular, a rare wood known as bodark, redwood, and laminated canvas-resin. For special finishes there are cork and also rubber floats.

Magnesium floats are more durable than wood, lighter in weight, and produce a smoother finish. Concrete doesn't cling to them.

Trowels. A wood float produces a gritty, nonskid surface—the kind you want on a sidewalk or driveway. A steel trowel produces a smooth, hard, slick surface—best for slabs on which you want to install thin-gauge flooring, or use for shuffleboard or dancing.

Troweling is the last step in finishing. Trowels are made in many sizes, but a 14" by 4" or 16" by 4" is best for most jobs.

A wood float (right) is used for support as steel trowel is used in final finishing of concrete.

Philippine mahogany float is an inexpensive favorite. Bevel edge helps prevent splintering and makes it possible to work in tight places. Just 3¹/₂" wide; it comes in 15" and 18" lengths. Goldblatt.

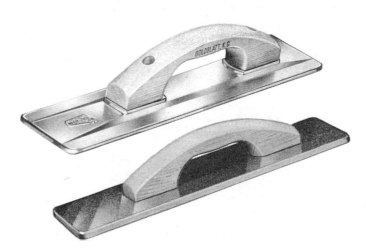

Magnesium and plastic floats by Goldblatt. Both come in several sizes. Magnesium float has a backbone for added strength. Laminated canvas resin float is molded under high pressure to extremely high density.

Rubber float for special finish has aluminum back, wood handle, and a dense sponge rubber face. A waterproof epoxy beading around the edge protects it from coming apart. Wal-Board.

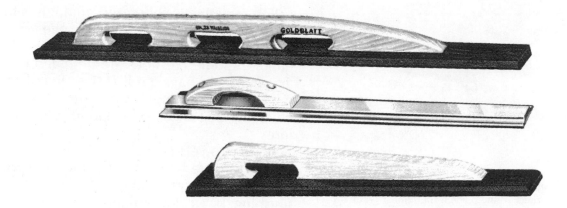

Tapered darbies in mahogany or magnesium. The 45″ mahogany darby (top) has three grips on handle, which make it especially easy to use. It tapers form $3^5/_8$″ at rear to $2^1/_2$″ at point. The 30″ magnesium darby (center) has almost the exact same taper, but features a single-grip wood handle. The 28″ darby at bottom is made of straight grain, kiln dried, imported mahogany.

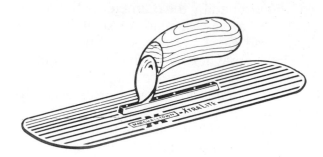

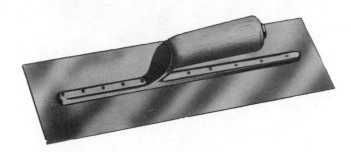

Pool trowel has round ends, and its stainless steel blade is so flexible you can bend it to almost any radius you need. It has a "camelback" handle. Goldblatt.

Easco #500 series trowels are designed for the professional. They feature blades of tempered spring steel, one-piece aluminum alloy mounting shank, with blades and shank secured with smoothly polished cold-rolled steel rivets. Natural finish hardwood handles. Sizes from 10″ to 16″, all 4″ wide.

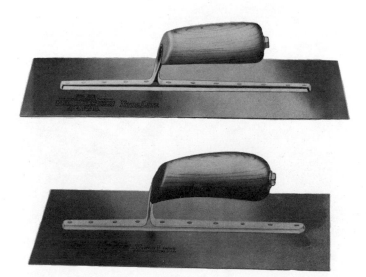

Marshalltown trowels have spring-steel blades, tempered, ground and polished. Malleable iron mounting provides extra stiffness. Natural finish basswood handle. Available in six sizes from 12″ x 4″ to 20″ x 4″. Available with straight handle (*top*) or California handle.

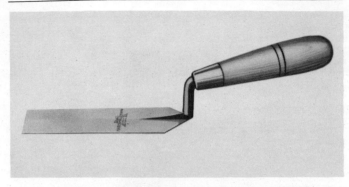

For those last finishing touches—margin trowels are just 1¹/₂" or 2" wide, 5" or 6" long. Forged in one piece from highest grade trowel steel. Hardwood handle. Marshalltown.

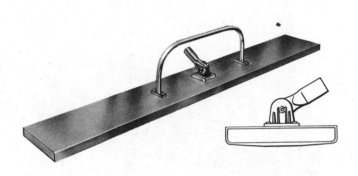

Six-foot magnesium bull float is designed especially for large concrete jobs. Because of its size, it levels and fills voids in the slab to produce a much flatter surface. It comes with a lifting bar for easy handling. Goldblatt.

For very large jobs, and difficult situations, there are Fresno trowels. These range from 24" by 5" to 48" by 5". They are for use with long handles. Some Fresnoes are designed to work at any angle and have a full 360° swing of handle in relation to the trowel. California-style Fresnoes have rounded ends and are for use next to curvatures.

Power trowels are used in finishing large areas or for concrete too stiff to handle otherwise. The machine doesn't completely eliminate hand finishing, but it does minimize it. You can adjust the blade pitch of a power trowel as you work, get to within ¹/₄" of obstructions. There are 28" trowelers, small enough to fit in a car trunk, very popular 34" and 36" models, and heavy-duty 42" and 46" machines for the really big operations. Size is determined by the diameter of the ring that protects the revolving blades. All these trowels are powered by 4-cycle gas engines and they weigh in at anywhere from 100 to 150 pounds.

There is even a power-trowel attachment for a drill. Goldblatt's pony trowel uses any slow-speed heavy-duty drill (¹/₂" or over) with chuck speeds under 500 rpm. It has a 20" ring and is rated at finishing up to 2000 square feet per hour. It's lightweight. It trowels by speed and friction, not weight. It will break down to fit in a car trunk, so you can take it anywhere.

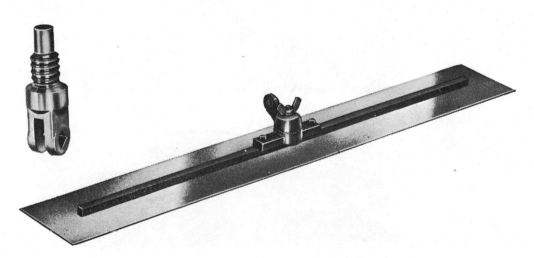

All-angle Fresno trowel and adaptor has a head that pivots 360° so you can work at any angle to the slab. Enables working at hard-to-get-at places with ease. Goldblatt.

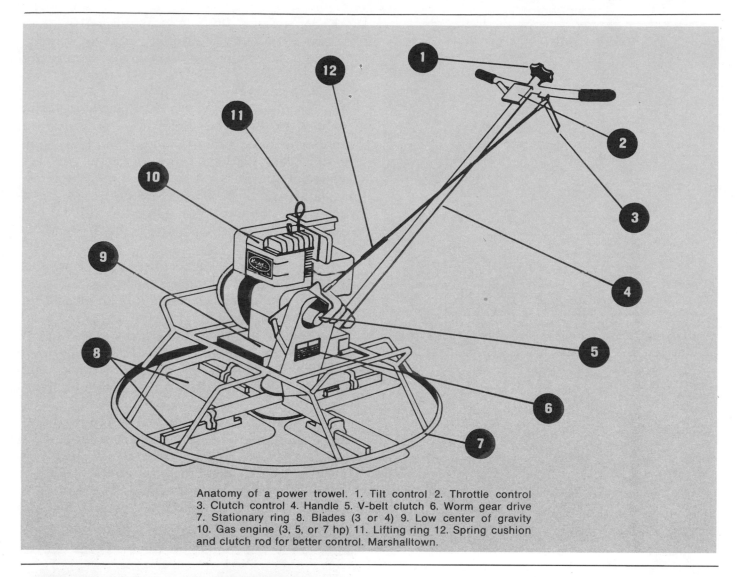

Anatomy of a power trowel. 1. Tilt control 2. Throttle control 3. Clutch control 4. Handle 5. V-belt clutch 6. Worm gear drive 7. Stationary ring 8. Blades (3 or 4) 9. Low center of gravity 10. Gas engine (3, 5, or 7 hp) 11. Lifting ring 12. Spring cushion and clutch rod for better control. Marshalltown.

The 34″ and 36″ power trowelers are the most popular, but there are also smaller and larger models. All have such safety features as "dead man's control lever," which stops blades the moment it's released. Choice of three or four-blade models. Choice of finish, combination, float, float shoe, grinding stone, and stone-holder blades available.

To get out over a slab, you can erect a wooden bridge of planks.

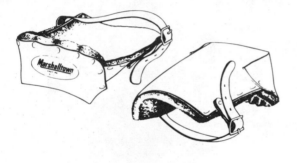

Kneepads. It's difficult to avoid getting down on your knees when finishing concrete. To make the job easier, there are kneepads of leather and felt, plastic, and rubber. Pads also prevent moisture from getting through your clothes and abrasion from wearing them out. When buying pads, check their fit to make sure they won't slip down when you walk or cut into your legs. Some hold in place with one strap, others with two.

Special finishers. Step and corner tools are available in matched pairs—one tool for finishing outside corners, the other for inside ones. These are available with no radius, $1/4''$ and $1/2''$ radius.

There are curved tools, gutter tools, base tools, and radius edgers for curved slabs.

When you finish a concrete job, and it's all set, you may find need for dressing down the work and correcting minor flaws. You may want to remove form and mold marks. For this there are rub bricks, fluted silicone-carbide bricks with handles. Fast cutters, they are available in 20 grit and 60 grit.

For chipping away at concrete, cutting holes, and making minor alterations, there are special concrete chisels. They are 10" to 12" long with bits $1 7/8''$ to $2 7/8''$ wide. If these aren't enough to do the job, there are high-powered rotary hammers, designed for breaking up old concrete and masonry.

Kneepads of plastic or rubber. Neolite kneepads (top) are lined with felt and shaped to fit the knee. One leather strap holds in place. Rubber cushion pad has soft rubber on the inside to act as cushion. Adjustable web straps.

Long-arm acid brush. With the 20" handle, you stay clear of the acid. The bristles are springy Palmyra fiber. Brush face is 5" x 6".

Six Masonry Brushes
by Goldblatt.

Long-wearing acid brush. The 8$^1/_4$″ x 3″ hardwood block has 18 x 7 rows of 1$^1/_4$″ Tampico fiber bristles. Supply your own handle.

Utility brush. Made of white Tampico fiber, 6$^1/_2$″ wide, 2″ thick and trimmed to 4″. Used for many purposes.

Bricklayer's brush. Medium soft hair. Overall length 13″.

Heavy duty acid brush. For use with muriatic or other acid in cleaning. Tampico fibers are 3″ long; handle is 14″ long. Leather binding.

Plastic-bristle acid brush. Brush is 8$^1/_2$″ long, handle 5″.

Textured surfaces. Brooming is an easy way of achieving a striated non-slip surface. It is only one of many surface effects possible. Rectangular and other designs can be cut with a groover. A flagstone effect may be cut with a bent pipe. Circular design is impressed with a cookie cutter.

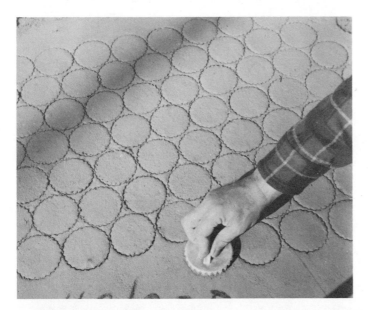

Ready. Aim. Fire! There's almost no effort involved in this "sure-fire" way of fastening to concrete. You just aim the Bostitch "Boss" forced-entry tool and squeeze the trigger. A .22 caliber charge does the rest.

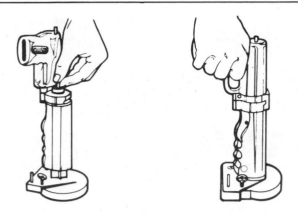

With their hinge-action design, the Bostitch forced-entry tool easily accepts pins and power loads. Once closed, the tool will not fire until depressed flush against work surface.

It's a 1½" rotary hammer for fast percussion-drilling in concrete. No air compressor is needed. Just plug into any 120V outlet. Milwaukee Electric.

The hammer for nailing to concrete. Concrete or masonry nails should be driven with a blacksmith hammer, like Vaughan model shown, or with other hammer whose face has been especially tempered to allow use on hardened nails.

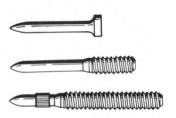

Fasteners for concrete may be headed (left) and have steel discs under the heads for increased bearing area. They may be threaded (center) for attaching of fittings or components after driving. Or they may have knurled shanks for increased holding strength in some applications.

Milwaukee's hard-hitting demolition hammer is powered by an electric motor; needs no air compressor. The 10.5 amp motor delivers 2000 blows a minute.

Manufacturers. Marshalltown and Harrington are two of the top names in trowels and allied equipment. One of the best sources for all masonry tools is Goldblatt of Kansas City, Kansas. Silvo Hardware is also a good mail-order source.

50.

MASONRY TOOLS

According to the dictionary, "A mason is one whose trade is building with units of various natural or mineral products, such as stones, bricks, cinder blocks, tiles, etc., usually with the use of mortar or cement as a binding agent." It's a durable way of building—just look at the pyramids!

The tools for laying brick, block, or stone are simple. If you don't already have them, you can improvise many of them.

MIXING TOOLS

Small amounts of mortar can be mixed in a bucket or tub. You can also mix it on a sidewalk or garage floor, though it's apt to be messy. More workmanlike is a mortar board. This may simply be a 3' by 3' wooden platform, made with a pair of 2 x 4s set on edge as a base, with tongue-and-groove boards or a piece of waterproof $3/4''$ plywood as a top. Better than such an improvised platform are mortar boards you can buy. They are usually made of fiberglass or polyethylene, are lightweight, won't absorb water and won't splinter. They have a lip to keep liquids from spilling over the edges.

A wheelbarrow is also useful for mixing mortar. Support the rear legs on bricks and its pan will be more level. Easier to locate where you want it are pans you can buy that look like the pan off a wheelbarrow. They may be made of plastic—which is an advantage. It's lighter than metal and easier to clean. Dried mortar can be knocked out of the pan with just a few hammer blows on the bottom. It's usually 30″ by 30″ and 7″ deep, with its sloped sides tapering to 16″ by 16″ at the bottom.

For mixing large quantities there are mortar boxes, typically of 16-gauge steel and in sizes that will hold from 6 cubic feet to 15 cubic feet. The 6-cubic-foot size is 42½″ long by 23″ wide, and weighs about 50 pounds.

A garden hoe can be used for mixing, but a mortar hoe is better. It has a bigger blade (10″) and two holes, which help the mixing action.

There are also special power mixers for mortar run by an electric motor or gas engine. Small concrete mixers are also adaptable to mixing mud, as mortar is known to professionals. You can move the mortar from the mixer to where you want it in a barrel or a bucket. Specially made for the purpose are flexible grout buckets made of polyethylene, with a 14-quart capacity. Goldblatt has a special ''bucket'' trowel! It's like a regular trowel with 4″ or so cut off its pointed end.

Pressed steel pan is better than boards or wood boxes. It has rolled reinforced edge, rounded at corners for safety. Top 29″ x 29″, bottom 16″ x 16″, vertical depth 7″. Jackson Mfg. Co.

Containers that won't rust, dent, leak or chip. Bucket (left) is made of flexible polyethylene, holds 14 quarts, and is specially designed for holding grout, which is mortar thin enough to pour. The 15 gallon rubber tub is used for mortar, plaster and small mixing jobs. Goldblatt.

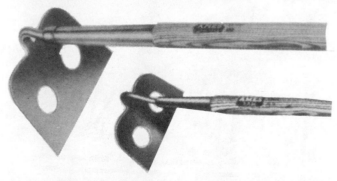

You can use a standard garden hoe for mixing mortar, but a hoe specially designed for the purpose is better. Standard mortar hoe (top) comes with blade 9″ x 6″ or 10″ x 6″. Blade, shank and ferrule are chromed; handle is 5½′ long. Homeowners' model has 7″ x 4¼″ blade, can also be used as a garden hoe. Ames.

A good trowel is a valuable asset. It cuts brick, spreads and scoops mortar, and can be used to tap bricks level. This London style trowel by W. Rose has blade that's 8″ long and 5″ wide at widest point.

TROWELS

Brick trowels generally range in length from 9″ to 13″ and are available with either wood or plastic handles. There are two dominant styles —the Philadelphia pattern and the London pattern. Think of the pointed end of the trowel as the toe and the part up near the handle as the heel. In the Philadelphia pattern, the heel meets the handle at about a 120° angle. In the London pattern, it meets at about 135°. It's called the low English "hang." London trowels are available with narrow heels (about $4^7/_8$″ wide) or wide heels (about $5^5/_8$″ wide). Most Philadelphia trowels range in width from $4^1/_2$″ to $5^1/_2$″.

Filling the joints of brickwork and stonework after they have been laid with mortar or cement is known as pointing. Trowels especially designed for this purpose are similar to brick trowels, except smaller. They range in length from $4^1/_2$″ to 7″ and in width from $2^1/_4$″ to 3″.

Other trowels, known as tuck-pointers or joint-fillers, have blades that are long, thin rectangles. They range in length from $6^1/_2$″ to $6^3/_4$″ and in width from $^1/_4$″ to 1″.

Mixing plaster is known as gauging, and for this, too, there is a special trowel. It's not as wide as a brick trowel—$3^3/_8$″—and is usually about 7″ long.

Tuck pointers and joint fillers are also known as caulking trowels. Their handles, characteristically, have a "high lift," to give you plenty of knuckle clearance.

Marshalltown pointing trowels for those finishing touches come in five sizes, from $4^1/_2$″ x $2^1/_4$″ to 7″ x 3″. Forged in one piece, with hardwood handle and polished steel ferrule.

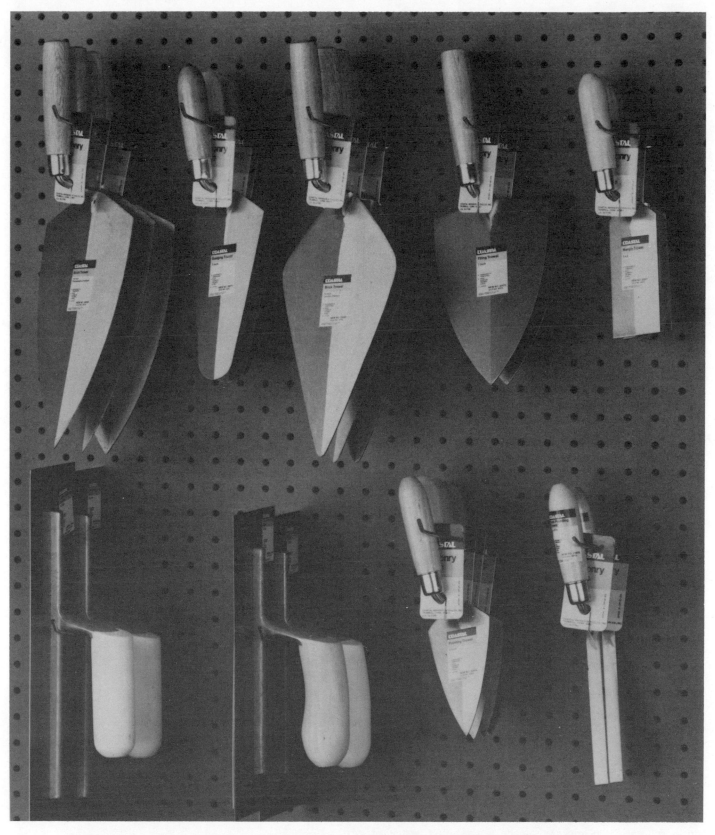

A variety of trowels by Coastal. Top row, from left: Philadelphia, gauging (for preparing or mixing plaster), London (round heel), tiling, and margin trowels. Bottom row: Cement finishing, plastering, pointing, and tuck pointing trowels. Coastal Abrasive & Tool Company.

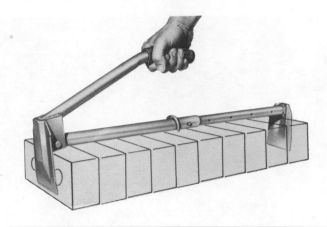

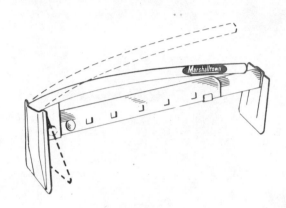

The easy way to carry bricks—brick handlers or tongs, easily adjusted to carry from 6 to 10 bricks. Goldblatt and Marshalltown make them.

Barrow will carry 120 bricks. It's made of hardwood, enameled orange. Double-disc steel wheel has 4.00 x 8", two-ply tubeless pneumatic tire, self-lubricating bearings. Weight is 65 lbs.

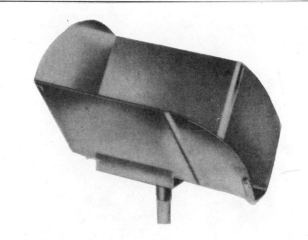

A hod is just the thing for carrying bricks up a ladder. Goldblatt has two sizes in aluminum.

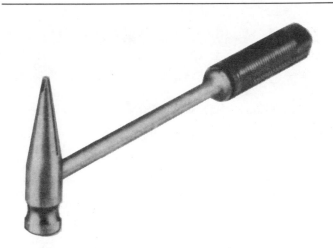

This tool breaks metal bands on brick bundles, and retains metal straps so they won't spring back and cause injury. Also good for opening shipping cartons. Will break metal bands up to 1″ wide.

TOOLS FOR CARRYING BRICKS

The traditional way to cary bricks was by a hod. Hods are still around. Instead of being made of steel, however, they are now of aluminum, which is lighter and eases the load on the shoulder when carrying a full hod up a ladder. Goldblatt has a 24″ by 14″ by 12″ hod which weighs 6³/₄ lbs. It comes complete with handle.

You will probably transport your bricks with a wheelbarrow, but it's not very efficient. There are special brick and tile barrows which carry up to 120 bricks. A similar design can easily be constructed on an old barrow frame.

Brick tongs are handy. They carry from six to ten bricks by varying the adjustment. They make brick carrying easier and faster.

Bricks sometimes come bundled with metal bands. Goldblatt has a special "band breaker" hammer that breaks the bands and holds them to prevent injury.

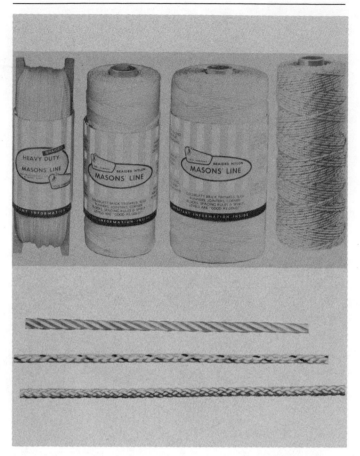

Goldblatt braided nylon line comes in easy-to-see white, green, or yellow. It won't sag, rot or mildew, and is ideal for all construction uses. Hardwood binder with built-in cutter holds 250' of line.

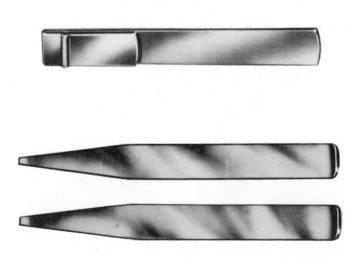

Inexpensive line pins and twigs. *Top:* This 4" snap-over line twig snaps over the line to eliminate sagging. There are 14 in an envelope. Goldblatt's bricklayers' 7" line pins are made of $^1/_8$" tempered tool steel. Four in an envelope. Goldblatt.

LINES AND LINE HOLDERS

Any chalk line or cord can be used to set up guides for laying brick or block, but masons's line is better. It's usually not made of cotton, which sags, stretches, and rots upon exposure to sun and rain, but of nylon or dacron.

Nylon line is the popular favorite. It's made in three colors—green, white, and yellow. Braided nylon line is superior to the twisted kind. The braid is though enough so that it won't break when accidentally hit by a trowel. Once it's taut, it stays taut. It won't sag.

Twisted nylon line is less expensive than braid is tough enough so that it won't break outwear cotton line. Typical braided nylon line tests up to 140 pounds.

Toughest nylon line of all (and most expensive) is braided nylon that has been impregnated and coated. But for super-strength you have go to dacron, which is used in highway work and other large jobs. It comes in 250- and 350-pound test, white only.

You can buy line in lengths from 100' to 1000'. A good choice is a 250' line that comes on a special plastic winder. If you're in doubt about color, yellow line has the advantage of high visibility.

You can support a line with a 10d nail, but line pins are better. One type is flat steel, 7" long and $^5/_8$" wide. It comes in a set of four. An English-made line pin, 6" long, has a 1"-diameter head to hold the line.

Masons use "twigs" to support lines. These are made of clock spring steel, and snap completely around the line. They are cheap and very useful. Size: 4" long and $^5/_8$" wide.

Some line stretchers for cement-block work adjust to fit all blocks from 4" to 12". You can stretch the line as tight as you like, and use the stretcher as a storage reel. Nonadjustable line stretchers come in four sizes to fit different size blocks.

Corner blocks are handy supports for lines. They can be made with an L-shaped piece cut from a 2 x 4. Manufactured ones may be of plastic. They are $4^1/_4$" long and, unlike wood, won't split. Other blocks are made of glass-reinforced nylon or aluminum.

Bricklayers' steel line pins are 6" long with 1" head to hold the line securely. Made of forged steel.

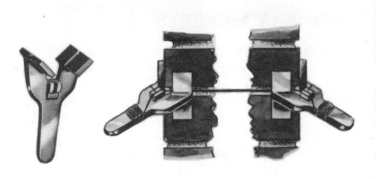

Bricklayer's corner blocks are very effective for holding lines. The line wraps around the stem, goes through the slot at the fork, then between the brick and the groove in the flat face of the block. Available in either reinforced nylon or slightly more expensive aluminum. Available by the pair from Goldblatt.

Home-made line holder is made with a 4" length of 2 x 3 cut into an L shape. It's held in place by line tension which you create by drawing string through hole until it's taut and winding it securely around two finishing nails.

STORY POLES

These are set up to establish a plumb line. Once the pole is plumbed, you have largely eliminated further plumbing work. It certainly cuts down on errors. You can improvise a pole, but nothing as durable, accurate, or light in weight as what you can buy.

Typically, a manufactured pole is 6' or 9' high, made of aluminum, with aluminum fittings for attaching and for carrying lines. These poles stay true, and standard and modular masonry-spacing scales are permanently engraved on them.

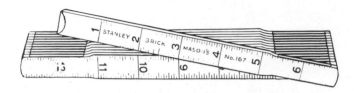

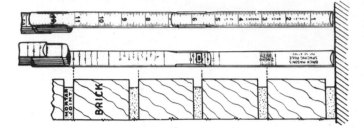

Brick masons' 6' rule with ten brick-spacing scales on one side and inches on the other. High-visibility black numerals on yellow. Strike plates and tips are brass-plated.

BRICKLAYER.

HAMMERS AND SETS

Brick hammers are designed for breaking, trimming, and cleaning brick. They are not intended for striking chisels or metal. Heads are available in weights from 12 to 24 ounces. Most hammer heads are quite similar in design, except for the "short head" hammer, a spacesaver. Handles may be of wood, tubular steel or solid steel. Metal handles invariably have a vinyl or other cushioning grip.

Scaling hammers are not only used for removing scale but for cleaning and refinishing old brick.

You can break a brick with the edge of a trowel or with a brick hammer. The lower front edge of the hammer, as well as its back end, are used for cutting, trimming, and cleaning brick. Brick chisels or sets are more accurate for cutting than either trowel or hammer. They come with blades that range from $2^{1}/_{2}''$ to $7^{1}/_{2}''$ in width. They are usually solid steel, but one British model has a grooved rubber grip.

Other cutters. When considerable fast, accurate cutting is a requirement, professionals use a masonry saw. Most will cut brick, tile, or block. It is especially good on materials that are difficult to cut, like tile and stone.

There's an hydraulic splitter for masonry that works by hydraulic pressure. You just pump the handle. Another type has a foot-operated hydraulic pump, so you can put your whole body behind the effort and develop up to 19 tons of cutting pressure. It will split even very hard stone.

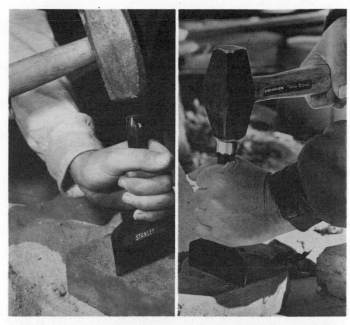

For clean, smooth breaks—Stanley brick chisel, of drop-forged tool steel, has a 3$^1/_2$" cutting edge and blade that's $^7/_8$" thick. It's 7$^1/_2$" overall. *Right:* Goldblatt set and Vaughan hand drilling hammer.

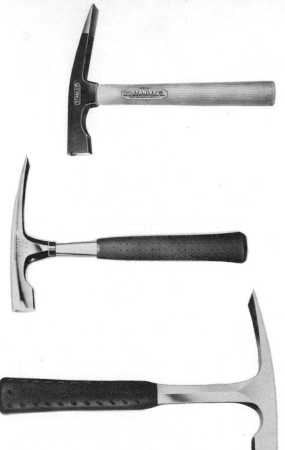

Bricklayers' hammers come in two weights—18 or 24 oz. They are 11" overall; handles are hickory. Use them for breaking, cleaning, or tamping bricks into place.

Chisel with rubber grip made in Sheffield, England. The grooved rubber gives you a better hold and it cushions hammer blows. It's 8$^3/_4$" long overall, with 5" long handle. Choice of 4" or 4$^1/_2$" cutting edge. Goldblatt.

For cutting brick, Goldblatt has a device called Elmer's Midget Helper. You pull down on the handle, and it will shave as little as $1/_4$" off the ends of a brick. A 12" rule and square are built into the tool. It's 26" high and weighs only 40 lbs.

There are many varieties of masonry saws, but most take up to 14" blade, and cut 2" brick, 4" tile, or 8" block. Reservoir pan has pump for delivering water for wet-cutting with diamond blades. Goldblatt is a good source.

Hydraulic cutter will cut brick or stone up to $3^1/_2$" deep and 8" wide. Exerts three-ton pressure. Weighs 51 lbs., is 12" wide, 20" long, 24" high. Goldblatt.

LEVELS

You can use a carpenter's level for doing masonry, but masons have their own favorites. For one thing, a 48" level is usually preferred. Masons also prefer wood levels, perhaps because they are comfortable to the touch in very hot weather and very cold. Mahogany is the popular choice. If it's bound in brass, so much the better.

One beautifully finished level, sold by Goldblatt, is of straight-grain mahogany bonded to an aluminum I-beam that extends the entire length of the level. Aluminum caps protect the wood against moisture where it is most damaging—the end-grain.

Of course, there are also magnesium levels and ones of cast aluminum. These offer the benefits of light weight, precision, and durability.

Mahogany level with brass binding is a favorite with masons. It's 48" long; available with either hand-holes or hand grooves. Fitted with four plumb vials, two level vials. Goldblatt.

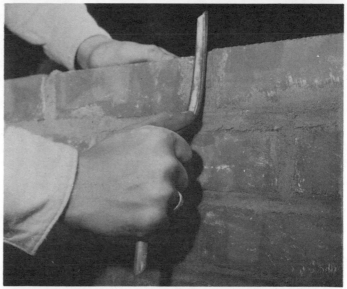

JOINT TOOLS

After laying block or brick, it's necessary to compact and smooth mortar in joints. There are a number of styles of jointers, runners, and rakers to do the job. Most are made of steel, but some are plexiglas.

Sled runners are for horizontal joints. The single runner is a V or half-round, depending on the joint desired. They run from 14″ to 24″ long, with widths of ½″ to ¾″.

It's two jointers in one! Each end of this heavy-duty convex jointer makes a different size joint. Maybe that's why this is the most popular jointer Goldblatt sells. It comes in five sizes ranging from ³/₈″ x ¹/₂″ to ⁷/₈″ x 1″. Overall length is 10¹/₂″. There are also styles for tuck pointing and joint filling. Goldblatt.

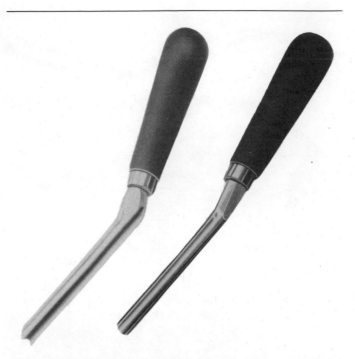

Easy-grip jointers with a comfortable handle. Convex tuck pointer (left) is 4 1/2" long. Concave tuck pointer is 3 7/8" long. Both are 1/2" wide. Easco.

Most jointers are two-ended. One end may be for a V, the other for a round joint. Or both ends may be for half-round joints, but of different sizes. One style of convex jointer is variable. It tapers from 5/8" at the end to 7/8" on the curvature, so you can handle different size joints.

Raked joints have a handsome shadow effect and lend a quality of depth and dimension. You can make your own joint raker. Merely drive a nail in a wood block, letting the head protrude to the desired depth you wish to rake. Easier to use, and with better control, are skate-wheel joint rakers. A hardened nail, adjustable to any desired depth, is used for raking. Smooth-running, 1"-diameter steel wheels bridge the joint, with the adjustable nail between them.

For stone, and other rough materials where you can't rake with a wheel joint raker, there is a combination raker-jointer. It is a 3/4" jointer at one end, a 5/16" joint raker blade at the other end.

A grapevine or colonial jointer produces a flat, recessed joint 1/8" wide.

Both Marshalltown and Goldblatt make these high-lift trowels for tuck pointing. Goldblatt's come in 1/4", 3/8", and 1/2" widths. Marshalltown's come in eight widths ranging from 1/4" to 1".

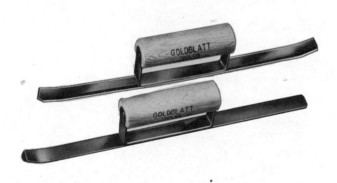

Sled runners for horizontal joints. Sled runner at top is for "V" joints; comes 14", 20" and 24" long. Half-round convex sled runner is for half-round sunken or rodded joints. Nine sizes, from 14" x 1/2" to 24" x 3/4".

Jointer for "grapevine" or "colonial" joints. It produces a flat joint with a concave trough running along its middle. The blade is 6" long, 1/2" wide, with a bit 1/8" wide to produce the concave trough.

A "V" sled runner is best for horizontal joints—and here's the tool that's best for striking the vertical or head joints. Sizes are 8 1/2" x 1/2" and 8 1/2" x 5/8".

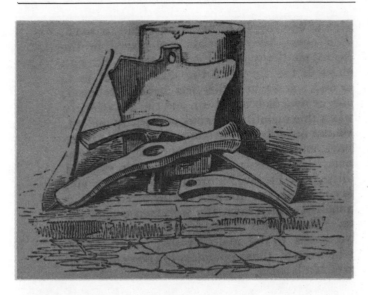

Building tools found at Pompeii.

A metal jointer can leave stains on white mortar, but a plexiglass rod jointer won't. It's 11$^3/_8$" long, comes in $^1/_4$", $^3/_8$", $^1/_2$", $^5/_8$", and $^3/_4$" sizes. Goldblatt.

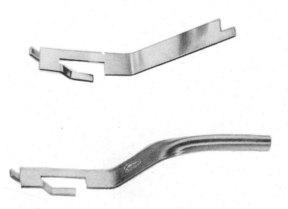

Special joint rakers for joints you can't rake with a wheeled jointer. Jointer at top rakes $^5/_{16}$" joints, throwing excess mortar out as you rake. For raking corners, you use the $^5/_{16}$" and $^3/_8$" tabs at either end. Combined raker jointer has a $^5/_{16}$" raker at one end, $^3/_4$" jointer at other. Goldblatt.

Skate-wheel joint rakers are available from Marshalltown, Harrington, and Goldblatt. Spade bolt holds nail at desired depth for raking. Square handled end can be used for rodding (smoothing) joints.

To make your own raking tool, all you need is a block of wood. Drive in a nail to desired depth.

A plugging chisel is used for removing mortar from brickwork joints so that plugs or wedges can be inserted. The plugs or wedges are then used as a base for attaching things. This imported plugging chisel is an English-made Eclipse.

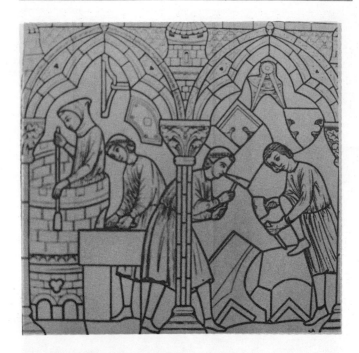

Essentially the same tools are used for building with blocks as are used in building with bricks.

To safely cut brick or block—protect your eyes. Use a hand-drilling hammer with specially tempered face that can strike steel with less danger of chipping or spalling. The bevel grind on striking face of chisel is added protection. Never use a mushroomed chisel without regrinding the bevel.

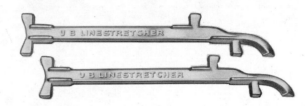

Line stretchers adjust to fit all block from 4″ to 12″. Made of cast aluminum, they have handy posts on which you can wind your line. Sold by the pair. Goldblatt.

You can improvise a line holder from a scrap block of wood along this design. Or you can buy line blocks made of plastic that do a similar job but are more durable. They'll never split.

Abrasive wheel cuts hard and soft masonry. It comes in $6^1/_2$", 7" and 8" sizes with universal bushing to fit diamond, $1/_2$" and $5/_8$" round shafts. Stanley.

Aluminum hawk by Marshalltown is useful to keep a supply of mortar at hand. It's 13" x 13", of 12-gauge hard-rolled aluminum with rounded corners. Trowel is a 14" x 4" "Iowa Cement" model, also by Marshalltown.

Skil introduced this totally new type of portable tool for drilling holes in concrete in 1959. Roto Hammer comes in many models and styles, and there is a complete range of bits and accessories to help you drill, set anchors, tuck point, chisel, bush, or demolish.

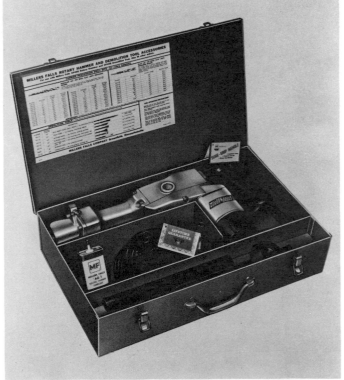

MANUFACTURERS

Goldblatt is a prime source for all masonry tools. Silvo is another good source for many items. Marshalltown is a top trowel manufacturer. Stanley makes hammers, levels, rules, and a number of other tools useful to masons. Chattanooga makes barrows, mortar pans, and boats.

Millers Falls double insulated rotary hammer has dual action. Its hammering stroke combined with power rotation speeds drilling through brick, masonry, etc. Accessories include mortar chisel for pointing, slotting tool for slotting and demolition, bushing tool for surfacing concrete, moil-point chisel for demolition drilling, etc.

51.

TOOLS FOR STONEWORK

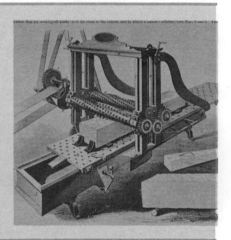

Stone is a natural material, and so was one of the first ever used—not only for building but for carving into ornamental shapes and sculpture. And it's durable, as Stonehenge, the pyramids, and the Colosseum in Rome all testify.

Early settlers in northeastern America built stone fences which served two purposes: they rid the fields of stone and provided enclosures. During ploughing, the farmer tossed aside stones that were turned up, or with a stoneboat and a horse or oxen hauled larger stones out of the way. In winter, when time was plentiful, he built with the stones.

Stone is tough to cut and often difficult to lay, but its beauty makes it worth the effort. It makes a handsome fireplace, a wall to support a carport or edge a garden pool. Deep raking of mortar joints shows off stone masonry to best advantage. Garden walls can be built dry—without mortar. It's just a matter of selecting the right stones and laying one to bridge the joint made by two below.

There are many varieties of stone used in construction, but none more beautiful than natural field stone. Deeply raked joints show off stone to best effect.

You don't need all these tools to work with stone, but you'll want some of them. Shown are sledge, stone hammers and stone ax, cold chisel, stone set, bullnose chisels and star drills.

**Six Models by
Woodings-Verona**

Hand drilling hammer comes in 2, 3, and 4 lb. weights, with a 10$\frac{1}{2}$" handle. The 4 lb. hammer is 4$\frac{1}{2}$" long with 1$\frac{5}{8}$" face.

Oregon striking hammer comes in 3 and 4 lb. weights with 16" handle, and in 6, 8, 10, and 12 lb. weights with a 36" handle. Nevada striking hammers are similar, but with somewhat longer heads.

Double-face blacksmiths' sledge is useful in making small rocks out of big ones. A 10 or 12 lb. weight is favored, but they're available up to 20 lbs.—if you can swing one that size.

Bush hammer weighs 4 lbs.; has a 1$\frac{3}{4}$" face and 16" handle.

HAMMERS

Hand-drilling or mash hammers are most useful in working with stone. They come in 2-, 3-, and 4-pound weights. It's the hammer to use with a bricklayer's set, as well as with chisels designed for use on stone. Most mash hammers have hickory handles, but you can get a one-piece steel head-and-handle hammer with a nylon-vinyl cushion grip.

Stone mason hammers have a flat face for breaking rock and a chisel end for chipping and trimming. A typical one weighs 4 pounds and has a 16" handle.

Bush hammers, used for dressing stone, have faces that are composed of pyramidal points or teeth. A typical variety has a 6"-long head with a 1$\frac{3}{4}$"-square toothed face at each end. Another kind of bush hammer, also known as a toothed concrete hammer, superficially resembles a bricklayer's hammer. It has a toothed face 1$\frac{1}{4}$" square. The opposite end of its long head is a chisel edge that's also toothed.

Oval-face stone sledge, 8 or 12 lb., has 36" handle. The smaller size is 7$\frac{1}{4}$" long with a 2$\frac{1}{8}$" face; the larger is 8$\frac{1}{4}$" long with 2$\frac{3}{8}$" face.

Single-face spalling hammer is excellent for trimming. It's available in 3 or 4 lb. weights with a 16" handle; 8 or 12 lb. weights with a 36" handle.

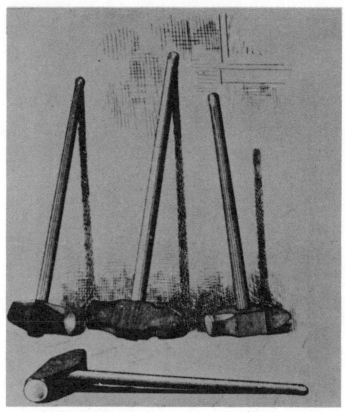

Drop-forged single-face heavy-duty hammer comes in six weights from $1^1/_2$ to 4 lbs. Polished face and peen. Rest of head is red-enameled. Channellock.

This model is similar to the one above except that it is double-faced and comes only in $1^1/_2$, $2^1/_2$, and 3 lb. sizes. Channellock.

Hand-drilling hammer (top) has black enamel finish, hickory handle. It comes in 2, 3 and 4 lb. weights and has an overall length of $10^3/_4$″. Engineers' hammer comes in $2^1/_2$ and 3 lb. weights with overall length of 16″. Its forged steel head has black finish. Both are by Stanley.

A hammer with three names—it's called a rock pick, prospectors' pick, or rockhound hammer. Has varied uses. Weighs 24 oz.; 13″ long overall.

Toothed masonry hammer has real bite. Also known as a bush hammer, it's 1¹/₄″ square, about 8″ long, and weighs about 2 lbs.

Powerful stone splitter has a foot-operated hydraulic pump that puts your entire weight behind the splitter blade. Develops up to 19 tons cutting pressure to cut all kinds of stone, block, brick. Throat 10″ x 8¹/₄″. Table height 40″. Shipping weight 165 lbs. Goldblatt.

CHISELS

Chisels for scoring or facing stone come with a plain or tooth edge, as shown in the illustrations. Cold chisels, star drills, and points or bullnose chisels are useful aids in various stone-working operations.

Trowels, plumbs, levels, rulers, lines, and other miscellaneous tools used in laying brick and block are equally useful in laying stone.

Pitching tool, for facing stones, is extra heavy duty. About 8″ long, it may have bit $1^3/_4$″, $2^1/_4$″, $2^1/_2$″, or $2^7/_8$″ wide.

Chisel forged from top quality, tempered tool steel. 9″ points come in $^5/_8$″, $^3/_4$″ and $^7/_8$″ diameters.

Stone masons' 8″ chisels come in $1^1/_4$″, $1^3/_4$″, $2^1/_4$″, and $2^3/_4$″ sizes, in plain or toothed style.

Building a stone wall. . .

BOOKS ON THE SUBJECT

You can learn most of what you need to know by observing an experienced stone mason at work, but important information is available in books on the subject—if you can find any. Look for Audel's *Masons and Builders Guide #4* (Theodore Audel & Co., 4300 W. 62nd Street, Indianapolis, Ind. 46268, 1949); *Dry Stone Walling,* by Col. F. Rainsford-Hannay (Faber and Faber Ltd., London, 1957); *The Forgotten Art of Building a Stone Wall,* by Curtis P. Fields (Yankee, Inc., Dublin, N.H., 1971); and *Building Stone Walls,* by John Vivian (Garden Way, Charlotte, Vt., 1976). A good chapter on stone masonry appears in *Handyman's Concrete and Masonry Guide,* by David X. Manners (Fawcett Publications, New York, N.Y., 1958).

MANUFACTURERS

Goldblatt has everything needed for stone masonry tools. Silvo also has many items. Marshalltown is a top trowel manufacturer. Stanley makes hammers, levels, rules and a number of other tools useful to stone masons.

ELECTRIC/ ELECTRONIC TOOLS

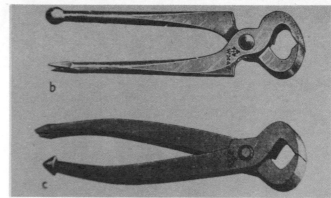

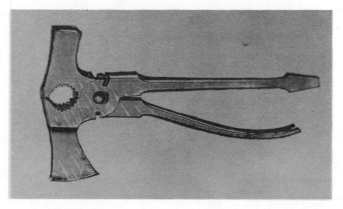

52.
TOOLS FOR WIRING

Electricity was once thought to be a kind of fluid. It is now understood to be caused by the presence and motion of charged particles. Obviously, to control and use electricity you need a system of wiring.

Wire was first made by hammering, and those who made it were known as wire smiths. In the mid-fourteenth century, the process of making wire by drawing steel was developed. That's how wire is still made today.

Installing residential wiring and related equipment requires a wide variety of tools, most of which are standard in an average collection—pliers, screwdrivers, hacksaws, drills, etc. These are discussed in other chapters. But a number of specialized tools are also needed, including specialized versions of standard tools.

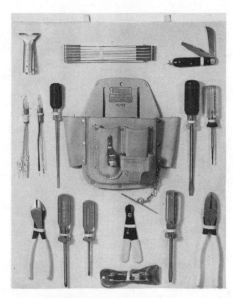

This 6-pocket pouch of cowhide holds a typical assortment of tools that are handy for completing almost any wiring job. Ric-Nor.

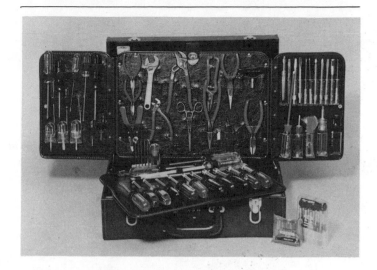

This Xcelite tool case for technicians and servicemen has 41 tools. Besides wire stripper/cutter, electrician's knife and electronic snips, it includes seven types of pliers, an adjustable wrench, straight nose seizer and a wide assortment of screwdrivers and nut drivers. Case measures $19\frac{1}{2}'' \times 13\frac{1}{2}'' \times 6\frac{3}{4}''$.

STRIPPERS

Most residential wiring is by armored, plastic, or nonmetallic sheathed cable. Some situations require metal conduit.

You can strip the insulation from a wire with a knife and there are special electrician's knives for the purpose. In many cases, special strippers, which cut both stranded and solid wire, do it quicker, easier, and better. They are less likely to damage the conducting wire.

Many strippers are combination tools, designed to do a variety of jobs in addition to stripping away insulation. They cut wire, crimp wires to make permanent solderless connections, act as long-nose pliers to loop wire ends and loosen or tighten small nuts. They may also cut bolts. A typical pair has insulating vinyl grips.

Rotary action wire-stripping plier is for all kinds of insulation, including fiberglass, asbestos and teflon. High-speed steel blades are infinitely adjustable. Housing is of high-impact plastic.

Pocket cable stripper is for circular or longitudinal cutting on small wire. Cutting depth is adjustable.

Automatic wire-stripping plier has special double-ground blades that make it especially effective on hard-to-strip insulations.

It's a longnosed plier, wire stripper, wire cutter, bolt cutter and wire crimper. No 908G Wire Tool by Channellock.

For stripping cable and heavy wire, the Channellock #10 skinning knife is a winner. Positive blade lock. With an unbreakable phenolic plastic handle.

This Ric-Nor tool is designed for fast, continual ripping of Romex and other cable. It's simple but effective.

Electrician's knife by Channellock does a variety of jobs—from stripping cable to turning screws. A lock keeps screwdriver blade from closing when in use. Riveted shackle. Unbreakable phenolic plastic handle.

Jiffy wire stripper for the home craftsman and hobbyist. Squeeze, twist, pull—and the wire is stripped. It's made of hardened spring steel. General.

Slide lock adjustment on General No. 68 adjustable wire stripper and cutter makes repetitive stripping easy. Hardened steel, black oxide finish, 5" long.

PLIERS

You can improvise with almost any pliers in doing electrical work, but lineman's or electrician's pliers do more jobs and do them better. They have big, square hard-biting jaws for twisting wire together and high-leverage edges for cutting them. Electrician's pliers usually have insulated handles, but don't depend on the insulation alone to protect you from shock.

Working in boxes, long-nose pliers are helpful. They are good at looping wire ends for terminal connections, and for operating in minimal space.

Some pliers are essentially wire clippers. They may be end cutters, or side cutters. Some are more like scissors or snips than pliers. There are a wide array of miniature and electronic pliers.

Pliers are described and illustrated fully in Chapters 54 and 60.

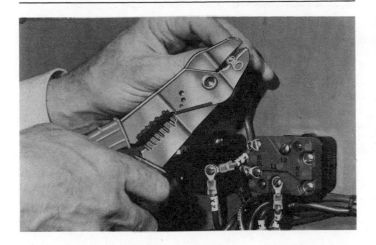

For insulated and non-insulated terminals, Vaco No. 1963 crimping tool handles 22- to 10-gauge cable, crimps solderless terminals. Bolt slicer handles six popular sizes.

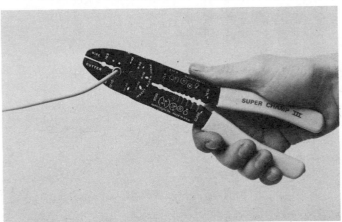

Amp Super Champ III handles everything. This versatile tool is for both insulated and uninsulated terminals, lugs, splices. A special feature is its in-nose wire cutter.

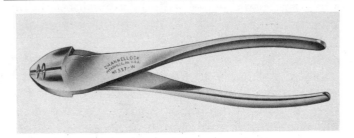

Electrician's wiring plier was especially designed by Channellock to speed the installation of electrical outlets. Cuts, strips insulation, and loops wire. Notches for 14- and 12-gauge wire strip insulation quickly, cleanly. Plastic grips optional.

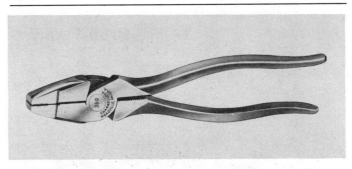

The extra power of this 9″ Channellock 369 plier comes from the joint being close to the cutters, which are perfectly mated.

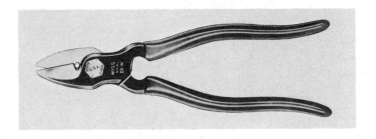

Solid steel shears will cut armored cable. Black handles fitted with red vinyl grips. Full length, 7″; length of cut, 1⅛″.

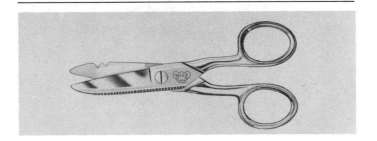

These 5″ Wiss electrician's scissors have a double stripping notch for 19- and 23-gauge wire. Scraper and file on back edge of blade. Hot drop-forged. Fully nickel plated.

SCREWDRIVERS

A variety of screwdrivers have application in electrical work. First on the list is the electrician's screwdriver—specially designed for installing electrical devices and attaching wires to terminals. Typically, it will have a round, thin shank and a cabinet blade. Crescent has them with blade lengths of 3″ to 10″. Blade diameters run from ¼″ to 3/16″. There are thinner blades on electronic screwdrivers—typically, 9/64″.

Often, screwdrivers are used in working near hot wire. For that reason you'll want screwdrivers with insulated handles, perhaps with an insulating shaft as well. Stanley makes them with a vinyl sleeving.

Other screwdrivers that are often useful in electrical work are shown in Chapter 57.

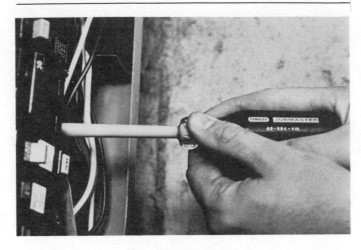

Screwdriver's vinyl sleeve is designed to insulate against up to 1000 volts AC. Comes in 3", 4", 6", and 8" lengths—all with cabinet tips and 8-flute black-cushion grip handles.

The "Z" Tang series of kits and components includes a medium- or heavy-duty handle that can be equipped with a wide variety of screwdriver, nutdriver, or Allen blades. A 5" extension and a 3-in-1 tapping tool blade are also available.

Ric-Nor triple tap is designed to clean or tap all common thread sizes. Each blade does three sizes. Setscrew and handle allows blade interchangeability. Shown is tool for $^6/_{32}$, $^8/_{32}$ and $^{10}/_{24}$ sizes. sizes.

Before electric current was understood, it was known to be a strange force that caused muscles to twitch.

CONDUIT TOOLS

If you work with conduit, you need a bender. One can usually be rented from stores selling electrical supplies or from a rental service store listed in the Yellow Pages.

If you try to bend conduit without a bending tool, you're likely to kink it, and it's difficult to pull wire past kinks. Improperly bent concuit may even break, producing a sharp, ragged edge that can dig into wire insulation and cause a short.

Sears sells an inexpensive bender for $^1/_2$" and $^3/_4$" thin-wall conduit. Sears also offers a portable or bench-mount conduit vise that's helpful in making clean, square cuts. Use it with a hacksaw fitted with a 24- or 32-tooth blade. A plumbing tubing cutter can also be used to cut thin-wall conduit. Cuts must be reamed to eliminate rough edges. Cutters and reamers are shown in Chapter 43.

To pull wire through conduit you need a fish tape. You can improvise with ordinary galvanized steel wire, but it lacks the springiness of tape and bends and kinks if you try using any length of it. Tape, made of tempered spring steel, comes in various lengths. Typical is 40' of tape on a reel with a built-in winder.

Tape is also useful in fishing wires and cable through existing walls. For some jobs you can get by with a straightened-out steel coat hanger with a hook bent at its end. Sometimes you'll want both the coat hanger and the tape.

Fish wire and drop chains are also used in feeding wires and cables between studs in existing walls. A drop chain consists of small chain links attached to a lead or iron weight. A variation employs a magnet which attaches itself to a second magnet attached to a lead wire.

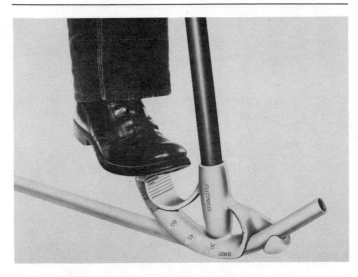

Ridgid conduit bender minimizes distortion. Comes in three sizes for $1/2''$ through 1" thin-wall conduit and $1/2''$ and $3/4''$ heavy-wall conduit. Markings indicate 30°, 45°, 60°, and 90° bends. Slip-resistant step. Handle not included.

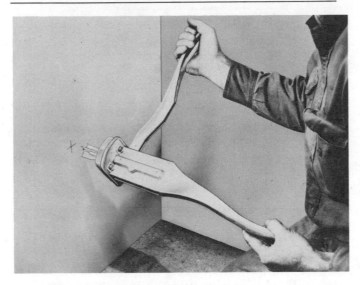

High-speed outlet hole cutter by Goldblatt is three times faster than a saw. Cuts holes in $3/8''$ and $1/2''$ wallboard cleanly. No torn paper to patch. Various sizes available.

ETCETERA

There are special hammers with long necks so you can drive nails inside boxes.

There is a special device that makes it quick and easy to cut outlet holes in plasterboard.

Locating studs is often a problem when remodeling or extending wiring. Typically, a stud finder consists of a magnet on a swivel. It is attracted to the nails that fasten the studs in place.

A fuse puller is designed for pulling and replacing cartridge fuses by hand.

This ratchet brace is meant for working in very tight corners and between joists. It doesn't require the 360° sweep of an ordinary brace. Measures 10" from handle end to shaft. Mahogany-tinted beech handle; nickel plated. Leichtung.

Channellock 18-ounce electrician's hammer has extra-long neck. Drop-forged steel, hickory handle.

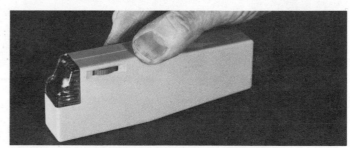

Electronic metal detector locates concealed wires. Indicator light comes on when sensing element detects metal, even when buried inside concrete. Also locates pipes, studs, reinforcing steel. Powered by 9-volt battery. Metrifast.

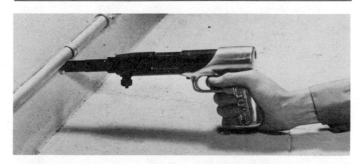

This Bostitch "Boss" low-velocity tool is for fastening conduit to concrete. Its .22-caliber cartridge will shoot fasteners equally well into steel.

53.
SOLID-JOINT PLIERS

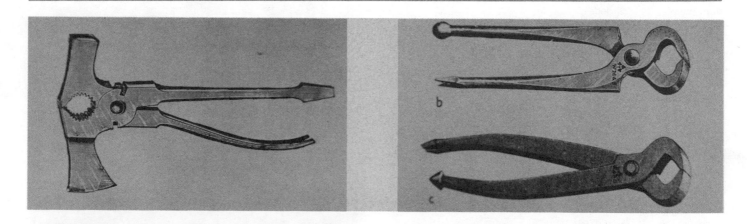

Pliers are direct descendants of old Roman pincers, dating back to the first century A.D. and earlier. The Romans used pincers in many trades, especially in blacksmithing. Tongs, tweezers, calipers, and forceps are close cousins of pincers and pliers and are equally ancient.

The big change in pliers came only recently. The age of electricity and electronics, which has given birth to many tools, has delivered none in wider variety than solid-joint pliers. It's a tool that has many jobs to do. Solid-joint pliers are for picking up, holding, looping, gripping, twisting, bending, forming, and cutting wire. Some are also for mechanical work, such as turning nuts, though slip-joint and adjustable pliers (see Chapter 60) are more commonly used for such purposes.

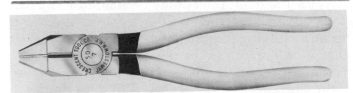

Crescent 7" side cutting plier is a sturdy tool for electrical work. Keen-edged cutters and spring-tempered handles. Also available in 6" and 8" sizes.

ANATOMY OF PLIERS

Pliers are a simple double-lever arrangement, with jaws and nose at one end and handles at the other. The fulcrum or pivot point is close to the jaws, which often include cutters, so that the mechanical advantage gained is great.

Plier noses may be square, tapered, or pointed. They may be short or long. They may be flat, round, tapered, duckbill, snipe, needle, offset, curved, or bent. Not all these terms are mutually exclusive.

Plier jaws may be side-cutting, diagonal-cutting, or end-cutting, or they may be without cutters.

Side cutters may be notched for stripping insulated wire. One type of needlenose plier has a side cutter only $^3/_{16}$" from the jaw tips. It's good for reaching into close quarters to pull or cut wire.

Some diagonal cutters are available without a top bevel on the knives to permit flush cutting. In others, thin diagonal cutters are ground down on the backside for reaching into confined places. Still other diagonal cutters have wire-skinning holes.

End-cutting pliers are designed for cutting off wire, nails, rivets, etc., close to work. There are angled flush, rounded flush, and transverse end cutters. There are longnose end cutters and short-nose angled end cutters. There are longnose tip cutters.

Plier jaws may be smooth or have scoring.

Plier handles may be plain, slip-on, molded plastic, plastic-dipped, or high dielectric insulated. Plastic-dipped handles are often for comfort only, not electrical insulation. Some plier handles have springs to open the jaws. Coil springs between the handles are found to speed production on assembly lines because plier jaws are always open and ready to go. They are also less tiring.

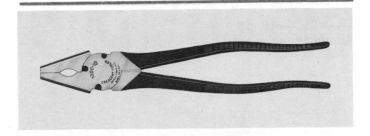

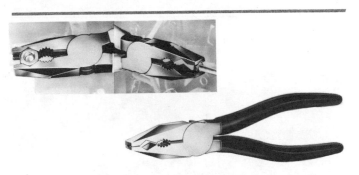

All-purpose flat nose "button" plier by Crescent includes a pipe grip and teeth in extreme tip of nose. It has three wire cutters, comes in 8", 10" and 12" sizes. Also useful in construction and maintenance of wire fencing.

Ordinary pliers can't be used to turn nuts. Here is an exception. Specially shaped openings and tips in side jaws grasp a range of nut sizes. It also cuts wire. Vinyl grips. Brookstone.

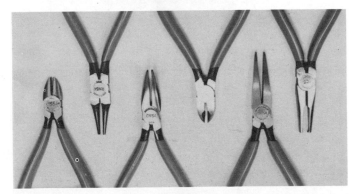

Six-piece mini-plier set by Diamond. Leichtung offers these 4" Copaloy electronics pliers in a handy suede pocket carrier (shown at top). *From left:* Transverse end cutting (for cutting close to printed circuits), duck bill (smooth jaws), flush cutting, curved needle nose (nose bent 60°), round nose (wire loop plier), and diagonal cutting plier.

Five Models By Ric-Nor

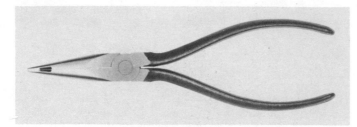

Long nose tip cutter

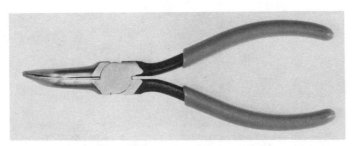

6″ curved nose

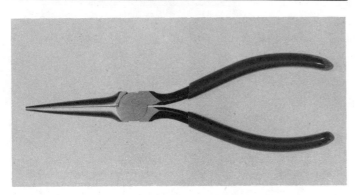

6″ needle nose

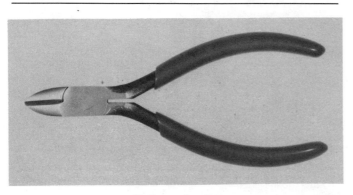

4″ diagonal cutter

As for material, pliers may be made of forged, stamped, or cast metal. Forged pliers are best because forging makes the grain of the metal follow the contour of the pliers, and this provides maximum strength. Stamped pliers may have grain, but it runs without regard to the contours. This provides only medium strength. Cast pliers have no grain structure at all, and are weakest.

Most pliers range in length from 4″ to 8″. The small and miniature sizes find special application in electronic work.

4″ end nipper

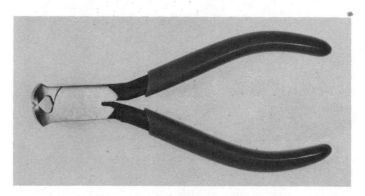

Plier designed by Leonardo da Vinci

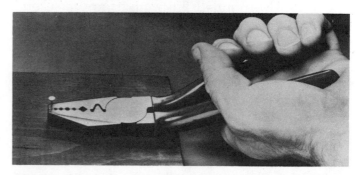

Offset holding plier is especially desinged for grasping and holding wires, nails, or rivets. Offset handles make it possible to hold jaws flush with surface. Vinyl-covered handles. Length 8″ overall. Brookstone.

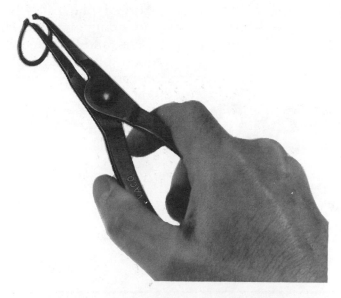

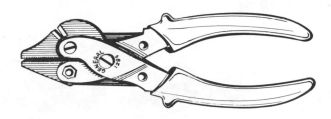

Many bearings, bushings and gears are held in place with snap rings. Pliers like these make it easy to snap the rings in or out. There is an internal style for contracting an internal ring to fit into a bore or housing, and an external style (shown here) for expanding an external ring over a shaft. Vaco.

Parallel jaw side-cutting plier is 6¹/₂" long and finished in bright nickel. Compound lever design provides a vise-like grip. Plastic-cushioned handles. Made in England by General Hardware.

NO! NO! NO!

● Never use pliers as a hammer, never hammer on the handles, or twist from side to side when cutting wire.

● Don't use pliers to hold objects in the flame of a torch; it may draw their temper and ruin them.

● Unless especially made for the purpose, don't use pliers for cutting hardened wire.

● Never use a pipe or otherwise extend the length of the handles to secure greater leverage.

● Unless specifically designed for it, don't use pliers on nuts or bolts. Use a wrench.

● Don't bend stiff wire with the plier tip.

Compound-action diagonal cutters made in West Germany by Moller. Plier is chrome vanadium steel with a polished head. So tough, it will cut piano wire. Its name, "Kraftgrip," means powerful grip. Handles have black/red japanned finish.

MANUFACTURERS

The importance of pliers as a tool is reflected in the number of companies engaged in making them. Crescent, Proto, S-K, Rosco, Channellock, Ric-Nor, Vaco, Diamond, and Truecraft are some of the major ones. Wilkinson from England, and Knipex and Werner Möller from West Germany, are top imports.

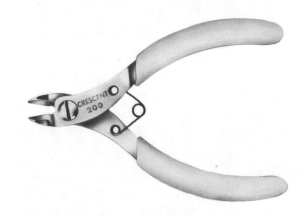

Stainless diagonal cutting plier is a specialist's tool for electronic and light electrical assembly work. Designed for cutting and trimming circuit boards and lead wires on capacitors, resistors and other electronic components. Crescent.

54.
SOLDERING TOOLS

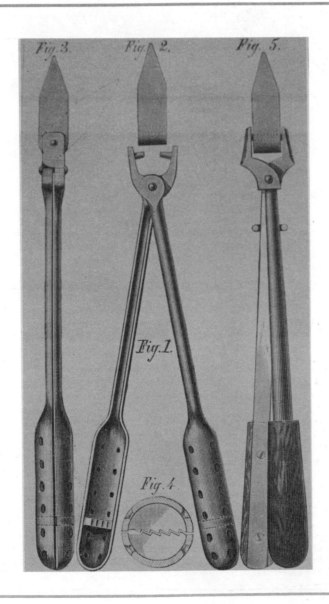

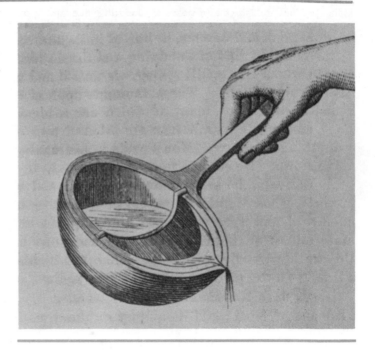

The soldering iron is an ancient tool. Two thousand years ago, ancient Romans were making water pipes by soldering together the long seams on narrow strips of lead. In Medieval times soldering irons were used to make stained glass windows. The *electric* soldering iron was invented in the Victorian era when tin roofs were made watertight by soldering.

Today, soldering tools enable you to assemble all kinds of equipment from kits, to do sheet-metal work, make jewelry and leaded windows and lamps.

HOW SOLDERING WORKS

Heat, properly applied, is the secret of successful soldering. It's the surfaces to be joined that must be heated, not the solder itself. The hot surfaces then melt the solder so that it flows smoothly and completely into the joint. Because different amounts of heat are required for different jobs, you may need more than one soldering tool.

Heat can be transmitted to a metal surface or joint with a torch, by a hotplate, or other means, but the most popular and preferred method is the iron. It does more than transmit heat. It enables you to manipulate the solder and do a neater job.

Electric irons have become so prevalent, the fact that there are nonelectric irons is sometimes almost forgotten. Nonelectric soldering irons, or coppers, to be heated by flame or forge, are commonly sold in three weights or sizes—$\frac{1}{2}$ pound for light work, 1 pound for medium-weight soldering and $1\frac{1}{2}$ pounds for heavy work. It's a good idea to buy them in pairs. Then you don't have to interrupt work when the iron cools. One iron can be heating while the other is in use.

ELECTRIC IRONS AND PENCILS

There are miniature, medium-duty, and heavy-duty electric irons. The power required to operate an electric iron is measured in watts. An electric iron, corresponding to the old nonelectric type, may have a $\frac{5}{8}''$ tapered chisel-style copper tip that heats to 900° and rates at 200 watts. Typically, it will measure about 15" long, have a hardwood handle that you clutch in your fist, and weigh about 2 pounds. Heavy-duty irons may run up to 300, 500, even 700 watts, and weigh 4 or 5 pounds. Tips may be "plug" or "screw" type and may be from $\frac{3}{8}''$ to $1\frac{3}{4}''$ diameter. In contrast, a typical lightweight pencil iron may be little more than 8" long and weigh only 2 ounces. As its name implies, it is designed to be held like a pencil.

Pencil irons usually feature stainless-steel barrels, nickel-plated copper tips, and heat- and impact-resistant handles. Most range from 25 to 80 watts, with 25- and 40-watt pencils being popular choices. Tip diameters may range from $\frac{1}{32}''$ to $\frac{1}{4}''$. They are ideal for hobbies and electronics.

Marksman series of Weller soldering irons includes three pencil types (2 to 4 oz.) rated at 25, 40 and 80 watts, and two heavy-duty models (10 to 11 oz.) at 120 and 175 watts. All are UL listed and feature stainless steel barrels and nickel-plated copper tips.

Wallbrand 200 watt iron for continuous heavy-duty soldering has a $\frac{5}{8}''$ tip. Ruggedly constructed; resistance wire is wound on pure mica. Allen-head set screw secures tip to barrel. Wall-Lenk.

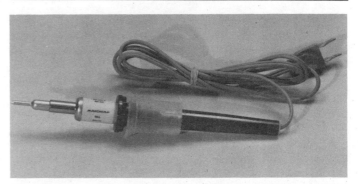

Custom-design your own! Start with a "Cool-grip" polypropylene handle, add 27, 42, or 50 watt heating element and light, medium or heavy-duty thread-on copper tip. Interchangeable heating units and tips make a complete soldering workshop. Radio Shack.

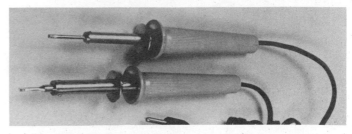

Because they are simpler than irons made for disassembly and repair, these Wallbrand "Triple-E" throwaway irons cost less, but they are reliable. Stainless steel barrel and set screws, polycarbonate handle, 25 watt $\frac{1}{8}''$ tip, or 42 watt $\frac{1}{4}''$ tip. Wall-Lenk.

Leakages or transient voltages may be too small to hurt the person doing the soldering, but they can damage voltage-sensitive components in electronic assemblies. Hexacon's Posi-Ground design minimizes this problem and also makes it easy to replace worn-out cord sets or burned-out elements.

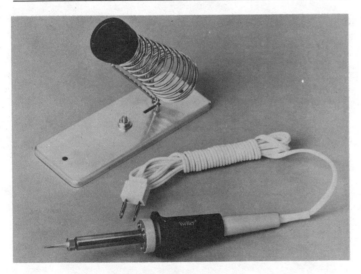

Weller's pencil-type irons have stainless steel barrels and offer a selection of eight interchangeable tips. In 25 and 40 watt general-purpose models with either two- or three-wire cord. Aluminum stand can be either free standing or mounted.

Designed to guard sensitive components from damage by milli-volt leakage, this Hexacon Dial-a-Temp soldering station offers temperature range from 350° to 950° at twist of dial. Controls, holder, tip-cleaning sponge and tray in one compact unit.

Especially designed for printed circuit electronics, or where sensitive components may be damaged by heat, there are controlled output models. Depending on the model, the desired temperature may be achieved by dial adjustment or changing the screw-in heating element. Tips are often screw-type and interchangeable.

Most pencil irons have no on-off switch. When you plug one into an outlet, it's on. To turn it off, you unplug it. Pencils take two to three minutes to reach working temperature. Some pencils come without stands, and this can represent a safety hazard when tips are hot. The answer is to buy or improvise a stand.

SOLDERING GUNS

Light-duty soldering pencils can join the stranded wires used in many household appliances. But when there's more metal to heat, you need a higher capacity, such as provided by a medium- or heavy-duty soldering gun.

These pistol-grip soldering tools have molded plastic housings that in most cases enclose a transformer. Their tips are also their heating elements, so they heat up in two or three seconds. Typically, they have a trigger switch that goes to "off" when you release pressure.

Some guns have hairpin-style tips and you have the choice of two heat levels. These may be 100/140 watts or 240/325 watts. Levels are controlled by a two-position trigger. Other guns have a tubular heating element or power head. By changing the tip, you can change the temperature. On a Weller solid-state soldering gun of this type, for example, one power head offers 600° and another has 700° capability.

CORDLESS IRONS

For jobs where no plug-in electrical source is available, there are cordless soldering irons. Weller makes one that comes with three different tips. It weighs under 6 ounces and heats up in 6 seconds to a tip temperature of 700°F. It uses nickel-cadmium batteries.

Cordless irons vary in the length of time it takes to recharge them. The fastest can go from "dead" to "full" in one hour. Others may take overnight,

You can assemble a three-temperature soldering iron tip yourself with Heathkit's model GH-17A. Stand with metal cage keeps iron secure. Turn dial for heat range desired. Six foot power cord. 120 volt AC.

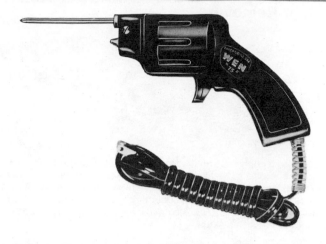

Lightweight 75 watt soldering pistol has a unique single post, which permits long reach and a clear view of work. Heats quickly. Like most guns, it has a built-in spotlight. Wen.

Cordless soldering pencil is just 7½" long, weighs only 6 oz. Will solder 35 to 100 joints per charge. Includes two nickel cadmium batteries, charger and tool rest.

Wen 100 watt transformer-type gun is extra thin—only 1¹¹/₁₆" wide. Heats in 2½ seconds. Feather-weight—only 19 oz. Comes with general-purpose long-reach tip.

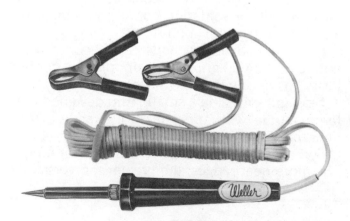

This Weller model TCP 12 field soldering iron comes with battery clips and a 12' cord. Operates on any 12 to 14 volt source and produces a tip temperature of 700°F.

Isotip cordless gun has a solder spool that automatically feeds when trigger is depressed, so soldering can be done with one hand. Heats in five to eight seconds, has built-in work light. Plug-in charger will fully recharge gun overnight. Choice of 16 different snap-in tips. Wahl.

Solder Removers

Electronic technician drill is ideal for removing solder from printed circuit boards as well as cleaning lead holes and revising/redesigning circuit boards. Operates at about 9000 rpm. Comes with three collets that accommodate drills and burrs with a shank size up to .125 ($^1/_8$"). Also available in a style that plugs into car cigarette lighter. Wahl.

Hexacon's tinned copper braid for removing solder comes in widths from $^1/_{32}$" to $^5/_{32}$" on spools of 5' to 100'. Extra-fine wire stranding increases capacity to hold solder. Use iron with enough heat to melt solder on connection within two seconds.

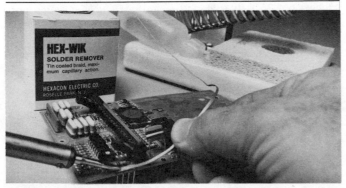

Left: Desoldering Vacu-Bulb cleans up solder. Easy-to-clean no-stick tip won't mar new connections. *Right:* Tip-cleaning sponge removes excess solder, keeps soldering tip clean for efficient heat transfer. Extends tip life. Radio Shack.

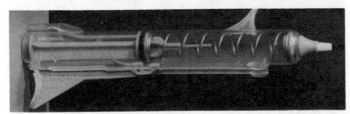

"Snortini" desoldering vacuum pump has one-hand action, makes it easy to desolder and rework miniature and micro-miniature circuits. Radio Shack.

but a partially discharged battery can often be restored to usefulness in an hour or two. Depending on the gauge of the wire, you can solder from twenty to a hundred joints per charge. Most attain soldering heat in five to ten seconds.

There's another type of soldering tool that's independent of the electric plug. It's one that works off a 12-volt battery. It comes complete with battery clips and a 12' cord. Tip temperature is 700°F.

WHAT TO LOOK FOR

Some guns have copper tips. Others have tips clad with nickel or iron. The latter may stay clean longer, but solid copper tips are easier to clean.

The built-in transformer makes a gun rather heavy. Some may weigh over 3 pounds. So balance is an important factor. Compare the feel of one gun with another. Check the weight of one gun with another. Extra weight can become very tiring, and even a few ounces can make a difference.

A pencil iron is likely to last longer than a gun. Drop a gun on a concrete floor and, because of its weight, it may be damaged beyond repair.

If you choose a gun with a hairpin tip, you'll have to avoid bearing down too heavily on it. Hairpin tips bend out of shape rather easily. They also can't get into tight places as readily as the tube-shaped types.

If you're going to be working inside a crowded chassis, choose a small-barrel, small-tip gun. Larger tips are good for mechanical joining, but they are not for soldering copper plumbing tubing. Tubing requires a torch.

In prolonged use, pencils can become pretty hot. Cork finger grips rate among the coolest. Sears has one with a metal ring. Ouch!

Most guns include a small lamp designed to illuminate the work area. It's not exactly a spotlight, but it helps.

Some guns offer two, others three heat ranges. The more heat ranges, the greater the versatility.

MANUFACTURERS

Hexacon and Weller are leaders. Other makers include Wall-Lenk, Wahl, Wen, Archer (Radio Shack), Millers Falls, and Black & Decker.

PART VI

MECHANIC'S/ METALWORKING TOOLS

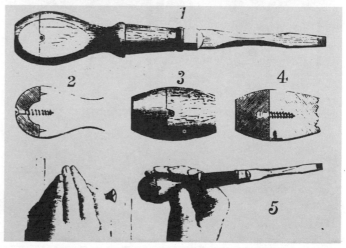

55.
SCREWDRIVERS

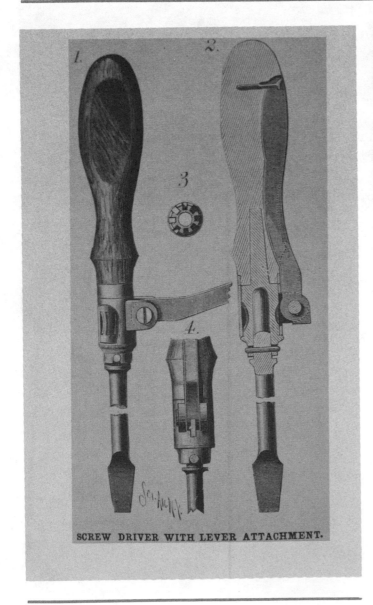

SCREW DRIVER WITH LEVER ATTACHMENT.

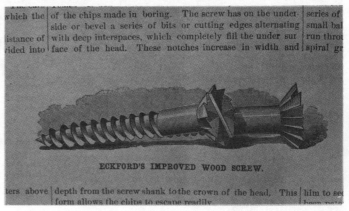

which the of the chips made in boring. The screw has on the under series of side or bevel a series of bits or cutting edges alternating small bal istance of with deep interspaces, which completely fill the under sur run throu ided into face of the head. These notches increase in width and spiral gr

ECKFORD'S IMPROVED WOOD SCREW.

ters above depth from the screw shank to the crown of the head. This him to se form allows the chips to escape readily.

Which came first, the screw or the screwdriver? The screw did—by many centuries. Before the slot-top screw we know today, there were screw bolts, turned by a wrench. Other screws had head holes and were turned by rods thrust through them. Still others were screws to be turned by thumb and forefinger. Then came the slot or slit screw and the screwdriver, or the turnscrew as it was called at first.

The first use of these screws was early in the seventeenth century on the plates of guns. Carpenters, however, didn't use wood screws until the mid-1700s. In 1775, the cast-iron butt hinge was invented, and it became the practice to attach it with screws rather than with nails or rivets. That gave a big boost to screwdrivers.

Blacksmiths were the first makers of screwdrivers. Typically, those early screwdrivers had two or more decorative "waists," and sometimes a hole in which a rod or bar could be inserted to assist in turning it. Screwdrivers were factory-made after 1850.

TYPES, SIZES, DESIGNS

A screwdriver is a simple tool, yet today it comes in more than 100 types, sizes, and designs.

Bassically, a screwdriver consists of a handle, ablade, and a tip. But the blade may be long or short, thin or thick, round or square.

The tip may be designed for a simple slot, the cross-slots of Phillips-head screws, or other specialized configurations.

If a screwdriver has a flat tip, it may have a "keystone" shape and taper to the tip, or it may have straight sides and no taper. The latter is known as a cabinet tip, for it is designed to drive screws deep into recessed holes without scraping the sides of the holes. To assist in holding screws, tips may be magnetized or equipped with other screw-holding devices.

The way a tip is ground is important. Its faces and edges should be cross ground. You can usually see the grind marks quite clearly. Cross grinding produces sharp sides and edges and a perfect bottoming fit. Tips that are ground lengthwise have a rounded edge that won't stay in the slot. It will grip higher in the slot and is more apt to break out than a tip that grips the bottom of the slot.

The best screwdriver blades are made of chrome vanadium steel. The tip must be hard, but not brittle. It should bend before breaking. If a tip is too soft it won't hold its sharp edges and rounded edges won't take hold. If tips are too soft they wear out quickly.

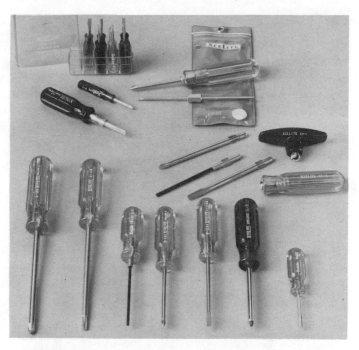

Clockwise from top left: Compact set in flexible plastic case with see-through cover, reversible blade kit in zipper case, regular and T handle with interchangeable blades, 2" regular, 3 1/2" Scrulox type, 4" regular round blade, 3" Phillips, 4" Allen hex socket type (1/8"), 6" clutch head type, and 6" Phillips. Xcelite.

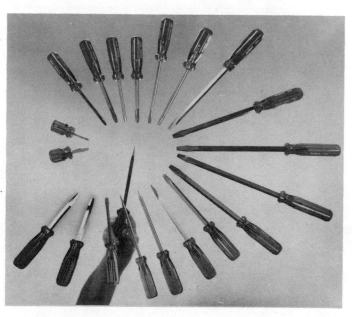

Round blade, square blade, slot and Phillips tips—all by Ridgid. Plastic handles are oversize, their ends designed so they won't dig into your palm.

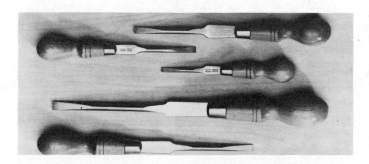

Cabinetmakers' screwdriver set. Lengths (ferrule to tip) range from 3" to 8". Oval handles are lacquered beech. Flat area below ferrule can accommodate a wrench for extra torque. Leichtung.

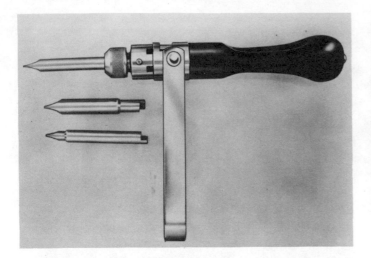

Ratchet screwdriver with lever that folds out for applying powerful torque. Adjusts to fit into tight or awkward places. Three-position ratchet will drive or remove screws, or lock in position. Comes with three flat bits, but Phillips bits are available. Brookstone.

Yankee combination spiral ratchet screwdriver and drill comes with a $1/4''$ bit for slotted screws. Its clear plastic handle contains a $5/32''$ bit for slotted screws and $5/64''$ and $7/64''$ drill points for boring small holes. Stanley.

Stanley furnishes four bits with this magazine-handle ratchet driver—two for slotted screws, two for Phillips screws. Three settings: rigid driver, and ratchet for setting or drawing screws.

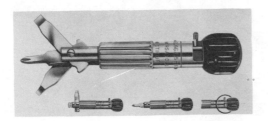

Ratchet "Versatool" by Shelton. The three tool-steel blades fold and retract when not in use. Universal ratchet in handle speeds work in either direction, or it can be locked. Pocket-size. Available from U.S. General Supply.

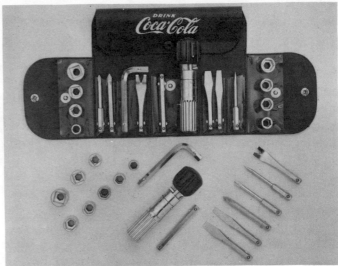

The complete ratchet kit! Almost everything you might want in screwdriver bits, sockets and awl points in a handy roll-up vinyl case. One ratchet handle powers all of them. Shelton.

Two ratchet imports from Sheffield, England. The blades of these Eclipse screwdrivers are made from a special alloy steel, with knurled finger grips for starting small screws. Blade lengths range from 3" to 6". Polished hardwood handles. Frog Tool Co.

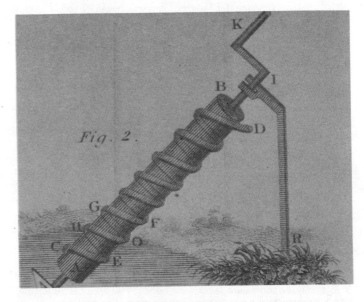

Archimedes' screw didn't require a separate driver.

THE HANDLE

Handles may be square, round, oval, or ridged. They may be made of wood, plastic, or rubber. If the screwdriver has interchangeable blades, the handle may be hollow and used as a storage compartment.

Plastic handles are generally safe from shock when dry and intact. If the handle should be cracked, foreign matter in the crack may make it conductive. Plastic handles are often covered by rubber or vinyl cushion grips. These may be conductive when damp.

Handles may include a ratcheting device. A single push on the handle of a spiral ratchet screwdriver will turn a screw almost three times. The direction of drive can be reversed or locked, making it a rigid screwdriver.

Some screwdriver handles take interchangeable bits. These will also accept nutdriver bits.

A bit brace can be used as a handle for screwdriver bits. A brace is a highly effective method of multiplying turning power, or torque.

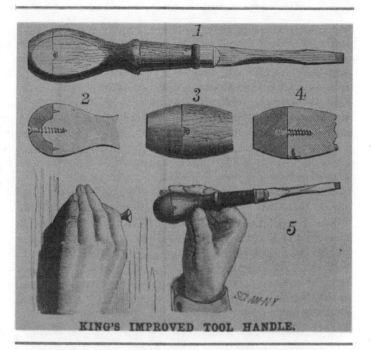

KING'S IMPROVED TOOL HANDLE.

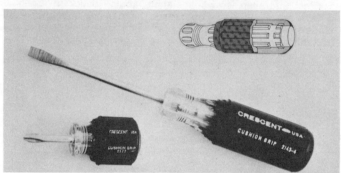

To provide maximum turning power with minimum effort, Crescent screwdrivers combine an oversize handle with a non-slip rubber "Cushion Grip." Shown are round blade and stubby Phillips, and there are also square blade and standard Phillips. Blade lengths from $1^1/_4$" to 12".

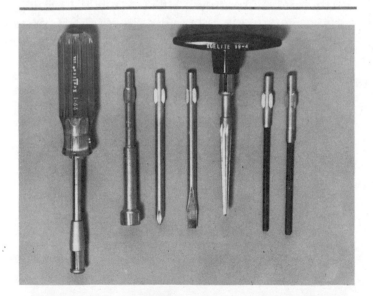

Xcelite has five handles—regular or tee, with or without reversible ratchet action, or stubby. They will accept 85 screwdriver, nutdriver and special-purpose shafts and blades. Two of the handles and six of the attaching devices are shown here.

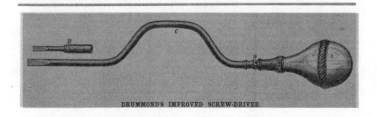

DRUMMOND'S IMPROVED SCREW-DRIVER.

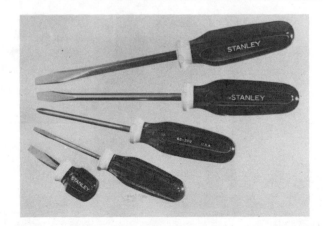

Stanley "Workmaster" screwdriver handle, of translucent plastic, has three fluted sides to fit the pocket formed by the hand when it grips the handle. In 16 sizes and four types: square-bar, standard, Phillips and cabinet.

Screwdrivers for Small Spaces

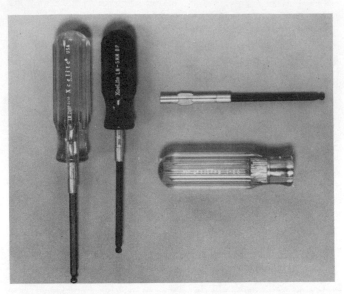

For reaching Allen screwheads at any angle—ballpoint hex socket drivers are available in both fixed handle and interchangeable blade styles. They'll engage screwhead at any angle. Metric sizes have black handles; inch sizes have amber handles. Xcelite.

Ratchet offset screwdrivers reach hard-to-get-at screws and exert strong leverage action. Made in three styles: with ¼" and ⅜" straight blades; with #1 and #2 Phillips type blades; with straight and Phillips-type blade. General Hardware.

The shaft on this Oxwall driver flexes so you can get at hard-to-reach places. Nickel plated.

General Hardware's offset screwdriver has four ¼" blades mounted at four different angles to permit short movements when turning space is limited. Indispensable for setting or removing hard-to-get-at screws.

TIPS ON USE

Screws are easy to drive and remove when the screwdriver tip fits perfectly in the slot. When a tip fits the slot completely, it exerts maximum torque. If a tip is too narrow for the slot, or too thin, it is likely to break out of the screw, damaging it and the sourrounding surface. A blade tip should fill at least three-quarters of the slot.

A screwdriver is made for screws, not for prying. If you use a light-duty screwdriver for prying, you'll bend it permanently. A medium-duty model does have some prying capability, and a heavy-duty model certainly has.

There's only so much a screwdriver can take. If you apply too much torque to a light-duty driver you may twist its tip. If you have a heavy-duty model with a square shank, you can turn the tool with a wrench, but if you overdo it you may break the screwhead or ruin the screwdriver's tip.

You can also get a grip on the flats of a blade tip with a wrench. But never use pliers on a screwdriver. They'll chew it up.

The term "turnscrew" still is applied to some screwdrivers made especially for wood screws. These have egg-shaped or oval handles, and the upper part of their blade is flattened to take a wrench.

Some old-timers say that a hammer can be used for starting screws. Most screwdrivers, however, are not designed to take such impact. An exception is where the shank extends all the way through the handle.

Offset model for turning screws in confined spaces. *Top:* Standard tip, 3" to 6⅛" long. *Bottom:* Different Phillips size on each end. Overall length 4¾" or 6". Proto.

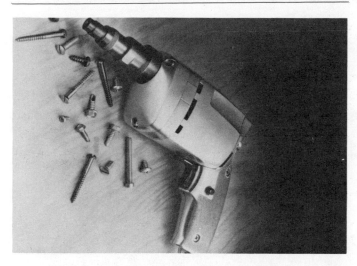

There are six models of Stanley power screwdrivers to choose from; three are clutch types. Pistol-grip screwdrivers take the time and work out of setting drywall screws, fastening in wood, fastening wood to metal, metal to metal, or fiberglass to metal. Variety of bits available.

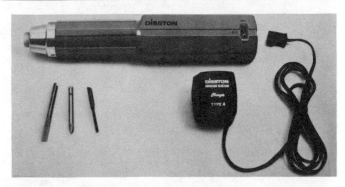

Disston cordless electric screwdriver will drive 80 one-inch screws into pine on a single charge without pre-drilling. Tough plastic case. Comes with charger, two slotted bits, two Phillips bits, and $\frac{1}{16}$" and $\frac{1}{8}$" drill bits. U.S. General Supply.

Eclipse pocket set for tiny screws contains screwdriver handle and six interchangeable blades with widths from .6 mm (.025 inch) to 2.5 mm (.1 inch). About $3\frac{3}{4}$" overall length.

MANUFACTURERS

Rosco Tools Inc. is the world's largest manufacturer of screwdrivers. There are many other companies which are not so large but still turn out quality products. Among them are Crescent, Stanley, Proto, Xcelite, Ridgid, Millers Falls, and BernzOmatic.

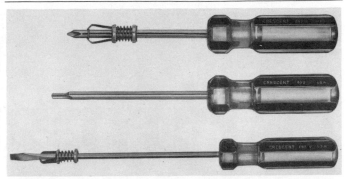

Crescent screw-holding drivers are just the thing for situations where you can't use two hands. Thumb control holds screw for one-hand start. Phillips, clutch-head, and mechanic's tips.

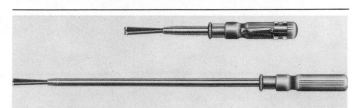

Quick-Wedge is the original screw-holding screwdriver. Double-split blade holds, starts, drives and sets the screw. Rugged tips won't bend or distort in normal use. Kedman Co.

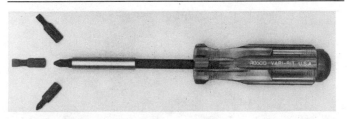

Powerful magnet built into the shank of this Roscoe Vari-Bit screwdriver holds interchangeable bits. Comes with two flat bits for slotted screws and two Phillips bits.

SCREW DRIVER ATTACHMENT.

This is a convenient and handy little countersink tool, to be attached to an ordinary screw driver and remain permanently affixed thereto, each implement being as readily used as if it had a separate handle. The reamer or countersink is placed alongside the screwdriver, and a slot in its shank provides for its being slid down when required for use, and up out of the way when the screw driver is needed. The inventor, Mr. W. G. A. Bonwill, of Dover, Del., proposes to use his improvement in conjunction with gimlets and other tools in use by carpenters, the application of it to which will readily be suggested in practice; but it will be found in its most appropriate place on a screw driver, that the hole, after being bored, may be reamed before the screw is inserted. It is a neat and convenient arrangement and will find favor with workers in wood.

Medical Uses of Carbolic Acid.

1. It is not proven that carbol is a general disinfectant.

2. It is of the greatest use to disinfect wounds.

3. It accomplishes this by destroying pus, etc., and by preventing inflammation.

56.
NUTDRIVERS

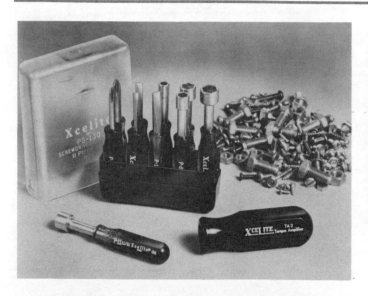

A special torque amplifier handle comes with these midget nutdriver and screwdriver sets. Slipped over the handle of the 3½" midget tools, it gives larger gripping surface, extended reach and increased driving power. Eight different assortments of nutdrivers and screwdrivers are available in stand-up plastic cases. Xcelite.

Nutdrivers, like screwdrivers, have a handle and a shank, but instead of a blade they have a socket. The socket fits hex nuts, hex bolts, and hex screws for easy starting and removing. In London, you might hear them called "nut spinners."

The radio industry undoubtedly gave nutdrivers their start. It was just the tool to get down in between tubes. You couldn't use a wrench; there wasn't enough space. A nutdriver offered wrench action plus the long reach of a screwdriver. Years before Stanley was making nutdrivers it was producing nutdriver bits for its Yankee ratcheting screwdrivers.

A nutdriver doesn't have the strength or power of a wrench. It is for nuts that don't have to be too tight, like those in an electronic chassis. Tightening and loosening with a nutdriver is limited to what you can do with your hand. It's undoubtedly why nutdriver capability is limited to $\frac{1}{2}''$, and why $\frac{1}{4}''$ is the most popular nutdriver size. Usually there is a nutdriver for each size nut.

ANATOMY

Typically, a nutdriver consists of a handle, a shaft, and a socket. Handles may be like those on screwdrivers. Most are plastic and shockproof. They may be fluted for firm grip. They may have a rounded end for pressure turning. They may be piggyback, with a large handle that slips down over a smaller one for extra gripping area and power. They may have a pistol-grip, with ratchet action. They may be ball shaped, T-handled or with a $\frac{1}{4}''$ female drive in the handle so that two or more tools can be fitted together for extra reach. They may be hinged, or flexible.

Betraying their blood relationship, handles may accommodate both nutdriver and screwdriver bits. They may also accept hex bits and drivers for hollow-head fasteners with hex recesses.

The nutdriver shaft may be hollow, to accommodate long studs. It may be flexible, to get into tight places. It may be extra long (18") for getting into walls and other hard-to-get-at places. Vaco has one nutdriver that's $21\frac{1}{2}''$ long—if you include the handle.

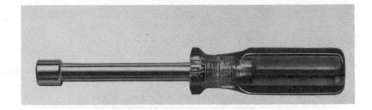

Hollow-shaft nutdrivers come in seven color-coded sizes from $\frac{3}{16}''$ to $\frac{1}{2}''$. You can buy them individually, or in a seven-piece set that comes in a pouch.

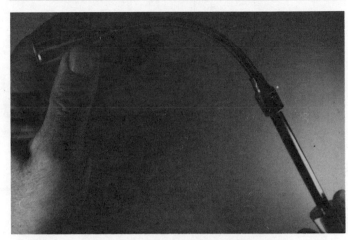

Proto flexible extension reaches places a rigid extension can't. It has an overall length of 6" and a $\frac{1}{4}''$ drive.

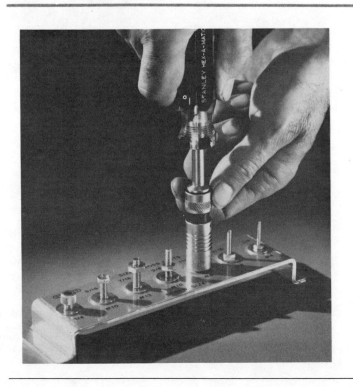

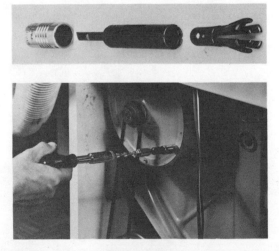

At left: Stanley's "Hex-a-Matic" handles five sizes of hex nuts ($\frac{1}{4}''$ to $\frac{7}{16}''$), five sizes of hex-head screws (No. 6 to $\frac{1}{4}''$), and five sizes of socket head cap screws (No. 8 to $\frac{5}{16}''$). It will also fit all metric size fasteners up to 11 mm. *Top right:* Collet chuck of driver disassembled to show action of its six fingers. *Bottom right:* "Hex-a-Matic" attachment to fit Stanley's Yankee Spiral Ratchet screwdriver.

Clear plastic handles of these Ric-Nor nutdrivers have color-code stripes for easy identification of sizes.

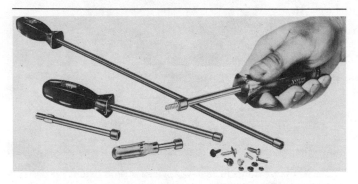

A permanent magnet in the socket of the Xcelite nutdrivers makes one-hand driving and removing easy. Styles range from a 3¹/₂" midget to a super-long 20³/₄". Plastic handles are color-coded for instant hex-opening identification.

By means of a special ring you can quickly tighten any nut or screw with your thumb or forefinger before applying full torque of the pistol grip handle. It saves wrist fatigue. Metrifast offers this 20-piece kit in a zippered vinyl case.

Sockets come in metric and standard sizes. Typical sets come in seven popular sizes from ³/₁₆" to ¹/₂" and metric sizes from 4mm to 11mm. So you can tell them apart easily, handles are color-coded as to size. There are miniature nutdriver sets in ten color-coded sizes from ³/₃₂" to ³/₈" by increments of ¹/₃₂".

Though most nutdrivers fit only one size nut, one type has multiple nesting hex sockets, so that one tool fits four or more sizes. Others have fingers which automatically lock in place when the driver is pushed down over a nut or screw. It has an infinite range of adjustment, will fit and hold even damaged or "burred" nuts and screws.

Some sockets are magnetic, to hold screws and nuts. There are also "Magnaserts" which make any socket magnetic.

Just as nutdrivers and screwdrivers overlap, so do nutdrivers lap over into socket wrench sets. You'll find handle and shank to which you attach sockets directly or by extension bars (typically, 1¹/₂", 3", 6"). Some tools have flex T-handles and crossbar or slide-bar handles.

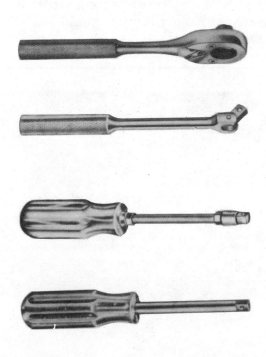

Where nutdrivers leave off and other socket wrenches begin is a gray area. The tools shown above accommodate a variety of sockets as well as standard and Phillips screwdrivers. From top—reversible ratchet, hinge handle, flexible socket driver and socket driver with ¹/₄" square female drive in handle.

Rusty, corroded or frozen screws, nuts, and bolts often cannot be loosened by ordinary screwdrivers or socket wrenches. That's when you need an impact tool. They are easy to use. You just attach a driver bit to the tool holder and pound with a hammer. The pounding is converted into torque.

Most of these hand-impact tools come in kits or sets that include a variety of straight and Phillips bits. Typically, they have $3/8''$ or $1/2''$ drives, which are reversible, so you can tighten as well as loosen. They'll also take hex socket wrenches and stud extractors.

You can also get $1/2''$ and $3/8''$ square drive electric impact wrenches. They use only special power-drive sockets.

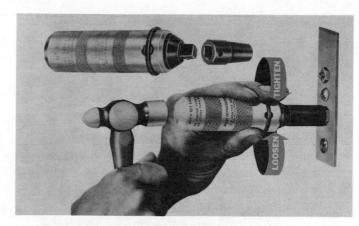

Impakdriver converts hammer blow into powerful torque to loosen frozen or rusty fasteners. It's 5" long, has reversible drive. Kit includes adapter, four screwdriver bits, three hex impact sockets. Choice of $3/8''$ or $1/2''$ drive. H.K. Porter.

MANUFACTURERS

Xcelite was a pioneer in the nutdriver field and is still a leader. Others include Stevens Walden, Proto, S-K, Vaco, Rosco, Ric-Nor, and Stanley.

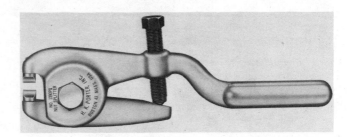

To remove a rusted or frozen nut, use this H.K. Porter nut splitter. It splits both sides of a nut at one time, without damage to bolt or thread. Just put it across nut with blades in position. Turn power screw with an impact or hand wrench. The nut splits free.

Use a screw extractor to remove screws, studs, other broken-off parts. Drill hole in part, insert extractor, use wrench to turn part out. Sold in sets of 10 and 15 to fit holes from $1/8''$ to $13/32''$. Brookstone.

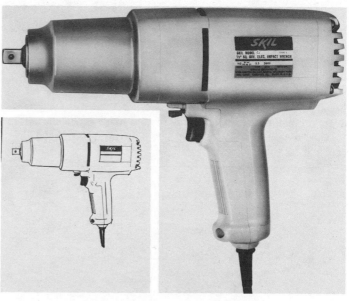

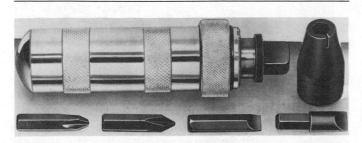

Impact driver for stuck screws breaks loose stubborn screws, nuts and bolts. Converts hammer blow to rotational impact. Reversible to set screws dead tight. Brookstone.

Skil's No. 821 heavy-duty impact wrench has a half inch square drive. Its 5.5 amp., $1/3$ hp motor delivers 2000 blows per minute, forward and reverse. Ball bearing construction. Double insulated.

57.

ADJUSTABLE PLIERS

The "Cee Tee" plier is of drop-forged steel, hardened and tempered, with a nickel-chrome finish. In 6" and 8" sizes. Crescent.

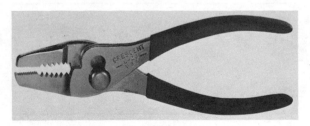

Crescent plier has a thin and straight nose that's especially useful in tight spots. Comes in 5", 6" or 8" lengths, with $^3/_4$", 1" and $1^1/_4$" capacities, respectively. Teeth are sha-a-rp!

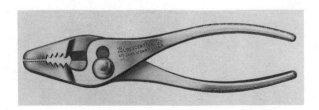

Crescent 6" slip joint, side cutting plier is of chromium-plated drop-forged steel. The cutter is sharp and strong. 1" capacity.

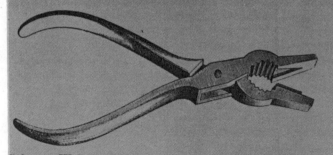

IMPROVED PLIERS.

Our engraving illustrates an improved form of pliers, its construction being calculated to greatly increase the general usefulness of the instrument. This tool was patented by

Sylvanus Walker, of New York, January 8, 1867. The engraving shows so plainly the form of the pliers that we need only remark that the jaws are plain at the ends, and have opposing grooves for holding a bolt longitudinally, and serrated transverse hollows for use as a wrench.

"To ply is to bend, fold, or mold," says the dictionary. And what tool does the plying? Why *pliers,* of course.

Join two oppositely curved pieces of metal to form jaws on one side and handles on the other, and you have a pair of pliers. Especially meant for gripping and turning of round things such as pipes, rods, and studs, they have sharp teeth. But for gripping flat-sided nuts, which teeth might mar, they are made with smooth jaws.

The business end of pliers may be extra thin, extra heavy, or bent—depending on what special jobs they are designed to perform. On the handle end, pliers may be knurled to provide a good grip, or they may be covered with fiber-impregnated plastic for a positive hold even under oily, sweaty conditions.

Slip-joint pliers, or combination pliers as they are sometimes called, are measured by their overall length, which usually ranges from 5″ to 10″.

THE SLIP JOINT

Like pincers, the first pliers had a fixed joint. Then some forgotten genius discovered that a "slip joint" could let a plier's jaws open wider, increasing its capacity. He made the rivet or pivot-bolt, holding the two lever-like arms together and serving as a fulcrum, so that it could slip from one slot to a second slot. But the slipping could take place only when the jaws are open wide. When the jaws are brought together, the flat side of the bolt is in the wrong position to move through the narrow two slots connecting the passage.

The slip-joint plier came in with the automobile. It was invented out of necessity. Old 4-cylinder engines had water pumps up front with a fan attached. To tighten the packing nut on the pump and stop leaks, you couldn't use a pipe wrench. Needed was a plier that would open extra wide. Thus the slip-joint came into being, and soon became useful to plumbers, electricians, and everybody else.

The 6½″ slip joint is the popular choice. The 5″ slip joint is a good choice for a small toolbox, glove compartment, or kitchen drawer.

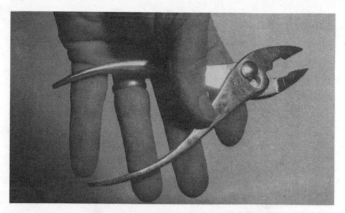

"Gas pliers" are so called because of their frequent use in loosening or tightening small-diameter gas pipe and fittings. If used on tight nuts, they are likely to chew them up, destroying their corners.

Heavy duty slip-joint side cutter is made for a rough life—and it can take it. Its milled teeth have a powerful bite. Sharp cutting edges; flush bolt. Polished head and black knurled handles. Crescent.

Soft-jawed pliers won't hurt finishes. They're made for grasping cylindrical objects from ½″ to 2½″ in diameter. Durable synthetic pads won't damage chromed pipe or fittings. Also useful in inserting dowels or for removing round parts from machinery. 9″ long. Brookstone.

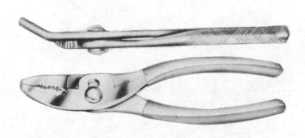

Thin bent-nose plier reaches around obstructions and goes where straight-nose pliers can't. The thin nose with 30° offset is the reason. Two jaw positions and a wire cutter. Chrome plated; with or without plastisol-dipped handles. About 6¾″ long. Proto.

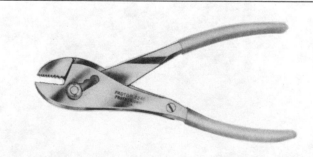

Three-piece compound-leverage design multiplies applied pressure ten times. Four-position slot allows four parallel jaw openings to 1¼″. Proto.

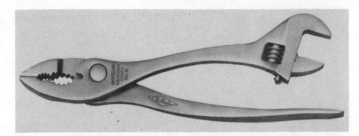

Originally designed for U.S. ski troops, this Diamond "Handyboy" combines plier, wire cutter, wrench and screwdriver. It's 6½" long with plier capacity 1", wrench capacity ½".

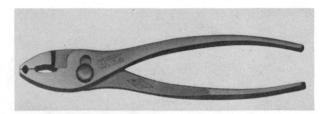

This 8" hose clamp plier is handy for applying and removing spring hose clamps, often used with washing machines and other appliances. Recesses in jaws grip ends of the spring. Diamond.

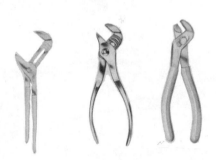

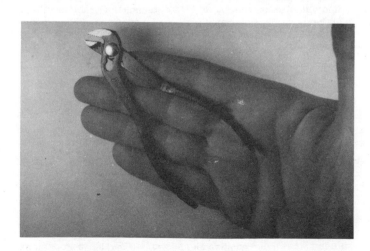

Midget pliers by Proto are less than 5" long.

THE MULTI-JOINT

If two slots were good, wouldn't more slots be better? It could permit an even wider range of adjustment. Thus the multi-position slip-joint plier came into being. It, in turn, led to the tongue-and-groove plier invented by Howard Manning in 1933.

Manning was in charge of tool and die design for a hammer manufacturer in Meadville, Pennsylvania. Seeking to take the pressure off the pivot rivet in slip-joint pliers and give it an even wider range of adjustment, he came up with the idea of using ribs and slots instead of holes. They called it the "Channellock" plier. Its patent ran out in 1970 and now everybody is making the tool.

Channel-joint pliers may have 5, 7, or 11 positions. You can get them up to 20" long with 5½" capacity.

The 10" size is a popular choice.

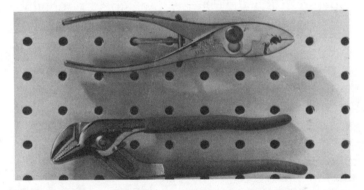

The 6" slip-joint plier offers two positions, and the 7" cushion-grip Multi-plier offers five. Both tools are by Crescent.

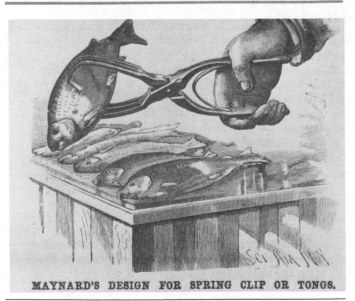

MAYNARD'S DESIGN FOR SPRING CLIP OR TONGS.

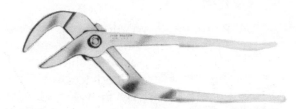

Why settle for five or ten positions? Ingenious gear-rack construction permits 40 parallel jaw positions. Handles objects up to 2⁷/₈″ in diameter. About 11³/₈″ long. Proto.

Spring-loaded bolt keeps jaws on this quick-set plier open for one-hand use. Eight positions to maximum of 2¹/₂″. Ratchet-type action. 6¹/₂″ and 10″ sizes. Cushion grip.

Parrot-nosed plier takes no backtalk. Its 75° offset nose makes it ideal for pipe and tubing work, or any job you can't tackle head-on. Four adjustments. About 7³/₈″ long. Proto.

Ridgid tongue-and-groove pliers are high in strength and light in weight. Lengths and capacities are 6¹/₂″ (⁷/₈″), 10″ (1¹/₂″), and 12″ (2¹/₂″). The plastic grips are for comfort, not electrical insulation.

Channellock plier has smooth jaws that are kind to polished and plated surfaces.

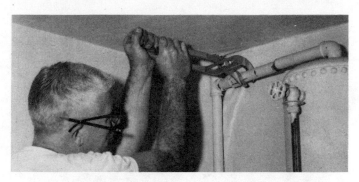

Channellock's 16″ model is useful in plumbing work.

10″ Crescent Multi-pliers come with straight or curved jaws, with 1¹/₂″ capacity and five positions. Chrome finish provides top resistance to corrosion. Weight is .87 lbs.

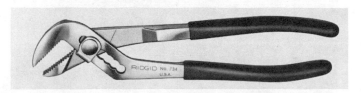

To prevent leaks around the rotating shaft, a nut is tightened against compressible packing. It's for that nut that this plier is intended. Its business end is thin, so it can get into tight places. 10″ long, with 0″ to 2″ capacity. Ridgid.

58.
WRENCHES

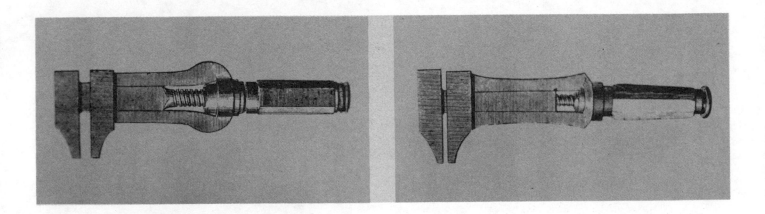

Wrenches are for wrenching. Originally designed for military use, they were employed for wrenching loose the steel bars and latticework of strong points and fortifications. Today, they are usually called on for gripping and turning heads of bolts, nuts, pipe, etc. There are seven principal varieties.

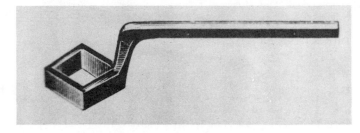

ADJUSTABLE OPEN-END WRENCHES

As the name implies, adjustable wrenches are designed to fit objects of various sizes. Although they are heavier than nonadjustable wrenches, they are usually weaker.

The monkey wrench, now all but extinct, was the first adjustable wrench. It is an effective tool when there is plenty of swing space, but it is awkward when the swing is less than 60°. The Crescent wrench, also called the adjustable open-end wrench, overcame this handicap.

It had its beginnings in Sweden in 1888. Karl Peterson, a Swede, brought the concept with him when he immigrated to the United States and in 1907 made a wrench with its head turned back at a 22° angle to the handle. Because its shape was like an open-end fixed wrench, it was very adept at close-quarter work. It needed only half the swing space of a monkey wrench. With automobiles beginning to appear on the scene in increasing numbers, the new tool was an instant success. Thus began the Crescent Tool Company, the creator of the Crescent wrench. It has had many imitators.

Adjustable open-end wrenches come in sizes ranging from 4", with a $\frac{1}{2}$" jaw capacity, to 24" with a $2\frac{7}{16}$" capacity. Larger sizes often have tapered handles to cut weight and give a better two-handed grip.

Crescent wrenches have a tension spring under their knurl to keep the jaw opening from changing adjustment. Proto makes adjustable wrenches with a "Clik-Stop" feature that locks the moveable jaw at any opening you select. You don't have to push any button. It's handle pressure that locks the wrench, and when handle pressure is released, the knurl turns easily to any other desired size opening. Proto adjustable wrenches have an especially thin head for getting into tight places.

Wrenches are available in a chrome finish, or a black rust-resisting finish that provides a comfortable nonslip grip. Crescent also offers a baked-on bright red plastic grip with a textured surface. Attractive, but an electrical insulation it is not.

Adjustable wrenches are designed to provide the convenience of a single tool with a wide range of capacity. As indicated before, they don't have the durability of fixed-opening wrenches.

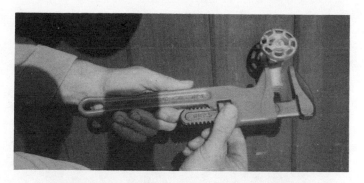

This 12" monkey wrench is strong, well balanced, and has narrow jaws for close quarters. Its drop-forged heat-treated hook jaw is replaceable. Made by Ridge Tool Company, one of the few still making monkey wrenches.

This adjustable double-head wrench, made in West Germany, is described as an "English pattern." In five sizes. Polished finish.

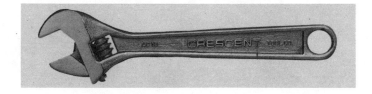

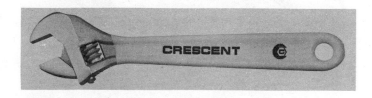

This is the original Crescent wrench. Open-panel design makes knurl adjustment easier. Made of alloy steel with chrome finish (sizes 4" to 24"), or black phosphate finish (sizes 4" to 18"), or with baked-on red plastic "Cushion-Grip" handle (sizes 4" to 12").

Bill Petersen, a blacksmith who came to the U.S. from Denmark in 1901 and settled in Dewitt, Nebraska, developed the Vise-Grip locking pliers.

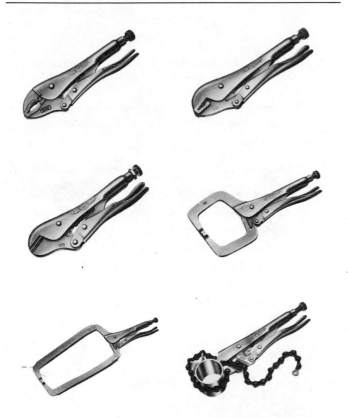

The Vise-Grip line includes: (top row) 5″, 7″, and 10″ curved-jaw pliers with wire cutter; 7″ and 10″ straight jaw; (center row) pinch-off tool that pinches off and locks on copper tubing, specially designed for the refrigeration industry; 11″ C-clamp; (bottom row) long-reach C-clamp, and chain clamp that locks around any shape and size.

They should not be struck with a hammer or an extension placed on their handle. Don't try to free a frozen nut with an adjustable wrench. If damaged, however, parts can usually be replaced.

When you buy an adjustable wrench, look for good workmanship. The rack teeth and knurl should be cleanly machined and smooth in action. There should be only very slight play. Be wary of cheaply plated knurls. Once the plating begins to flake off, knurl action will be impaired. If you buy wrenches made by a reputable manufacturer, you may find it easier to get replacement parts.

LOCKING WRENCHES

Locking, lever, or cam-action wrenches look like a pair of pliers. A bolt in one handle adjusts the jaw opening. Compound hinging increases leverage and locks the jaws in an extremely powerful grip. It is said that a 10″ model can exert a 1-ton thrust at the jaws. Typically, the jaws snap open when a release trigger is pressed.

A blacksmith named William Petersen, who arrived from Denmark in 1901 and settled in DeWitt, Nebraska, is credited with developing this handy tool.

Vise-Grip locking pliers come with straight or curved jaws and a wire cutter. With straight jaws without wire cutter, they come 7″ and 10″ long. They are available in special forms, such as locking "C" clamps, chain clamps, welding clamps, sheet metal, and pinch-off tools.

It's four tools in one—a powerful hand vise, clamp, pipe wrench and plier. Besides locking on nuts and serving as a wrench, it can pull headless nails and cotter pins, twist wire, hold small pieces while grinding, add leverage to a screwdriver, hold sheet metal for soldering or riveting and much, much more.

OPEN-END WRENCHES

This is the simplest type of wrench, consisting only of a bar of metal and a fixed jaw at one or both ends. Most open-end wrenches have a different-size head at each end. The heads are angled at 15°. This permits complete rotation of a hex nut in a 30° swing by merely flopping the wrench. A good practice is to buy a set with six wrenches ($^3/_8$″ through 1″) or 9 wrenches ($^1/_4$″ through $1^1/_8$″). For work on machine-screw nuts, found in home appliances and electronic gear, you can get a set of ignition wrenches with openings of $^7/_{32}$″ through $^7/_{16}$″. They are also useful in car repair.

Oxwall wrench set consists of five drop-forged, chrome-plated open-end wrenches packed in handy storage clip. Sizes: $^5/_{16}$″ by $^{11}/_{32}$″ to $^5/_8$″ by $^3/_4$″.

BOX WRENCHES

These wrenches completely encircle bolt heads and nuts. Because they go all the way around, they can be made smaller in relation to their openings than open-enders and have equal strength.

Inside the box you may find twelve notches or points instead of a hex. This means you can take hold on a six-sided bolt head or nut at a variety of positions without having to flop the head. It also means a surer grip. But you can't use a box wrench unless you have clearance to get over the top of the nut. Their greater holding power makes them better for breaking loose stubborn bolts and nuts or giving them a final turn.

Some box wrenches have ratchet action, which means a sacrifice in strength and a bulkier head. Others have a single head with the other end of the handle designed for striking with a hammer, within reasonable limits. Handles, otherwise, may be straight or offset. The latter gives better clearance for knuckles and for swing in general.

Best buy is a starter set of six tools, which means twelve separate openings ($^3/_8$″ through 1″).

Roller Ratchet wrench is faster than a box wrench, grips tighter than an end wrench. Especially designed for use in close quarters. Swagelok Roller Ratchet Wrenches automatically equalize torque over the five corners of a hexagon nut.

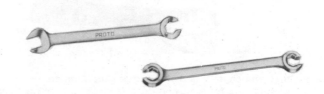

Flare nut wrenches are designed to turn nuts and fittings on compressors, brake and hydraulic lines, and other types of tubing systems. Combination wrench is the same size on both ends. Double-end flare nut wrench has different sized six-point openings on each end.

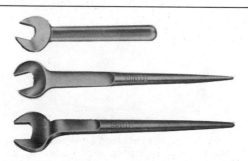

Heavy-duty industrial wrenches. Engineers' wrench with 15° angle head (top) comes with nominal openings of $^3/_8$″ (4″ long) through $2^1/_4$″ (20″ long). Construction wrenches (below), straight and offset, have tapered handles for aligning bolt and rivet holes.

COMBINATION WRENCHES

These have a box head at one end and an open end at the other, both of the same size. Because open enders are faster, and box heads are more secure, this tool gives you the best of each. Some combination sets have staggered-sized opening.

SOCKET WRENCHES

These combine detachable heads or sockets with a wide variety of handles. They come in "socket sets."

Sockets may be regular or extra deep. Socket openings may be square, or 6-, 8-, or 12-point. Capacities range from $^3/_{16}$″ to $3^1/_8$″. Special sockets are used with power drives and impact wrenches.

Hand socket wrenches all have square drives ranging from $^1/_4$″ to 1″. Most popular is the $^1/_2$″ drive, and a good buy is fourteen 12-point sockets ($^7/_{16}$″ through $1^1/_4$″) and an L-shaped handle.

Other handles include flex head, reversible ratchet, sliding "T", flew and flex head ratchet.

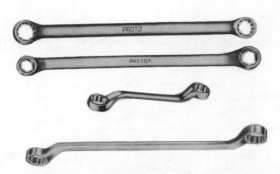

Four useful box wrenches (from top): 12- and 6-point straight shank; short and long offset wrenches.

Striking box wrench (top) and slugging box (bottom) are designed to be struck and are for removing or replacing stubborn nuts and bolts in restricted places. Finished in rust resistant black oxide.

When obstructions rule out use of standard wrenches, this 12-point Proto obstruction box wrench may come to the rescue. Three combinations: $^7/_{16}$" by $^1/_2$", $^9/_{16}$" by $^5/_8$", and $^5/_8$" by $^3/_4$".

Proto crowfoot wrench for places with vertical clearance but little or no horizontal clearance has $^3/_8$" square drive; comes in twelve sizes from $^3/_8$" to $1^3/_8$".

TORQUE WRENCHES

Torque wrenches are used where proper tightening of nuts, bolts, and other fasteners is critical.

One type sounds an audible signal when the preset torque is reached. Others indicate torque on a dial, scale, or by electric light signal. A micrometer adjustable type lets you preset torque. It clicks when torque is reached. Most torque wrenches have square drives and use regular detachable sockets. They come in both ratcheting and nonratcheting types.

Lowest cost are flexible-beam wrenches. Next are dial-indicating types and torque-limiting wrenches. These have no dial or scale, but release when the preset torque is reached.

Spanner isn't just the English name for a wrench. Here in the U.S. it's a wrench that gets a grip by means of a pin or hook that fits in holes. A spanner may come with a kit for installing a lock or servicing an appliance.

Handy all-purpose Oxwall bone wrench has ten sizes—five at each end. It's good to fall back on when you can't find any other wrench that fits.

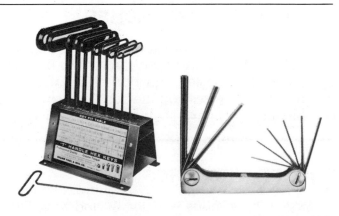

You can get keys for all hex socket screws with T handles for greater torque, or in a fold-up style for greater convenience. Elkind Tool and Mfg. Co.

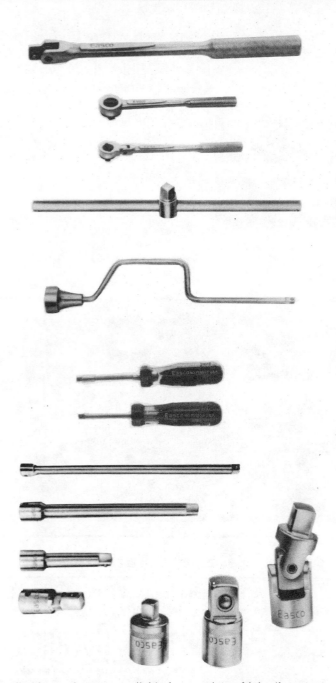

Handles for sockets are available for a variety of jobs (from top): flex handle; ratchet and flex ratchet handle; slide-T-handle; speeder; flex and nonflex spinner handle; extension bars; universal joint; reducing increasing adapters.

MANUFACTURERS

Leaders include Crescent, Channellock, Proto, S-K, Husky, Indestro, Vaco, and BernzOmatic.

Among top imports are Britool and King Dick from England and Möller and Knipex from West Germany.

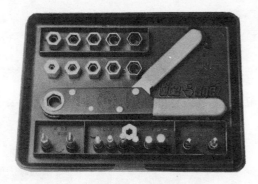

This 22-piece tool kit contains a ratchet squeeze wrench for standard and metric sockets, standard and Phillips screwdrivers, and Allen wrenches. Consumer Tool Company.

Ric-Nor socket set contains compact 12-piece $^3/_8"$ drive. Features reversible ratchet handle and comes in steel case.

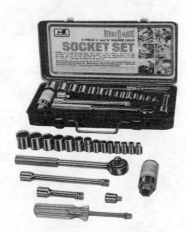

The 21-piece BernzOmatic set has $^1/_4"$ and $^3/_8"$ drive, is available in fractional or metric sizes. The 40-piece set (not shown) contains both fractional and metric sizes. It, too, has $^1/_4"$ and $^3/_8"$ drive.

59.

GRINDERS/ POLISHERS

BROWN'S OIL-STONE STAND.

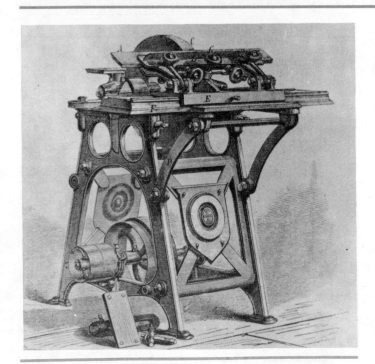

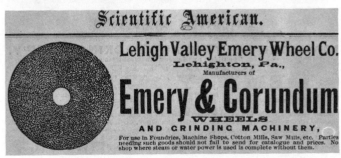

Soldiers of old sharpened their swords against stone walls, and the scorings that were made are still visible on ancient structures around the world. Later, a piece of sandstone, set into a block of wood, was used for sharpening. It was not until the sixteenth century that the wheel entered into the picture and the revolving grindstone, turned by a crank or treadle, became the most popular sharpening device.

SHARPENING STONES

Carving tools, chisels, gouges, turning tools, plane irons, axes, knives, and scissors are some of the edge tools that require sharpening. They can all be sharpened by hand by means of special stones.

These stones, often referred to as whetstones, are usually kept in a retaining block and covered when not in use. The retaining block protects the stone's edges, and allows the stone to be clamped into a vise without danger of breaking. The cover protects the stone against dust and dirt which would impair its cutting action. A popular size for stones is 2" by 8" by 1".

Sharpening stones may be of natural or man-made material. Some of the best natural sharpening stones come from the Ozark Mountains of Arkansas. These stones are mined from novaculite strata, a rock composed essentially of microcrystalline quartz. It occurs in varying qualities of hardness and cutting ability. Washita is the coarsest and one of the fastest cutting of the Arkansas stones. Used alone, it can give a keen, usable edge. Soft Arkansas is the best general-purpose stone and provides a good edge on a variety of cutlery as well as woodworking tools. The densest novaculite rock is Hard Black Arkansas. It is slow cutting and must be used in combination with softer stones, but it can provide a fine finish.

Man-made stones are usually aluminum oxide or silicon carbide and are made in an electric furnace. A typical sharpening stone made of silicon carbide will be coarse on one side, fine on the other, but it is also separately available in coarse, medium, and fine grits.

Silicon carbide stones may be used dry, with oil, or with water. Water should never be used on a natural stone, or on a very fine-grained artificial stone. Oil should be used—and plenty of it. The purpose of the oil is to float away the grinding particles and keep the pores of the stone from becoming clogged and the surface glazed. If the pores become clogged with dirt, the tool edges can't make proper contact with the stone. You can use a special sharpening oil, light machine oil, #10 motor oil, or a blend of half oil and half kerosene.

Slip stones are stones shaped for the special conformation of the tool to be sharpened. They may be triangular, round, oval, or other shape.

Arkansas sharpening stones (from top): soft paddlestone; 7" x 1½" x ¼" bonded to a 14" cedar paddle; Arkansas stone honing oil; three-in-one 6" stones—Washita, soft Arkansas, and white hard Arkansas mounted on cedar block with dust covers; soft in cedar box; surgical black hard; Washita.

An array of heavy-duty sander-grinders is available from Milwaukee. There are nine models to choose from. Tool shown here, equipped as a grinder, may also be equipped as a sander.

Stanley honing guide sets beveled blade at the correct angle. Takes blades 1⅛" to 2⅜" wide. Chrome-plated steel with nylon rollers.

Oxwall offers six assorted wire wheels with 1/4″ shanks that chuck into an electric drill.

World's first double-insulated bench grinder, from Wen, has 6″ wheel, 1/2 hp 4-amp motor. Dynamic brake for fast stops. Plastic housing has no-glare mar-resistant finish.

Readi-Grinder is a 4-in-1 fixture. It will drive a grinding wheel, wire brush, buffing wheel and sanding disc, using your own electric drill as a power source. Jimkraft Corp.

Millers Falls bench grinder with 7″ by 1″ wheels and 1/2 hp motor. MF also offers 6″, 8″, and 10″ bench models. Plastic eye shields provided on all as standard equipment.

Unlike other stones which are held stationary while the edge is moved over them, a slip stone is rubbed along the edge of the tool to be sharpened.

After stone sharpening, final finishing may be done with a hone stone or a leather strop.

HAND-POWERED GRINDERS

The old-fashioned grindstone wheel lives on. Typically it is made of sandstone, and its weight gives it the momentum that keeps it turning at a steady speed.

Water is used on a grindstone to keep the tool edge cool as it is sharpened, so the danger of drawing out its temper is minimized. Though a rough cutter, the grindstone does an excellent job of reshaping an edge, removing nicks, or putting a final cutting edge on an axe. For most tools sharpened on a grindstone, final finishing must be done on a whetstone, or by honing and stropping.

In modern, miniature form, there are small hand-powered grinders that can be clamped to the edge of a bench or table. Their abrasive wheel, typically 6″ by 1″, is made of aluminum oxide and can be turned at 1500 rpm. The only problem is that it can be awkward to hold the tool being sharpened with one hand while turning the crank with the other. A tool rest, adjustable by means of a wingnut, can help some.

PORTABLE GRINDERS

Available in horizontal models and as angle grinders, these powerful tools are ideal for all kinds of metal sanding and grinding applications, such as smoothing castings, welds, and general metal fabricating work. Typical wheel sizes are 5″, 7″, or 9″. Wheels may be of aluminum oxide for really tough cutting assignments, or silicon carbide for softer materials, such as masonry. They are available in disc or cup forms.

Some portable grinders are especially designed for die-grinding, finishing molds, deburring and doing other precise grinding. Other compact models are excellent for less demanding applications, such as automotive refinishing. Some are double-insulated and require no grounding.

Among top makers are Milwaukee Electric, Millers Falls, and Skil.

BENCH GRINDERS

Power grinding and wire brushing can be done with an electric drill, a drill press, or with a flexible shaft powered by a jigsaw or other source, but the tool especially made for these operations is the bench grinder.

A typical bench grinder has two aluminum oxide wheels, ranging in size from 4″ by $\frac{1}{2}$″ to 8″ by 1″. Usually, one wheel will be medium coarse and the other medium fine. It is an excellent tool for sharpening edges, cleaning up casting, smoothing welds, and grinding off rivets. When sharpening tools, to remove the wire edge that results from grinding, it is necessary to whet the tool on an oilstone. Grinding wheels have a tendency to become dull and glazed. When this happens, they can burn the tool being sharpened. Wheels can be resurfaced, or you can get replacement wheels.

Two kinds of stands are available for grinder mounting. One is of tubular steel with four spreading legs. Better is the pedestal type with a tubular steel post rising from a heavy cast-iron base, which may be bolted to the floor. The standard height for mounting a grinder is 32″.

A bench grinder may be equipped with buffing wheels. With compound, the wheels can be used for a variety of polishing and finishing operations. Typically, a buffing wheel is made of thirty layers of spiral-sewn muslin with raked edges. Two or more wheels can be used in tandem for wide work. Popular size diameters are 4″, 6″, and 8″.

An adjustable tool holder gives excellent control in grinding operations. Sears has one of steel and aluminum, with 3″ travel and fine feed adjustment, that fits all Sears Craftsman grinders.

Milwaukee heavy-duty bench grinders come in 6″, 7″, 8″, and 10″ wheel sizes, $\frac{1}{4}$, $\frac{1}{3}$, $\frac{1}{2}$, $\frac{3}{4}$ or 1 hp with choice of eye shields or optional pedestal. Shields must be used when operating grinders.

Like an airplane propeller, the wheel of this grinder is invisible at full speed. Grinding is done against underside of wheel. Lamp shines through slots directly onto workpiece so you can observe the actual surface being ground—which makes it much easier to do a good job. Leichtung.

McGraw Edison 6″ bench grinder with hone features built-in drill sharpening guides, shadowproof eyeshields, water tray, fine and coarse wheels. Die-cast aluminum housing, 3-conductor cord.

Stanley 7″ grinder offers two speeds. Use 1800 rpm for sharpening chisels, plane irons, etc., 3600 rpm for ridge and burr removal, buffing and polishing. In $\frac{1}{3}$–$\frac{1}{2}$ hp. Comes with plane iron and chisel grinding attachment and two tool rests.

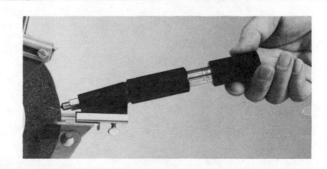

Dymex grinding-wheel dresser quickly dresses any grinding wheel. Micrometer insures accurate advancement of diamond tip. Body and handle made of ABS plastic. Dymex Marketing.

60.
METALWORKING TOOLS

Though metalworking is one of the earliest crafts known to man, many of the tools and techniques for forming and joining metal are strictly of this century.

Metal may be cut cold with a chisel, snips, shears, or an abrasive cutoff wheel, depending on the kind of metal and the circumstance.

COLD CHISELS

This wedgelike tool with a cutting edge at one end is thousands of years old. It's called a cold chisel because it's used on cold metal. A modern cold chisel is hot-formed from fine alloy steel and heat-treated to obtain a superb combination of hardness and toughness. It will cut any metal softer than itself: wrought iron, cast iron, steel, brass, bronze, copper, and aluminum.

Chisels commonly come in four styles. 1. The classic cold chisel has a tip like a screwdriver. 2. Cape chisels have a V-point and are for cutting narrow grooves, such as keyways and slots. 3. Diamond-point chisels are for cutting V-grooves and square inside corners. 4. Round-nose chisels are for cutting grooves where an oval shape is desired.

Cold chisels are available in at least twelve sizes with width of cut from $1/4''$ to $1^3/_{16}''$. A good buy for the homeowner is a five-piece set with cuts ranging from $5/_{16}''$ to $5/_8''$. Better yet is a twelve-piece set that includes seven punches in addition to the five chisels. These may include starter, pin, line-up, center, and prick punches. In effect, a punch is a chisel that comes to a point.

A starter punch is good for knocking a rivet from a hole after its head has been cut off.

A pin punch has a long, slender point and is good for knocking out pins.

A line-up punch is for lining up holes on two parts being fitted together.

A center punch can make a starting point when drilling metal. It can also mark the alignment of metal parts before you disassemble them.

Prick punches are like center punches but have a longer taper and a sharper point.

SNIPS

Tinner's snips are strong hand shears designed to cut sheet metal, wire screen, and lighter materials such as roofing. They come in standard, circular-cutting, and combination patterns.

The standard pattern is the most used type. It is for cutting straight lines or circles of a fairly large radius. Circular-cutting snips are for cutting patterns or curves. A combination pattern will cut curves as well as straight lines. It is available in a

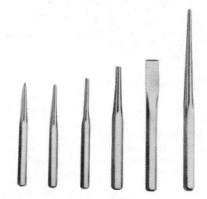

Easco punches and chisels (from left): *prick punch*, for scribing, punching starting holes for sheet metal screws, and aligning holes in two or more metal sheets; *center punch*, useful for marking centers of intersecting lines, centers for screws and drilling; *pin punch*, for driving out pins and rivets; *starting punch*, useful for installing pins and rivets; *cold chisel*, in sizes from $3/_8''$ to $3/_4''$; *drift punch*, for enlarging holes or bringing holes in line to receive bolts or rivets.

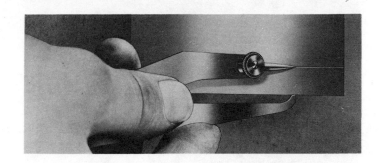

"Jenny" calipers with a firm friction joint will hold position without blade. Adjustable point. Sizes (from center of joint to point) are 4" and 6".

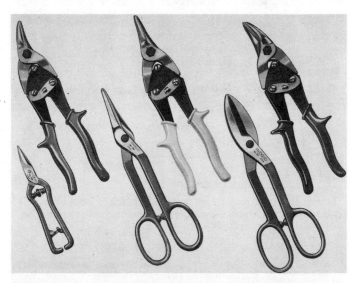

Aviation snips cut metal with ease. Top row: left-cutting, straight-cutting, right-cutting. Bottom row: light metal-cutting shear, duck-bill snips, straight snips. Duckbill and straight snips come in 7", 10", and $12^1/_2''$ lengths. Ridgid.

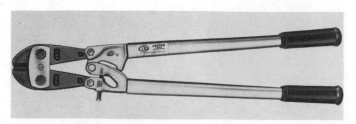

Here is the most widely used H.K. Porter cutter. Comes in 14" to 42" length. Will cut soft steel, hard steel, iron, non-ferrous metals, reinforcing rod, bolts, rivets, screws, wire, stainless steel—everything except hard guy strand.

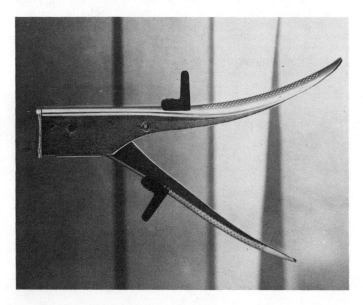

Nibbling tool cuts sheet metal up to 18 ga., $^1/_{16}$" (.046 max.) copper, aluminum, and plastic. Just start with a $^3/_8$" hole and nibble to shape and size desired. Made by GC Electronics, available at Radio Shack.

Tubular-frame hacksaw (top) provides a place to store blades. This one has aluminum handles, takes 12" blades. Jab saw (below) is designed for use on low-clearance jobs.

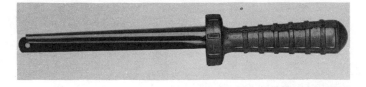

heavy-duty style designed to provide powerful leverage for heavy work. Typically, tinner's snips are available in lengths of 7", 10", and $12^3/_4$", with cuts of $1^5/_8$", $2^1/_8$ and $2^3/_4$".

Aviation snips were developed for use in the aircraft industry when metal replaced fabric for wing covering. Now they are used for many purposes, especially in roofing, airconditioning, and other types of ductwork installation.

They come in three styles—straight, left- and right-cutting. Typically, they are about $9^3/_4$" in overall length and have plastic grips in lively colors.

Aviation snips follow scribed lines with ease. For example, in cutting an opening in a duct, a small hole is punched in the center of an area and from this hole the snips spiral out to the scribed line.

Some snips are made of aluminum alloy with replaceable blades of hard, high-carbon steel. They are more corrosion-resistant than forged snips and have a high leverage ratio that makes for easier cutting. For limited use, there are snips that are merely stamped out of metal.

HACKSAWS

To hack, according to the dictionary, is to cut, chop, or sever with heavy, irregular blows. Combine "hack" with "saw" and you have a tough cutting tool—the hacksaw. It comes in several variations.

Most hacksaws have flat or tubular frames and are adjustable to take 10" and 12" blades. A tubular frame provides blade storage inside the tube. For certain types of heavy work, a nonadjustable 12" hacksaw is the answer. It's more rugged. For low-clearance work there are a number of special frames and holders, as shown in the photographs.

The proper type of hacksaw blade is important. Follow the manufacturer's recommendations. Work to be cut should be held rigidly and so placed that a number of teeth engage throughout the cut. Never let the teeth straddle the work. It's a good way to break them.

Power hacksaws and cutoff saws are used in commercial and industrial applications. You can cut light metal with a saber saw and a 32-tooth tungsten blade.

FORMING TOOLS

Metal may be formed by means of hammers, mallets, and bending devices. Because polished metal surfaces are damaged by steel hammers, special soft-faced hammers or mallets are often used in such applications.

The ball peen (or pein) is the hammer usually used for striking or beating metal. The striking end of the hammer head, opposite the face, is spherical in shape. The rounded end is often used for riveting, but also for enlarging, straightening, or smoothing. Light hammering or peening is a technique for strengthening a metal surface.

A ball peen hammer with a 12 oz. head is best for average use, 6 oz. for light duty and 16 oz. for heavy, but you can get them from 4 oz. to 32 oz.

RIVETERS

Rivets are 4000 years old, but it has been only since the early 1960s that they have become as easy to use as screws. Instead of hammering, you merely squeeze a handle. The hollow rivets used don't hold as well as solid rivets, which you set by hammering, but they serve for most household purposes, and you don't need access from the rear to set them. That's why they are called "blind" rivets. They are a popular means of joining metal as well as other materials.

Blind rivets are most commonly available in aluminum and steel. There are also rivets of copper, stainless steel, Monel, and brass, with a variety of platings and finishes. All are popularly known as "pop" rivets. Pop Rivets is the trademark of U.S.M. Corporation which introduced the tool. Vaco calls their rivets Pow. Richline makes Snapo, and Marson makes Klik-Fast.

Other companies involved in the business include Avdel Corp., Celus Fasteners, Inc., Rivco, Inc., and Southco, Inc.

WELDERS

Welding is often the best or only way to join metal. It may be done with gas or electric equipment.

Some metals which can't take welding, such as cast iron, may be joined by brazing, which in effect is like soldering with brass. There is scaled-down equipment for small jobs.

Power metal shear zips through sheet steel (up to 18 gauge) at an average rate of 15' per minute—with no distortion. Continuous metal curl leaves edges smooth, and free of burrs. Has a 1/4 hp motor. Brookstone.

"Iron Mike" portable power hacksaw requires motor, pulley, and belt to provide 120 strokes per minute. Takes any flexible 10" hacksaw blade. Use fully enclosed guards. Arco Mfg. Company.

Compact 2 hp saw has surface speed of 12,000 fpm, cuts 4" steel pipe in less than 10 seconds. Integral vise is adjustable from 0-45°. Guaranteed Muffler Supply Company Co.

This tool bends metal like cooked spaghetti. Accepts wire and rod gauges up to 5/16" and flat steel up to 1/8" by 1". Brookstone.

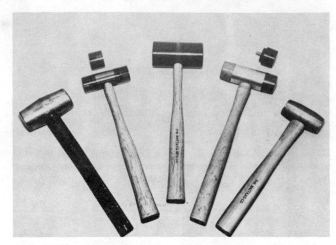

No-mar hammers (from left): lead; steel head with replaceable cellulose press-on-tip; high-density plastic; aluminum or zinc head with replaceable plastic screw-in tips; brass head. Plus Mfg. Co:

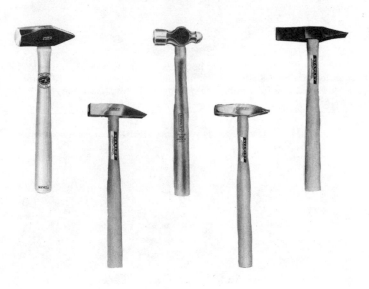

For metalworking hammers (from left): blacksmith's hammer; tinner's setting hammer; ball peen hammer; riveting hammer; scaling hammer.

The village blacksmith can still buy an anvil from Milwaukee Tool and Equipment Co., maker of blacksmith and tinmetal tools. tools.

Mini-torches are useful for hobby work. One type uses propane gas from standard 14.1-ounce cylinders and solid-oxygen pellets, which give off oxygen when they are ignited. Together they produce an oxygen-propane flame of 5000° F for brazing, light welding, and cutting thin-gauge sheet metal. Another type combines a torch fired by a MAPP gas cylinder and an oxygen cylinder (which holds 20 cubic feet and is refillable).

For tough jobs and professional results you need standard gas-welding or arc-welding gear.

Arc welding is extremely fast and it's easily self-taught. Transformers convert the juice from a 30-amp circuit to the higher amperages delivered by the welder. You attach one clamp to your work or the metal table on which your work rests. The other clamp holds a welding rod. When you touch it to the work, it in effect completes a short circuit, producing a powerful arc which you maintain as you weld. The arc is hot—about 7000° F. It's great on heavy stuff, but thin metals disintegrate under its blast.

Gas-welding equipment may cost about the same as that for arc welding, but there are tanks to rent or lease and refill, which makes it more expensive. But it does more things and offers more control. It's unexcelled in cutting, easily knocking off jobs that would be impossible with chisel or hacksaw.

A typical light-duty gas outfit consists of: (1) pressure regulators to reduce the high cylinder pressures to safe working pressure; (2) gauges to show the pressure in the cylinders and the working pressure of gas being delivered to the torch tip; (3) hoses to carry oxygen and fuel to the torch; (4) the torch, which is equipped with valves for control, a mixer seated in the torch head, and various-sized interchangeable tips.

Gas welding is not a difficult skill, but instruction is recommended. Adult classes in welding may be found almost anywhere, and in no more than eight sessions you'll be ready to strike out on your own and know which equipment is best for you.

Vise-Grip locking sheet-metal tool is almost indispensable for holding, bending, forming, crimping.

Portable forge has hand-operated blower. The 18″-diameter hearth is of heavy sheet steel. Ideal for light use. Weighs only 33 lbs. For bench use, lower legs can be removed. Buffalo Forge Co. Co.

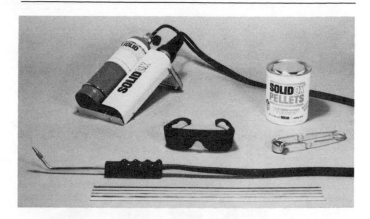

For light brazing, welding, and cutting, Solidox Apollo Torch Kit combines propane and oxygen to produce a 5000°F flame. Kit includes rods, glasses, and lighter.

These riveting guns take ¹/₈″, ⁵/₃₂″, and ³/₁₆″ rivets. All operate by mechanical means except the heavy-duty Trojan riveter, which works by hydraulic action.

This 230-amp AC arc welder is designed for use in the home shop, hence its name. Wards also sells a 295-amp AC welder and an inexpensive 50-amp arc welder plus arc torch.

Propane-oxygen torch by BernzOmatic welds, brazes, solders, cuts up to ¹/₄″ steel, ³/₄″ bolts. Everything shown is included in the kit except the propane or Mapp gas fuel.

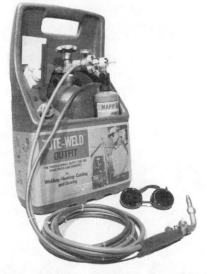

Tote-Weld outfit, which weighs just 25 pounds, can be used for light-to-medium-duty welding, cutting, and heating projects. Polystyrene case carries refillable 20-cubic-foot oxygen cylinder and a 1 pound, 8.8-cubic-foot disposable cylinder of Mapp gas.

61.
HOBBY/CRAFT TOOLS

In the tomb of King Tutankhamen, pegs capped with gold buttons were used to fasten an ivory veneer to a casket. It's an example of an early craft. A craft is simply a manual art requiring special skill. When a craft is not a main occupation, but is an activity or interest pursued for pleasure or relaxation, it's a hobby.

Today, model making, carving, engraving, and gem polishing are popular hobbies, and there are many others. Almost all require special tools and equipment.

ROTARY HOBBY TOOLS

Essentially, these are hand-powered units designed for performing many light craft operations—sculpting, wood carving, and polishing jewelry, to name a few. Often they are referred to as grinders, but in addition to abrasive wheels they can drive drills, routers, rotary rasps and files, wire and bristle brushes, sanding drums and discs, polishing wheels and pads, and tiny circular saws. They can be used for working wood, plastics, ceramics, ferrous and non-ferrous metals, glass, leather, stones, and gems.

In use, most rotary tools are held pencil-fashion or cupped in the hand. Almost all models come with one $3/_{32}''$ collet and one $1/_8''$ collet. A collet is simply an enclosing collar that you tighten on bits in much the same way as you tighten geared key chucks. A built-in lock pin prevents the motor from turning as the chuck is tightened. Most are tightened with a small wrench that comes with the tool. Some collets are tightened only with the fingers.

Unmounted cutters, felt wheels, buffs, etc., can be held in a mandrel. It's just a shaft with a holding device. Some hobbyists use cutters their dentists consider worn out. They may not be good for teeth, but they're still good for wood or soft metal. Ask your dentist for his old ones.

Dremel is the biggest manufacturer of small rotary grinders and their trade name is Moto-Tool. Weller has the Mini-Shop, and J.C. Penney offers the quite similar Micro Workshop. Ward's rotary tool is called Powr-Kraft. It is essentially similar to Dremel designs. Sears has one called Li'l Crafty, but it is rather slow and clumsy.

Several manufacturers offer simple stands for holding the grinder, freeing both your hands to do the work. The stand may have a swivel so you can adjust the tool to almost any desired position—vertical, horizontal, angled, or inverted so you can use it as a shaper. A stand gives you more control than working freehand.

Most of the tools are quite noisy, but some are noisier than others. You may want to compare them. Also check out how quickly they heat up. Some models tend to heat up excessively, especially with prolonged or heavy use.

Power is important for many grinding and routing jobs, so keep this in mind, too, when making a selection. But, remember, this is not a heavy-

Dremel Moto-Tool kit handles hundreds of hobby and craft jobs. Includes Moto-Tool and over 30 accessories—cutters, sanders, grinders, brushes, polishers. For model and pattern making, carving, jewelry work and more.

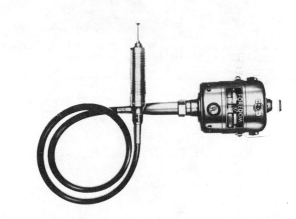

Hang-up flex shaft tool, one of the famous Foredom miniature power tools that are used by top crafts people, is available in 1-speed, 2-speed, variable speed, with a complete line of hand pieces and accessories. Leichtung.

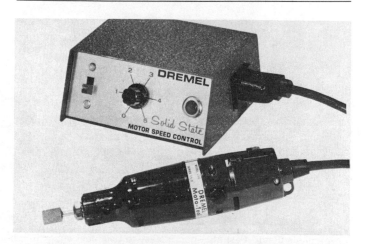

Lightweight (2 lbs.) solid-state speed control for any Moto-Tool accessory project. Enables you to reduce speed with tools such as wire and bristle brushes. Up to 5 amps.

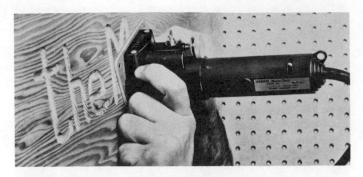

Create unique lettering and designs with this router attachment that converts any Moto-Tool into a router for shaping, edging, chamfering, routing, rabbeting, dadoing. Calibrated depth control.

This tool is used to install eyelets in leather, fabric, or lightweight plastics. Comes with 100 assorted eyelets. Oxwall.

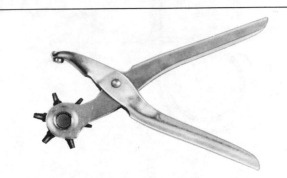

Revolving hole punch features six sizes. For use on plastic, canvas, leather, paper. Smooth action, comfortable grip. Oxwall.

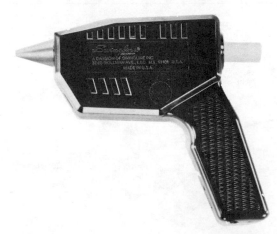

Swingline's Electri-Fast glue gun is easy to use. Just apply thumb pressure to hot-metal glue stick to make it flow. Releasing pressure stops glue. No clamping necessary; bonds in 60 seconds. Also handy for caulking/sealing.

duty tool. It's meant for delicate and miniature work. Find out which accessories are offered. You may want to select a tool that provides the advantage of a drill press stand or router attachment.

Because this is a tool with many small parts, you need a case. Almost all manufacturers offer them, but some are better than others and it's a good idea to have one that's durable and well-designed.

For safety, goggles are recommended. You never know when chips or other debris may fly in your face—and eyes.

FLEXIBLE SHAFT OUTFITS

Similar in the operations it performs to the rotary hand tool is the flexible shaft. The difference is that the power source is separated from the tool by a shaft that is almost a yard long. This means heat generation is not a problem and the lightweight hand piece makes it easier and less tiring to do intricate jobs.

As its name implies, the flex shaft is flexible. There is a core which turns inside the shaft casing. Most motors and power tools provide too much torque for use with the kind of flexible shaft we're talking about here. A flex shaft is powered by a high-speed motor that has a light touch.

Perhaps the best known of the flexible-shaft miniature power tools is that made by Foredom. Foredom is known for its large variety of interchangeable hand pieces—eleven of them. A Foredom hand piece boosts the speed of the motor $2^{1}/_{2}$ times—up to 35,000 rpm. Foredom also offers seven collets from $^{1}/_{16}$" to $^{1}/_{4}$" in a kit.

SPECIAL TOOLS

There is a vast array of special tools for each particular craft, whether it be working with silver or polishing rocks. There are many special variations of standard tools. There are special hammers, saws, punches, marking and forming devices, shears. Some tools, with multiple applications, such as staplers and glue guns, find wide-spread application in crafts, particularly in furniture and cabinetmaking and in upholstery.

A wide variety of special tools is available for working in miniature. You can get lighted tweezers, miniature clamps and even miniature torch and welding equipment.

CARVING AND SCULPTURE

Three power tools used regularly by wood-carvers are the band saw, table saw, and drill press. But the lathe and chain saw also find application. For roughing-out large sculptural pieces, a chain saw is unexcelled.

For hand tools, besides the usual collection of planes, saws, drills, clamps, rifflers, rasps, and files, there are special chisels, a number of which are shown in the illustrations.

The best carving tools are hand-forged. The process of hammering steel while it is hot aligns the molecules in the metal so that an edge is easier to obtain and maintain. Tools must be absolutely sharp so that the wood fibers are sliced not torn. All carving tools are bevel-ground.

Most sculptors and woodworkers use a mallet made of wood, and Lignum Vitae, a heavy tropical wood, is usually the preferred choice. Typically, it will have a durable ash handle.

For chip carving or whittling there are special sets of knives, typically made of fine German steel with polished white beech handles.

Good sources for sculptors' and woodcarvers' tools are Leichtung, Woodcraft, Garrett Wade, and Craftool. The latter is also a splendid source for all other types of creative craft tools and equipment. It offers an unusually attractive full-color catalog. Other important sources for craft tools are the Borel and Dixon companies.

WORKBENCHES

A good workbench puts it all together. It is a key tool in almost all crafts. It must be sturdy, of proper height, and with appropriate holding devices, such as bench dogs and vises. The work area should be smooth and durable and there should be a place for tools. The kind of work you do, and the space available, will be controlling factors in the size of your bench.

The bench is the focal point of operations. It sets the tone for all you do. So you want to be proud of it. Many of the best benches are European made, often of kiln-dried European red beech, a hard, dense wood, heavy in weight. Swedish silver birch and Swedish pine may also be used, particularly in drawer construction. A good

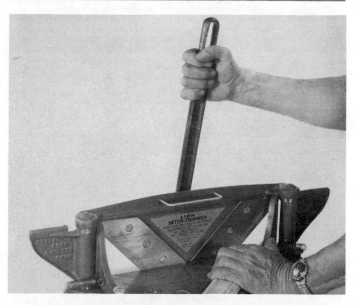

Lion Miter Trimmer takes the skill out of making picture frames. Accurately miters, squares, bevels all moldings at any angle—45° to 90°. With a special attachment it also measures pieces to exact length. Pootatuck Corp.

A stapler is almost indispensable in upholstery and many other craft operations. Here are five kinds made by Roberts. Top model is electric. Gun at lower right will drive staples into hardwoods, plastics, even soft metals.

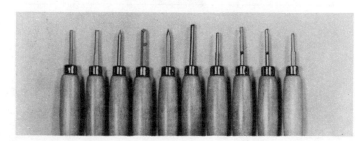

Miniature turning tools cut wood, plastics, metals. For modelers, clock and instrument makers, and other workers in miniature. Use with any kind of lathe. Ten handy shapes. Each tool about 6″ long overall. Brookstone.

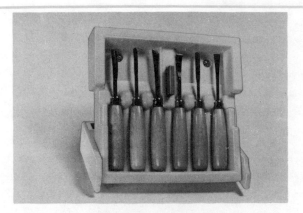

This Stanley set for carving soft wood, soap, plastic, or linoleum incudes $^3/_8''$ straight, bent, and skew chisels, a $^5/_{16}''$ gouge and $^3/_{32}''$ U and V tools. Storage case hangs on wall or stands on work area.

Miniature torch for welding, soldering, and brazing items too small for a regular torch. Use with oxyacetalene, oxyhydrogen or oxypropane gases. Comes with five interchangeable tips, $5^1/_2'$ of color-coded hose. Torch without tip is $4^3/_8''$ long. Brookstone.

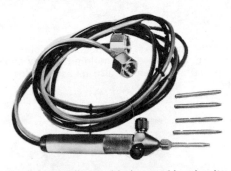

A chain saw isn't just for cutting firewood. It's the indispensable tool for large-scale wood sculpture, and the model shown is a favorite for totem-pole making. Homelite offers a booklet with 22 furniture, play equipment, and decorative projects that can be made quickly and easily with a chain saw.

With this 8-piece chip carving set you can make almost any kind of cut a whittler or chip carver would want. Hardwood handles are 5" to $6^1/_2''$ long. Blades are an easy-to-sharpen alloy that takes and holds a razor edge. Leichtung.

bench is like a piece of fine furniture. Often it is lacquer sealed.

Workbenches are usually from 24" to 30" wide and from 4' to 7' or more long. The working surface should be even with your hip joint, or 30" to 34" on average. This permits you to work without stooping. Storage provided under the bench can help prevent the bench top from becoming cluttered with tools.

If you would like to build your own bench, a good source of information is my book *Complete Book of Home Workshops,* a Popular Science Book published by Harper & Row.

Maintenance of benches requires periodic application of boiled linseed oil to all exposed wood surfaces, including the underside of the bench. Wood moves. This means all bolts and screws should be periodically checked and tightened, especially the stretcher bolts. The stretchers are the long members that brace the legs.

Miniature engraver combines hammer and chisel, weighs only 5 ounces, but will engrave all but hardened steels. Works off flexible shaft. Impact rate, controlled by foot rheostat, 300 to 1500 strokes per minute. The Ngraver Co.

Lervad bench, distributed by Leichtung Inc., is the world's standard for excellence. Made of Danish beech. Whether you build grandfather clocks, make models, carve, do leatherworking, or build fine cabinets and furniture, there's a style and size for you. This model 610 is 60" long.

INDEX